Dickinson's Misery

Dickinson's Misery

A THEORY OF LYRIC READING

Virginia Jackson

PRINCETON UNIVERSITY PRESS

PRINCETON AND OXFORD

Library of Congress Cataloging-in-Publication Data

Jackson, Virginia Walker, date
Dickinson's misery : a theory of lyric reading / Virginia Jackson.
p.   cm.
Includes bibliographical references (p.) and index.
ISBN 0-691-11990-2 (acid-free paper) — ISBN 0-691-11991-0 (pbk. : acid-free paper)
1. Dickinson, Emily, 1830–1886—Criticism and interpretation—History—20th
century.   2. Women and Literature—United States—History—19th Century.
3. Lyric poetry—History and criticism—Theory, etc.   4. Dickinson, Emily,
1830–1886—Technique.   5. Poetics—History—19th century.   I. Title.

PS1541.Z5J33 2005
811'.4—dc22   2004052466

British Library Cataloging-in-Publication Data is available

Publication of this book has been aided by a grant from the Abraham and Rebecca Stein
Faculty Publication Fund of New York University, Department of English.

This book has been composed in Palatino

Printed on acid-free paper. ∞

pup.princeton.edu

Printed in the United States of America

1   3   5   7   9   10   8   6   4   2

FOR SADYE AND WALKER

FOR YOPIE AND MARTIN

Contents

List of Illustrations

Acknowledgments

I AM FORTUNATE to have many people to acknowledge, and to be able to do so in print. The National Endowment for the Humanities, Princeton University, Boston University, New York University, and especially Rutgers University and the Center for the Critical Analysis of Contemporary Culture are institutional names for the support that has made this book possible. I am grateful to the Abraham and Rebecca Stein Faculty Publication Fund of New York University, Department of English, for a grant that subsidized the lavish number of illustrations in this book. The remarkable staff at the Houghton Library at Harvard, the Boston Public Library, the American Antiquarian Society, Mount Holyoke College, the New York Historical Society, the Yale University Library, and particularly Daria D'Arienzo in Archives and Special Collections at Amherst College helped me to see what I needed to see, and helped me to figure out what it was I was seeing, and how to show some of it to others.

An early version of chapter 3 appeared as "Dickinson's Figure of Address" in *Dickinson and Audience*, edited by Martin Orzeck and Robert Weisbuch (Ann Arbor: University of Michigan Press, 1996): 77–103; it is reprinted in expanded form by permission of the University of Michigan Press. A portion of chapter 4 was previously published as "'Faith in Anatomy': Reading Emily Dickinson" in *Dwelling in Possibility: Women Poets and Critics on Poetry*, edited by Yopie Prins and Maeera Shreiber (Ithaca and London: Cornell University Press, 1997): 85–108; it is reprinted in altered and expanded form by permission of the editors and of Cornell University Press.

The Dickinson letters are reprinted by permission of the publishers from *The Letters of Emily Dickinson*, Thomas H. Johnson, ed., Cambridge, Mass.: The Belknap Press of Harvard University Press, Copyright © 1958, 1986 by the President and Fellows of Harvard College. The Dickinson poems are reprinted by permission of the publishers and the Trustees of Amherst College from the following volumes: *The Poems of Emily Dickinson*, Thomas H. Johnson, ed., Cambridge, Mass.: The Belknap Press of Harvard University Press, Copyright © 1951, 1955, 1979, 1983 by the President and Fellows of Harvard College; *The Poems of Emily Dickinson: Variorum Edition*, Ralph W. Franklin, ed., Cambridge, Mass.: The Belknap Press of Harvard University Press, Copyright © 1998 by the President and Fellows of Harvard College.

This book is about the people, objects, accidents, and institutions left out of lyrics as they are handed down, and since this book itself has taken so many forms over the years, I wish I could account for all of the practical social relations that brought it into being. Instead, a few names will have to stand for many places and individuals even the longest list will inevitably omit. Many teachers and colleagues directly and indirectly enabled this project: David Bromwich, Robert Fagles, Stephen Yenser, Calvin Bedient, Shuhsi Kao, Douglass Fiero, Earl Miner, and A. Walton Litz may be surprised (if they are still surprisable) to find traces of their ways of thinking about poetry still evident here; Susan Mizruchi, Diana Henderson, April Alliston, Tomoko Masuzawa, Martha Nell Smith, Priscilla Wald, Karen Sanchez-Eppler, Amy Kaplan, Beth Povinelli, Jonathan Goldberg, Emily Apter, Eliza Richards, Margaret Carr, Elizabeth Wingrove, Max Cavitch, Michael Moon, Robert Gibbs, Barbara Johnson, John Guillory, Lynn Wardley, Michael Cohen, Phillip Harper, Eric Santner, Una Chaudhuri, Nancy Ruttenburg, Mary Poovey, Patricia Crain, Jay Grossman, Diana Fuss, Eduardo Cadava, Lawrence Buell, and Tricia Lootens have each and all made contributions in different ways, at different times and in different places. Adela Pinch has inspired me, in person and in print. For several years, Mary Loeffelholz has been the best friend and smartest interlocutor anyone thinking about Dickinson could have. A late-breaking reading by Jonathan Culler made the ending stages of this book the beginning of a conversation. I thank Helen Tartar, the gifted editor to whom so many authors owe so much, for her support of this book. Mary Murrell deserves an award for her patience with and advocacy for this book; I hereby give it to her. I am very grateful to Jonathan Munk, editor and poet. I have been fortunate indeed in my readers, editors, and collaborators, and fortunate to have been part of a community of extraordinary readers and writers and talkers at Rutgers. This book owes its present form to conversations with Brent Edwards, Jonathan Kramnick, William Galperin, Harriet Davidson, Cheryl Wall, Colin Jager, George Levine, Jonah Siegel, Myra Jehlen, Barry Qualls, Elin Diamond, and Michael McKeon. Carolyn Williams can think one's own thoughts and twist them around her own faster than anyone I've ever met. Michael Warner's reading of these pages is so intimately a part of them now that his name should appear on the title page.

As companions for the life of the mind, no one could ask for better fellow travelers than Neni Panourgia and Stathis Gourgouris, exemplary souls. The spiritual and intellectual energy and generosity of Meredith McGill have sustained me within and without the walls of Rutgers; Andrew Parker's talents as someone to think with are well known. Elizabeth Wanning Harries, Jennifer Whiting, Karsten Harries, and Elizabeth Langhorne have included me with surprising (and welcome) grace. In this paragraph I have begun the protocol of thanking my closest kin; my lovely mother, Eunice Harris, my stepfather, William Harris, my sister, Julia Jackson, and brother Frank Valente have been marvels of patience and support over the years. They have given me the great gift of taking for granted what has often seemed to me a leap of faith; no writer of a book could ask for more. Then, as Stathis would say, there are those people who *are* my life: Most of all, this book reflects a deep and lifelong collaboration with Yopie Prins, who anticipated every word I wrote and spelled it back to me, letter by letter; the words I have to thank her she already knows. It also reflects and is reflected in two lives that have made it and my life infinitely richer than either would have been without them. I dedicate this book to Sadye and Walker Teiser because I promised, and because in their own ways they are the lyrical subjects that transcend it while their everyday lives have informed each word. Sadye inspires me daily to live up to her shining example; Walker challenges me to keep up with his. Finally, I wish that I had words to thank Martin Harries. He shares in this dedication, since he is the genius, the genie, the re-enchantment (though I know that he won't accept any of those words). To say that he has made this book and my life possible is not to say half enough; it's a good thing that the other half we don't have to say.

Abbreviations

A	Dickinson Papers, Amherst College Library Special Collections. Amherst, Massachusetts
AAS	American Antiquarian Society. Worcester, Massachusetts.
BM	Mabel Loomis Todd and Millicent Todd Bingham, eds. *Bolts of Melody: New Poems of Emily Dickinson.* New York: Harper & Brothers, 1945.
CC	Sharon Cameron. *Choosing not Choosing: Dickinson's Fascicles.* Chicago: University of Chicago Press, 1992.
F	R. W. Franklin, ed. *The Poems of Emily Dickinson.* Variorum Edition. 3 volumes. Cambridge, Mass.: The Belknap Press of Harvard University Press, 1998.
FR	R. W. Franklin, ed. *The Poems of Emily Dickinson: Reading Edition.* Cambridge, Mass.: The Belknap Press of Harvard University Press, 1999.
H	Dickinson Papers, Houghton Library. Harvard University, Cambridge, Massachusetts
J	Thomas H. Johnson, ed. *The Poems of Emily Dickinson: Including variant readings critically compared with all known manuscripts.* 3 volumes. Cambridge, Mass.: The Belknap Press of Harvard University Press, 1955.
L	Thomas H. Johnson and Theodora Ward, eds. *The Letters of Emily Dickinson.* Cambridge: The Belknap Press of the Harvard University Press, 1958.
LT	Sharon Cameron. *Lyric Time: Dickinson and the Limits of Genre.* Baltimore: Johns Hopkins University Press, 1979.
MB	R. W. Franklin, ed. *The Manuscript Books of Emily Dickinson.* Cambridge: The Belknap Press of Harvard University Press, 1981.
OC	Ellen Louise Hart and Martha Nell Smith, eds. *Open Me Carefully: Emily Dickinson's Intimate Letters to Susan Huntington Dickinson.* Ashfield, Mass: Paris Press, 1998.
Poems 1890	Mabel Loomis Todd and T. W. Higginson, eds. *Poems by Emily Dickinson.* Boston: Roberts Brothers, 1890.
SH	Martha Dickinson Bianchi, ed. *The Single Hound: Poems of a Lifetime.* Boston: Little and Brown, 1914.

Dickinson's Misery

Beforehand

SUPPOSE YOU ARE sorting through the effects of a woman who has just died and you find in her bedroom a locked wooden box. You open the box and discover hundreds of folded sheets of stationery stitched together with string. Other papers in the bureau drawer are loose, or torn into small pieces, occasionally pinned together; there is writing on a guarantee issued by the German Student Lamp Co., on memo paper advertising THE HOME INSURANCE CO. NEW YORK ("Cash Assets, over SIX MILLION DOLLARS"), on many split-open envelopes, on a single strip three-quarters of an inch wide by twenty-one inches long, on thin bits of butcher paper, on a page inscribed "*Specimen of Penmanship*" (which is then crossed out) (fig. 1). There is writing clustered around a three-cent postage stamp of a steam engine turned on its side, which secures two magazine clippings bearing the names "GEORGE SAND" and "Mauprat." Suppose that you recognize the twined pages as sets of *poems*; you decide that the other pages may contain poems as well. Now you wish you had kept the bundles of letters you burned upon the poet's (for it *was* a poet's) death. What remains, you decide, must be published.[1]

Let this exercise in supposing stand as some indication of what now, more than a century after the scene in which you have just been asked to place yourself, can and cannot be imagined about reading Emily Dickinson. What we cannot do is to return to a moment before Dickinson's work became literature, to discover within the everyday remnants of a literate life the destiny of print. Yet we are still faced with discerning, within the mass of print that has issued from that moment, what it was that Dickinson wrote. As many readers have noticed (or complained), the hermeneutic legacy of Dickinson's posthumous publication is also first of all a "sorting out": so J. V. Cunningham remarked after what he diplomatically called "an authoritative diplomatic text" of Dickinson's extant corpus appeared for the first time in 1955, that "it is easier to hold in mind and sort out the plays of Shakespeare or the novels of George Eliot, for they have scope and structure."[2] In the pages that follow, Cunningham's response will come to seem symptomatic of the century's ongoing attempt to construct the scope of Dickinson's work, to make out of the heterogeneous materials of her practice a literature "to hold in mind" and to hand down—to sort her various pages into various poems, those various poems into a book.

But what sort of book? The frustration of readers like Cunningham is also their invitation, for the syntax perceived as missing from the "almost

1

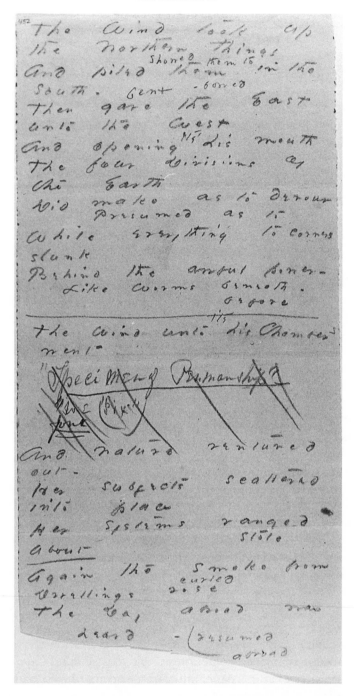

Figure 1. The text that Dickinson penciled on Mary Warner's penmanship practice sheet is now Franklin's poem 1152, "The wind took up the northern things." Courtesy of Amherst College Archives and Special Collections (ED ms. 452).

1,800 items in the collected poems" is theirs to supply. We might say of the range of Dickinson's texts considered together what Norman Bryson says of the objects in trompe l'oeil painting, that they may "present themselves as outside the orbit of human awareness, as unorganised by human attention, or as abandoned by human attention, or as endlessly awaiting it."[3] Yet of course what this comparison to painting suggests is that such an effect is just that: Dickinson's "items" have been successively and carefully framed to give the impression that something, or someone, is missing. While the recovery of Dickinson's manuscripts may be supposed to have depended on the death of the subject, on the person who had, by accident or design, composed the scene, the repeated belated "discovery" that her work is yet in need of sorting (and of reading) may also depend upon the absence of the objects that composed it. These objects themselves mark not only the absence of the person who touched them but the presence of what touched that person: of the stationer that made the paper, of the manufacturer and printer and corporation that issued guarantees and advertisements and of the money that changed hands, of the butcher who wrapped the parcel, of the manuals and primers and copybooks that composed individual literacy, of the expanding postal service, of the modern railroad, of modern journalism, of the nineteenth-century taste for continental literary imports. All of these things are the sorts of things left out of a book, since the stories to be told about them open out away from the narrative of individual creation or individual reception supposed by my first paragraph. This is to say that what is so often said of the grammatical and rhetorical structure of Dickinson's poems—that, as critics have variously put it, the poetry is "sceneless," is "a set of riddles" revolving around an "omitted center," is a poetry of "revoked . . . referentiality"—can more aptly be said of the representation of the poems as such.[4] Once gathered as the previously ungathered, reclaimed as the abandoned, given the recognition they so long awaited, the poems in bound volumes appear both redeemed and revoked from their scenes or referents, from the history that the book, as book, omits.

Take for example the second number in the "authoritative diplomatic text" to which Cunningham referred, Thomas H. Johnson's *The Poems of Emily Dickinson: Including variant readings critically compared with all known manuscripts*. The poem is printed, with its comparative manuscript note, as follows:

2

There is another sky,
Ever serene and fair,
And there is another sunshine,

Though it be darkness there;
Never mind faded forests, Austin,
Never mind silent fields—
Here is a little forest,
Whose leaf is ever green;
Here is a brighter garden,

Where not a frost has been;
In its unfading flowers
I hear the bright bee hum;
Prithee, my brother,
Into *my* garden come!

MANUSCRIPT: These lines conclude a letter, written on 17 October 1851, to her brother Austin. ED made no line division, and the text does not appear as verse. The line arrangement and capitalization of first letters in the lines are here arbitrarily established.

Once "arbitrarily established" as a lyric in 1955, these lines attracted a number of close readings—the response a lyric often invited after the middle of the twentieth century. By 1980, the lines had circulated for a quarter of a century as "a love poem with a female speaker," which is to say that they were read according to a theory of their genre that included the idea of a fictive lyric persona.[5] Feminist criticism took up the problem of metaphorical gender in the lines, and several critics placed them back into the context of the letter to Austin, but after its publication as a lyric, the lines were not again interpreted (at least in print) as anything else (though they had been published as prose in 1894, 1924, and 1931—and were again published as a poem "in prose form" in Johnson's own edition of Dickinson's letters in 1958).[6]

In 1998, Harvard issued a new edition of *The Poems of Emily Dickinson* in both variorum and "reading" versions, now more authoritative and more diplomatic, thanks to the detailed textual scholarship of R. W. Franklin. Franklin's edition does not include the end of Dickinson's 1851 letter to her brother as one of the 1,789 poems in the reading edition, but he does list it in the variorum in an appendix of "some prose passages in Emily Dickinson's early letters [that] exhibit characteristics of verse without being so written" (F, 1578). As the manuscript of the letter attests (fig. 2), the lines were indeed not inscribed metrically, though they can certainly be read as a series of the three- and four-foot lines characteristic of Dickinson. Interestingly, Franklin prints the text as a series of such lines, thus printing what has been read rather than what was written, what may be interpreted rather than what may be described—though he also marks the

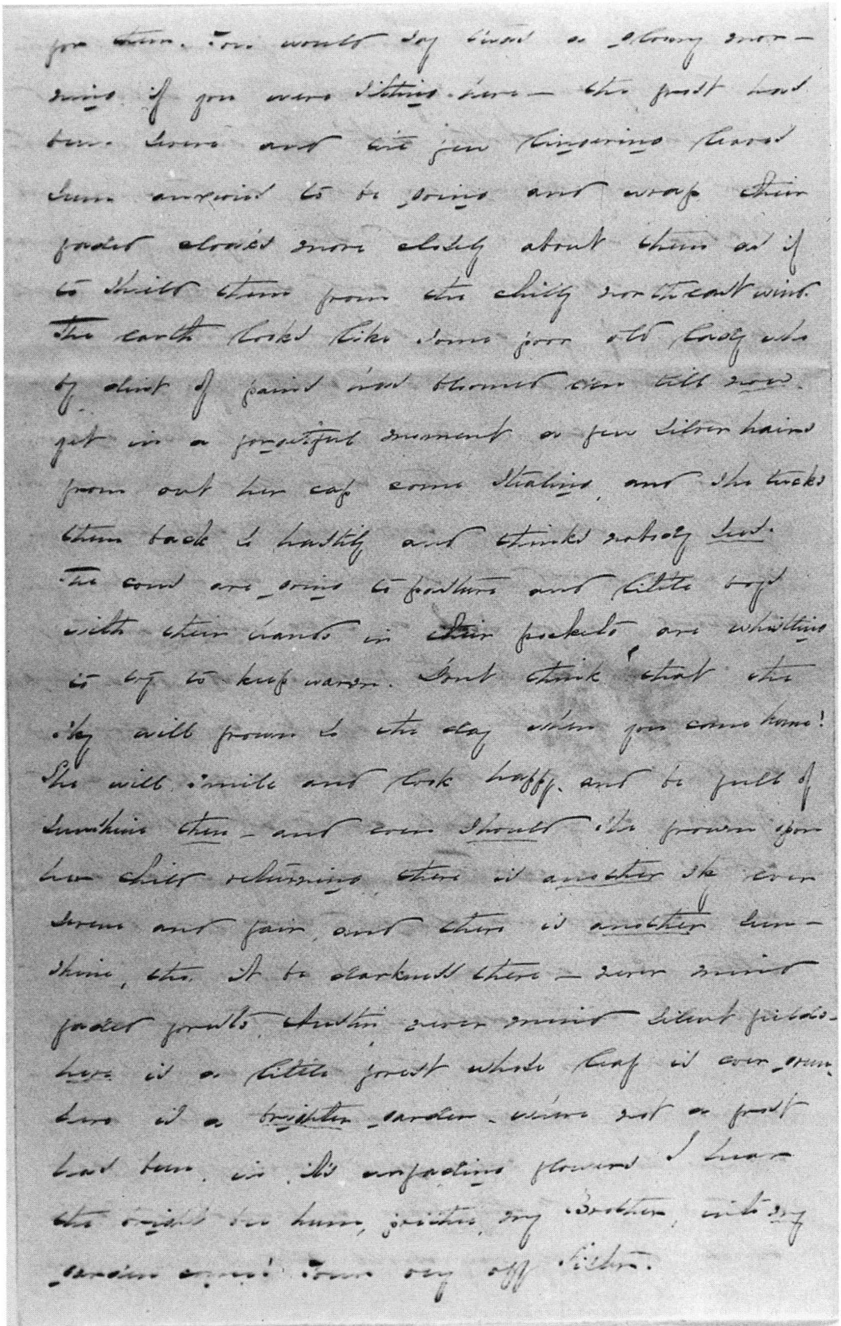

for them. You would say t'was a gloomy morning if you were sitting here — the frost had been here and hit the few lingering leaves and they seem anxious to be going and wrap their faded cloaks more closely about them as if to shield them from the chilly north east wind. The earth looks like some poor old lady who by dint of paint and flowers has held up till now, yet in a graceful moment a few silver hairs from out her cap come stealing, and she tucks them back so hastily and thinks nobody sees. The cows are going to pasture and little boys with their hands in their pockets are whistling to try to keep warm. Don't think that the sky will frown so the day when you come home! She will smile and look happy, and be full of sunshine then — and even should she frown upon her child returning, there is another sky ever serene and fair, and there is another sunshine, tho' it be darkness there — never mind faded forests, Austin, never mind silent fields — here is a little forest whose leaf is ever green, here is a brighter garden, where not a frost has been, in its unfading flowers I hear the bright bee hum, prithee, my Brother, into my garden come! Your very aff Sister.

Figure 2. Emily Dickinson to Austin Dickinson, 17 October 1851. The "poem" appears at the bottom of the page. Courtesy of Amherst College Archives and Special Collections (ED ms. 573, last page).

difference between interpretation and description by making a section in his book for poems that he does not include as poems. Is the end of Dickinson's early letter, then, after 1998, no longer "a love poem with a female speaker"? Was it never such a poem, since it was never written as verse? Was it always such a poem, because it could always have been read as verse? Or was it only such a poem after it was printed as verse? Once read as a poem, can its generic reception be unprinted? Or is that interpretation so persistent that it survives even when the passage is not described as a poem?

The many answers to these questions could be posed as statements about edition (the many ways in which Dickinson has been or could be published) or statements about composition (the many ways in which Dickinson wrote). While the fascinating historical details of Dickinson's production and reception will be central to this book, I will be primarily interested in what such details tell us about the history of the interpretation of lyric poetry (primarily in the United States) between the years that Dickinson wrote (most of the 1840s through most of the 1880s) and the years during which what she wrote has been printed, circulated, and read (from the middle of the nineteenth through the beginning of the twenty-first century). In view of what definition of poetry would Dickinson's brother have understood the end of his sister's letter to him as a poem? Did it only become a poem once it left his hands as a letter? According to what definition of lyric poetry did Dickinson's editor understand the passage as a lyric in 1955? What did Dickinson's editor in 1998 understand a lyric poem to be if it was not the passage at the end of the 1851 letter? Can a text not intended as a lyric become one? Can a text once read as a lyric be unread? If so, then what is—or was—a lyric?

The argument of *Dickinson's Misery* is that the century and a half that spans the circulation of Dickinson's work as poetry chronicles rather exactly the emergence of the lyric genre as a modern mode of literary interpretation. To put briefly what I will unfold at length in the pages that follow: from the mid-nineteenth through the beginning of the twenty-first century, to be lyric is to be read as lyric—and to be read as a lyric is to be printed and framed as a lyric. While it is beyond the scope of this book to trace the lyricization of poetry that began in the eighteenth century, the exemplary story of the composition, recovery, and publication of Dickinson's writing begins one chapter, at least, in what is so far a largely unwritten history. As we have already begun to see, Dickinson's enduring role in that history depends on the ephemeral quality of the texts she left behind. By a modern lyric logic that will become familiar in the pages that follow, the (only) apparently contextless or sceneless, even evanescent nature of Dickinson's writing attracted an increasingly professionalized attempt to secure and contextualize it as a certain kind (or genre) of literature—as what we might call, after Charles Taylor, a lyric social imaginary.[7] Think of the modern imaginary construction of the lyric as what allows the term to move from adjectival to nominal status and back again. Whereas other poetic genres (epic, poems on affairs of state, georgic, pastoral, verse epistle, epitaph, elegy, satire) may remain embedded in specific historical occasions or narratives, and thus depend upon some description of those occasions and narratives for their interpretation (it is hard to understand "The Dunciad," for example, if one does not know the characters involved or have access to lots of handy footnotes), the poetry that comes to be understood as lyric after the eighteenth century is thought to require as its context only the occasion of its reading. This is not to say that there were not ancient Greek and Roman, Anglo-Saxon, medieval, Provençal, Renaissance, metaphysical, Colonial, Republican, Augustan—even romantic and modern!—lyrics. It is simply to propose that the riddles, papyrae, epigrams, songs, sonnets, *blasons*, *Lieder*, elegies, dialogues, conceits, ballads, hymns and odes considered lyrical in the Western tradition before the early nineteenth century were lyric in a very different sense than was or will be the poetry that the mediating hands of editors, reviewers, critics, teachers, and poets have rendered as lyric in the last century and a half.[8]

As my syntax indicates, that shift in genre definition is primarily a shift in temporality; as variously mimetic poetic subgenres collapsed into the expressive romantic lyric of the nineteenth century, the various modes of poetic circulation—scrolls, manuscript books, song cycles, miscellanies, broadsides, hornbooks, libretti, quartos, chapbooks, recitation manuals, annuals, gift books, newspapers, anthologies—tended to disappear behind an idealized scene of reading progressively identified with an idealized moment of expression. While other modes—dramatic genres, the essay, the novel—may have been seen to be historically contingent, the lyric emerged as the one genre indisputably literary and independent of social contingency, perhaps not intended for public reading at all. By the early nineteenth century, poetry had never before been so dependent on the mediating hands of the editors and reviewers who managed the print public sphere, yet in this period an idea of the lyric as ideally unmediated by those hands or those readers began to emerge and is still very much with us.

Susan Stewart has dubbed the late eighteenth century's highly mediated manufacture of the illusion of unmediated genres a case of "distressed genres," or "new antiques." Her terms allude to modern print culture's attempts "to author a context as well as an artifact," and thus to imitate older forms—such as the epic, the fable, the proverb, the ballad—

7

while creating the impression that our access to those forms is as immediate as it was in the imaginary modern versions of oral and collective culture to which those forms originally belonged.[9] Stewart does not include the lyric as a "distressed genre," but her suggestion that old genres were made in new ways could be extended to include the idea that the lyric is—or was—a genre in the first place. As Gérard Genette has argued, "the relatively recent theory of the 'three major genres' not only lays claim to ancientness, and thus to an appearance or presumption of being eternal and therefore self-evident," but is itself the effect of "projecting onto the founding text of classical poetics a fundamental tenet of 'modern' poetics (which actually . . . means *romantic* poetics)."[10]

Yet even if the lyric (especially in its broadly defined difference from narrative and drama) is a larger version of the new antique, a retro-projection of modernity, a new concept artificially treated to appear old, the fact that it is a figment of modern poetics does not prevent it from becoming a creature of modern poetry. The interesting part of the story lies in the twists and turns of the plot through which the lyric imaginary takes historical form. But what plot is that? My argument here is that the lyric takes form through the development of reading practices in the nineteenth and twentieth centuries that become the practice of literary criticism. As Mark Jeffreys eloquently describes the process I am calling lyricization, "lyric did not conquer poetry: poetry was reduced to lyric. Lyric became the dominant form of poetry only as poetry's authority was reduced to the cramped margins of culture."[11] This is to say that the notion of lyric enlarged in direct proportion to the diminution of the varieties of poetry—or at least that became the ratio as the idea of the lyric was itself produced by a critical culture that imagined itself on the definitive margins of culture. Thus by the early twenty-first century it became possible for Mary Poovey to describe "the lyricization of literary criticism" as the dependence of all postromantic professional literary reading on "the genre of the romantic lyric."[12] The conceptual problem is that if the lyric is the creation of print and critical mediation, and if that creation then produces the very versions of interpretive mediation that in turn produce it, any attempt to trace the historical situation of the lyric will end in tautology.

Or that might be the critical predicament if the retrospective definition and inflation of the lyric were either as historically linear or as hermeneutically circular as much recent criticism, whether historicist or formalist, would lead us to believe. What has been left out of most thinking about the process of lyricization is that it is an uneven series of negotiations of many different forms of circulation and address. To take one prominent example, the preface to Thomas Percy's *Reliques of Ancient English Poetry* (1765) describes the "ancient foliums in the Editor's possession," claims to have subjected the excerpts from these manuscripts to the judgment of "several learned and ingenious friends" as well as to the approval of "the author of *The Rambler* and the late Mr. Shenstone," and concludes that "the names of so many men of learning and character the Editor hopes will serve as amulet, to guard him from every unfavourable censure for having bestowed any attention on a parcel of Old Ballads."[13] Not only does Percy not claim that historical genres of verse are directly addressed to contemporary readers (and each of his "relics" is prefaced by a historical sketch and description of its manuscript context in order to emphasize the excerpt's distance from the reader), but he also acknowledges the role of the critical climate to which the poems in his edition *were* addressed.[14] Yet by 1833, John Stuart Mill, in what has become the most influentially misread essay in the history of Anglo-American poetics, could write that "the peculiarity of poetry appears to us to lie in the poet's utter unconsciousness of a listener. Poetry is feeling confessing itself to itself, in moments of solitude."[15] As Anne Janowitz has written, "in Mill's theory . . . the social setting is benignly severed from poetic intentions."[16] What happened between 1765 and 1833 was not that editors and printers and critics lost influence over how poetry was presented to the public; on the contrary, as Matthew Rowlinson has remarked, in the nineteenth century "lyric appears as a genre newly totalized in print."[17] And it is also not true that the social setting of the lyric is less important in the nineteenth than it was in the eighteenth century. On the contrary, because of the explosion of popular print, by the early nineteenth century in England, as Stuart Curran has put it, "the most eccentric feature of [the] entire culture [was] that it was simply mad for poetry"—and as Janowitz has trenchantly argued, such madness extended from the public poetry of the eighteenth century through an enormously popular range of individualist, socialist, and variously political and personal poems.[18] In nineteenth-century U.S. culture, the circulation of many poetic genres in newspapers and the popular press and the crucial significance of political and public poetry to the culture as a whole is yet to be appreciated in later criticism (or, if it is, it is likely to be given as the reason that so little enduring poetry was produced in the United States in the nineteenth century, with the routine exception of Whitman and Dickinson, who are also routinely mischaracterized as unrecognized by their own century).[19]

At the risk of making a long story short, it is fair to say that the progressive idealization of what was a much livelier, more explicitly mediated, historically contingent and public context for many varieties of poetry had culminated by the middle of the twentieth century (around the time Dickinson began to be published in "complete" editions) in an idea of the lyric as temporally self-present or unmediated. This is the idea aptly expressed in the first edition of Brooks and Warren's *Understanding Poetry* in 1938: "classifications such as 'lyrics of meditation,' and 'religious lyrics,' and 'poems of patriotism,' or 'the sonnet,' 'the Ode,' 'the song,' etc." are, according to the editors, "arbitrary and irrational classifications" that should give way to a present-tense presentation of "poetry as a thing in itself worthy of study."[20] Not accidentally, as we shall see, the shift in definition accompanied the migration of lyric from the popular press to the classroom—but for now we should note that by the time that Emily Dickinson's poetry became available in scholarly editions and university anthologies, the history of various genres of poetry was read as simply lyric, and lyrics were read as poems one could understand without reference to that history or those genres.

The first and second chapters of this book will trace the developing relation between lyric reading and lyric theory in the United States over the nineteenth and twentieth centuries by focusing on the circulation and reception of Dickinson's remains. What makes Dickinson exemplary for a history of the lyric in which I wish to chronicle a shift in the definition (or undoing) of the genre as an interpretive abstraction is that there is so little left of her. Yet, as we shall also see, the persistent sense that something *is* left—those handsewn leaves, those pieces of envelopes pinned at odd angles—keeps recalling modern readers to an archaic moment of handwritten composition and personal encounter, a private moment yet unpublicized, a moment before or outside literature that also becomes essential to modern lyric reading in post-eighteenth-century print culture.[21] As Yopie Prins has written, "if 'reading lyric' implies that lyric is already defined as an object to be read, 'lyric reading' implies an act of lyrical reading, or reading lyrically, that poses the possibility of lyric without presuming its objective existence or assuming it to be a form of subjective expression."[22] This is as much as to say that while any literary genre is always a virtual object, there may be ways to read the history of a genre on the way to becoming such an object. Still, as Prins implies, the object that the lyric has become is by now identified with an expressive theory that makes it difficult for us to place lyrics back into the sort of developmental history—of social relations, of print, of edition, reception, and criticism—that is taken for granted in definitions of the novel.[23] The reading of the lyric produces a theory of the lyric that then produces a reading of the lyric, and that hermeneutic circle rarely opens to dialectical interruption. In his famous version of "lyric reading," Paul de Man cast such an interruption as theoretically impossible: "no lyric can be read lyrically," according to de Man, "nor can the object of a lyrical reading be itself a lyric."[24] While this is as much as to say (as de Man went on to say) that "the lyric is not a genre" (261) in theory, *Dickinson's Misery* shows how

10

poems become lyrics in history. Once we decide that Dickinson wrote poems (or once that decision is made for us), and once we decide that most poems are lyrics (or once that decision is made for us), we (by definition) lose sight of the historical process of lyric reading that is the subject of this book. Precisely because lyrics can only exist theoretically, they are made historically.

Since most of that historical process has taken place in relation to Dickinson in the United States, the subtitle of this book could be "American Lyric Reading," but it is not the national identity of the lyric imaginary that Dickinson comes to represent that I want to emphasize here. As we shall see, for over a century readers of Dickinson have been preoccupied with her work's exemplary American character, and that aspect of the public imagination of Dickinson will be central to the pages that follow. There *is* an account of the lyricization of specifically American poetry to be written, especially since there has been no comprehensive view of that history since Roy Harvey Pearce's *The Continuity of American Poetry* in 1961. Pearce takes for granted that Puritan epitaphs, elegies, anagrams and meditations, Republican epics, satires, dialogues in verse, pedagogical exercises, versified commencement addresses, protest songs, contemporary ballads, odes, and commemorative recitation exercises can all be read as lyrics—indeed, one might argue that it is lyric reading that makes possible the "continuity" of Pearce's title. Such a close affiliation between lyricization and Americanization will come to seem familiar in these chapters, though there is much to be said about the relation between national and generic identity that will fall outside the chapters themselves. I will be arguing that while the national as well as the gendered, sexed, classed, and (just barely) raced identities at play in Dickinson's writing have been examined to different ends in recent criticism, the generic lens they must all pass through has been treated as transparent.[25] This book attempts to make the only apparently transparent genre through which Dickinson has been brought into public view itself visible. Some of the work of doing so might at times seem microscopic, since it entails a focus not on big ideas—poetry, America, person- and womanhood—but on the small details on which those ideas precariously (though surprisingly tenaciously) depend.

Consider, for example, one overlooked detail in the history of reading Dickinson—a bit of ephemera that tempts while it also resists lyric reading. Like so many of Dickinson's letters, the rather long 1851 letter to Austin that closes with the lines that Johnson "arbitrarily established" in 1955 as a lyric and that Franklin then decided were not a lyric contained an enclosure: a leaf pinned to a slip of paper inscribed "We'll meet again and heretofore some summer 'morning'" (fig. 3). The "little forest, whose leaf is ever green" to which the lines-become-verse point is and is not the

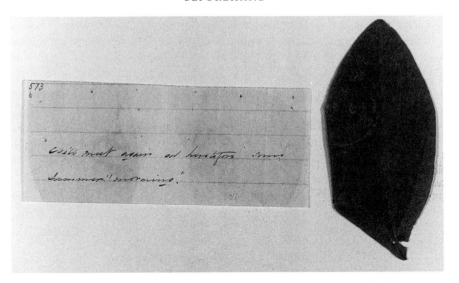

Figure 3. Emily Dickinson to Austin Dickinson, 17 October 1851. The postscript was pinned where the hole appears in the leaf at the bottom of the picture; the postmark on the leaf matches the postmark on the envelope that contained it. Courtesy of Amherst College Archives and Special Collections (ED ms. 573, enclosure).

leaf that Austin held in his hand, and that difference is the enclosure's point. Whether or not the lines at the end of the letter are printed as a lyric, the now-faded leaf that left its imprint on the line attached to those lines cannot be printed—though it is here, for the first time, reproduced, and thus unfolded from Dickinson's letter and folded into the genre of literary criticism. Now addressed not to Austin but to my anonymous reader (to you), not the leaf itself but a copy of its remains, Dickinson's enclosure becomes legible as a detail of a literary corpus. Or does it? While for Austin the leaf popped out of the letter as an ironic commentary on the time and place the familiar correspondents did not but may yet have shared (if only on the page, or between quotation marks) on the October day when the letter was sent ("some summer 'morning'"), by the time that you (whoever you are) encounter the image of the leaf in this book about Dickinson you will understand it instead as a reminder of what you cannot share with Dickinson's first readers, an overlooked object lyrically suspended in time. What may seem lyrical about it is the apparent immediacy of our encounter with it: editors and printers and critics and teachers may have transformed Dickinson's work into something it was not intended to be, but a leaf is a leaf is a leaf. Yet Dickinson's message pinned to the leaf asks its intended reader to understand that a leaf taken out of context is not self-defining; it won't remain "ever green" but will (as it has) fade to brown. Dickinson could not have foreseen that the faded leaf would end up in a college library, or that her intimate letter to her brother would one day be addressed to the readers of the 1955 *Complete Poems of Emily Dickinson*. She could also not have foreseen that the leaf in the library would bear the trace of its transmission stamped by a hand not Dickinson's nor any reader's own. *Dickinson's Misery* is about the way in which the confusion between the pathos of a subject and the pathos of transmission evoked by the leaf rather accurately predicts the character of the poet who will come to be read heretofore as Emily Dickinson. This book is also about the way in which that confusion has come to define, in the last century and a half, not only an idea of what counts as Dickinson's verse but of what does and does not count as literary language—and especially of what does and does not count as lyric language. Let the postmark on the leaf that mediated the encounter between Dickinson and her intimate reader also stand for the institutions that exceed as they deliver literature—modes of cultural transmission that make even an old leaf legible.

My title, *Dickinson's Misery*, is intended to gain significance as this book progresses. As my account of the historical transmission of Dickinson's writing takes us further and further away from a direct encounter with that writing, "Dickinson's Misery" may evoke the pathos not of Dickinson herself but of her writing as a lost object, a *texte en souffrance*.[26] Yet while Derrida may be right that writing always goes astray—or is, by definition, disseminated in order to become literature—*published* writing does not wander away on its own: it is directed and addressed by some to others. In my first chapter, "Dickinson Undone," I will consider recent editorial attempts to release Dickinson's writing from the constraint of earlier editorial conventions and to rescue the character of that writing from institutional mediation—even from the constraint of the codex book itself. I will argue that recent attempts to liberate Dickinson from the unfair treatment of editorial hands are dependent on an imaginary model of the lyric—a model perhaps more constraining, because so much more capacious, than those Dickinson's early genteel editors supposed. The aspects of Dickinson's writing that do not fit into any modern model of the lyric—verse mixed with prose, lines written in variation, or lines (like the one pinned to the leaf) dependent on their artifactual contexts—have been left to suffer under the weight of variorum editions or have been transformed into weightless, digitized images of fading manuscripts made possible by invisible hands. In my second chapter, I will measure the distance between the circulation of Dickinson's verse in several spheres of familiar and public culture in the nineteenth century and the circulation of ideas of the lyric in academic culture in the twentieth century. The more we know about the circumstances of the nineteenth-century composition and reception of

Dickinson's poems, the less susceptible they seem to the theories of lyric abstraction that emerged in twentieth-century critical culture. From genteel criticism to New Criticism to de Man's lyric theory to the pragmatic backlash against literary theory and the new lyric humanism, ideas of the lyric in the century during which Dickinson's work proliferated in print constructed and deconstructed the genre in which Dickinson's writing has been cast, but in doing so they tended to widen rather than close the distance between that genre and that writing. The remaining chapters then attempt to bridge that distance, or to claim that Dickinson's work may help us to do so. In my third chapter, I will compare Dickinson's figures of address—her sociable correspondence—to the forms of address that have been attributed to her texts as a set of lyrics. In my fourth chapter, I will explore Dickinson's forms of self-reference, especially literal or physical self-reference, in the context of nineteenth-century American intellectual culture and in the context of twentieth-century feminist discourse. In my final chapter, I will bring those modern feminist concerns to bear upon the nineteenth-century sentimental lyric, an often forgotten genre of vicarious identification that itself may span the distance between Dickinson's writing and the image of the poet she has become. In all of the chapters, my concern will be to trace the arc of an historical poetics, a theory of lyric reading, that seeks to revise not only our understanding of Dickinson's work but our contemporary habits of poetic interpretation.

Dickinson's Misery tries to do many things, but one thing it does not try to be is a reception history. Scholars have already compiled excellent critical histories of Dickinson's reception, though there is much more to be done, especially on the history of Dickinson's popular readership, yet that is not my project in this book.[27] Here I am interested instead in the models of the lyric that governed Dickinson's edition and reception. I could have chosen to chronicle those models strictly chronologically—the aesthetic model of the 1890s, the Imagist model of 1914, the modernist model of the 1920s, the culturally representative model of the 1930s, the pedagogical model of the 1940s, the professional model of the 1950s, the subversive model of the 1960s, the conflicted model of the 1970s, the feminist model of the 1980s, the materialist and queer models of the 1990s, and the public sphere and cyberspace models of the beginning of the twenty-first century— but as this list suggests, such a chronology quickly devolves into a thematic catalogue of types of lyrics while leaving the generic character of those lyrics relatively stable. This book instead combines reception history, book history, literary history, genre theory, and one genealogy of the discipline of literary criticism to destabilize an idea of the genre of which Dickinson's work has become such an important modern paradigm. Editors, reviewers, teachers, and readers may make up versions of a genre to suit their place and time, but they do not do so from scratch. My subtitle, "A Theory of Lyric Reading," is meant to suggest that genre is neither an Aristotelian, taxonomic, transhistorical category of literary definition nor simply something we make up on the spot to suit the occasion of reading. What a reading of Dickinson over and against the generic models through which she has been published and read can tell us about the lyric as a genre is indeed that history has made the lyric in its image, but we have yet to recognize that image as our own.

Dickinson Undone

BIRD-TRACKS

IN OCTOBER 1891, Thomas Wentworth Higginson published an article that may be read as a miniature portrait of Dickinson's reception as a lyric poet. The article, not ostensibly on the poetry but on "Emily Dickinson's Letters," responded to what Higginson called "a suddenness of success almost without a parallel in American literature" (that is, the commercial success of his own first edition of Dickinson's *Poems* the year before) by making public the poet's private letters to her future literary editor. After printing the first one (figs. 4a, 4b), from April, 1862, which (now) famously begins,

MR. HIGGINSON—*Are you too deeply occupied to say if my verse is alive?*,

Higginson remarks in the *Atlantic* article, "The letter was postmarked "Amherst," and it was in a handwriting so peculiar that it seemed as if the writer might have taken her first lessons by studying the famous fossil bird-tracks in the museum of that college town." Dickinson's inaugural letter to Higginson has been remembered and reprinted so often that her self-introduction to the abolitionist, women's rights activist, former Longfellow student at Harvard, magazine editor, and literary insider now appears to have been addressed to us. Yet Higginson is the one who makes the letter seem to have been publicly addressed to a private individual rather than privately addressed to a public figure when he invents a story about his own encounter with unfamiliar writing: according to this story, first the reader notices the postmark on the envelope, then the character of the hand (which was not actually yet "so peculiar" in 1862), and then he puts the two together. By way of this anecdote, Dickinson's editor—whom she had addressed as her "Preceptor" in response to Higginson's own public letter "To a Young Contributor" in that month's *Atlantic*—makes his mediating role in the recognition of Dickinson's poetry as American literature disappear.[1] The interest that by the time of Higginson's 1891 article readers had already demonstrated by buying out six printings of Dickinson's *Poems* in the volume's first six months of publication (a phenomenon much publicized at the time in several cities—as one E. J. Edwards remarked after noting that it was impossible to buy a copy of the *Poems* in

New York a few days before Christmas, 1890) is presupposed in Higginson's fable of a first, innocent encounter with Dickinson's handwriting.[2] What Higginson also supposed in that first encounter and what every reader since Higginson has assumed is that what Emily Dickinson wrote was lyric poetry. But how do we know that lyrics are what Dickinson wrote? What definition of the lyric turns words on an envelope into a poem?

Although he goes on to claim that "the impression of a wholly new and original poetic genius was as distinct on my mind at the first reading . . . as it is now," it was the public demand for more information in print that occasioned the editor's rendition of his first impression. By the time that Higginson told his story of trying to decipher Dickinson's peculiar hand, Mabel Loomis Todd had already transcribed and carefully copied and Roberts Brothers had typeset and many booksellers had sold many volumes of Dickinson's verse. It is thus possible to say that in Higginson's narrative, print precedes handwriting: the story he weaves about Dickinson's manuscript is really a story about the poems already in print.[3] Yet print is not the only defining feature of Dickinson's writing in Higginson's account: his fable of the identity between that writing and the spirit of its place makes writing seem to precede what it represents. In this fiction, Emily Dickinson learned to write not at Amherst Academy or Mount Holyoke Seminary but in the museum of the college her family helped to establish. The product of an institution within an institution, Dickinson's originality appears to Higginson a copy of a prehistoric natural form—a form that was, not incidentally, the trace of the figure of the bird that Dickinson (and almost everyone else in the nineteenth century) associated with lyricism. Subtle and fanciful as Higginson's imaginary scenario may be, it is also an image of Dickinson's lyric reception—a reception that Higginson figures as already encrypted in Dickinson's writing, fixed into timeless generic form and rescued, excerpted, and placed on public display by a private cultural institution.

Higginson's edition, criticism, and promotion of Dickinson has been much criticized by later editors, critics, and promoters of Dickinson. Either Higginson is accused of failing to recognize Dickinson's greatness by not bringing her into print during her lifetime, or he is accused of having made the volume he did publish posthumously an image of his own idea of what Dickinson's poems should have been. Most readers would agree that Dickinson's early editors imposed conventional poetic form—including titles, regular rhyme, and standard punctuation—on the published verse that in manuscript evaded or swerved away from such conventions, and most would also agree that editors since Higginson have brought Dickinson's published work ever closer to its original scriptive forms, so

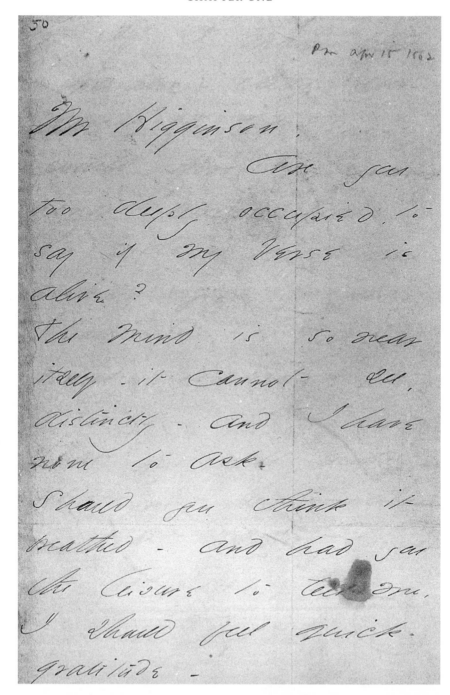

Figure 4a. Emily Dickinson to Thomas Wentworth Higginson, April 1862. Boston Public Library/Rare Books Department, Courtesy of the Trustees (Ms. AM 1093, 1).

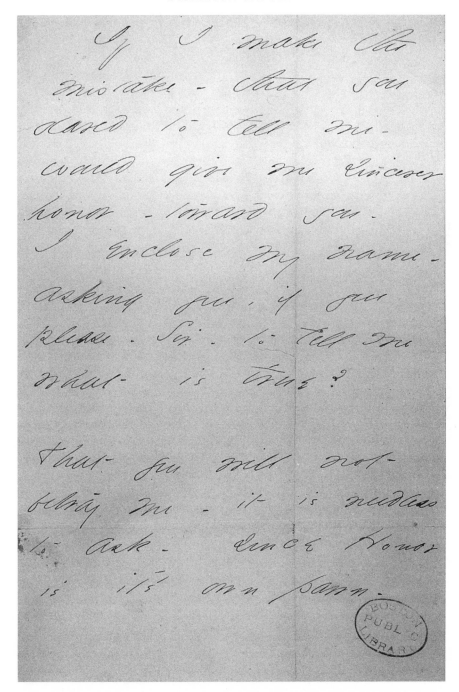

Figure 4b. Emily Dickinson to Thomas Wentworth Higginson, April 1862. Boston Public Library/Rare Books Department, Courtesy of the Trustees (Ms. AM 1093, 1).

that in moving forward from the nineteenth to the twentieth to the twenty-first century we have gradually moved back to discover the "original poetic genius" early editors failed adequately to represent in print. Increasingly, that revelation has taken the cast of what Mary Loeffelholz has called "the unediting of Dickinson," a growing fascination over the last decades (after R. W. Franklin's publication of *The Manuscript Books of Emily Dickinson* in 1981) with the details of Dickinson's handwriting and with the ready-to-hand artifacts on which she wrote. "The full significance of Dickinson's writing," Jerome McGann predicted in 1991, "will begin to appear when we explicate in detail the importance of the different papers she used, her famous 'fascicles,' her scripts and their conventions of punctuation and layout."[4] Yet as editors and critics have returned their attention to Dickinson's papers bound and unbound, to her peculiar hand, and to the "layout" between the two, the question lurking in Higginson's 1891 description of Dickinson's manuscript has resurfaced: what was it that Emily Dickinson wrote?

Higginson's image of fossilized bird-tracks contains a (rather beautiful) notion of the lyric as the form informing Dickinson's scriptive character—a very late-nineteenth-century image of lyric reading. Later editors have certainly come a long way since Higginson, and the lyrics they decipher in Dickinson's manuscripts have changed character, yet although at the time of this writing many debates rage over the literary forms immanent in Dickinson's writing, there is and always has been uniform consensus that Emily Dickinson wrote lyric poems. While versions of Dickinson's lyricism have shifted as interpretive communities have shifted, some version of the genre everyone since Higginson has assumed Dickinson wanted her writing to become has been discovered to be already there. Like Higginson in 1891, most readers have found it impossible to read Dickinson's manuscripts as if they had not already been printed as poems. Yet Higginson *had* read just such manuscripts—and had not, until Dickinson's death, printed her work as a series of poems. Did Higginson not recognize a poem when he saw one? If we imagine the now historically impossible scenario (conjured on the first page of this book) of "discovering" Dickinson's as yet unprinted manuscripts, would we recognize a Dickinson poem if we saw one?

For the moment I would like to set aside strictly formal answers to that question. Hymnal meter, the occasional pentameter line, stanzaic breaks, regular and irregular rhymes, and rhetorical patterns define much of Dickinson's writing as *poetic* in a very broad sense of the term—in the broadest sense, as language not unversified. Many manuscripts—especially the "fascicles," or hand-sewn booklets, but also such separate sheets as the ones Dickinson enclosed to Higginson when she asked if her verse was "alive"—contain only such forms, and many more contain such forms within or alongside others, commonly in the genre of the familiar letter. Yet, as we have seen, although *poetic* and *lyric* have come to seem cognate, they are not necessarily—and certainly have not historically been thought to be—so. The instance of the letter to Austin attached to the leaf demonstrates one obvious way in which a later editor turned cadenced prose into a printed lyric. Whether such a lyric may have been imagined by Dickinson or her brother we cannot say—but we can say that it is not visible on the manuscript page as it is in Johnson's edition. If the lyricization of poetry has led us to read the lyric, as Michael Warner has put it, "with cultivated disregard of its circumstance of circulation, understanding it as an image of absolute privacy," it is also worth noting that our ability to cultivate such disregard depends on the print circulation of lyrics as such.[5] Neither the leaf nor its accidental postmark is printable, and neither could be included in a volume of Dickinson's poems. The lyric reading practiced by every editor since Higginson has actively cultivated a disregard for the circumstances of Dickinson's manuscripts' circulation. By being taken out of their sociable circumstances, those manuscripts have become poems, and by becoming poems, they have been interpreted as lyrics.

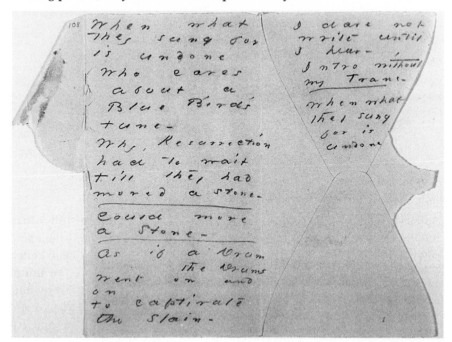

Figure 5. Courtesy of Amherst College Archives and Special Collections (ED ms. 108).

Sometimes, however, a piece of Dickinson's writing illustrates the historically fictive process of lyric reading not because it has become an imaginary poem but because it has not become—at least in print—a poem at all. About 1881, or thirty years after Dickinson wrote *"Here* is a little forest, whose leaf is ever green" and attached a little green (now brown and postmarked) leaf to her letter, she pencilled some lines—this time separated, after a fashion, as verse—on the inside of a split-open envelope that was addressed (by her cousin) to herself (fig. 5). Here are the lines, printed as literally as possible:

When what   I dare not
they sung for   write until
is undone   I hear—
Who cares   Intro without
about a   my Trans—
Blue Bird's   ——————
tune—   When what
Why, Resurrection   They sung
had to wait   for is
till they had   undone
moved a stone—

——————————

Could move
a stone—

——————————

As if a Drum
The Drum
went on and
on
to captivate
the slain—

As far as we know, these lines were not much read by anyone other than the envelope's addressee between their discovery in 1886 and their first publication in 1945. From 1945 until the present, they have been called various things: a worksheet, a variant, a fragment, and, once, an unfinished poem.[6] One thing they have never been called is a poem. Why not? If pieces of letters, riddles, recipes, notes, botanical descriptions, complaints—if almost anything Dickinson wrote has been turned by some editor into a poem, why not this? And what can the fact that this is one of Dickinson's versified manuscripts that has not been printed as a poem tell us about what it is we recognize as a lyric?

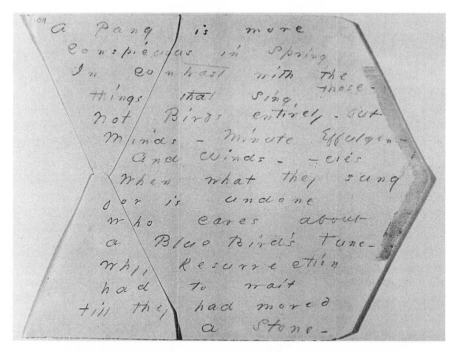

Figure 6. Courtesy of Amherst College Archives and Special Collections (ED ms. 109).

I do not (or do not simply) pose these questions rhetorically; Dickinson's scholarly editors have good answers to them. Both Johnson and Franklin publish in their collected *Poems* another set of lines on a split-open envelope (addressed to Dickinson's sister, "Vinnie") from the same period (fig. 6). I will again transcribe the lines as they were written:

> A Pang is more
> Conspicuous in Spring
> In contrast with the
>   those—
> things that sing,
> Not Birds entirely—but
> Minds—minute Effulgen—
>   —cies
>   And winds—
> When what they sung
> For is undone
> Who cares about
> A Blue Bird's tune—
> Why, Resurrection

had to wait
till they had moved
a Stone—

Since the last lines on this envelope are the first lines on the envelope in figure 5, they might be read as a revision or later version. Johnson thought that they *were* written later, dating the lines in figure 5 "about 1877" and the lines in figure 6 "about 1881." Johnson was allowed to see the manuscripts (then in the possession of Millicent Todd Bingham) on only two occasions, though he had photostats of them. Franklin, who had more liberal access to the manuscripts (now in the Amherst College Library) dates both "about 1881" (as had Bingham). Though roughly contemporary by his estimate, Franklin prints only the lines in figure 6 in his Reading Edition, and prints the lines in figure 5 as a variant of Poem 1545 in his variorum edition. In general, Franklin's understanding of the principles that guided what he tellingly calls "Dickinson's workshop" dictates his choice of the last complete version—preferably a fair copy or fascicle inclusion—for publication. His edition is guided by the assumption that "the distinction between genres was Dickinson's own" and that the text of a poem must be separable from its artifact.[7] This is to say that Franklin is the best and latest in a long line of editors who have assumed that what Dickinson aspired to write were individual, discrete, more or less polished lyric poems and that she wanted them to be printed as such. Yet what makes one of the envelopes in figures 5 and 6 look later, more individual, more highly crafted, more *printable* than the other?

The handwriting on the envelope inscribed with "A Pang . . ." (fig. 6) is slightly larger than that on the other envelope, and although Dickinson's writing did become larger and more widely spaced as she grew older, within the same year there could be many variations. The text in figure 5 might also seem more tentative than that in figure 6, since an entire line is given in variation, but as we shall see, the sheets in the fascicles often include several variants, and yet are considered fair copies. Both sets of lines may be scanned in the alternating three- and four-foot patterns typical of Dickinson's writing; formal criteria will not separate finished poem from draft. In fact, if what one wants to publish is a formally complete lyric, it is difficult to find in all of the Dickinson corpus a poem that closes with the repetition of its first lines, as does the text in figure 5: "When what they sung for is undone . . . when what they sung for is undone." Such repetition could certainly be read as a refrain, one of the oldest formal devices of the lyric. If we were to continue to read figure 5 along these lines, we could draw on such authoritative theorists of lyric form as Barbara Herrnstein Smith and John Hollander, who both point out that "the modern lyrical refrain derives in good part from the medieval carol burden," where the repeated lines "announce that a song will be sung and then that it has been sung."[8] In contrast, the text in figure 6 ends in what is the middle of the text in figure 5, and if it was written later, it does not include the variant for "they had moved a stone" ("could move a stone"). But the lines that begin the text in figure 6 that appear nowhere in figure 5—

> A Pang is more
>   Conspicuous in Spring
> In contrast with the
>   those—
>   things that sing,
> Not Birds entirely—but
> Minds—minute Effulgen—
>   —cies
>   and winds—

are beautiful, and so may give the impression that they were added to the lines that begin "When what they sung for" as a more developed and finished composition. I could continue to give interpretive reasons for describing either envelope as a lyric, and those reasons would participate in a phenomenology of lyric reading that moves the text into the present-tense world of the poem itself, once we decide what that is. A comparison of the two envelopes thus not only raises questions about the conventions of literary entextualization (to which we shall return), but those questions also lead to another, more basic one: if either text can be read as a lyric, then how do we recognize a lyric poem when we see one?[9]

If my reader is by now impatient with the hermeneutic fundamentalism of that question, you are not the only one. In the section of the *Aesthetics* on poetry, Hegel seems to have anticipated a similar aversion:

> To define the poetic as such or to give a description of what is poetic horrifies [*abhorrezieren*] nearly all who have written about poetry. And in fact if a man begins to talk about poetry as an imaginative art without having previously examined what art's content and general mode of representation is, he will find it extremely difficult to know where to look for the proper essence of poetry. But the awkwardness of his problem especially increases if he starts from the individual character of single works and then proposes to assert some universal derived from their character and supposed to be valid for the most varied *genres* and sorts of poetry. Along these lines the most heterogeneous works count as poetry. If this assumption is presupposed and the question is then raised: By what right should such productions count as poems? the difficulty just named enters at once.[10]

Most of us would agree with Hegel that to derive a general conception—a *genre*—from a single example is a logical mistake; on the other hand, few of us have a synthetic theory of Beauty and the Ideal that would allow us to avoid such mistakes. Yet pragmatically, the difference between being able or unable to answer the question, "By what right should such productions count as poems?" is (even for Hegel) less a question of one's transcendental theories than it is a question of temporality. According to Hegel, relief from the horrors of poetic definition—articulation of "the poetic as such" as well as of "the most varied *genres* and sorts of poetry"—is allowed by an earlier moment when generic difficulties that one *would* have encountered if one had not "previously examined" aesthetic theory have already disappeared. By the time that Hegel invokes these practical difficulties, they are fortunately fictive. But Hegel's precedent, metapragmatic, temporally decisive moment seems to be exactly what is in question in both the historical determination and the figurative power of Dickinson's lines on the envelopes. Dickinson's lines return us to what Hegel identified as "the awkwardness of the problem" of reading the lyric, especially since that awkwardness is, awkwardly, what the lines that have never been published as a poem are about.

"When what they sung for . . ."

If generic recognition depends on hermeneutic promise, then the lines in figure 5 are a poem many times over. Although these lines have never been described as a lyric, we could interpret them as an exemplary lyric—indeed, as several different exemplary lyrics. But is a lyric by interpretation made? As Hegel would say, one's answer will depend upon what theory of the lyric has been previously assumed. But as Hegel also suggests, such a theory is not assumed at will, but assumed in time. Paul de Man may be right to conclude in theory (along Hegelian lines) that "no lyric can be read lyrically, nor can the object of a lyrical reading be itself a lyric," but, as we shall see in the next chapter, that theory is a set-up for an inevitable historical process. While de Man's false maxim seems to beg the question of what we mean by "lyric," it leaves open the question of what it is to "read"—lyrically or otherwise—or of who reads when.[11] Consider three theoretically historical readings of the lines that have never been printed as a lyric.

If we were to follow the late-nineteenth-century, aesthetic strain of reading implicit in Higginson's remarks, we might say that the first lines on the envelope in figure 5 invoke not birdsong's full-throated ease but the pathos of the moment when the song's occasion is over. The question

("Who cares?") is not a question about anyone's recognition of the song it-self but about whether "[t]he world should listen then—as I am listening now"—that is, about whether song has an afterlife. As my allusions to Keats and Shelley suggest, this sort of lyric reading of Dickinson assumes that by 1881 Dickinson's own lyric reading of romanticism and several versions of postromanticism may be taken for granted; a bluebird's (or a nightingale's or a sky-lark's or a bobolink's or a darkling thrush's) tune would always already have been for Dickinson (as for Higginson) a lyric poem. In the chapters that follow I will have much to say about Dick-inson's preoccupation with the trope of birdsong as the strain of inhu-man lyricism turned to poetic type by the romantics and "fossilized"—excerpted and contextualized—by Victorian poets.[12] In the condensed phrase "inhuman lyricism" I mean to recall the nineteenth century's asso-ciation of birdsong with a pure expressive capacity the human poet cannot own, and also to point out that it would follow that the nineteenth-century reading of this figure would not be as a synonym for poetic voice but as a song the poet cannot voice. In the early nineteenth century, birdsong was not poetic personification but lyric antipersonification (Keats could not become the nightingale, Shelley could not pretend to be the skylark), yet by the time of Dickinson's publication at the end of the century, birds and poets were often conflated with one another. So Thomas Aldrich could re-mark in 1892 and 1903 that "Miss Dickinson's stanzas, with their impossible rhyme, their involved significance, their interrupted flute-note of birds that have no continuous music, seem to have caught the ear of a group of early listeners. A shy New England bluebird, shifting its light load of song, has for a moment been taken for a strange nightingale."[13] Aldrich's complaint against what he had called in 1892 Dickinson's "versicles" ("I don't know how to designate them") is that they evoke "no continuous music"; for him, Dickinson is more bird than human rather than too human to be bird.

Yet lest that (obviously gendered) capacity be mistaken for an achieve-ment of the romantic lyric ideal, Aldrich borrows Dickinson's own habit-ual substitution of the American for the British bird and turns her distinc-tion (as well as her popularity in the 1890s) against her. Keats and Shelley may have wished for the voice of the nightingale, but according to Aldrich, readers at the end of the nineteenth century thought that Dickin-son *had* such a voice—though by his critical lights, her domestic "flute-note" never reached lyric heights. While for the romantics, the nightin-gale's inhuman lyricism granted it transcendence, Aldrich's attribution of birdlike lyricism to Dickinson denies her the artistry of the human poet and thus his immortality ("oblivion," he wrote in 1892, "lingers in the im-mediate neighborhood" [Lubbers, 94]). Dickinson could not have read Aldrich before writing the lines in figure 5, and Aldrich could not have

27

read those Dickinson lines, though he certainly did read another poem Dickinson's editors entitled "The Bluebird" (to which we shall return) in the 1891 *Poems* (F 1484). Like Higginson, then, Aldrich makes a figure of natural expression out of what is already edited verse in print—and then asks his readers to mistake his figure for Dickinson's. The homology between his bluebird and Dickinson's may indeed tempt us to read Aldrich's interpretation back into the lines in figure 5 as evidence that the answer to

> Who cares
> about a
> Blue Bird's
> tune—

is "We do!" But to hail the text in this way would be to repeat Aldrich's mistake and assume that the Blue Bird's tune had already become Dickinson's poem.

For Aldrich, of course, Dickinson's "versicles" *had* already been printed as individual poems, so his resistance to reading them as artistically achieved lyrics was predicated by their publication and reception as such. Though Aldrich's was by no means the common opinion of the 1890s, the fact that he had succeeded William Dean Howells (and Higginson) as editor of the *Atlantic Monthly* in 1881 made his views influential, at least for the genteel, nonacademic arbiters of literature who had begun to position their taste against that of the mass reading public.[14] For critics like Aldrich to complain that Dickinson's verse was "formless" was to register reservations not only about Dickinson as a poet but about the sudden popularity of her poetry as well as about Higginson's and Howells's enthusiastic embrace of Dickinson's published work. It was also to take a measured step away from the emerging academic criticism of scholars like Francis Stoddard (professor in the new department of English at New York University) who had begun to respond to charges that Dickinson's verse was "formless" by generating what would become a pedagogically influential model of organic poetic form. In January 1892 (the same month and year in which Aldrich's first review of Dickinson appeared) Stoddard could write that "Miss Dickinson's poems may be formless, or they may be worded to so fine and subtle a device that they seem formless, just as the spectrum of a far-off star may seem blankness until examined with a lens of especial power."[15] Although the practice that Stoddard advocated would not be called "close reading" in the United States until the twentieth century, his assumption that interpretation itself (and, not accidentally, at least metaphorically scientific methods of interpretation) could reveal organic aesthetic spectra speaks volumes about the history of that practice in the interpretation of lyric poetry.[16] Yet, like Aldrich's resistance to what he took to be Dickinson's lack of form, Stoddard's revelation of form was predicated by the *Poems*, already, by January 1892, in print ten times over. Whatever fine lines of the spectrum close attention might reveal, the generic identity of Dickinson's writing was not really in question for readers responding to the published poems. Of the many strains of lyricism readers discerned in Dickinson's writing, only one or two years after the publication of the *Poems* no reader could doubt that lyric poems were what Emily Dickinson had written.

This is to say that the problem of the generic recognition of the lines in figure 5 is (as it is in Hegel) a question of time rather than a question of form. If we were to pursue the line of close reading begun in the late nineteenth century and developed in twentieth-century lyric pedagogy, we might note that recognition is also the problem and time is also the question in these lines: we could read the preposition "for" as either what precedes the bird's song (that "for" or because of which the bird sang) or as what comes after, the effect of the song (what the bird sang "for" or to). It may seem an interpretive stretch worthy of Stoddard to say that Dickinson's line condenses a central problem in the theory of poetic representation (i.e., is a poem written in response to an historical event or in view of the response of a reader?), but the lines that follow the opening rhetorical question insist on the decisive role of temporality in the interpretation of form. The temporal gap between the first cause of the Blue Bird's tune and its aftermath—the moment when the occasion of the song comes "undone"—is first made analogous to the three days between Christ's death and resurrection, an interregnum figured by the stone that must be moved in real time in order for transcendental temporality to take hold. As if that analogy were not enough to ponder (does the theological await the powers of the secular? What has the new temporal order of the Resurrection to do with the ephemerality of birdsong?), the lines add another: "As if a Drum / the Drums / went on and / on / to captivate / the slain—." This is a difficult double analogy: on one hand the drumbeats parallel the birdsong and "the slain" parallel the ones who may no longer care "about a Blue Bird's tune." On the other, "the slain" are the bodies before resurrection, though these bodies do not seem to await an event in historical time to be redeemed. The pun on "captivate" makes "the slain" seem captive as well as dead, and "a Drum / the Drums" that go "on and / on" play in counterpoint to "the Blue Bird's tune": there is nothing transcendent or redemptive in the compulsive march that the drums continue to urge on those no longer animate enough to be compelled. Yet "As if" marks the perverse analogy as hypothetical; what "the slain" can no longer accomplish in history they might sustain in fiction.

The direction of the close reading I have just begun could lead us away from Stoddard's late nineteenth-century formalist proto–close reading toward a twenty-first-century form of post–close reading, from an early attempt to take the lyric out of the confusion of history to recent attempts to return the fine lines of the lyric to the broad outline of social history. If we were to read the manuscript that has never gone public as a poem, we might observe that the notion that the redemption of history depends on a sustainable theological fiction would have been common in New England twenty years before the lines appear to have been written. We might then go on to read Dickinson's twisted and condensed version of this notion as a deferred, ironic commentary on such lines as Julia Ward Howe's in "The Battle-Hymn of the Republic":

> In the beauty of the lilies Christ was born across the sea,
> With a glory in His bosom that transfigures you and me;
> As he died to make men holy, let us die to make men free;
> While God is marching on.[17]

If we were to align Dickinson's lines with this most enduringly public of nineteenth-century American poems, we might say that Dickinson's poem is its antithesis.[18] If we were to follow the line of redemptive logic in Howe (and, by implication, in Northern liberal intellectual culture in the early 1860s), we could place Dickinson's antiredemptive vision against it, and thus place her lines back into the nineteenth-century American history that conditioned them.[19] Doing so would offer us another exemplary lyric reading: in this reading, the lines have become not only formally self-reflexive (and thus reveal the rewards of close reading) but they lyrically condense the critical (and still, in 1881, critically unresolved) theological and intellectual dilemmas that surrounded the causes and effects of the official state violence that blasted the American nineteenth century into two parts (and thus reveal the rewards of an historicist reading that can incorporate temporality into the problem of form).

Yet the historicist reading, like the formalist reading, must begin by assuming that the lines in figure 5 comment upon history *as a lyric poem comments upon history* by freezing an historical moment into apt rhetorical form—that is, that like Howe's poem, they turn the privacy of perception toward a print public sphere. If the lines in figure 5 stopped on the left side of the envelope, a good argument could be made that such a freeze-frame or snapshot effect is exactly what they accomplish, but don't finish accomplishing, which is why they constitute the draft of a lyric rather than a lyric complete in itself. Yet the lines on the right-hand flap of the envelope present problems for both formal and cultural interpretations, since they return us to the problem of what or when or who it is we are reading in the first place. That question quickly becomes a question not just of rhetorical but also of quite literal context.

LYRIC CONTEXT

The literal problem in deciding whether the lines in figure 5 are or are not a lyric poem emerges most clearly when we try to read the lines in the context of one another. When, in his variorum edition, Franklin prints the lines as variants of those in figure 6, he separates as a quatrain,

> When what they sung for is undone
> Who cares about a Blue Bird's Tune—
> Why, Resurrection had to wait
> Till they had moved a stone—

and notes that this "quatrain is followed by five lines that are at least related in part, since the ultimate one is a repetition of the first line of the quatrain":

> As if a Drum went on and on
> To captivate the slain—
> I dare not write until I hear—
> Intro without my Trans—
>
> When what they sung for is undone. (F 1353)

If we scan the lines as written on the envelope, it is hard to tell why Franklin would consider the lines before the horizontal line separating the variant lines a separable quatrain and would then arrange the remaining lines as two couplets followed by the single "repetition." Yet if we recall that the lines were first printed in 1945 as an "unfinished" version of those in figure 6, Franklin's rationale becomes clearer. The first lines in figure 5 seemed to Bingham in 1945 separable from the lines that follow them because they are also the last lines in figure 6; once figure 6 had been printed as a finished poem, then the frame of publication itself determined that the repeated lines could be excised as a quatrain. Interestingly, unlike Franklin, Bingham printed some of the succeeding lines in figure 5 as another quatrain:

> As if the drums went on and on
> To captivate the slain—
> I dare not write until I hear—
> When what they sung for is undone. (BM 618)

Although only printed among the "Poems Incomplete and Unfinished" rather than as a finished lyric, Bingham's version of the lines in figure 5 looks like the other Dickinson lyrics in her edition: two symmetrical quatrains in alternating tetrameter and trimeter lines. Beneath Franklin's printed version of the manuscript in figure 5, then, lurks another poem already in print—even if it was not printed as a poem. By printing Dickinson's writing on the model of the poetry already in print, Franklin decides the genre of the lines—or the genre they don't quite manage to become—in advance. Bingham made the lines in figure 5 look like a draft of those in figure 6 by forming them into stanzas and by deleting the most troublesome line in order to do so: "Intro without my Trans—." Although Franklin does print that line, he does so in what appears in print as one of several scattered lines after the initial apparently intact quatrain, though in the manuscript the lines are no more or less set apart than the others. In publishing both what they consider the finished lyric in figure 6 and the draft lyric in figure 5, Bingham and Franklin make print itself the context in which the genre of the text will be recognized. But how would we recognize a lyric in the lines in figure 5 if we had not seen them first in print, or (to imagine an equally historically impossible situation) if we had not already decided that Dickinson wrote poems?

Perhaps a better question than *how* would be *why* we should take Dickinson's lines out of their manuscript and into printed contexts. One simple answer to that question is tautological: in order to print them, and we print them in order to read them. In context, many of Dickinson's lines are literally illegible. Consider for example the lines in figures 7a and 7b, which run down the front and back of two pages torn from a small memo tablet. The recto lines read,

> But that
> defeated accent
> is louder now
> than him
> Eternity may
> imitate
> the Affluence
> of time
> ~~Ecstasy~~
> of time
> But that
>   arrested
> suspended sylla

ble—
Is wealthier
than him

But Loves
dispelled
Emolument
Finds no
Ha
Abode in
him—
Has no re
trieve in
him

On the verso of the second sheet, we can (just barely) make out some lines that have little to do with the memo pages' series of "but . . ."s:

for Light would
certainly find it
~~and I think~~ I
~~did and~~
so
perchance I believe
did—
and
Love first
last of all things
Made
Of which this
our
living world is
but the shade
[vertically across the bottom of the page:]
possibly I did
text book—<u>Airy</u>
Bring your own
your text Book—
—Be sure to bring
suit—you—
on which
to the agile topic though that I add
to all my other subjects on which to consult you

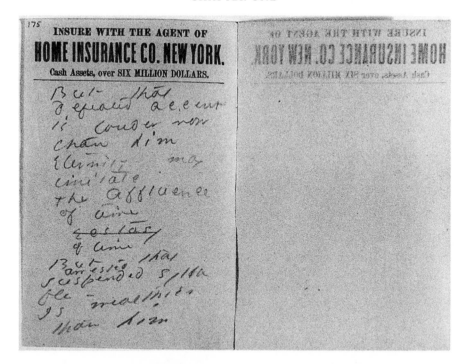

Figure 7a. Courtesy of Amherst College Archives and Special Collections (ED mss. 175, 175a).

The first lines to be published from the many odd lines running along the sheets at odd angles in figures 7a and 7b were, oddly enough, taken from the center of the least legible, most heterogeneous page; they were printed by Bingham in 1945 in a section simply entitled "Fragments":

627

> Love first and last of all things made
> Of which our living world is just the shade.
> (BM 317)

The more legible set of lines on the front of the sheets was then published by Bingham in an essay on the "Prose Fragments of Emily Dickinson" in 1955—seventy years after the memo pages were found in the locked box.[20] In their first appearance in print, these lines were cast not as a poem but as what Bingham described as "successive attempts to overtake an idea" in prose. Johnson followed Bingham by printing the recto lines in the section of "Prose Fragments" in his 1958 Letters (L 915) and went on to publish the verso lines not as a poem but as another prose fragment, though he points out that the lines that Bingham had already published as a verse fragment "recall the Prelude to Swinburne's 'Tristram of Lyonesse,' which opens:

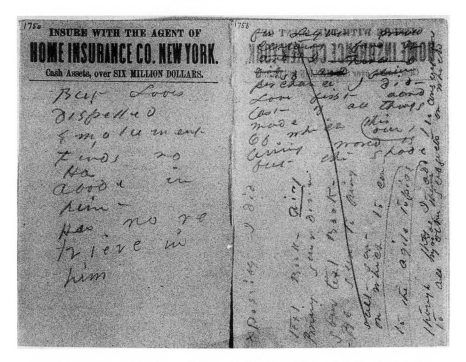

Figure 7b. Courtesy of Amherst College Archives and Special Collections (ED mss. 175, 175a).

'Love, that is first and last of all things made, / The light that has the living world for shade" (L 917–18). Although no longer printed as a poem, by 1958 a poem had been recognized in Dickinson's lines—though it was not a poem first written by Dickinson, and it was not—at least in Swinburne's context—a lyric. Thirty-five years later, in 1993, William H. Shurr published *New Poems of Emily Dickinson*, a glossy volume that claims to recover "the prose-formatted poems" that have remained hidden in Dickinson's prose.[21] Shurr accepts Bingham's and Johnson's characterizations of most of the HOME INSURANCE CO. NEW YORK pages as "one of [Dickinson's] prose fragments," but suggests that this fragment in prose contains "an overlooked workshop poem in which Dickinson has not yet decided between two alternate lines to give the final shape to a thoughtful quatrain:

486

Eternity may imitate
The Affluence (Ecstasy) of time
But that arrested (suspended) syllable
is wealthier than him
But Loves dispelled Emolument

Finds (Has) no Abode in him—
(Has no retrieve in him)."[22]

By 1993, then, a poem not attributable to another poet had finally been recognized in Dickinson's lines; it had been over a hundred years, but as
Bingham eloquently described the moment of recognizing the genre one
had already decided was immanent, "after laboriously puzzling out a
word, a line, a stanza, letter by letter, with all the alternatives, one is re-
warded by seeing, suddenly, a perfect poem burst full-blown into life"
(BM xv). But whose poem (and whose life) is it? When did it become a
poem? And where is the poem—on Dickinson's memo page or on the
"new" printed ones?

In the 1998 variorum, Franklin followed Shurr by printing as his Poem
1660 a quatrain drawn from the recto lines in figures 7a and 7b, but he de-
parted from Shurr by giving final shape to a *different* quatrain, which appears alone in his 1999 reading edition:

> But that defeated accent
> Is louder now than him
> Eternity may imitate
> The Affluence of time.
> (FR 1660)

In his variorum edition, Franklin dates the manuscript "about 1884" and
notes that "also present is a prose draft beginning 'Possibly I did' that includes a quotation from Swinburne" (F, note to 1660). He then goes on to
print the lines that follow the first four lines on the recto pages as variants
of his printed quatrain. In order to make the point that they are variants
and not independent prose or verse lines, Franklin reprints in brackets
what he takes to be the precedent lines for which Dickinson sketched several possible endings, which he separates with printer's bullets:

> But that suspended syllable—
> Is wealthier than him
>
> •
>
> [But that] arrested [syllable—]
> [Is wealthier than him]
>
> •
>
> But Love's dispelled Emolument
> Finds no Abode in him—
>
> •
>
> [But Love's dispelled Emolument]
> Has [no Abode in him—]
>
> •

[But Love's dispelled Emolument]
Has no retrieve in him
Affluence of time <Ecstasy> of time.
(F 1660)

My reader can see for herself the difference that printing makes to the many possible lyrics that may be read out of the pages in figures 7a and 7b; clearly it is Franklin who has made of Dickinson's scattered lines these pseudocouplets, thus making visible in print the genre Hegel would say that he had assumed. Although he did not decide to print the lines in figure 5 as a poem, Franklin did decide to print some of the lines in figures 7a and 7b as poetry, and further decided that the other lines are poetic variants or prose. We will return to the complex problem of reading Dickinson's proliferating variant lines, but Franklin's reading edition saves us from that problem altogether by printing only the one excised quatrain. In doing so, he follows established and not at all unusual editorial precedent in choosing between several manuscript possibilities.[23] He also follows the tradition of Dickinson's editors in assuming that what we want to discern among those possibilities is an individual poem. And, as Franklin wrote in reply to Susan Howe's now famous suggestion that Dickinson's manuscripts are themselves "artistic structures," individual poems depend on discrete sets of lines. In response to Howe's opinion that Dickinson's manuscript line breaks were significant yet ignored in print, Franklin wrote that remarking "line breaks depended on an 'assumption' that one reads in lines. He asked, 'What happens if the form lurking in the mind is the *stanza*?'"[24]

We will return to Howe's deeply lyrical interpretation of the difference between Dickinson-in-manuscript and Dickinson-in-print, but what the preceding pages have demonstrated is that a history of reading Dickinson lyrically has been made possible by a history of printing Dickinson lyrically. Since, as we saw in Hegel, all "texts are interdiscursive with respect to other text occasions, especially to relatively originary or precedential ones with respect to which a 'reading,' for example, is achieved," then we might say that the precedential text that has served as a point of reference for all readers and editors of the texts in figures 7a and 7b, whether read in lines or stanzas, as visually significant or metrically conventional, as figurally or formally or historically lyrical, is the imaginary or originary lyric poem in print that Dickinson did not write.[25] The example of the HOME INSURANCE CO. NEW YORK sheets and their many editorial versions may seem to have taken us far afield from the interpretation of the lines on the right side of the envelope in figure 5 (lines that are still hanging fire, I hope, over these pages, and to which we will return, returning as well to the lines that have now intervened in figures 7a and 7b), but they also return us to the hermeneutic problem of just how interdiscursive the "text occasion" of Dickinson's writing can be. While print versions of Dickinson's writing might lead us to believe—indeed, have led generations of readers to believe—that the difficulty of reading Dickinson is that her brief lyrics hover one after the other on the white page out of context, the difficulty of reading Dickinson's manuscripts is that even in their fragmentary extant forms, they provide so much context that individual lyrics become practically illegible.

Hybrid Poems

In his book *The Editing of Emily Dickinson* (his first on the subject, written prior to his becoming the editor of Emily Dickinson) in 1967, Franklin himself eloquently characterized the interpreter's dependence on acontextual "poems" that the critic must not admit are editorial fictions:

> The contemporary critical climate rules that we consider the poems as poems, and here the difficult problem arises: just what *is* the relationship between the author and his work? Critically, we say that a work of art is not commensurate with its author's intentions, yet the basic text is recovered, edited, and printed on the basis of authorial intention (so that the critic can then go to work with the theory that it is not commensurate with those intentions). It is an anomaly within our discipline and one that is not always recognized. . . . A poem, one might argue, is a poem is a poem. Clearly, even an altered poem *is*. And within the context of poetry in general, criticism of such a poem is perfectly valid. The error, the deception, comes in passing off these poems as Emily Dickinson's. They are Dickinson-Todd-Higginson's. They are, quite simply, poetry. . . . But we are not commonly organized in our pursuit of literature to talk about literature per se. Fortunately or unfortunately, authors are our categories, and there is little place for hybrid poems. . . . Academically raised in an era that believes in the sacredness of the author's text and that also believes in criticism divorced from authorial intention, we face a quandary with the Dickinson texts . . . any approach that is exclusively author-oriented will fail editorially. . . . If, then, we want the poems in a readers' edition, we are forced to make decisions. But this, too, can lead to the impossible. "Those fair—fictitious People" [now F 369] exists in a semi-final draft with twenty-six suggestions that fit eleven places in the poem. From this, 7680 poems are possible—not versions but, according to our critical principles, poems.[26]

As an aspiring critic, Franklin could see that a reading of Dickinson in manuscript is mathematically impossible; as an editor, he needed to take the poem out of its scriptive context in order to make a reading possible. In 1998, Franklin published only one of the 7,680 poems possible "according to our critical principles." Franklin's editorial decision on a single Dickinson-Franklin lyric would have been impossible according to Franklin-the-critic, because by the middle of the twentieth century, the "critical climate rule[d] that we consider the poems as poems," or "within the context of poetry in general." What remains to be said is that the critical climate given such juridical (not to say institutional) power in 1967 ruled that we consider all poems as lyric poems, and all lyric poems as "verbal icons." According to Wimsatt and Beardsley's influential description of the poem as verbal icon in 1954 (one year before the first scholarly edition of Dickinson's complete poems), to read a lyric is "to impute the thoughts and attitudes of the poem immediately to the dramatic *speaker*, and if to the author at all, only by way of an act of biographical inference."[27]

I will have much more to say in the next chapter about the New Critical lionizing of Dickinson as an ideally iconic (that is to say, acontextual) lyric poet, and much in the chapters that follow about the still dominant twentieth-century reading of Dickinson's poems (and of all poems) as a series of performances by fictional speakers or dramatic personae. For now we may simply note the distance between Higginson's and Aldrich's nineteenth-century figuration of Dickinson's writing as an author's attempt to represent birdsong and Franklin's view of the New Critical divorce from authorial intention. According to Franklin, "there is little space for hybrid poems" because after the nineteenth century lyrics are taken to be the utterance of a single subject, and after the middle of the twentieth century, that subject is not imagined as the author who, historically, inscribed the text. As Wimsatt and Beardsley wrote, "Judging a poem is like judging a pudding or a machine. One demands that it work. It is only because an artifact works that we infer the intent of the artificer" (71). Franklin's complaint against such New Critical principles of interpretation anticipates Foucault's famous description of the author as "the principle of thrift in the proliferation of meaning"—with the important distinction that when twentieth-century critics such as Wimsatt and Beardsley read poetry, they want books to obey an economic law that they want the poems within those books to defy.[28]

What critics want when they read lyric poetry, Franklin sensibly remarks, is not to have their author and have her, too. "According to our critical principles," if an author wrote a line, the critic is bound to interpret it as part of a poem whether or not the author intended the line to be read as such. If the line "works," that means that the author intended it to work. Such principles, Franklin suggests, ignore "the principle of thrift" that what Foucault would call the "author function" imposes on "the proliferation of meaning." The 7,680 poems—Imagine!—that become possible, and printable, according to mid-twentieth-century lyric logic seem to Franklin a foolishly profligate proposition, as indeed they may be. The principle on which the poem is manufactured cannot be so liberally interpreted, or the poem (like a pudding or a machine) loses value in the literary economy. But while Franklin follows the logical contradiction inherent in his era's literary criticism to what he takes to be its absurd extreme, he is saved from what Hegel called "the awkwardness of the problem" because before he reached that extreme he had already decided that what Dickinson wrote was literature—not "literature per se," but lyric poems.

But are lyric poems in manuscript the same poems in print? While Franklin's 1998 Harvard edition of the *Poems* would seem to argue that this is the case, his comments in 1967 point to the opposite conclusion, and indeed when in 1981 he and Harvard published a facsimile edition of *The Manuscript Books of Emily Dickinson*, he wrote that "the manuscripts of this poet resist translation into the conventions of print" (MB ix). Yet in his introduction to the facsimile edition, everything that Franklin says orients the manuscripts toward the horizon of print:

> Emily Dickinson, although she did not publish, wrote nearly eighteen hundred poems and organized the largest portion of them with her own form of book-making: selected poems copied onto sheets of letter paper that she bound with string. In her isolation and poetic silence, these manuscript books, known as fascicles, may have served privately as publication, a personal enactment of the public act that, for reasons unexplained, she denied herself. In time the poems became an extended letter to the world, gradually published after her sister, Lavinia, upon finding the manuscripts, set about with determination to get them printed. Yet no edition of the Dickinson poetry has followed the fascicle order; indeed for much of the complex manuscript history the fascicles have been in disarray, divided between families and, finally, between libraries. This edition makes the manuscript books of the poet available for the first time, restored as closely as possible to their original order and, through facsimile reproduction, presented much as she left them for Lavinia and the world. (MB, ix)

As Jerome McGann has pointed out, Franklin's facsimile edition "acquires its significance by seizing the privilege of its historical backwardness."[29] Yet although, as Margaret Dickie long ago remarked, such regression may aim to take Dickinson's "work back to the point at which her sister, Lavinia, discovered the fascicles and from which every editor since

Mabel Loomis Todd has tried to rescue her," its apparent erasure of Dickinson's print history presupposes that history, and the legibility of its manuscript images depends on the poems' prior existence in print.[30] If Franklin's publication of Dickinson's "manuscript books" redresses what he had characterized in the 1960s as the New Critical error of divorcing poems from poets' intentions, then it does so not only by reclaiming the literal evidence of Dickinson's own compositional and editorial practices, but by presenting those practices to the public as evidence of Dickinson's desire to be an author—that is, to see her poems in print. For Franklin, poems in fascicle manuscript are the same poems in print because lyric poems are for him by definition private compositions intended "for . . . the world." If Dickinson wrote lyric poems, then she intended them to be read as such—and, as all of his editorial work makes clear, Franklin is quite sure that Dickinson wrote discrete lyric poems, separable one from another.[31] Franklin's speculation that the fascicles were for their author a "personal enactment of the public act that, for reasons unexplained, she denied herself" mirrors on the level of authorial intention what his idea of the lyric genre already assumes: lyrics in print represent privacy to a public readership; it follows that publishing privacy is what all lyrics want to do, so Dickinson left the poems "for Lavinia and the world." Having found the destiny inscribed in their genre, the poems may now be restored to "the fascicle order," since that is the order closest to that their author intended.[32] Yet what Franklin cannot explain is the relation between the inherent intention of the genre (to be read while pretending not to be) and the apparent intention of the author (not to be read while pretending to be).

The contradictions attendant on Franklin's publication of the manuscript books (as opposed to Howe's reading of the manuscripts themselves, to which we shall return)—handwriting not quite in print yet mass-produced, compositional order restored yet the identity of individual already printed poems left intact, the author's intentions represented but not determined—have been addressed most powerfully and at greatest length by Sharon Cameron. As the professional reader of Dickinson most dedicated to the difficult issue of Dickinson's lyricism, Cameron has consistently asked how Dickinson's writing might exemplify ideas of the genre itself. In her first book on Dickinson, *Lyric Time: Dickinson and the Limits of Genre* (1979), Cameron suggested that "the temporal problems in Dickinson's poems are frequently exaggerations of those generic features shared by all lyrics, and that it is precisely the distance some of these poems go toward the far end of coherence, precisely the outlandishness of their extremity, which allows us to see, literally magnified, the fine workings of more conventional lyrics" (LT 23). Thus Cameron articulated what had been implicit in Dickinson's reception since 1890: as the hypostatized lyric had come to stand for poetry in general, so Dickinson had come to stand for the hypostatized lyric in general. Late in the history of distressed lyric criticism, Cameron could presuppose, as Hegel might say, a common assumption that "conventional lyrics" shared "generic features," and that what Dickinson's poems did was to take up those conventions and push them to their limits. The central convention at stake for Cameron in 1979 was the lyric's representation of isolated spots of time. "Unlike the drama, whose province is conflict," Cameron wrote, "and unlike the novel or narrative, which connects isolated moments of time to create a story, multiply peopled and framed by social context, the lyric voice is solitary and generally speaks out of a single moment in time" (LT 23). Most readers in 1979 would have shared Cameron's assurance that the solitude of the lyric voice was its transhistorical feature; like the broad taxonomic distinctions between the drama and the novel with their definite articles, this form of lyric reading did not depend on any particular historical situation or lyric subgenre. In Cameron's early reading, the lyric's generic solitude and temporal isolation mirrored the serial isolation of the discrete lyrics in Johnson's 1955 *Poems*, and *Lyric Time* proceeds through a series of brilliant interdiscursive readings of those isolated representations of personal and temporal isolation.

After the publication of Franklin's *Manuscript Books*, however, Cameron revised the phenomenology of reading implicit in Johnson's print edition and elaborated in her own interpretation. In *Choosing Not Choosing: Dickinson's Fascicles* (1992), Cameron elaborated instead the deeply problematic experience of reading lyrics that cannot be isolated from one another—a problem introduced by the altered images in Franklin's fascicle edition. Given Dickinson's practice of arranging poems in sequences, of suggesting but not excluding variants, of repeating lines in different parts of a fascicle, of arranging fascicles as collections yet not (as far as we know) announcing the rationale of her collections, of privately publishing and yet, privately, not publishing those collections, the interpreter of the fascicles must ask, as Cameron so succinctly does ask, "What *is* the poem?" (CC 5).

Or *where* is the poem? The question that Cameron allows the fascicles to pose is, again, how to recognize a poem when we see one—in context. As she writes, she means "to ask how reading a lyric in sequence is different from reading a lyric as independent, for to do the latter is to suppress the context and the relations that govern the lyric in context—a suppression generating that understanding of Dickinson's poems as enigmatic, isolated, culturally incomprehensible phenomena which has dominated most Dickinson criticism, including my own" (CC 5). Yet "what happens when context—when the sequence—is not suppressed" (CC 19)? One might think that the first thing that would happen for a reader as rigorous as

Cameron would be that the idea of the lyric as the genre theoretically determining Dickinson's practice would itself be thrown into question. Yet Cameron's second book on Dickinson holds tenaciously to the lyric as the genre governing Dickinson's composition and, more suggestively, governing the interpretation of that composition. While in her first book she argued that Dickinson's isolated lyrics exaggerated the isolated temporality of the lyric itself, in her second book on Dickinson she argues that "Dickinson's fascicles trouble the idea of limit or frame on which . . . our suppositions of lyric fundamentally depend" (CC 5). It should follow that if all lyrics depend on limits or frames, and Dickinson's writing turns out not to have such limits or frames, then Dickinson did not write lyrics—or did not write poems that conform to "our suppositions of lyric." But that is not Cameron's conclusion.

Instead, Cameron takes her supposition of "what is definitional of the genre" from Allen Grossman's "Summa Lyrica," which was published in the same year as Cameron's *Choosing Not Choosing* (1992) by her colleague at the Johns Hopkins University.[33] Grossman describes his text as "a primer or handbook of commonplaces . . . designed to befriend the reader of poetry (always supposing that the reader of poetry needs a hermeneutic friend) by constructing a culture in which poetry is intelligible." Grossman is brilliantly open about his assumption that the principle of intelligibility at stake in the definition of the lyric is the principle of interpretation rather than the practice of composition; a poet himself, he is concerned about "the function of poetry . . . for everybody," his ambition no less than "to obtain for everybody one kind of success at the limits of the autonomy of the will." Grossman's humanist enterprise influences not only the interpretive ambition of Cameron's readings, but also her ambitiously fundamental view of the genre those willful readings construct. "Lyric is the most continuously practiced of all poetic kinds in the history of Western representation," Grossman writes; "as the kind which imitates man alone, lyric is the first and last poetic sort."[34]

Grossman and Cameron are in good historical company in seeing the lyric as poetry writ large—and they also share the modern presumption that the lyric (that is, poetry) will not be culturally intelligible unless the interpreter makes it so. Thus Cameron's book on Dickinson's fascicles takes Grossman's proposition that "the frame of the poem" defines the lyric as the limit case and turns that definition of the genre inside out: if lyric is "the first and last poetic sort," and "assumptions about boundedness are so fundamental to our suppositions about lyrics as in effect to become definitional of the genre," *and* "Dickinson's fascicles trouble the idea of limit or frame on which, as Grossman reminds us, our suppositions of lyric fundamentally depend," then, Cameron concludes, the interpreter of the fascicles must expand her notion of the lyric to encompass a larger version of its frame (CC 5). Like Grossman, who supposes that "the reader of poetry needs a hermeneutic friend," Cameron supposes not only that Dickinson wrote lyric poetry but that she did so in view of a hermeneutic future. If Franklin publishes the fascicles in order to reveal the order of the poems as Dickinson intended it, Cameron interprets the fascicles in order to reveal that intention as indeterminate, and thus open to infinite nuances of interpretation, since "the difficulty in enforcing a limit to the poems turns into a kind of limitlessness" (CC 6). Cameron takes seriously the suggestion that in 1967 Franklin considered absurd: she attempts to read the multiplying variety of poems made possible by what she takes to be the relation between poems and variants in the fascicles, and thus enters into the hermeneutic problem that Hegel identified as so awkward and that Franklin discounted. And because she tries to hold a definition of the lyric stable in relation to that very unstable or speculative problem, Cameron turns the material context of Dickinson's manuscript books into a limitless opportunity for lyric reading.

Thus far in this chapter, I have been arguing that an imaginary version of the lyric in print informs late nineteenth- and twentieth-century interpretations of Dickinson, and I have suggested that in the same period increasingly professionalized literary interpretation creates an idea of the lyric as poetic norm. That dialectical process reaches a fascinating turning point in Cameron's work on Dickinson's fascicles, since "it may well be the case," Cameron speculates, "that Dickinson did not publish her poems because she literally did not know whether to publish them as a sequence or as single lyrics. Or because she could not publish them in both forms at once" (CC 54). As Cameron notes, while her book produces "an empirical argument about how the fascicles work, and about what the fascicles are, the basis of that argument is, and could only be, speculative" (CC 7n6). But one starting point for Cameron's argument that in the fascicles Dickinson wanted to represent both poems in and poems out of sequence, both individual lyrics and one big indeterminate lyric—in short, that the fascicles allowed Dickinson "to choose not to choose" whether or not to write individual lyrics—is not at all speculative: it is the prior existence of Dickinson's poems in print, the historical precedence of print publication to Franklin's manuscript publication. Cameron's frequent comparison of Dickinson's poems to modern poems by Yeats, Whitman, Stevens, and Rilke assumes the fascicles' separation into individual lyrics for the purposes of interpretation.[35] And the way in which Dickinson's writing is printed in *Choosing Not Choosing* itself illustrates the lyric reading that the individual chapters of the book pursue. Not only are poems printed and analyzed in their forms and according to their numbers in Johnson's 1955 edition in Cameron's text, but the selected fascicles within Cameron's book are printed from Johnson's edition; only one fascicle (number 20) is then reprinted by Cameron in manuscript facsimile as an appendix.

As we have seen, the precedence of print to manuscript certainly makes the manuscripts more legible, yet as we have also seen, the prior existence of the poems in print makes it difficult for any reader to consider Dickinson's writing as anything other than a set of lyrics. The enumeration and separation of the texts in Johnson's print edition (reprinted in Cameron's analysis of that edition) imply an interpretation of the poems as single lyrics, while the sequence of lines that run along sequences of pages in the manuscript fascicles (reproduced by Franklin and again reproduced by Cameron) appear implicated in the context of one another across the page. Cameron chooses to interpret the context of the fascicles as an elaboration of Dickinson's lyrics—that is, to read literal context as proliferating figurative text. Other, much less interesting, recent attempts to interpret the fascicles have rendered them not as an elaborately lyrical sequence and cross-sequence but as narrative sequence; given the amount of text contained in the manuscript books and the number of variant lines, one can imagine the emergence of a critical literature around the fascicles almost as capacious as the work that has collected around the print editions of Dickinson.[36] Yet to foresee that hermeneutic future is also to suppose that Dickinson's writing was always oriented toward it. That is, of course, what any edition of Dickinson must suppose, whether in print or manuscript facsimile—or must suppose if it is an edition of Dickinson's lyric poems. Before we return to the manuscript on the split-open envelope that has not yet been published as a Dickinson poem, we should turn to the most recent attempts to take Dickinson's work out of the double bind of generic edition—to give an even greater hermeneutic future to Dickinson's poetry by taking her writing not only out of print but out of the book.

Dickinson Unbound

The electronic archive projects launched in the last decade of the twentieth century on the World Wide Web promise to use new media to reimagine Dickinson's message. The Dickinson Electronic Archives (henceforward DEA) (http://www.iath.virginia.edu/dickinson/) presents itself as "a new type of critical resource" devoted to "examining the extent to which the poem as printed object has shaped the interpretation, circulation, reputation, and transmission of Emily Dickinson's writings and of how reconceiving them as scribal objects profoundly alters one's experience of her literary presentations." What web media can do that print media cannot is to "digitize images of [Dickinson's] manuscripts and provide diplomatic transcriptions and notes in searchable electronic form, thereby enabling new kinds of critical inquiry unimaginable within the constraints of the book, the machine that has made the object, 'Dickinson's poem,' and that has determined how that object is seen, interrogated, and theorized." What distinguishes Dickinson-on-the-screen from Dickinson-on-the-page, such statements suggest, is the difference between an idea of genre-as-medium and genre-as-work.[37] Yet will a new conception of Dickinson's genres as media shift the reception of that writing as lyric poetry? It is worth noticing that the institutional, juridical power over interpretation with which Franklin credited "the contemporary critical climate" is in the editorial statement of the Dickinson Electronic Archive assigned to print itself; Web publication is cast here as the liberation of Dickinson's writing from the policing gaze of the print public sphere. What for Franklin was critical self-deception is for the Dickinson Editorial Collective (henceforward DEC) (general editors Martha Nell Smith, Ellen Louise Hart, Marta Werner, and Lara Vetter) the "capital-driven" deception of the impersonal codex "machine." While Franklin claimed in 1967 that readers cannot have both Dickinson's poems in legible print form and a book with only her name on it, the DEC claims to release Dickinson's poems from the constraining medium of the book altogether, virtually restoring them to their original status as "scribal objects" at the same time that the DEA wants to generate an alternative terminology for those objects ("Emily Dickinson's writing," "literary presentations") commensurate with the new possibilities of access allowed by the new medium of the Web and its altered phenomenologies of writing and reading. Yet does the alternative medium or that medium's alternative terminology enable us to think of Dickinson's work as anything other than the lyric poetry made by a century of print machines?

Emily Dickinson wrote on all kinds of ready-to-hand paper; some of what she wrote was printed during her lifetime in mid-nineteenth-century newspapers (including a paper in Brooklyn, New York, used to raise money for Union troops) and in the "No Name" series of gilt volumes of contemporary poems; some of the manuscripts that survived after her death were copied by hand and then transcribed letter by letter on Todd's World typewriter; between 1890 and 1998 thirteen editions and countless reprinted editions of Dickinson's poems were printed and sold in the United States; in the 1990s, the DEA began to unprint the manuscripts and display their images on computer screens around the world. On one hand, this simplified series represents a progressive narrative of ever greater public access to those papers in the locked box; on the other hand, it represents a progressive abstraction of the pages Dickinson wrote, a movement away from the author as "the principle of thrift" toward an economy apparently out of anyone's control. As Harold Love has written,

> a sub-spectrum along the axis chirography-typography-electronography might be formed thus: authorial holograph, scribal transcript, typewritten transcript without corrections, words printed from copper or steel engraved plates, computer printout, lithographic printing, raised surface printing, baked clay tablets, braille, skywriting with aeroplane, words seen on a TV screen or VDU, neon sign—by each of which the sign is progressively removed from an assumed source of validation in the movement of the author's fingers and relies instead for signifying power on its locus within an autonomous universe of signs.[38]

Dickinson's writing has been represented in all of these ways, and more—but does the medium change the message? If the message is taken to be determined by the author's hand (as Franklin would like critics to admit), then the answer is no; if the message inscribed by that hand becomes a part of a text that generates proliferating interpretations (as Cameron would lead us to think), then the answer is yes and no; if the semiotic spectrum in which the message is placed by its medium is indeed self-organizing (as the DEC imagines it might become), then the answer is yes. On the first view, if Emily Dickinson intended to write lyric poems, then a chirographic, lithographic, skywritten, or digitally displayed poem is a poem is a poem; on the second view, handwriting allows more interpretive range than does printing, and so may change the shape of the poem, but does not change the genre itself; on the third view, the reception of a particular medium determines the message's genre.[39] The medium changes the genre—or so the DEC claims—by becoming its context. It may be too early to tell what new intersections between genre and medium might be made possible by the Web, but it is already clear that whatever the developing possibilities may turn out to be, the new media return the problem of genre in Dickinson to an old division between private context and public context—and specifically, to a division between private and public temporality.

It is, of course, a highly mediated and highly capitalized illusion that the Web makes publicly available "an autonomous universe of signs": not everyone has Internet access, and those that do must pay for it or be granted the means by institutions; the signs displayed on the Web are encrypted by technology professionals and their relation to other signs is determined by the links established by the creators of the website and by the creators of the other websites accessible through those links. In the case of the DEA, anyone with access to the World Wide Web can see the site, but you will need a password in order to read most of what is on the site. The DEC is well aware of the contradictions posed by its elected medium: the Collective wants to be a community effort sponsored by many editors and users, yet its structure is designed by a few editorial hands; it wants to be infinitely accessible, but most users will lack the password and will therefore be denied access (though one editor has asked me to publish the password here, in the interest of a greater public accessibility as of 2004: the "username" required is **dickinson** and the password is **ink_on_disc**). There is no question that the DEA is a tremendous resource for readers of Dickinson, and it will certainly change the collective reading of Dickinson in ways none of us can foresee. But will it change our reading of Dickinson's genre—or will readers still go to the Web as they have to the print editions in order to read more Dickinson poems? Won't readers still view—because they already expect to view—these poems as lyrics? Will the medium of the Internet have any effect on the imaginary lyric model that has guided the editing and interpretation of Dickinson for so long?

Some of the versions of Dickinson available in the DEA do seem to present alternatives to the tradition of lyric reading (especially the parts of the site authored by Martha Nell Smith on Dickinson's collaboration with Susan Gilbert Dickinson, to which we will return in chapter 3); some alter slightly the genre of the lyrics Dickinson wrote (for example, the section entitled "Letter-Poem, a Dickinson Genre") but all parts of the site describe Dickinson as a lyric poet. According to the evidence so far on the electronic Dickinson sites, the greater range of access they promise is not actually a greater range of genre or interpretation, though accessibility may seem to offer new ways of reading by promising a shift in temporality.[40] All of the versions of Dickinson posted by various hands on the Web partake, by virtue of their medium, of the new time frame of Web discourse: a text available at a click, an illusion of simultaneous production and reception, a public world of individual access viewed by the "global village" in the privacy of home or office. Most importantly, that access will appear unmediated and immediate, and will not appear to unfold through time. Whereas we know that the first edition of Dickinson's poems (or Dickinson-Todd-Higginson's poems) was printed by Roberts Brothers in Boston in 1890 (just before the passage of the international copyright law) in a white and gray gift book edition edged in gold leaf, the images of old manuscripts on the computer screen are as new as your screen. The inscription and successive publication dates of each manuscript on the site are meticulously noted, but the site itself seems to hover in electric air. The introductory image for the section "Letter-Poem, a Dickinson Genre" (fig. 8), for example, superimposes a typescript transcription of Dickinson's manuscript on a filmy image of that manuscript, and superimposes both

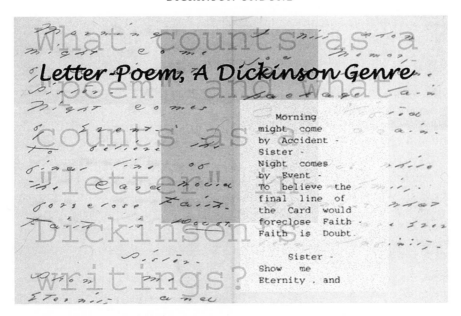

Figure 8. Cover page for the "Letter-Poem" section of the Dickinson Electronic Archives. Courtesy of the Dickinson Electronic Archives.

transcript and manuscript on an enlarged background image of a printed page of critical prose about the relation between Dickinson's poems and letters. Theoretically, we can now read these formerly discrete levels of discourse and media simultaneously, thanks to the immediacy of Web transmission. Whereas print editions like Franklin's must choose between manuscript and print—or, like Cameron's book, choose not to choose between manuscript and print, and so go back and forth between one sort of page and another—manuscript and print may be represented at the same time on one Web "page." We will return to the many implications of the convergence of private and public space and time in the electronographic representation of Dickinson, and we will return in a moment to the generic difficulties of reading the versified lines on the split-open envelopes with which we began—difficulties generated by the ways in which the manuscripts' material or historical aspects (their media) as well as their figurative content (their message) do allow us to speak of them as discourse unfolding in time. But first we should note that the capacity for historical temporal development—unfolding through time—is just the way not only Web discourse but lyric discourse is seldom understood. That is, while the electronic versions of Dickinson may aim to shift our idea of what it was that Dickinson wrote by altering what we read and how we read it, the immediacy of Web presentation closely allies all of Dickinson's writing with postromantic theories of lyric representation.

In an electronic archive entitled *Radical Scatters* and linked to the DEA (though it offers even more limited access than does the DEA, since it requires a site license that may be purchased only by institutions), Marta Werner, one of the editors in the DEC, has explicitly articulated the coincidence between the temporality of Web representation and the temporality of postromantic lyric reading. The primary aim of *Radical Scatters,* as Werner puts it, is "to foreground Dickinson's extrageneric compositions"—the "late fragments" that include such cross-written surviving pages as those in figures 7a and 7b (though she does not include the lines in figure 5 as a "fragment").[41] Werner's site is a fascinating exemplification of the difference between description and interpretation and of the costs of moving from one to the other; in the presentation and transcription of the texts themselves, the site is meticulous and objective: one click will turn Dickinson's practically illegible script to legible print and back again (a great service, and the transcription here of figure 7b would have been impossible without it), and the citational field that surrounds each "fragment" is elaborate (there is even a "hand library" that archives the approximate dates of the many shifts in the character of Dickinson's writing). In sections separated from the bibliographic (or manugraphic, or webographic) empiricism of the archive proper is Werner's reading of the fragments, which are, writes Werner, "like souls, neither touching nor mingling, never composing a set, these positionless fragments depict the beauties of transition and isolation at once. Belonging to the chronology of the instant, a book of them would have to present them as a discontinuous series, a 'book from which each page could be taken out.' " This is not a reading of Dickinson's poems as iconic print artifacts removed from their makers (or the reading Franklin caricatured as New Critical); neither is it a reading of Dickinson's fascicle poems as unbounded lyrical possibility (or the reading pursued by Cameron), but it *is* an emphatically lyric reading. According to Werner, Dickinson's late fragments "inaugurate a lyric nondiscourse scattered in an infinity of singular articulations and manifested finally as an *absence d'oeuvre.* Untitled, unauthorized, and extrageneric, these whispers at the outer edges of Dickinson's work ask 'Where do I exit and go and how do I proceed?' "

As Werner interprets them, the parts of Dickinson's manuscripts not recognizable as poems are more lyrical than the lyrics they are not. The "chronology of the instant" is the oldest chronology in the book not only for Dickinson's lyrics but for the lyric as such; as we have seen, a "discontinuous series" of such instants is exactly what the print versions of Dickinson's poems have always represented: one instant after another, each surrounded by the white space of the page. The space surrounding the "souls" on the computer screen is thrillingly black, and the traditional investment of lyrics with an inner life translates into the literal animation of the electronic medium: with a click on a torn corner or virtual straight pin, the reader/user can make the "souls" spin, unfold, attach and detach to and from other souls or move nearer to or farther from view (rather like the sexual intercourse of angels in *Paradise Lost*). Following Susan Howe's lead in *My Emily Dickinson* and *The Birth-mark* Werner's site spectacularly lyricizes precisely those Dickinson texts that have not been printed as poems (though they have sometimes been printed as letters); perhaps precisely because they have not been printed as lyrics, Werner can read them as hyperlyrics. The "fragments" that have not been identified as printed poems or as letters may remain for Werner "extrageneric" and therefore perfect exemplars of the lyric as a creature of modern interpretation.[42] The *"absence d'oeuvre"* or perfectly abstracted book that dissolves into its own performance would be for Werner—as it was for Mallarmé—the ideal fate for the lyric that no longer has to mean but be. This is to say that Werner ventriloquizes a history of lyric interpretation in presenting Dickinson's "lyric nondiscourse" to view and in so doing she gives that discourse the voice of the lyric as such (though the words are, appropriately, from Novalis): "'Where do I exit and go and how do I proceed?'" The implied answer, of course, is, as Werner puts it, "to the ends of the lyric"—that is, straight to you.[43]

Werner's lyrical reading of the outer edges of Dickinson's work as unmediated, free-floating, instantaneous hyperlyricism is in fact the way that Dickinson has been read for well over a hundred years. As I shall argue in greater detail in the third chapter on "Dickinson's Figure of Address," at least since Higginson's introduction of the first edition of Dickinson's poems as "something produced absolutely without the thought of publication, and solely by way of expression of the writer's own mind" (*Poems* 1890, iii), the interpretation of Dickinson's poems as un- and therefore self-directed has long made them the perfect fit for the characterization of lyric poetry as discourse immediately and intimately addressed to the reader precisely because it is not addressed to anyone at all. In the next chapter, I will examine the theoretical implications of modern thinking about the lyric as the public circulation of privacy, but first it is important to notice that the print, facsimile, and web editions of Dickinson—that is, *all* editions of Dickinson—turn Dickinson's private writing practices public, whether they do so in the medium of print, photographic reproduction, or digital hypertext. The exposure of Dickinson's private hand to the public gaze has thrilled readers since the nineteenth century, and though new Web technologies may provide more spectacular means for such exposure, it is not technology itself that determines interpretation. My argument that the imaginary lyric in print informs even unprinted editions of

Dickinson is not an argument about print per se; the electronic attempts to undo Dickinson's print history amply demonstrate the limits of techno- logical determinist arguments. The fact that Werner's immensely techno- logically accomplished representation of the unprinted Dickinson ends in a fundamental form of lyric reading demonstrates that reading's depen- dence on the cultural mediation of any medium—whether print, pixels, or skywriting. As long as there is a cultural consensus that Dickinson wrote poems *and* as long as poems are considered essentially lyric *and* as long as the cultural mediation of lyrics is primarily interpretative and largely academic—indeed, as long as lyrics need to be interpreted in order to *be* lyrics—then the media of Dickinson's publication will not change the message.

The new Web presentation can deliver images of the archive no one who has not visited the institutional archives of Dickinson's manuscripts has seen, and Web images do give a better idea of Dickinson's compositional practices than any previous edition could.[44] That increased access to the visual archive is itself immensely valuable—but does it make each of us an historian or a viewer? What kind of readers of those images do we be- come? We have yet to see if the screening of the archive will give us access only to images or to a critical sense of the archive as (in Brent Edwards's words) "a discursive system that governs the possibilities, forms, appear- ance, and regularity of particular statements, objects, and practices."[45] This second, interpretive view of the archive is the archive we construct as readers of a moment by definition different than our own—and, by defi- nition, perhaps not viewable via the medium of the computer screen's il- lusion of immediacy. The alternative to that illusion may be closer to the interpretation imagined by Michel Foucault as a critical "archeology," an analysis that "deprives us of our continuities; it dissipates that temporal identity in which we are pleased to look at ourselves when we wish to ex- orcise the discontinuities of history. . . ."[46] No edition of Dickinson will es- sentially change the interpretation of Dickinson if it is an edition of Dick- inson's *poems*. It is not the medium but the genre that determines the message. And what determines genre?

The hermeneutic ambition of recent print, facsimile, and Web-based editions of Dickinson suggests one answer to the question of genre, the question that, as Claudio Guillén has put it, bridges "the gap between crit- ical theory and the practice of literary criticism."[47] Of the many formal and historical influences on the formation of literary genres, the most persis- tent is the influence of critical theory itself—in Dickinson's case, the influ- ence of what I am calling "lyric reading." The theoretical existence of liter- ary genres makes possible the practical existence of literary criticism. All editions of Dickinson to date seek to undo the limiting perspective of previous editions in order to give Dickinson's poems a newer (and, by implication, better) interpretation. I have been suggesting that they do so because our idea of what a lyric is requires that Dickinson's private compositions be made ever more public and ever more immediately accessible—ever more *readable*. That is, the representation of Dickinson's work has depended on a critical theory of its genre (as privacy gone public, as present-tense immediacy, as an invitation to interpretation), and in turn critical theories of genre have determined the representation of Dickinson's work (as privacy gone public, as spots of time in the middle of a page or the center of a screen, as addressed to the interpreter). But what if everyone since Higginson has been wrong? What if Dickinson did not write lyric poems?

THE ARCHIVE

Those "fossil bird-tracks" in the Amherst Museum in Higginson's *Atlantic* article have turned into apt images of what every visitor to the Dickinson archive has expected to find: the poems' essential lyricism, resident in the peculiar traces of the poet's hand. Recent editorial and critical attempts to undo earlier print representations of Dickinson's manuscripts have reinscribed Dickinson's lyricism in every torn corner and watermark of her pages, thus repeating Higginson's gesture and participating in a later version of the discursive system that governs all statements about all aspects of Dickinson's writing as statements about lyric poems. In order to allow the archive to disrupt rather than confirm that system, to deprive us of our continuities, we will need to alter not only our view of Dickinson's materials as they emerge into view but we will need to change our interpretation of the genre into which we tend to fit those materials. That is not easy to do—or to undo.

We might begin by noticing those continuities of the lyric into which Dickinson's writing, on closer view, does not seem to fit: rather than turning privacy public, her work tended to take all kinds of public and private, artificial and natural materials into the everyday life of a private person. Rather than give us immediate access to the private perceptions of that person, the literate traces of that everyday life tend to emphasize our distance from the time and place of her practice—of her culture. Rather than address themselves to an horizon of literary interpretation in the future (to future literary critics), Dickinson's manuscripts were addressed to particular individuals or to herself. Let us return, for example, to the lines on the split-open envelope with which we began (fig. 5). The fact that this is a rare instance of a Dickinson manuscript that has never been published as a Dickinson poem (or even as an extrageneric lyric fragment) may seem to give us the opportunity to read this archival fragment as something else. Yet, as we have seen, while the lines, when printed or reproduced as a lyric, generate several possible lyric readings, it is hard to say what kind of reading they might generate if we regard them not as a poem but as, say, an envelope. That is because we do not *read*—in the strong sense of the verb that has, to some degree since the nineteenth century and certainly since the 1940s in the United States, defined the job of the literary critic— envelopes in the way that we *read* poems.[48] When Higginson began his essay on Dickinson by reading her envelope as evidence of her lyricism, he was not only identifying Dickinson as a lyric poet but identifying himself as a lyric reader. On the other hand, the lines on the split-open envelope in figure 5 are not an address; they are lines written on the inside rather than the outside of the envelope, and they are not directed to anyone we can identify. They fall into the alternating tetrameter and trimeter lines now associated with Dickinson's poems and in the nineteenth century associated with hymns as well as with a great deal of popular poetry, especially ballads. If scanned as three tetrameter lines followed by six alternating trimeters and tetrameters, the lines sustain a delicate series of slant variations on *n* sounds: undone / tune / (wait) / stone / on / slain / (hear) / Trans / undone. As we have already noted, the refrain or framing line gives the series the effect of closure or formal integrity. This is to say that even as a manuscript not printed as a poem, these lines exemplify the formal definition we attribute to poems. And as if that were not enough to make them a poem, they take the subject of birdsong as their theme and then associate that lyric type with the lyric "I." The combination of such traditionally (even redundantly) lyric form and content invites, as we have seen, several different possible lyric readings. Thus if a lyric is defined as a self-reflexive aesthetic whole, there can be no question that the lines in figure 5 that have never been printed as a lyric are a lyric.

Yet the fact that figure 5 has not been published as a poem may mean that self-reflexive form does not (*pace* modern generalizations about the self-reflexive postromantic lyric), after all, itself determine our theory of genre. Instead, as Carolyn Williams has recently suggested, the "law of genre," may be better understood as "the play of formalism and deformation in sociocultural terms."[49] Williams's understanding of genre would be a very un-Hegelian way of making the abstract category of genre contingent on social circulation rather than on a priori aesthetic criteria. In order to do so, she suggests that we "think of 'discourse' and 'genre' as a dialectical pair, one foregrounding synchronic study and the other foregrounding diachronic study; one emphasizing historical discontinuity and the other emphasizing historical continuity; one tending (potentially, but not necessarily) toward the thematic and the other toward formalistic oversimplifications" (520). The advantage of Williams's way of thinking about genre is that it does not separate form from history. To say that lyrics are part of the Dickinson archive is not necessarily to say that the discursive system of the lyric inevitably governs everything that can be said about Dickinson's work. Dickinson may have used the nineteenth-century lyric as one of many discourses she employed in her writing, but that does not mean that what Dickinson wrote inevitably eventuates in the genre of the lyric. It is the literary criticism since Higginson that has created the discourse of lyric reading that in turn editors and readers have recognized in Dickinson. If, as Williams suggests, discourse and genre are a dialectical pair, then discourse is not something that is imposed on genre but is made out of genres.[50] Thus to read figure 5 as an old envelope need not mean not also reading the lines on the envelope as lyrical, and to read them as lyrical is not necessarily to read them as a lyric. As the most formally defined of modern literary genres, the lyric has been misunderstood as the genre most isolated from history—indeed, as the exemplary model of literary genre as a category separable from history. But Dickinson's work may be a model for an alternative approach in which the reading of genre and the reading of history are mutually implicated in each other.

As we shall see in the next chapter on lyric reading, that mutual implication has proven difficult to think about for literary critics. The source of the difficulty is on one hand the historical transformation of "genreness" itself. Michael McKeon eloquently phrases "the modern shift in the idea of genre—from an enabling hermeneutic to a constraining taxonomy," and notes that this shift "is coextensive with the emergence of the novel. . . . The novel crystallizes genreness, self-consciously incorporating, as part of its form, the problem of its own categorical status." This modern shift in notions of genre reflects, in other words, what Bakhtin called "the novelization of genre," by which he did not mean that traditional genres all become more and more novelistic, but that in modernity genre itself becomes a mutable—though far from disappearing—category rather than "some sort of stylization of forms that have outlived themselves."[51]

Thus one difficulty for critical thinking about the lyric is that a contingent, developmental view of genre is so intimately tied to the novel that the lyric becomes the novel's other, assigned to an outmoded stylization rather than a dynamic process. The other side of this difficulty is that in fact the lyricization of poetry works very differently than the novelization of genre: whereas novelization has made genre a more socially enmeshed concept, lyricization has taken traditional poetic genres out of circulation. When Clifford Siskin writes that "the lyricization of the novel" began in Austen, for example, he means to argue that the historicity of genre makes all genres intergeneric—that is, that the romantic lyric influences the nineteenth-century novel and that the novel influences the lyric. It is certainly true that, as Siskin states, "poetry and the novel . . . cannot be known in isolation from each other" in the nineteenth century, but post-romantic lyric discourse shapes another view of genre altogether: when we read a text as a lyric, we consent to take it out of circulation and, in a sense, out of generic contingency.[52] If the novel is the modern genre par excellence because it takes all genres into itself and celebrates generic contingency, lyric is the modern antigenre, since it is at once too formally distinct to be anything other than a literary genre, and yet it pretends not to be any particular literary genre. John Stuart Mill, the touchstone theorist of the lyric in Anglo-American modernity, makes the intentional performance of such an illusion explicit in a passage that immediately follows his famous distinction between eloquence as *heard* and poetry as *overheard*, a distinction that defines all poetry as "soliloquy": "It may be said that poetry which is printed on hot-pressed paper and sold at a book-seller's shop, is a soliloquy in full dress, and on the stage. It is so; but there is nothing absurd in the idea of such a mode of soliloquizing. . . . The actor knows that there is an audience present; but if he act as though he knew it, he acts ill."[53]

According to Mill, the circulation of poetry "on hot-pressed paper" is exactly what the generic conventions of the lyric cannot acknowledge—that is, the lyric can no more acknowledge its literal circumstance than can the actor, and is at the same time no less dependent than that actor on the generic recognition of the audience it must pretend is not there. Thus the difficulty of thinking about the lyric as implicated in historical contingency is that the discourse that surrounds the genre must admit without acknowledging the defining effect of that contingency.

Dickinson's lines on the envelope in figure 5 both exemplify and ponder the difficulty of thinking through lyric historicity, of shifting the lyric archive. If "a Blue Bird's tune—" is, as I have suggested, a figure for lyric convention, then the question that the lines pose is a question of their own survival. Since they have not survived as a lyric on hot-pressed paper, we might conclude that they fail to answer the question. Certainly the lines that offer various figures for lyric survival amplify rather than solve the problem: the ephemerality of birdsong by definition does not last, but Resurrection is, by definition, what does. In Dickinson's version, however, recognition is what Resurrection "had to wait" for; the stone is moved not in order to allow Christ's body to escape (that has already been accomplished by unseen hands) but so that the apostles can witness its disappearance. As in Mill's figure of the actor's soliloquy, in Dickinson's figure of the historical contingency of the Resurrection, the public confers definition. Or does it? If drumbeats play to the dead (whether they have been resurrected or not), then their audience (not incidentally, the victims of public violence) cannot recognize them. The lines on the right flap of the envelope (fig. 5) acknowledge that the double bind of lyric circulation suspends the writer's address to the reader between mutually exclusive poles: if "I dare not / write until / I hear—" what the generic conditions for reading what I write might be, then the lines depend on an afterlife of translation. Uncertain of that afterlife, the lines remain in temporal suspension: "Intro without / my Trans—." Indeed, their afterlife has depended on a series of historically contingent versions of lyric reading, including the reading I have just performed. Yet until I just dared to write that these lines take up the subject of lyricism itself, they had not been translated into the lyric they claim they cannot become.

Since self-reflexiveness is one of the central criteria of lyric discourse, my reader might say that I have just done exactly what I set out not to do: I have made an old envelope into a new Dickinson lyric. Despite my intention to read it as an envelope, I have interpreted it as a lyric—indeed, I have made it a metalyric. Thus we might conclude that the reason for us to think that Dickinson wrote lyric poems is that even though she did not publish most of her work on hot-pressed paper as a series of lyric soliloquies, an envelope never published as a lyric can be interpreted as such. Further, the historical accidents that have kept this manuscript from publication make it the figure of the lyric par excellence: the soliloquy we now "hear" because it was definitely not performed for us. On this view, genre is a consequence of interpretation (the writer may *act* as if her writing is not addressed to us, but it is up to us, as sophisticated readers of the genre, to know that it is). But it is precisely this discourse of lyric interpretation that Dickinson's lines on the envelope query. What makes such interpretation possible? Fundamentally, a lyric reading practice supposes that poems are written in view of a future horizon of interpretation, a "Trans—." Everything about Dickinson's work contradicts that supposition: either she actually sent lines to friends or she wrote them on household scraps like the split-open envelope. Yet as Cameron suggests, the fascicles are the exception to both rules; if Dickinson made books, then was she not indulging in a form of self-publication in view of future or at least imaginary readers of those books?

If we think of the fascicles as books of poems, then the discourse of lyric reading would dictate that we answer yes to that question. After Lavinia Dickinson found the sheets tied with string in Dickinson's bedroom after her death, she called them "volumes"; Mabel Loomis Todd, Higginson's editorial collaborator (and the person who did all the practical editorial work, as her daughter, also a Dickinson editor, would point out) coined the term "fascicles" (often, "little fascicles"), preferring the botanical term for a bundle of stems or leaves to Lavinia's image of a series of bound books.[54] Lavinia's assumption from the beginning was that if the pages tied with string were "volumes," then the writing within them must be "poems," and that while other manuscripts might be personal and therefore should be destroyed upon the death of the person (she had already burned hundreds), poems in books were intended for print.[55] Cameron's argument that the fascicles are "definitive, if privately published texts" extends Lavinia's assumption that poems should be treated as if intended for publication, though as we have seen, Cameron suggests that Dickinson sought to expand the possibilities of the lyric by not printing, and so not choosing, individual lyrics. But what if the fascicles are—or were—not books at all, or not "volumes" either meant for or kept from publication? If not, would that mean that the writing inside them is neither a series of lyrics nor one big lyric?

When Higginson introduced Dickinson's *Poems* in 1890 by writing that her verses "belong emphatically to what Emerson has long since called 'the Poetry of the Portfolio,' " he was referring to Emerson's suggestion in 1840 that there be "a new department in poetry, namely, *Verses of the Portfolio.*"[56] With Emerson's phrase Higginson took Emerson's lyrical notion that "manuscript verses" exhibited "the charm of character," that they were "confessions . . . for they testified that the writer was more man than artist, more earnest than vain"—that is, that the writer of such verses was Mill's perfect actor, utterly unaware of his audience. Yet the majority of portfolio makers in New England in the nineteenth century were women who did not write with a view toward or away from publication; rather, the many forms of the portfolio in the period tended to take the materials of the culture into the literate life of the private individual. Barton Levi St. Armand has pointed out "the essentially private nature of the portfolio genre, its function as a loose repository of musings, views, portraits, copies, caricatures, and 'studies from nature' that made it truly an idiosyncratic 'Book of the Heart.' The portfolio . . . had close affinities with the schoolgirl exercises of the album, the herbarium (in which Dickinson was adept), and the scrapbook."[57]

Although St. Armand dubs such collections "private," it is important to note that such privacy literally included publicly circulated material; in many instances, the copybook practice typical of school albums consisted of writing out poems already in print, or of pasting printed poems beside manuscript copies. In the handsewn school notebook of Georgina M. Wright, for example (fig. 9), Mount Holyoke Female Seminary Class of 1852, class notes face a page of handwriting exercises partially obscured by pasted poems cut from the newspaper (the same weekly local paper in which Dickinson's poems would first appear). Dickinson attended Mount

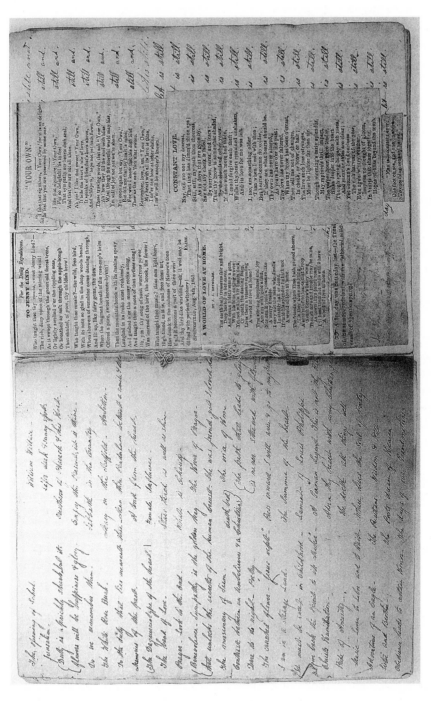

Figure 9. Notebook of Georgina M. Wright, Mount Holyoke Female Seminary Class of 1852. Courtesy of Mount Holyoke College and Special Collections.

Holyoke in 1847 and 1848, and though her school notebooks probably went up in Lavinia's fire, the habit of sewing pages together to create manuscript books would have been part of her practice there. Like other things at Mount Holyoke, it was a practice that extended domestic culture into the school; as the facing pages from a notebook kept by members of the Page family in Boston between 1823 and 1827 illustrate (figure 10), the domestic transcription of poetry resembled school exercises—just as school exercises resembled domestic literacy.[58] Both also resemble the fascicles— so much so that we may conclude that such collections are not *like* the fascicles, but are what the pages now called "Dickinson's fascicles" *are*—or *were*. That difference in temporal definition is a difference in genre: if lyrics are private performances in public, "sudden flashes" of present-tense immediacy, and utterances addressed to future interpreters, then Dickinson's manuscripts are not lyrics. Though the fascicles were for the most part, as far as we know, collections of Dickinson's own verse, they were collections from different occasions, various correspondences. They undo each criterion of lyric discourse by reversing it: they take public materials into privacy; their material, artifactual circumstances and, often, their figurative content emphasize temporal difference rather than simultaneity; if they are now addressed to literary interpreters, Dickinson is not the one who inscribed the envelope.

Yet if even such a fragmentary critical archaeology suggests that Dickinson's writing undoes lyric discourse, it also suggests that Dickinson's writing has come to epitomize lyricism by being removed from its circumstances of circulation by unseen editorial hands. It may seem funny to insist on Dickinson's private (or non-)circulation of her own writing as an historical condition of generic exchange, but Cameron, Howe, Smith, Werner, and others who urge editorial revision of the Dickinson canon are right to point out that the difference between the isolated Dickinson lyric in print and the experience of reading Dickinson's intricate manuscript compositions changes one's view of the writing in ways we have yet to explain. As we saw in the instance of the HOME INSURANCE CO. NEW YORK memo pages (figs. 7a, 7b), part of that difference depends on the surplus value of literal context the manuscripts provide: lines from Swinburne may appear in excerpted, lyricized form beside what seem to be personal notes or parts of a letter, but editors like Shurr and Franklin can find quatrains and couplets in even such riddled manuscripts. Yet in removing such lines from their historical "text occasions," editors have also changed the way in which we read them. In print editions, lines such as "the Affluence / of time" or "Loves / dispelled / Emolument" may appear invitations to metaphorical translation, evidence of Dickinson's famous blend of abstract and concrete nouns, of economic and poetic terms, of suggestively

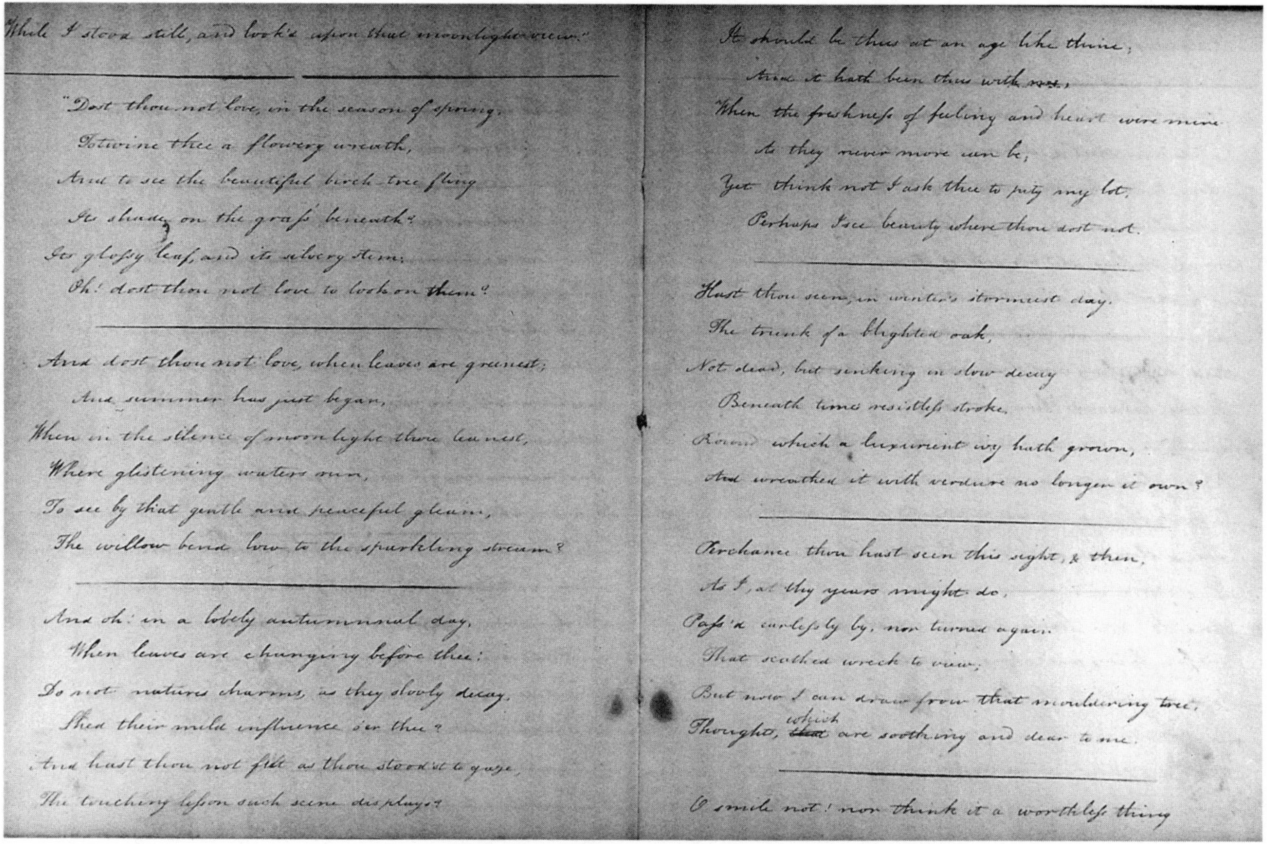
While I stood still, and look'd upon that moonlight view."

"Dost thou not love, in the season of spring,
To twine thee a flowery wreath,
And to see the beautiful birch-tree fling
Its shade on the grass beneath?
Its glossy leaf, and its silvery stem;
Oh! dost thou not love to look on them?

And dost thou not love, when leaves are greenest,
And summer has just begun,
When in the silence of moonlight thou leanest,
Where glistening waters run,
To see by that gentle and peaceful gleam,
The willow bend low to the sparkling stream?

And oh! in a lovely autumnal day,
When leaves are changing before thee;
Do not natures charms, as they slowly decay,
Shed their mild influence o'er thee?
And hast thou not felt as thou stood'st to gaze,
The touching lesson such scene displays?

It should be thus at an age like thine;
And it hath been thus with me,
When the freshness of feeling and heart were mine
As they never more can be;
Yet think not I ask thee to pity my lot,
Perhaps I see beauty where thou dost not.

Hast thou seen, in winter's stormiest day,
The trunk of a blighted oak,
Not dead, but sinking in slow decay
Beneath time's resistless stroke,
Round which a luxurient ivy hath grown,
And wreathed it with verdure no longer its own?

Perchance thou hast seen this sight, & then,
As I, at thy years might do,
Pass'd carelessly by, nor turned again
That scathed wreck to view;
But now I can draw from that mouldering tree,
Thoughts, ~~that~~ which are soothing and dear to me.

O smile not! nor think it a worthless thing

Figure 10. Page family notebook, 1823–27. Courtesy, American Antiquarian Society.

inappropriate prepositions and verb forms. In the textual economy of the memo sheets, however, "Emolument" and "Affluence" pun on the insurance company's ad. The agent of the company's "Cash Assets, over SIX MILLION DOLLARS" may promise one sort of affluence, and the payments the agent offers constitute one sort of emolument, "but Loves / dispelled / Emolument" is, by contextual implication, uninsured.[59] The distribution of such memo sheets to wealthy private home owners like the Dickinsons represented the implication of public business enterprise in domestic private life, a symptom of the development of what Gillian Brown has dubbed American "domestic individualism."[60] As the manuscript books enfolded home into school and school into the home, Dickinson's use of the memo sheets as writing material turned the public appropriation of privacy inside out. Not incidentally, at least some of the lines on the sheets claim that "Love," that most cherished of domestic sentiments, is not subject to claims of capital and commodity—though the sheet on which those claims are written may be.

As we shall see in the chapters that follow, Dickinson's use of commercial advertisements, pasted clippings, other people's poems, bits of fabric, dead insects, pressed flowers, accidental blots, and collections of her own lines as companions for her writing not only expand that writing's field of reference but should expand our notion of the genre on which her lines so often comment. In the next chapter, I will consider the developments in twentieth-century lyric theory that make it so difficult for us to compass that expansion in our idea of the lyric itself. But before we move on to the century of theoretical speculation on the lyric that would accompany the expanding circulation of Dickinson's lyrics in and beyond print, one final example from the archive that might stop such speculation in its fossil bird-tracks is in order. Perhaps just before she wrote the lines on the split-open envelope (fig. 5) that begin "When what / they sung for / is undone—," Dickinson wrote a related series of lines that survive in four different manuscript versions. Three of the manuscripts were sent to familiar correspondents: Frances Norcross, Dickinson's cousin, made a transcript of a version sent to her, a version in pencil was sent to Dickinson's friend Sarah Tuckerman at around the same time, and on May 12, 1879, Helen Hunt Jackson wrote to Dickinson: "I know your "Blue bird" by heart—and that is more than I do any of my own verses.—I also want your permission to send it to Col. Higginson to read. These two things are my testimonial to its merit."[61] Clearly Jackson, maven of print circulation that she was, thought of the manuscript Dickinson sent to her as a lyric that could be detached from its address to her and circulated to other readers— notably, to a reader to whom Dickinson also sent many poems, the man who would edit and inaugurate the poems' public circulation as individual lyrics. And clearly, by sending versions of the same manuscript to several persons, Dickinson herself indicated that the lines were not intended for one reader—as, say, a personal letter might be—but could circulate independently of particular readers or a particular material context. Though this sociable exchange of verse does not approach the anonymous circulation characteristic of the print public sphere, it does represent an increasing detachment of the text from its conditions of circulation. Why not, then, just print and interpret the lines as an independent lyric?

The lines have indeed been just so printed and interpreted since Higginson and Todd edited the 1891 *Poems.* Franklin's most recent printed version renders them as Poem 1484:

> Before you thought of Spring
> Except as a Surmise
> You see—God bless his Suddenness—
> A Fellow in the Skies
> Of independent Hues
> A little weather worn
> Inspiriting habiliments
> Of Indigo and Brown—
> With specimens of song
> As if for you to choose—
> Discretion in the interval—
> With gay delays he goes
> To some superior Tree
> Without a single Leaf
> And shouts for joy to nobody
> But his seraphic Self—

The lines are directly addressed, but since we know that each of at least three different people thought that she was the unique addressee (thus Jackson's request for Dickinson's permission) and was not, we might conclude that they are not addressed as historical but as fictive discourse. As Barbara Herrnstein Smith has usefully defined the distinction, when we interpret an historical or "natural" utterance, "we usually seek to determine its historical determinants, the context that did in fact occasion its occurrence and form. . . . The context of a fictive utterance, however, is understood to be *historically indeterminate.*"[62] By this logic, once we decide that Franklin's Poem 1484 was not a Dickinson letter but a Dickinson poem—that is, once we decide on the text's genre—then the circumstances of its original circulation and composition matter less than our interpretation of the text itself. Once we decide that a text is "historically indeterminate" and therefore fictive, we infer that the text asks us to make of it what we will. Indeed, as we have begun to see, such moments of what Dickinson's lines call "Discretion in the interval—" characterize the history of the lyricization of Dickinson's writing. But whose "Discretion" is it? In what is now Poem 1484, the bird that sings to himself is Mill's perfect figure of the actor who acts well because he takes no notice of his audience. Yet the difference between Dickinson's bird and Mill's actor is that Dickinson's "you" is the one who puts the bird on stage. Your interpretation of the timely announcement of spring as a performance intended for you is a mistake: though you may experience the "specimens of song / As if for you to choose—," that *as if* makes all the difference. Your mistake is a fiction that you enjoy, and since the bird is unconscious of it, you might as well. The lines that begin "When what / they sung for / is undone" may worry about the afterlife of lyricism, but the lines that begin "Before you thought of Spring" do not.[63] Why should we?

In the chapters that follow, I will not continue to worry about whether or not Dickinson wrote lyric poems. I shall leave that up to you. What I will explore instead are Dickinson's intricate uses of lyricism in her writing, and the ways in which her writing has come to exemplify assumptions about lyric interpretation. As we shall see, some of those assumptions have nothing to do with the texts published as Dickinson's lyrics, some of them do, and some of them are just historically inappropriate. But all of the genre mistakes associated with Dickinson's writing are instructive—and all of them lead us further and further away from a conclusion about how Dickinson's work *should* be edited, either in print, in facsimile, or as an electronic archive. The fact remains that Dickinson's private composition and circulation of her writing makes that writing exemplary of the lyric in modernity *and* exemplary of how far modern forms of acontextual lyric reading miss its mark.

The fourth extant manuscript version of the lines that begin "Before you thought of Spring" were written on the back of a wrapper for John Hancock writing paper (figs. 11a, 11b). As you can see, Dickinson wrote "Blue Bird" on the printed side advertising the hot-pressed paper inside the wrapper. Whether the inscription represents her answer to the lines' riddle or the title of her poem we cannot say. If the words are a title, then this is one of the few instances in which Dickinson actually titled one of her own poems—an instance that would suggest that she thought of her writing as a set of discrete lyrics.[64] And now that the wrapper is itself printed (for the first time) here, next to the lines known for over a century as a Dickinson poem, you will also notice that as evidence of Dickinson's authorial title or signature, it bears her "John Hancock." You may also notice that once that name comes to suggest a pun, then "Byron" is also a poet's name, and the "Number One Note" that the bird on the verso side utters may be

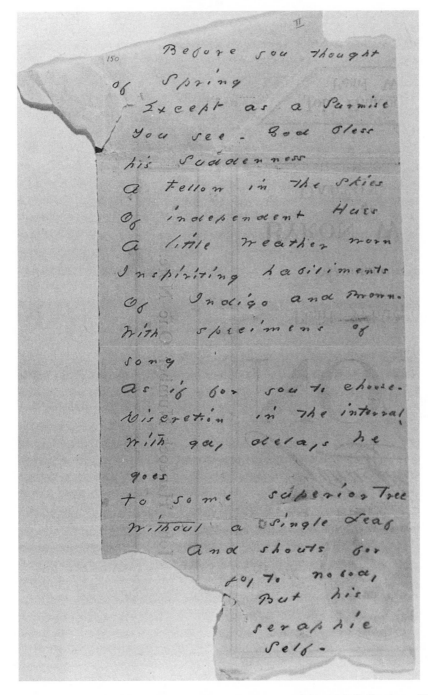

Figure 11a. Courtesy of Amherst College Archives and Special Collections (ED ms. 150).

Figure 11b. Courtesy of Amherst College Archives and Special Collections (ED ms. 150, verso).

literalized on the printed side of the page—so literalized that it has been stamped in small print, "Copyright Secured." Of course, while you are imagining these associations, you will realize that you are merely reading a found page lyrically; the maker of the wrapper certainly did not intend for you to interpret those signs in that way, in the fictive discourse of that genre. Like the bird who sings "to nobody," the wrapper is just advertising paper. Yet now that the wrapper has been published as part of a Dickinson poem, associations between literal accident and figurative meaning invite surmise. What you have just done is what I call "lyric reading," and it is a double bind. In the next chapter, we will explore some coincidences between literal reference and figurative meaning in the verse Dickinson circulated to her familiar correspondents, and then we will turn to later versions of lyric reading that took poems out of such contingent relations and so made everything that was not a lyric disappear.

Lyric Reading

"My Cricket"

In the issue of the *Springfield Republican* for March 23, 1864, a small notice announced that

> In Flatbush, N.Y., last Sunday, William Cutter, a farm laborer, attempted to shoot Anne Walker, a servant in Judge Vanderbilt's family. He fired twice, one of the balls passing through her sleeve and the other lodging in her hip. Cutter also shot at Mrs. Vanderbilt, who ran to the assistance of the girl, inflicting a very severe, and probably mortal wound in the abdomen. Cutter's attentions to Miss Walker had been discarded by her, and hence his attempt at revenge.[1]

The account was reprinted from the *Brooklyn Eagle;* Samuel Bowles, the editor of the *Springfield Republican*, forwarded the *Eagle* article to Susan Gilbert Dickinson, commenting that "it is all horrible, & tears, & tortures, & sets all fundamental ideas afloat." Vanderbilt was Susan Dickinson's friend from school, and the interest of her personal connection to the victim was enhanced when the incident became a public event—so public that when Vanderbilt survived, Henry Ward Beecher reportedly called her the "visible evidence of spiritual life."[2] In September 1864, Emily Dickinson wrote to Susan, "I am glad Mrs.—Gertrude—lived—I believed she would—Those that are worthy of Life are of Miracle, for Life is Miracle, and Death, as harmless as a Bee, except to those who run—" (L 2:294).

To Gertrude Vanderbilt herself, whom she had never met, Dickinson addressed several lines. She may have sent verses to Vanderbilt because of Vanderbilt's friendship with Susan Dickinson, or perhaps because through that connection three Dickinson poems had just appeared in the *Drum Beat*, a paper published during the two weeks of a fund-raising fair sponsored by the Brooklyn and Long Island Fair for the Benefit of the U. S. Sanitary Commission (to improve conditions for Union troops).[3] In making transcripts in 1891 of the lines sent to Vanderbilt, Mabel Loomis Todd echoed Vanderbilt's private involvement in public matters when she noted that they were "to Mrs. Vanderbilt, after she had met with a serious accident at the close of the war—."[4] Todd's confusion of private and public events, accident and intention foretold the fate of Dickinson's letters to

Susan's Brooklyn friend: the four of which Todd made transcripts were all published as poems over the next sixty years.[5] Two of the letters seem to refer directly to Vanderbilt's "serious accident" and recovery. One of them was published as a letter in 1894, 1924, and 1931, and then as a poem in 1955 (J 830):[6]

> To this World she returned
> But with a tinge of that—
> A Compound manner,
> As a Sod
> Espoused a Violet,
> That chiefer to the Skies
> Than to Himself, allied,
> Dwelt hesitating, half of Dust—
> And half of Day, the Bride.
>> Emily

Another has never been published as a letter, and was first published as a poem in 1945 (BM 193):

> Dying—to be afraid of Thee—
> One must to thine Artillery
> Have left exposed a friend—
> Than thine old Arrow is a Shot
> Delivered straighter to the Heart
> The leaving Love behind—
> Not for itself, the Dust is shy.
> But—Enemy—Beloved be—
> Thy Batteries divorce—
> Fight sternly in a dying eye
> Two Armies, Love and Certainty,
> And Love and the Reverse—
>> Emily

Dickinson then copied both sets of lines onto the sort of bifolium sheets she had formerly bound in the fascicles, but after 1865 apparently arranged without binding.[7] Did the copies of the letters no longer refer to Vanderbilt? Were they ever specifically addressed to Vanderbilt? Once lifted out of the fabric of personal and public sociability in which they were originally embedded—away from Vanderbilt as cause célèbre, from the scandal of the rich white woman's dangerous employees, from Vanderbilt's implication in the war and related social causes, from Susan's friendship with her, from Dickinson's presumption of intimacy with Vanderbilt (though not with her servant) through her intimacy with Susan, from Bowles's familiar address to Susan and his editorial and personal involvement with the Dickinsons (especially Emily), from the way friends made their way into newspapers and newspapers made their way into homes, from the coincidence between the war and Vanderbilt's "accident"—the lines no longer seem to refer to an historical occasion. Without the signature, and printed as they now appear in Franklin's edition, they look like lyric poems.

As I suggested in the previous chapter, whatever the lines *were* before they were collected and published, their existence in modern volumes may mean that the lines now *are* lyrics—at least for the purposes of interpretation. In this chapter, I will consider one of the most curious purposes of lyric interpretation during the period in which Dickinson's poems have appeared in print: a great deal of lyric reading in the twentieth century attempted to restore lyrics to the social or historical resonance that the circulation of lyrics as such tends to suppress. And since, from the perspective of modernity, that interpretation is always a recovery project, the resonance that reading restores to lyrics—especially to Dickinson's lyrics—tends toward pathos. Thus when some of the lines that begin "Dying—to be afraid of Thee—" became Poem 831 in Johnson's 1955 edition of Dickinson's *Poems*, Shira Wolosky could write in 1984 that in the poem, martial "conflict becomes an image of Dickinson's inner strife concerning an afterworld," and so conclude that Dickinson's poetry was not just "private and personal" but engaged in the suffering and dilemmas that characterized (Northern) intellectual life during the Civil War.[8] If one begins with the poem in print and if one assumes that a poem is the visible evidence of inner life, then it does seem as if the "Artillery," the "Shot, the "Batteries," and the "Armies" are figures borrowed from the period's literal strife as vehicles of personal expression. Yet if one begins with the Vanderbilt incident, Dickinson's expression may seem no less personal, though its vehicles will seem less figurative. Dickinson's language may aggrandize domestic violence into political and metaphysical contest, but such exaggeration is part of the point of the letter to Vanderbilt—it makes explicit the associations that Bowles and Beecher and Todd all implied. Yet once the letter becomes a lyric, and once the lyric is printed and opened to lyric reading, those public and private associations and their literal and figurative certainties are reversed.

Versions of the other two letters to Vanderbilt take up the confusion between literal reference and lyric reading even more explicitly—and, as we shall see in this chapter, in ways that are telling for the history of lyric interpretation in the United States in the last century. The ambitious modern theories of the lyric that emerged in the twentieth century may be far removed from the circumstances of Dickinson's writing, and far removed from (if implicit in) most practical criticism of Dickinson, but they all, in different ways, took up the problem of the lyric's removal from modern culture; to return to Grossman's phrase in *Summa Lyrica*, they all aimed to construct "a culture in which poetry is intelligible" (207). The assumption behind such theoretical construction is always that we no longer live in such a culture. But Dickinson did. In another note sent to Vanderbilt, of which only Todd's transcript survives (fig. 12), the verse was "intelligible" to its addressee precisely because its literal referent was enclosed in the envelope:

> They have a little odor
> That to me is metre, nay 'tis poesy
> And spiciest at fading celebrate
> A habit of a laureate.
> (F 505)[9]

If Vanderbilt understood the wit of the lines in relation to an enclosed bouquet from Dickinson's garden or conservatory, then how do we understand the lines without the enclosure? Dickinson herself opened the question when she copied the lines into a fascicle (fig. 13), though of course if the fascicles were personal collections, she would have known the original referent.[10] Millicent Todd Bingham was the first to publish the lines as verse in 1945 in her book defending her mother's editorial work on the Dickinson manuscripts, though it is perhaps significant that she used them as an epigraph to a chapter entitled "Creative Editing."[11] We could decide that the exact referent for the pronoun makes no difference—that when printed as Poem 88 in *Bolts of Melody* or Johnson's Poem 785 or Franklin's Poem 505, the point of the lines is that "metre" and "poesy" (or "melody") are metaphors. But they only become metaphors when they are no longer puns on the relation between flowers and poems, a relation that, as Vanderbilt and Dickinson and any other nineteenth-century reader would know, usually worked the other way around (so that "flowers" would be a term used to refer to poems rather than "poems" becoming a term one uses to refer to flowers).[12]

If comparisons between Dickinson's printed lyrics and their manuscript forms merely continued to yield reversals of literal and figural fortune, they would be worth making, but they would not be very suggestive for a theory of modern lyric reading. Yet several versions of the lines in the fourth letter to Vanderbilt suggest much more than such a reversal: the history of their familiar circulation as well as the history of their publication and later reception open into the central issues in twentieth-century lyric theory—indeed, the story of their transmission exemplifies the emergence of the lyric as a creature of modern interpretation and its shift

71

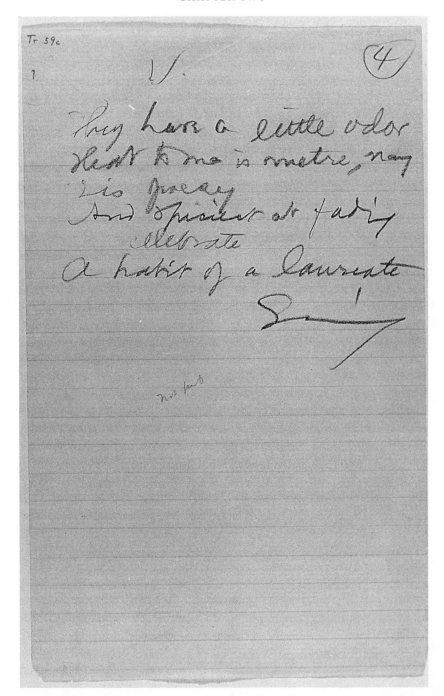

Figure 12. Mabel Loomis Todd's transcript of the note to Gertrude Vanderbilt that is now Franklin's poem 505. Courtesy of Amherst College Archives and Special Collections (ED ms. Tr. 59c).

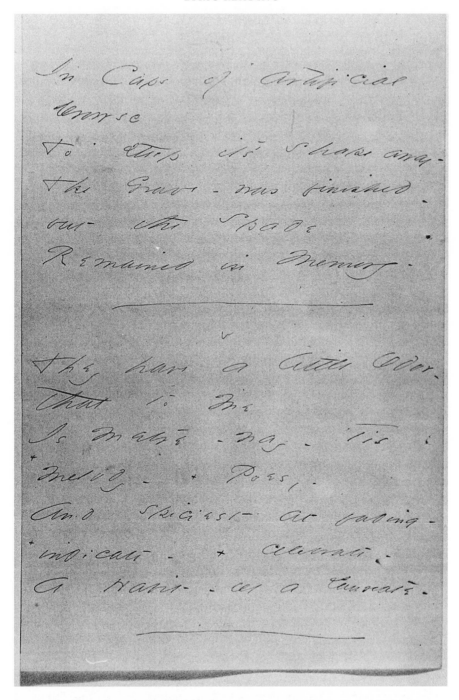

Figure 13. "Fascicle" copy of lines in fig. 12, lower half of page. Courtesy of Amherst College Archives and Special Collections (ED ms. No. 81-9, verso).

toward personal and cultural abstraction. That story began rather modestly when, in the summer of 1865, Dickinson sent some of the most beautiful lines she ever wrote to Flatbush:

> Further in Summer than
> the Birds—Pathetic from the
> Grass—a Minor Nation
> celebrates it's unobtrusive Mass—
> No Ordinance be seen—
> So gradual the Grace
> A pensive Custom it
> becomes Enlarging loneliness—
> 'Tis Audiblest, at Dusk—
> When Day's attempt
> is done and Nature nothing
> waits to do but terminate in Tune—
> Nor difference it knows
> Of Cadence, or of
> Pause—but simultaneous as
> Same—the Service emphasize—
> Nor know I when it
> cease—
> At Candles, it is here—
> When Sunrise is—that
> it is not—than this, I know
> no more—The Earth has many
> keys where Melody is not
> Is the Unknown—
> Peninsula—Beauty is Nature's
> Fact—but Witness for Her
> Land and Witness for Her
> Sea—the Cricket is Her
> utmost of Elegy, to Me—[13]

If, as I suggested in the last chapter, birdsong represented for Dickinson and for the period as a whole a lyricism unattainable by the human poet, then we might say that the cricket's song is even "further" removed from the capacity of human expression than is the nightingale's or skylark's or bluebird's. By this logic, the crickets can express what the writer cannot, or can, as part of nature, themselves become the signs of seasonal wane, of summer's passing. Thus these lines, unlike the lines in the other letters to Vanderbilt, do not seem to refer to any historical circumstance or literal enclosure known to the two women. On the contrary, their theme of seasonal change as well as their use of the cricket as poetic figure place them squarely in the abstract temporality and figurative referentiality of the lyric.

Or so it now seems to us. As it happened, another set of lines that were published in the *Drum Beat* twelve days before Vanderbilt was shot bear a relation to the lines now known to most readers of Dickinson's poems as "Further in Summer than the Birds." In the first edition of Dickinson's *Poems* in 1890, Higginson and Todd gave the following lines the title "Indian Summer," though they were entitled "October" in the final issue of the *Drum Beat* issued on March 11, 1864:

> These are the days when birds come back,
> A very few, a bird or two,
> To take a backward look.
>
> These are the days when skies resume
> The old, old sophistries of June,—
> A blue and gold mistake.
>
> Oh, fraud that cannot cheat the bee!
> Almost thy plausibility
> Induces my belief,
>
> Till ranks of seeds their witness bear,
> And softly, through the altered air,
> Hurries a timid leaf.
>
> Oh, sacrament of summer days,
> Oh last communion in the haze,
> Permit a child to join!
>
> Thy sacred emblems to partake,
> Thy consecrated bread to take,
> And thine immortal wine!
> (F 122 [B])

Whether or not Vanderbilt was responsible for the *Drum Beat* publication of Dickinson's poems, both she and Dickinson would have read the poem reprinted above in that paper.[14] If Dandurand and Franklin are right that the lines that begin "Further in Summer than the Birds" were sent to Vanderbilt late in the summer of 1865, then they would have been written over a year after the lines about late season birds were published in 1864. Like the crickets in the later lines, the birds in the lines that appeared in the Brooklyn paper are signs of change—though the fall birds are misleading, seeming to signal summer rather than winter. What is striking when one puts the lines next to one another (something no editor of Dickinson has done) is the somewhat inappropriate language of Christian ritual that characterizes both sets. The language is "somewhat inappropriate" in the sense that in the *Drum Beat* poem, what is frankly called a "mistake" in the sixth line becomes a "sacrament of summer days" in the thirteenth; in the lines that begin "Further in Summer than the Birds," the "unobtrusive Mass" celebrated by the "Minor Nation" of Crickets is a strangely elaborate figure for cricket song. In both the poem published in the *Drum Beat* and in the lines sent to Vanderbilt in 1865, the activities of birds and crickets are described as highly ritualized Christian observance—so highly ritualized that they seem absurd activities for even anthropomorphized birds or crickets.[15] If in the romantic lyric birdsong was (and it was) a figure for the native culture of nature, in Dickinson's lines birds and crickets clearly do not belong to the culture of "sacrament," "communion, "Mass," and "Ordinance" used to describe them. Dickinson's lines place Christianity, cultural iconography, nature, and writing at odd angles to one another.

That incongruity would have been important in the United States in 1864 and 1865. We need only recall once again that most popular of Union Civil War poems, "The Battle-Hymn of the Republic," to see that "[w]hile God is marching on" in Howe's call to arms, "trampling out the vintage where the grapes of wrath are stored," the apostrophe to the "sacrament of summer days" in Dickinson's *Drum Beat* poem does not suppose that those days' "immortal wine" is anything but an autumnal illusion. Now, since the lines appear to have been first sent to Susan Dickinson in the 1850s, it is unlikely that Dickinson originally intended them to resonate with the discourse that intensified with the war; it was only their accidental publication in 1864 in a paper devoted to the Union cause that made the untimely "sacrament of summer days" potentially analogous to a divinely sanctioned ray of hope in a darkening season.[16] And if the beginning of the last year of the war was a hybrid season, then the summer after the end of the war was a season of stark contrasts. The immense relief that the war was over was followed so swiftly by Lincoln's assassination and the registration of such enormous national loss (including the loss of the identity of "the nation" itself) that, as Louis Menand has written, martial victory seemed to have come at the cost of "a failure of culture, a failure of ideas."[17] If Dickinson did send the lines that begin "Further in Summer than the Birds" to Vanderbilt in the summer of 1865, then the "Minor Nation" of crickets observes an Old World Catholic "Custom" unavailable to the ravaged modern Protestant culture of Dickinson's place and time.[18] Unlike the suffering modern American postwar nation, the pathos of the crickets' "Minor Nation" finds coherent cultural expression; their natural ceremonies may be invisible, and they may not be metrical, but the last lines describe them in the rhetoric of classic nationalism (". . . for Her Land . . . for Her Sea . . .") as the Earth's "Elegy." Yet while the elegy is apt, the sacramental language used to describe it is evidently not: is "a Minor Nation" a nation at all? Is an "Ordinance" that cannot be "seen" still a rite or statute? Is a "pensive Custom" no longer a custom because no longer ingrained habit? Is a "Tune" without "Cadence" or "Pause" a song?

Those questions may be rhetorical, but the last lines sent to Vanderbilt, beginning "The Earth has many / keys," appear to reverse their direction, or put them to rest. In these lines, human "Melody" cannot be imposed on nature, which is suddenly (and strangely, after having been made into a Catholic nation with its own customs) "the Unknown— / Peninsula—." As Joanne Feit Diehl has pointed out, Dickinson's lines may echo Keats's sonnet "On the Grasshopper and the Cricket" and its opening assertion that "[t]he Poetry of the earth is never dead."[19] If so, however, then unlike Keats's cricket by the hearth, Dickinson's cricket does not sing of nature's persistence within culture but of a natural death that culture cannot repair. That reversal of the first lines' emphasis might be why Bingham printed them separately as Poem 139 (Johnson followed suit in 1955 and made "The earth has many keys" the last poem in his collection, Poem 1775, an error that led several later interpreters to treat the poem invented by a modern editor as Dickinson's own last poem).

Now, the cricket's elegy may be or may have been simply the elegy of summer's passing, and its elevated or outlandish description no more than that. Yet the summer of 1865 was full of elegies for nature that were elegies for the culture lost with Lincoln and the war. Whitman's great pastoral elegy "When Lilacs Last in the Dooryard Bloom'd" may now be the best known of such poems, a spring elegy on the occasion of the events of April 1865, and the most beautiful lines ever written on the relation between seasonal redemption, Christian myths of resurrection, and cultural reformation. Yet there were many less distinguished elegies published that summer in the aftermath of the war. In the July 1865 issue of the *Atlantic Monthly* a sonnet appeared, bearing a somewhat out-of-date title:

ACCOMPLICES.

Virginia, 1865.

The soft new grass is creeping o'er the graves
   By the Potomac: and the crisp ground-flower
   Lifts its blue cup to catch the passing shower;
The pine-cone ripens, and the long moss waves
Its tangled gonfalons above our braves.

Hark, what a burst of music from yon wood!
   The Southern nightingale, above its brood,
In its melodious summer madness raves.
Ah, with what delicate touches of her hand.
   With what sweet voices, Nature seeks to screen
The awful Crime of this distracted Land.—
   Sets her birds singing, while she spreads her green
Mantle of velvet where the Murdered lie,
As if to hide the horror from God's eye![20]

The war over, "accomplices" seems the wrong word for the signs of natural recovery the sonnet describes. Yet, as becomes (all too) clear in the closing sestet, the grass, flowers, moss, and birds of postwar Virginia are in cohoots with the Union's former enemies by themselves regenerating a pastoral scene to "screen" the war's casualties. "The Murdered" appear all the more murdered (as opposed to, say, *fallen* in battle) in contrast to the apparent peace of the pastoral scene.[21] Not the instruments of divine will (like Howe's "grapes of wrath") but attempts "to hide the horror from God's eye" (still identified with the wounded Union's perspective), the sonnet mourns the fact that natural expression is not cultural expression— or if it is, it is the expression of the wrong culture, the wrong poetry of the wrong earth. "The Southern nightingale" could not exist in nature in North America, but as romantic poetic figure it becomes the laureate of "this distracted Land," a rough analogy to the cricket's function as "Witness for Her / Land" in Dickinson's lines. Unlike "The Earth" in "Further in Summer than the Birds," however, Virginia in 1865 was, according to the sonnet, still removed and led astray from the Union, a condition that nature could not repair. The problem in the *Atlantic* sonnet is that nature is not naturally elegiac; "its melodious summer madness" is the wrong tune for the cultural season, or for what will now, the poem suggests, count as the perspective empowered by the state to decide that the South's actions were criminal.

The perspective of the sonnet itself is not hard to locate: as a rather elaborate combination of Italian and Elizabethan forms in Wordsworth's modern mode (including couplets within as well as at the end of the sonnet), the poem claims the privilege of its high-middlebrow *Atlantic* publication (a rough equivalent to the contemporary weekly *New Yorker* poems) to present what later in the century in another genre the same magazine would call "local color." In contrast, in Dickinson's 1865 lines to Vanderbilt, "Beauty is Nature's / Fact" rather than the sign of individual or cultural pathos, though "the Cricket" can still seem the "utmost of Elegy, to Me—."[22] That last prepositional phrase, signed "Emily" in the original manuscript, qualifies the problem of whether nature actually mourns and makes it a matter of personal, rather than cultural, perspective. The question is then how that personal perspective circulates, of what forms it takes, of what culture it may create.

We do not have a record of Vanderbilt's reply to Dickinson's "Further in Summer than the Birds," if she wrote one. We do know that Dickinson sent a similar set of lines to her cousins, Louise and Frances Norcross, perhaps also in 1865, but that manuscript has been lost. In 1866, Dickinson sent some of the same lines to Higginson (figs. 14a, 14b), accompanied by a note:

> Carlo died—
> E. Dickinson
> Would you instruct me now?[23]

Carlo, Dickinson's Newfoundland dog, would have been about sixteen years old in 1866.[24] Since her first letter to him in 1862, Dickinson had been asking Higginson for "instruction" in writing, so perhaps she meant to present her lines as evidence of her attempt to write an elegy. But an elegy for what, or for whom? If Vanderbilt might have understood the lines sent to her in 1865 in the context of the aftermath of the war, did Higginson understand them as an elegy for a dog? In the version of the lines sent to Higginson, neither the invocation of national witness in the final lines to Vanderbilt nor the word "elegy" appears:

> Further in Summer
> than the Birds
> Pathetic from
> the Grass
> A minor nation
> celebrates
> It's unobtrusive Mass.
> No Ordinance be
> seen
> So gradual the
> Grace
> A pensive Custom
> it becomes
> Enlarging Loneliness.
>
> Antiquest felt
> at noon
> When August
> burning low

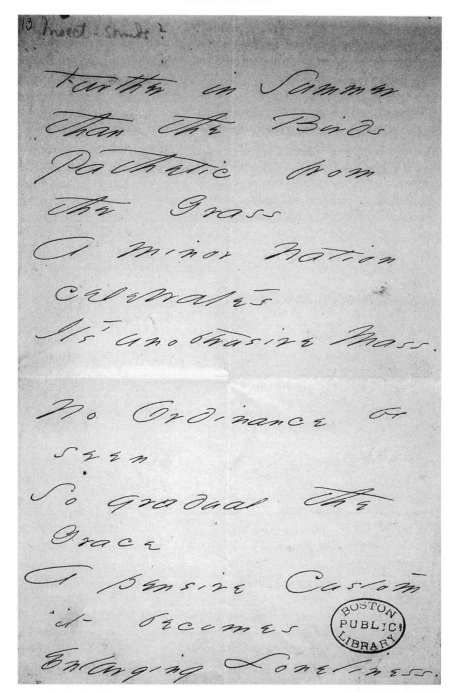

Figure 14a. Emily Dickinson to Thomas Wentworth Higginson, 1866. Boston Public Library/Rare Books Department, Courtesy of the Trustees (Ms. AM 1093, 22).

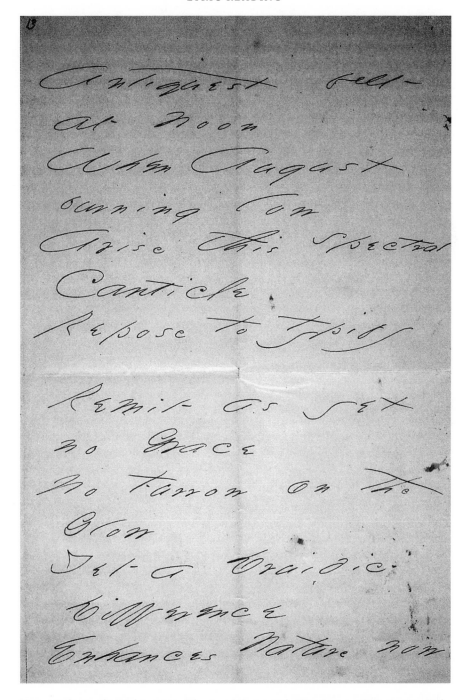

Figure 14b. Emily Dickinson to Thomas Wentworth Higginson, 1866. Boston Public Libaray/Rare Books Department, Courtesy of the Trustees (Ms. AM 1093, 22).

Arise the spectral
Canticle
Repose to typify

Remit as yet
no Grace
No Furrow on the
Glow
Yet a Druidic
Difference
Enhances Nature now[.]

Since Dickinson sent the lines to Higginson in late January 1866, they certainly did not refer to a current natural season, and if they may have resonated with a cultural season in the summer of 1865, then that resonance must have been fainter in the winter of 1866. Dickinson's rather abrupt note to Higginson at the beginning of 1866 was actually the first letter she had sent to him since she had written to him in early June 1864, after learning that he had been wounded in battle in July 1863 and had left the Union army in May 1864.[25] Dickinson herself was in Cambridge under the care of a doctor for eye trouble in 1864; she had written to Higginson to ask if he were "in danger," commenting that "Carlo did not come, because he would die, in Jail" (L 290). Thus the letter of 1866 picks up the thread of the dog's health, but may also continue the oblique reference to the consequences of the war. The lines to Higginson that differ from those in the letter to Vanderbilt not only take out the earlier explicit reference to "elegy" but place the consequences of seasonal change earlier and further within the discourse of natural sympathy than did the lines to Vanderbilt. The first new line, "Antiquest felt," puns on the Old World "Mass" and "Ordinance," but shifts the language of outmoded "Custom" to the realm of individual sensibility, and that shift also changes what the ritual of the crickets is said to "typify." The symbolic function of cricket song has moved away from the register of natural national "witness" in the lines to Vanderbilt; in the lines to Higginson, the still vaguely Catholic "Canticle" represents midday "Repose." But whose repose? The abstraction of the lines to Higginson align the day's apex with individual pathos and then align both with an even older, more culturally misplaced religious rite, a "Druidic / Difference." The lines are certainly more abstract than were the lines sent to Vanderbilt, but the relation between natural and cultural expression—or the problem of what form expression should take—has become more acute.

If that problem may have attached itself to the historical climate in the seasons just after the war, or even to the death of Carlo in 1866, it would have presented itself very differently seventeen years later when Dickinson sent the lines she had sent to Higginson to Thomas Niles. Niles was the chief editor at Roberts Brothers, the publisher that would issue the first volumes of Dickinson's poems in the 1890s. He had initiated a correspondence with Dickinson in 1878, after he had published a Dickinson poem in the anonymous collection *A Masque of Poets*.[26] In 1883, Dickinson wrote to thank him for a copy of the Roberts Brothers' edition of Mathilde Blind's *Life of George Eliot*, writing, "I bring you a chill Gift—My Cricket and the Snow" (L 813). She then included the lines she had sent to Higginson in 1866 in the letter before her signature (figs. 15a, 15b, 15c), and separately enclosed the lines that became "It sifts from Leaden Sieves—" (F 291). Though Niles apparently addressed Dickinson several times, asking for "a M.S. collection of your poems, that is, if you want to give them to the world through the medium of a publisher" (L 813b), she sent only what she called such "gifts," naming them as if they were the objects they described: "My Cricket and the Snow," or "the Bird . . . a Thunderstorm—a Humming Bird . . . a Country Burial" (L 814). Dickinson's objectification of her writing mirrored her own practice of including objects with or within the writing; like the pressed flowers, dead insects, assorted clippings, or illustrations that often accompanied the lines she addressed to particular correspondents, the "gifts" sent to Niles were marked by the singular rather than the commodity form—or at least that is the way Niles himself seems to have understood Dickinson's intention. "I am very much obliged to you for the three poems which I have read & reread with great pleasure," he wrote to Dickinson in 1883, "but which I have not consumed. I shall keep them unless you order me to do otherwise—" (L 814a). The intimacy supposed by the exchange of the singular object obliges its recipient to keep it, and his relationship to the giver, to himself.[27] But we know that the verse Dickinson referred to as "My Cricket" was not a singular object—on the contrary, it was a text she had circulated to various correspondents over the course of over sixteen years. By sending it to Niles, a publisher she would never meet, did she not intend to widen those conditions of circulation, to go public? If the difference between a singular object and a commodity is the exchange value of that object, then we would have to say that by sending her verse to Niles, Dickinson was potentially increasing the exchange value of her writing, or bringing it closer to the commodity form.[28]

Yet as history would have it, not until seven years later, after her death, did Niles and Roberts Brothers publish in what Austin Warren would later call "slim grey volumes" the verse that Higginson would so emphatically characterize as "something produced absolutely without the thought of publication, and solely by way of expression of the writer's own mind"

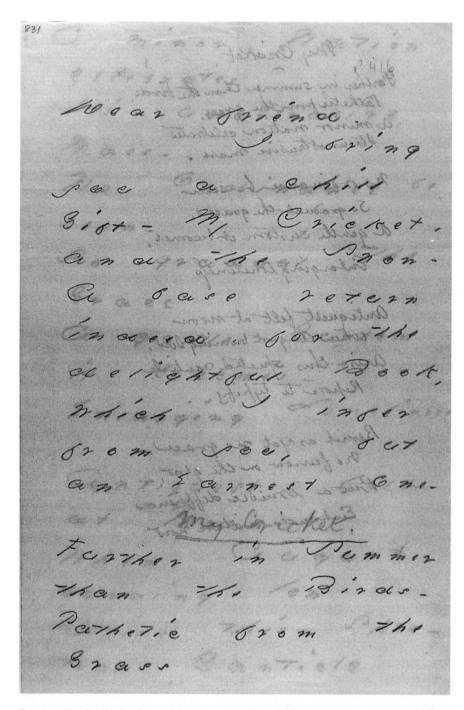

Figure 15a. Emily Dickinson to Thomas Niles, 1883. Todd's transcript of lines, which she copied onto the verso of the first sheet of the letter, is visible in the photograph above; Todd also penciled in the later title. Courtesy of Amherst College Archives and Special Collections (ED mss. 831, 831a, 831b).

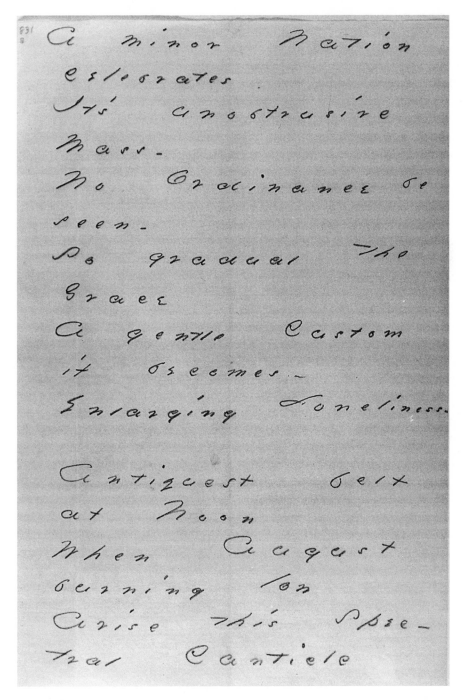

Figure 15b. Emily Dickinson to Thomas Niles, 1883. Courtesy of Amherst College Archives and Special Collections (ED mss. 831, 831a, 831b).

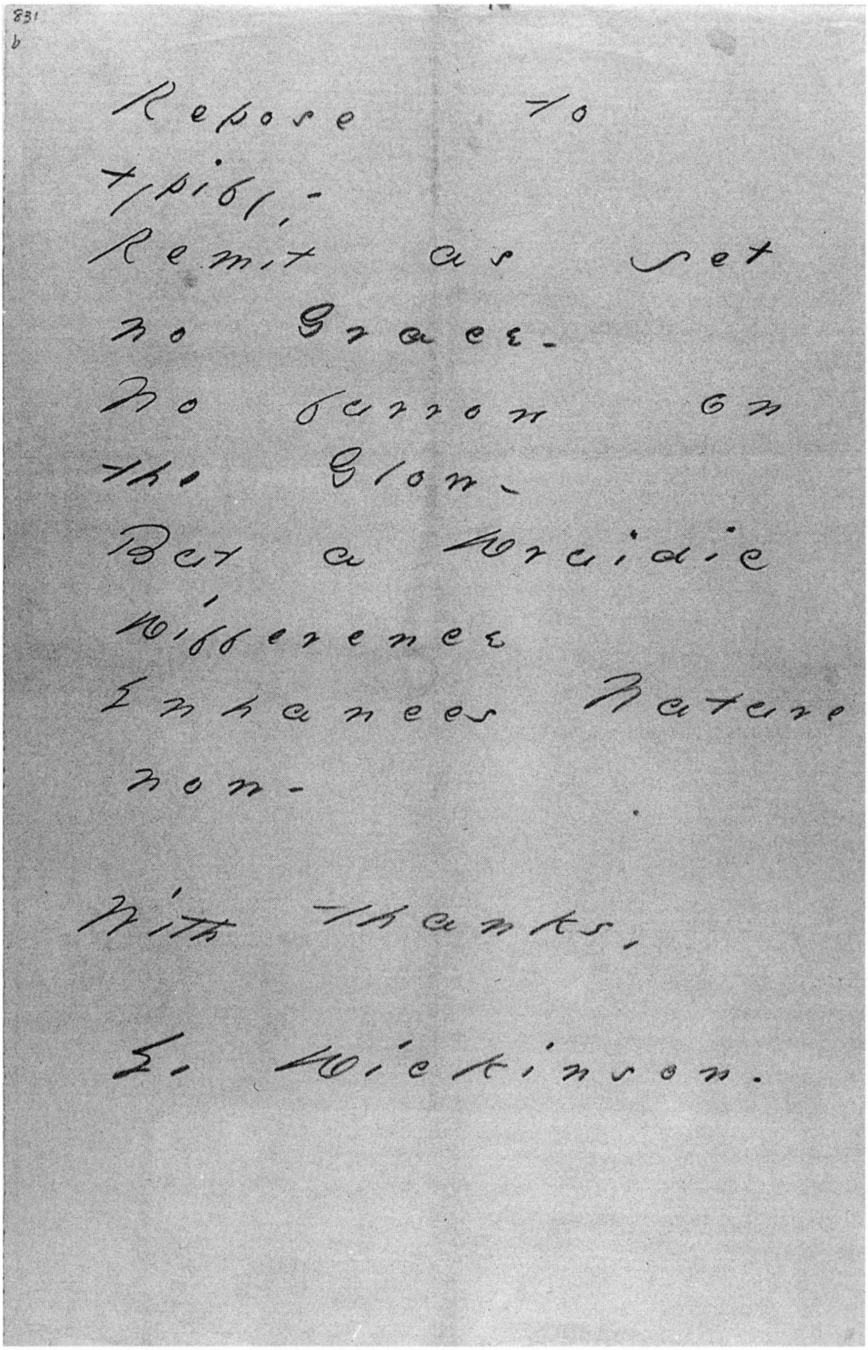

Repose   to
typify -
Remit   as   set
no   Grace -
No   ferror   on
the   Glow -
But   a   Druidic
Difference
Enhances   Nature
now -

With   Thanks,

E.   Dickinson.

Figure 15c. Emily Dickinson to Thomas Niles, 1883. Courtesy of Amherst College Archives and Special Collections (ED mss. 831, 831a, 831b).

(*Poems* 1890, iii).[29] Whatever Dickinson's own intentions may have been, the fact that Niles chose not to publish her poems until they could be circulated as if not intended for public circulation increased their commodity value beyond anyone's expectations. The practical editor of that first edition, Mabel Loomis Todd, transformed Dickinson's reference to her lines into a penciled title, and lineated the poem directly on the manuscript (fig. 15a). Whatever genre we might assign to Dickinson's lines during the years they were exchanged between Dickinson and various individuals, they became lyrics in 1890. The maze of particular practical-social relations to which they pointed before they were published as lyrics became a much more abstract and simplified social relation after publication determined their genre.

Before that happened, however, Dickinson sent the lines that she had sent to Vanderbilt and Higginson and Niles to one other person. Although Dickinson could not have known it in 1883, the woman to whom she addressed this last manuscript (figs. 16a, 16b), Mabel Loomis Todd, would become the first and in many ways most influential hands-on editor of Dickinson's poems. Todd would be the one to take apart the fascicles, to make transcripts of lines in various correspondences, to sort most of what Todd later wrote "looked almost hopeless from a printer's point of view."[30] Yet Todd's familiarity with Dickinson's manuscripts began after Dickinson's death; since Todd was Dickinson's brother's lover, Dickinson's sister-in-law and lifelong intimate, Susan Gilbert Dickinson, the recipient of most of the manuscripts Dickinson herself circulated, did not share most of her cache of manuscripts with Todd and Higginson. By late summer 1883, the affair between Austin Dickinson and Mabel Todd had been going on for about a year, long enough for it to have become a matter of social concern; when Todd was spending the summer of 1883 in New Hampshire, the letters between the two alternated between businesslike "cover" letters and passionate secret confessions that they asked one another to "destroy."[31] One such enclosure of August 1883 from Austin to Mabel is a small scrap of paper:

> Can you endure this silence longer?
> *I cannot*
> I said too much when I said you needn't write
> 'Tis too dreadful
> *Do speak*[32]

It was during this time of separation and tension between her brother and Mabel Todd that Emily Dickinson sent the lines that begin "Further in Summer / than the Birds—" to New Hampshire addressed formally to "Mrs. Prof. Todd," signing them "Brother and Sister's Emily, with love—."

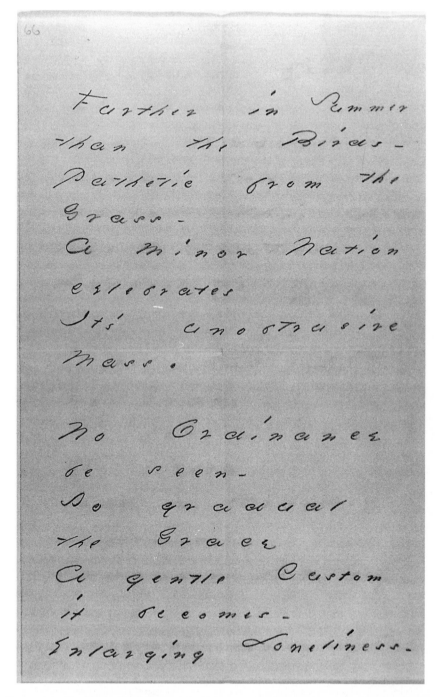

Figure 16a. Emily Dickinson to Mabel Loomis Todd, 1883. Courtesy Amherst College Archives and Special Collections (ED mss, 66, 66a).

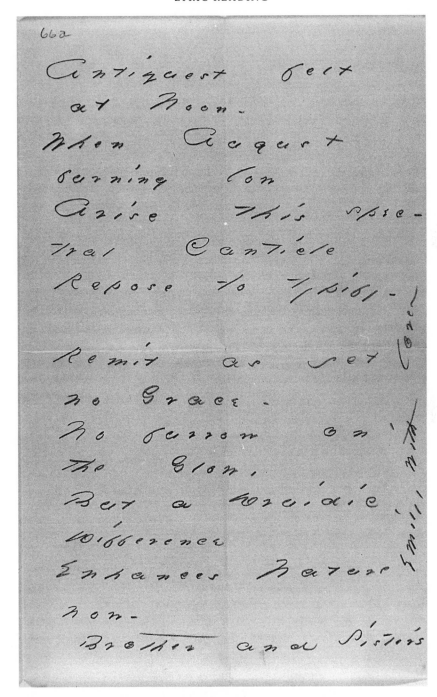

Figure 16b. Emily Dickinson to Mabel Loomis Todd, 1883. Courtesy Amherst College Archives and Special Collections (ED mss, 66, 66a).

Enclosed within the lines was a small square of white paper, and enclosed in that square was a dead cricket, which has miraculously survived in the archive in disarticulated fragments (fig. 17). If the reference to "My Cricket" in the letter to Niles may have suggested that Dickinson had begun to reify her writing in view of a wider, less personal circuit of exchange, then her enclosure of the cricket in the intimate exchange of the lines addressed to more intimate correspondents suggests a very different view of their range of reference, or of the pathos they may have expressed for their reader.

This is to say that while the problem of lyric reference might seem to have been what was at stake in the preceding pages, the overlapping or incongruous details, seasons, public and private histories, battles and pets, sex scandals and insect remnants, books, newspapers, and all sorts of familiar letters that surrounded the lines later published as a Dickinson lyric could not be said to be what the lines are "about." In fact, those contingencies may never have been the subject of the lines, but in any case they could only have formed part of what the lines *were* about; that is, the stories that could be unfolded from them may or may not have been relevant to the lines' potentially miscellaneous subjects (and objects) in the past. Once the lines were published and received as a lyric, those several and severally dated subjects and objects and their several stories faded from view, since the poem's referent would thereafter be understood as the subject herself—suspended, lyrically, in place and time.

That lyrical suspension may seem to be where Dickinson's lines on the cricket were always headed, detaching themselves over and over from whatever circumstances clung to them and readily attaching themselves to others. Yet, as we shall see, one of the most interesting aspects of twentieth-century critical thought about lyric subjectivity was the lack of such particular attachments; for literary theory in the United States in the twentieth century, the isolated lyric subject tended to become a social, even an historical and cultural, abstraction. In Dickinson's case, that meant that the densely woven fabric of social relations from which her verse was removed when it was edited and published as a series of isolated lyrics was replaced by a theoretical concept of "the social" as such; the lyric subject then became the personification of that concept. So, for example, when David Porter wrote in 1981 that what was by then Johnson's Poem 1068 "is a masterpiece in the art of the aftermath," he did not mean the aftermath of Vanderbilt's accident, or of the Civil War, or of any particular summer, or of Higginson's wounds, or of Carlo's death, or of Dickinson's brother's love affair, or of the life and death of a cricket, but Dickinson's own "preoccupation with afterknowledge, with living in the aftermath."[33] That preoccupation, in turn, typified for Porter "an extreme,

Figure 17. This cricket (now dismembered, though artfully rearticulated by the photographer) was enclosed with fig. 16 in the small square of paper on which it is pictured, and on which it has left its mark. Courtesy of Amherst College Archives and Special Collections (ED. ms 66, enclosure).

perhaps terminal, American modernism of which [Dickinson] is the first practitioner" (1). Thus, in what was by then a tradition of lyric reading, the subject of the poem became an abstract person accessible to modern readers.

As we have begun to see, such claims for Dickinson as representative have been made consistently for over a century, and some of them may even be true, but what concerns me here is what such statements suppose about the genre of Dickinson's work. For as Dickinson also became representative of the lyric, the lyric in turn came to represent a distinctly twentieth-century form of interpretation, and the aftermath of this interpretation removed lyric poetry from everything it may or may not have been about and made it about modern lyric reading—about fictive rather than historical persons, and, inevitably, about the historical pathos attached to those fictions.

Lyric Alienation

In 1938, Yvor Winters published an essay entitled "Emily Dickinson and the Limits of Judgment."[34] The essay bears an epigraph taken from the poem published in 1891 under the title "My Cricket":

> Antiquest felt at noon
> When August, burning low,
> Calls forth this spectral canticle,
> Repose to typify.[35]

As Winters's essay unfolds, the epigraph comes to stand for both Dickinson's and her twentieth-century readers' critical blind spots. According to Winters, both Dickinson and her modern readers underestimate the value of lyric poetry: Dickinson because "no poet of comparable reputation has been guilty of so much unpardonable writing"; and Dickinson's readers because "one cannot shake off the uncomfortable feeling that her popularity has been mainly due to her vices; her worst poems are certainly her most commonly praised" (283). The punch line is that "as a general matter, great lyric poetry is not widely read or admired" (283). For Winters, "My Cricket" is an instance of Dickinson's lyric power, *not* the sort of thing that the public would appreciate, and the sort of poem Dickinson herself rarely achieved.

Winters is not just interested in elevating this particular poem, but in placing lyric itself in such an elevated position that it must be alienated from both ordinary poet and ordinary reader. That elevation was for Winters a moral stance, a perspective that made him controversial among the literary critics that John Crowe Ransom would dub "New" in 1941.[36] As

Winters put it, his "theory of literature" was "absolutist" in the sense that he believed that "the work of literature, in so far as it is valuable, approximates a real apprehension and communication of a particular kind of objective truth." He goes on: "The form of literature with which I am for the most part concerned is the poem; but since the poem exhausts more fully than any other literary form the inherent possibilities of language, what I say about poetry can be extended to include other literary forms with relatively unimportant qualifications" (11). Winters's lyricization of poetry ("the poem" rather than any particular kind of poem) thus extended to a lyricization of literarature tout court, with the result that the reading of lyric became for Winters, as for New Criticism generally, the test case, the zero-sum game, of literary interpretation, and literature became the test case of cultural interpretation.[37]

The importance of the lyric to the New Critics has become the most characteristic—and oft caricatured—aspect of the mid-twentieth-century criticism that continues to have a formative influence on the study and, especially, the pedagogy of literature in the United States. As Mark Jeffreys has written, "lyric became a metonymy for New Critical ideology" in the literary critical eras that emerged as New Criticism began to loosen its hold; but as my attribution of grasping agency and Jeffreys's attribution of the term "ideology" to New Criticism indicate, that metonymy was hardly a neutral or purely contingent association.[38] It would be more accurate to say that lyric became a *metaphor* for the New Criticism, in the sense that both the genre and the critical perspective on that genre came to stand for one another—so much so that the ahistoricism attributed to New Critical close reading became confused and identified with an inherent ahistoricism of the lyric genre itself. Yet while many studies have exposed just how historical New Criticism actually was (as a conservative reaction to the new Left of the 1930s, as a post-Reconstruction Southern phenomenon, as a product of Eliot's literary theology, as an institutional grab for power in the postwar university), few have focused on how historically inflected the still-prevalent New Critical notion of "the lyric" was.[39]

One place to notice that inflection is in the New Critics' embrace of Dickinson. In Winters's reading of the poem he knew by the title "My Cricket," lyric isolation is actually the subject of the interpretation. Winters' reading is worth citing in its entirety because it frames Dickinson's lines in exactly the terms that would be so influential, not only for the interpretation of Dickinson but for the interpretation—and formation—of the genre:

In the following poem, we are shown the essential cleavage between man, as represented by the author-reader, and nature, as represented by the insects in the late summer grass; the subject is the plight of man, the willing and freely moving entity, in a universe in which he is by virtue of his essential qualities a foreigner. The intense nostalgia of the poem is the nostalgia of man for the mode of being which he perceives imperfectly and in which he cannot share. The change described in the last two lines is the change in the appearance of nature and in the feeling of the observer which results from the recognition of the cleavage:

> *Farther in summer than the birds,*
> *Pathetic from the grass,*
> *A minor nation celebrates*
> *Its unobtrusive mass.*
>
> *No ordinance be seen*
> *So gradual the grace,*
> *A pensive custom it becomes,*
> *Enlarging loneliness.*
>
> *Antiquest felt at noon*
> *When August, burning low,*
> *Calls forth this spectral canticle,*
> *Repose to typify.*
>
> *Remit as yet no grace*
> *No furrow on the glow,*
> *Yet a druidic difference*
> *Enhances nature now.*

The first two lines of the last stanza are written in the author's personal grammatical short-hand; they are no doubt defective in this respect, but the defect is minor. They mean: There is yet no diminution of beauty, no mark of change on the brightness. The twelfth line employs a meaningless inversion. On the other hand, the false rhymes are employed with unusually fine modulation; the first rhyme is perfect, the second and third represent successive stages of departure, and the last a return to what is roughly the stage of the second. These effects are complicated by the rhyming, both perfect and imperfect, from stanza to stanza. The intense strangeness of this poem could not have been achieved with standard rhyming. The poem, though not quite one of her most nearly perfect, is probably one of her five or six greatest, and is one of the most deeply moving and most unforgettable poems in my own experience; I have the feeling of having lived in its immediate presence for many years. (292–93)

The scrupulous formalism for which the New Critics, and especially Winters, became known is abundantly evident here, as is the cultivated appreciation of each formal feature. As R. P. Blackmur wrote of Winters in 1940, "his observations carry the impact of a sensibility which not only observed but modified the fact at hand; and we feel the impact as weight, as momentum, as authority."[40] That presumption of moral authority alienated Winters from much of the contemporary critical culture with which he was in conversation.[41] But the important thing about his formalist, somewhat picky reading of Dickinson is that its aim is to establish her as "one of the greatest lyric poets of all time" (299). What Winters wanted to isolate and secure was the *literary* Dickinson—or Dickinson as definition of the literary, and especially of the lyric. He accomplishes that isolation in his full critical (and aesthetically italicized) citation of the poem and in his demonstration of its craftsmanship. The one "defect" that Winters finds in Dickinson's artistry are two small lines "in the author's personal grammatical shorthand." Winters quickly dismisses the lapse as "minor," but his remark speaks volumes by the time we get to his reading's stunning conclusion: the "personal" touch interferes with the critic's own personal identification with the poem's portrait of isolation. What matters for Winters's reading of the poem is not when it was written, how it was written, or who read it—in fact, for the image of literary isolation he wants to find in the poem, it is just as well that he does not know any of that. If he did, the lines would seem insufficiently lyric.

The ways in which Winters's investment in Dickinson's abstract alienation is also an investment in a certain definition of the lyric become even clearer when we notice that Winters's essay was in part a response to an essay on Dickinson that Allen Tate had published in 1932. Entitled "New England Culture and Emily Dickinson," Tate's essay also identifies Dickinson's work as definitively literary, going so far as to claim that in order to appreciate Dickinson, one must have "a highly developed sense of the specific quality of poetry—a quality that most persons accept as the accidental feature of something else that the poet thinks he has to say. This is one reason why Miss Dickinson's poetry has not been widely read."[42] Tate's conclusion is a counterfactual statement: as we have seen, Dickinson's poetry *had* been widely read by 1932, most recently in a flurry of attention surrounding Aiken's and Bianchi's editions in 1924. But what is interesting about Tate's assertion is why it matters that his view of Dickinson rests on that fiction. As his title suggests, Tate wants Dickinson to represent not only "the specific quality of poetry" but to personify culture, namely American intellectual culture before and after what Tate calls by the Southern title "the War between the States." As others have pointed out, Tate's view is certainly informed by his own regional loyalties, and the form that regionalism takes in his version of Dickinson is that her work becomes regionally representative. In the passage that Winters cites from Tate just before his reading of "My Cricket," Dickinson's local culture becomes evident in her relation to nature:

> The enemy of all New Englanders was Nature, and Miss Dickinson saw into the character of this enemy more deeply than any of the others. The general symbol of Nature, for her, is Death, and her weapon against Death is the entire powerful dumb-show of the Puritan theology led by Redemption and Immortality . . . we are renewed by Nature without being delivered into her hands. When it is possible for a poet to do this for us with the greatest imaginative comprehension, a possibility that the poet himself cannot create, we have the perfect literary situation. Only a few times in the history of English poetry has this situation come about: notably, the period between about 1580 and the Restoration (159).

Vanderbilt and Norcross and Higginson and Niles and Todd would be surprised by Tate's view of Dickinson's "weapon against Death," but perhaps that is because they shared Dickinson's culture. Tate's view is possible only from a temporal and regional purchase outside that culture—indeed, it is the otherness of "all New Englanders" in his account that allows his characterization of "the entire powerful dumb-show" in which they were, apparently, puppets. Tate's Dickinson becomes the voice of that "dumb-show," a poet able to redeem not nature but culture itself: a Shakespeare, a Milton.

What Dickinson also redeemed for the New Critics was the profession of literary criticism. If Winters's response to Tate was to personalize the cultural alienation that Tate attributed to Dickinson, Blackmur's response a year before Winters's was to objectify alienation: "Mr. Tate builds up a pretty good historical prejudice and makes it available in the guise of insight," Blackmur wrote, and he went on to identify Tate's partial account of intellectual history as

> the prejudice contained in the idea of imagination being fed and dying, or for that matter living or doing anything whatever—that is to say, a prejudice about the nature of poetry itself as the chief mode of the imagination. Poetry is composed of words and whenever we put anything into poetry—such as meaning or music; whenever poetry is affected by anything—such as the pattern of a culture or the structure of a stanza; whenever anything at all happens in poetry it happens in the medium of words. It is also near enough the truth to say that whenever we take anything out of poetry, either to use it or to see just what it is, we have to take

it out in the words—and then put it right back before it gets lost or useless. The greatness of Emily Dickinson is not . . . going to be found in any-
body's idea of greatness, or of Goethe, or intensity, or mysticism, or historical fatality. It is going to be found in the words she used and in the
way she put them together; which we will observe, if we bother to dis-
criminate our observation, as a series of facts about words.[43]

Blackmur's manifesto may certainly be read as what is now a truism
about New Criticism: he insists on divorcing poetry from the sources of
self-expression, rendering the poem a pure text to be read by the scientifi-
cally detached observer of linguistic "facts" (one can hear structuralism
and poststructuralism rustling in the wings beyond Blackmur's performance). But Blackmur's phrase for his abstraction of poetry as pure language is curious: "whenever we take anything out of poetry, either to use
it or to see just what it is, we have to take it out in the words—and then put
it right back before it gets lost or useless." Why would we have to take
anything out of poetry? What would it mean to take something out of poetry? What is it that we could take out? Could we say that Dickinson's familiar readers "took something out" of her verse (even when it did not
contain dead crickets)? If they did, why or how would they "put it right
back"? Winters's response to Blackmur was to cast as subjective experience the objective scene of reading that Blackmur describes. Winters scru-
tinized the formal elements of the poem in order to abstract them and thus
identify with their subject; Blackmur's version of an intersubjective relation to the poem is selective and utilitarian: rather than live in the poem's
presence, he fiddles with its parts. Thus Blackmur concludes his evalua-
tion of Dickinson by claiming that "she never undertook the great profession of controlling the means of objective expression" (223). Blackmur
wants Dickinson to be a professional because he wants literary critics to be
professionals, which is to say that the intersubjective function of the poem
for Blackmur is not to reflect Dickinson's own intellectual culture or to reflect the individual taste of the reader but to create academic culture.[44]

One of the foundational texts of the culture that Blackmur projects as
the lyric's proper sphere was published in the same year as Winters's
essay on Dickinson (1938), a year after Blackmur's, and six years after
Tate's. In the first edition of *Understanding Poetry: An Anthology for College
Students*, Cleanth Brooks and Robert Penn Warren specifically reject moral-
ist, subjectivist, historically representative, and purely mechanical approaches to poetry, instead recommending that we—that is, "we" teachers
and students in college classrooms—think "of a poem as a piece of writing
which gives us a certain effect in which, we discover, the 'poetry' in-
heres."[45] It is an interestingly tautological recommendation. We read a

poem in order to discover "'poetry'"? Like Winters, Tate, and Blackmur, Brooks and Warren identify poetry as lyric, they identify the lyric as the literary, and they specify the literary as what they want to teach the student in turn to identify in poetry. The logic represents a seamless rationale for literary studies as a separate academic discipline. But what is this "'poetry'" in quotation marks that English professors teach students to discover in poems? Dickinson is one of the poets Brooks and Warren select to analyze as an exemplary instance of the poetry in the poem. Their explication of "After great pain a formal feeling comes—" emphasizes the imagery of the poem line by line in order to lead to the following conclusion: "the formality, the stiffness, the numbness . . . is an attempt to hold in, the fight of the mind against letting go; it is a defense of the mind" (471). Could not the reader have come to that conclusion by reading the first line? Perhaps, but according to Brooks and Warren, the reader could not have discerned the "'poetry'" of that conclusion, since such discernment requires that the imagery of each line be made the site of not just one reader's intersubjective experience but the common reference point for a select group of individuals who need to be directed to experience particular moments of intersubjectivity—of "reading." As Brooks and Warren put it in their introduction, "poetry is not an isolated and eccentric thing, but springs from the most fundamental interests which human beings have" (25). The purpose of *Understanding Poetry* is to direct students' individual interests toward a common goal, a common culture of the class. That is where, after 1938, "'poetry'" will be found.

As the many different cultural sites where Dickinson's poetry was found collapsed into the community of professional (or apprentice) readers, so the contingent details, referents, genres, enclosures, circumstances, addressees, occasions, secrets, and textures of her work were collapsed into an idea of the lyric generated by that community. It would be interesting to compare the abstractly useful model of the lyric that the New Critics developed in their conversation around Dickinson to Adorno's introductory apology in "Lyric Poetry and Society" (1957) to the effect that his title might make his audience think that "a sphere of expression whose very essence lies in either not acknowledging the power of socialization or overcoming it through the pathos of detachment . . . is to be arrogantly turned into the opposite of what it conceives itself to be through the way it is examined."[46] American readers have sometimes mistaken the object of Adorno's address here as New Criticism, especially since Adorno's essay first appeared in translation in the American Marxist journal *Telos* in 1974 next to an article by John Fekete on "The New Criticism: Ideological Evolution of the Right Opposition."[47] But New Criticism never pretended that the lyric is not social in nature—it simply claimed that the social is only available in the lyric through linguistic and personal abstraction, since words and fictive personae are what the poem (or the book or class in which we receive the poem) gives us to read. Adorno comes to a strangely similar conclusion: "the paradox specific to the lyric work, a subjectivity that turns into objectivity, is tied to the priority of linguistic form in the lyric; it is that priority from which the primacy of language in literature in general (even in prose forms) is derived" (43). Yet the world of difference between the reasons that the New Critics and Adorno come to the conclusion that the lyric is an alienated, or objectified, formal structure that renders personal expression abstract may account for why Adorno's view of lyric has not had much influence on American criticism and pedagogy.[48] His idealist view of the genre itself is derived from the European romantic tradition, in which the "genreness" of the lyric is not what is at stake in its interpretation. Benjamin's interpretation of Baudelaire is the more immediate subtext of Adorno's essay, and Benjamin's version of "A Lyric Poet in the Era of High Capitalism" (like the New Critics' reading of Emily Dickinson, also a product of the 1930s) would also seem to have found curiously little purchase in American lyric reading—though, as we shall see, American critics continue to try to integrate Frankfurt School thought about aesthetic abstraction into poetic interpretation.[49]

Instead, another European critic who then studied with the latter-day New Critic Reuben Brower (who coined the phrase "close reading") and was the formative influence on the post–New Critical Yale School of lyric interpretation combined the European idealization of the lyric with the American academic will to power through interpretation.[50] Paul de Man did not take up Emily Dickinson as his lyric example (he took up no American literary examples), but since I take the notion of "lyric reading" from de Man's interpretation of the genre, I shall consider his construction (which he claimed was a deconstruction) of the lyric in some detail. The complicated shorthand genealogy I have just given for de Man's approach to the lyric also betrays the extent to which the lyric became the creature of twentieth-century criticism: by the time of the conversation between Tate, Blackmur, and Winters over Dickinson in the 1930s, academic critical culture had already replaced the sociable versifying and verse-reading culture of Dickinson's contemporaries. The consequences and history of that shift have been the implicit subjects of these pages; in order to tell the full story, we would need to retrace the emergence of professional literary criticism out of familiar culture's path toward the genteel literary criticism that brought Dickinson's work into circulation. But since my purpose here has not been to trace a reception history but instead to trace in and through Dickinson a history and theory of lyric reading, de Man's post–New Critical focus on lyric reading itself becomes important to consider here. For although de Man did not write about Emily Dickinson, he followed the New Critics' emphasis on the lyric by writing about virtually nothing but lyric reading, and his theory of lyric reading will bring us straight back to Dickinson as representative of the very reading practices de Man tried to take apart.

LYRIC THEORY

When de Man suggested that "no lyric can be read lyrically, nor can the object of a lyrical reading be itself a lyric" in 1979 in "Anthropomorphism and Trope in the Lyric" (*The Rhetoric of Romanticism* 254), he was making the argument of *Dickinson's Misery* in reverse. I have been suggesting that New Critical readings of texts like "Further in Summer than the Birds" (or "My Cricket") created an abstract personification in place of the historical person, and consequently created an abstract genre accessible to all persons educated to read lyrically in place of the verse exchanged by people with varying degrees of access to one another who may have read according to their own historical referents. I have also been suggesting some ways in which we might recover some of the practices that preceded critical lyric reading, and even some ways to retrieve some of those material historical referents. But because de Man began from the perspective of twentieth-century lyric reading, he took a different theoretical tack. For de Man to prove that the lyric was a modern critical fiction, he needed to begin by declaring that it did not exist: "The lyric is not a genre, but one name among several to designate the defensive motion of the understanding, the possibility of a future hermeneutics."[51] How could the genre for which de Man's own essay was named not exist? While the primary and much-debated aim of the essay was to question the phenomenal or experiential subject of lyric utterance (the infamous deconstructive dismantling, or death, of the subject), another and less noticed effect of the assertion that "the lyric is not a genre" is that critical reading has made it so. What de Man's reading performed was not the disappearance of the lyric subject, but the appearance of the critical subject of the lyric.

De Man proclaimed the death of the lyric with such bravado that it may obscure the fact that the latter contention that genres are not born but imperfectly made was hardly new by the end of the 1970s. In *Beyond Genre*, ten years before de Man's essay was published, Paul Hernadi had suggested that an essential account of the lyric genre seemed not to exist: "As for lyric poetry, I am not aware of any widely shared concept of its generic structure. While deep insights have been attained with regard to certain kinds of non-dramatic, non-narrative writing, critics do not seem to have succeeded in providing a unified conceptual map of this 'no man's land.'"[52] Likewise, René Wellek had at around the same time complained that "lyrical theory" had led to "an insoluble psychological cul de sac." According to Wellek, "the way out is obvious. One must abandon attempts to define the general nature of the lyric or the lyrical. Nothing beyond generalities of the tritest kind can result from it. It seems much more profitable to turn to a study of the variety of poetry and to the history and thus the description of genres which can be grasped in their concrete conventions and traditions."[53] Given this context of an unravelling lyric hermeneutics already beginning to forfeit the name of its object ("no man's land," "the variety of poetry") we can begin to see that de Man's sentence was (as he might put it) set in motion by a performative ("the lyric is not a genre") masquerading as a statement of fact. This statement could only be said to be "true" if "the possibility of a future hermeneutics" had not already come to pass and begun to be surpassed. If "there is no significant difference between one generic term and another" because "all have the same apparently intentional and temporal function" (261), that *apparent* function makes all the difference. Since the lyric was already firmly in place as a critical convention—as a basis for the production and reception of poetry—saying that it did not exist would not unmake what literary tradition had already made. "Generic terms such as 'lyric'" may be, as de Man argued, "at the furthest remove from the materiality of actual history" (262), but they are also themselves historical.

But rather than historicize the idea of the lyric, de Man chose to emphasize the alienation of that idea from history. De Man's reading of the lyric later became associated with the inherent ahistoricism of high literary theory in the academy, yet at the end of "Anthropomorphism and Trope in the Lyric," it was history, of all things, that de Man thought might be salvaged from his deconstruction of the lyric. If generic terms are, according to de Man, "always terms of resistance and nostalgia," (262), was de Man's point that "non-lyrical, non-poetic, that is to say, prosaic, or better, *historical* modes of language power" (262) *could* be recovered from their idealized or "defensive" or resistant or nostalgic categories of "understanding"? How? What would "the materiality of actual history" look like on the page? Like a flower, like an ad, like a dead cricket? The irony of de Man's assertion that the genre that was his criticism's central preoccupation did not exist is that Paul de Man—proper name for the scandals of late twentieth-century academic literary theory—appears to have intended to restore to his own and others' constructions of the lyric an aspect of contingent, perhaps even historical, practice.

This, at least, is one implication of de Man's lyrical unreading of Baudelaire's "canonical and programmatic sonnet 'Correspondances'" (243). Like Benjamin, de Man took up Baudelaire as the iconic modern poet, and

101

he selected that poet's most iconic poem. The adjectives attached as introduction betray at the start that what is at stake in de Man's interpretation was what he elsewhere distinguished as "the canonical '*idée reçue*' of the poem," as opposed to "the poem *read*."[54] Yet how could a poem possibly be *read* apart from its "*idée reçue*" or detached from its identity as *a poem?* The question should sound familiar to readers of *Understanding Poetry* as well as of the previous chapter of this book. Since the entire trajectory of de Man's essay is, as Jonathan Culler has remarked, "in effect, if not in principle, a reading of lyric" in the sense that it is "an exposition of [the genre's] constitutive conditions," this turns out to be in de Man, as in Brooks and Warren and in "Dickinson Undone," not only a tricky but perhaps a trick question.[55] The conditions that make "Correspondances" a convenient paradigm for examining the lyric's "constitutive conditions" are the conditions of the sonnet's reception *as* paradigmatically lyrical, and this reception is, according to de Man, already inscribed in the intersubjective logic of the poem itself. In other words, in order to expose the lyric as a modern critical fiction, de Man adopted the very strategy of modern literary criticism: a close reading of the iconic modern poem as a purely linguistic artifact. The crux of this logic rests in the repetitively analogical structure of the lyric's rhetoric, a structure that, as de Man reads it, comes to an abrupt halt in the sonnet's final tercet in precisely the term for identity by analogy, the word "comme" (which, as de Man informs us, is not incidentally "the most frequently counted word in the canon of Baudelaire's poetry" [248]). In order to see how in de Man's *very* close reading a monosyllable could be seen to allow a reading that it then disallows, we need to consider the sonnet in its entirety:

> La Nature est un temple où de vivants piliers
> Laissent parfois sortir de confuses paroles;
> L'homme y passe à travers des forêts de symboles
> Qui l'observent avec des regards familiers.
>
> Comme de longs échos qui de loin se confondent
> Dans une ténébreuse et profonde unité,
> Vaste comme la nuit et comme la clarté,
> Les parfums, les couleurs et les sons se répondent.
>
> Il est des parfums frais comme des chairs d'enfants,
> Doux comme les hautbois, verts comme les prairies,
> —Et d'autres, corrompus, riches et triomphants,
>
> Ayant l'expansion des choses infinies,
> Comme l'ambre, le musc, le benjoin et l'encens,
> Qui chantent les transports de l'esprit et des sens.

The pillars of Nature's temple are alive
and sometimes yield perplexing messages;
forests of symbols between us and the shrine
remark our passage with accustomed eyes.

Like long-held echoes, blending somewhere else
into one deep and shadowy unison
as limitless as darkness and as day,
the sounds, the scents, the colors correspond.

There are odors succulent as young flesh,
sweet as flutes, and green as any grass,
while others—rich, corrupt and masterful—

possess the power of such infinite things
as incense, amber, benjamin, and musk
to praise the senses' raptures and the mind's.[56]

According to de Man, in the course of these lines "the transcendence of substitutive, analogical tropes linked by the recurrent 'comme,' a transcendence that occurs in the declarative assurance of the first quatrain, states the totalizing power of metaphor as it moves from analogy to identity, from simile to symbol to a higher order of truth" (248). To paraphrase: the identities that seem to be so seamlessly accomplished in the opening quatrain ("La Nature *est* un temple . . .") are the results of an elaborate verbal performance motivated by an apparently threatening "totalizing" desire inherent in the very rhetorical structure of metaphor, which depends on the grammatical structure of analogy and leads inevitably to the generic structure of "a higher order" of symbolic, or lyric, value ("truth"). That this "higher order" precedes the "substitutive, analogical tropes" that make its existence possible allows it to seem to be a cause when it is in fact, de Man argues, an effect. And yet even if we grant this reversal, we are left with the question of how an effect can also be causal: if metaphors may have desires (or "totalizing power") then so may genres. The fact that "Correspondances" is a sonnet means that all of its "confuses paroles" will be read as if they were ("comme") their rhyming terms, "symboles." Thus the formal architecture (or "temple") of the poem will, generically, donate the effect of a significant intention to the words—and therefore to the subject—it contains and confuses.

Wary of this confusion, de Man proceeds carefully "à travers" each line of the poem, in a movement caught in the ambivalence he himself notes in the phrase "passer à travers," which can mean to "cross" the wood but also "to remain enclosed in the wood" (248). This ambivalence reaches its crisis—in the poem as in de Man's reading of it—when, a belated Dante, "à travers des forêts de symboles" in both senses, the critic arrives at the final "comme" in the poem: "Il est des parfums frais comme . . . / Doux comme . . . / /—Et d'autres . . . // Ayant l'expansion des choses infinies / *comme* l'ambre, le musc, le benjoin et l'encens." At this point, de Man remarks, in a performative statement of his own: "Ce comme n'est pas un comme comme les autres" (249). Lapsing from his lapidary English prose into "the declarative assurance" of Baudelaire's French (and, oddly, into an English pentameter rhythm in the French if pronounced as prose, and into Baudelaire's alexandrine if the line is pronounced as verse), this statement does much more than it says. While in one sense the declaration breaks away from the analogical movement of the preceding seven lines of the poem, in another it is entrapped by their "confuses paroles" so utterly that it is reduced to an imitative stutter ("comme . . . Comme comme . . ."). Here indeed the lyric and its interpretation, or, literally, the language of the poem and the language of the interpreter are difficult to tell apart. The French sentence that occurs nowhere in the poem "sounds" like Paul de Man, the smuggler of French theory into American literary studies, taunting his American readership. Thus at the climax or aporia of his strongly persuasive challenge to an essentially anthropomorphic or intentional subject of the lyric, the critic is suddenly possessed by that subject. In the most literal sense—in the sense peculiar to this shift in literacy—what this sentence enacts is exactly the sort of identification that de Man describes as "anthropomorphism," which

> is not just a trope but an identification on the level of substance. It takes one entity for another and thus implies the constitution of specific entities prior to their confusion, the *taking* of something for something else that can then be assumed to be *given*. Anthropomorphism freezes the infinite chain of tropological transformations and propositions into one single assertion or essence which, as such, excludes all others. It is no longer a proposition but a proper name, as when the metamorphosis in Ovid's stories culminates and halts in the singleness of a proper name, Narcissus or Daphne or whatever. (241)

Taking one entity for another—French for English, performance for statement—de Man's sentence eventuates in exactly the sort of metamorphosis he deconstructs on the level of an evocatively linguistic substance. Rather than taking apart the expressive subject, his reading gives the genre a critically expressive subject. No longer a proposition, the sentence culminates and halts in an identification to which we should give the name "lyric": a genre resurrected from its theoretical abolition in the doubled proper name of "de Man" and (or as) "Baudelaire." That momentary metamorphosis—as de Man's prose freezes into Baudelaire's verse, and reader and writer exchange places—complicates the concluding move of de Man's essay, after ce comme qui n'est pas un comme comme les autres becomes comme un autre de Man qui est comme un autre Baudelaire. Following his show-stopping line (worthy of the accoutrements of the séances of which Baudelaire's verse was so fond), de Man goes on to soberly explicate the rhetorical difference between this final "comme" and the instances preceding it, concluding that while the other "commes" link "the subject to a predicate that is not the same: scents are said to be like oboes, or like fields, or like echoes," the same word in the last tercet "has two distinct subjects" (249). If joined to the first of these subjects, "l'expansion," "comme" would function "like the other 'commes,' as a comparative simile." Yet by this point in the extended sentence of the final two tercets, "comme" also refers back to "parfums": "Il est des parfums frais . . . / /— Et d'autres . . . // . . . / comme l'ambre, le musc, le benjoin et l'encens." In the latter case, "comme" comes to mean "such as, for example" and thus enumerates rather than analogizes the attributes of its subject. It is as much as to say that "'Il est des parfums . . . / / Comme (des parfums)'" (250).

While such a distinction between exemplification and analogy makes impressive sense of the strangeness of the penultimate catalogue of scents, the conclusion that the poem ends in a tautology is also only a weaker version of the confusion between "the two distinct subjects" named prose and poetry or de Man and Baudelaire, a confusion performed by the French sentence that hovers between or gives one over to the other. Likewise, de Man's extended comparison between "Correspondances" and Baudelaire's later sonnet "Obsession," a comparison intended to demonstrate that the later poem lyricizes the earlier sonnet's resistance to lyric reading, stages as a merger of two texts the marriage that has already occurred between the two subjects. If, as de Man writes, "the relationship between the two poems can . . . be seen as the construction and the undoing of the mirrorlike, specular structure that is always involved in a reading" (252), a more striking exemplification of that relationship may be the mirrorlike, specular structure of the sentence that had already prescribed the phantasmatic recovery of the lyric subject in the confused practice of de Man-Baudelaire.

In effect, "Obsession" could be said to read "Correspondances" as a parody of de Man's rather possessed or obsessed reading of "Correspondances." It is actually in the literal sense a *parody* or ode parallel to the earlier sonnet, the apostrophe latent in the first poem's abstractions having emerged as a direct first-person invocation:

> Grands bois, vous m'effrayez comme des cathédrales;
> Vous hurlez comme l'orgue; et dans nos cœurs maudits,

Chambres d'éternel deuil où vibrent de vieux râles,
Répondent les échos de vos *De profundis.*

Forest, I fear you! in my ruined heart
your roaring wakens the same agony
as in cathedrals when the organ moans
and from the depths I hear that I am damned.[57]

According to de Man, the opening of "Obsession" reverses that of "Correspondances": "it naturalizes the surreal speech of live columns into the frightening, but natural, roar of the wind among the trees" (254). What the direct address to the "Grands bois" does, according to de Man, is to anthropomorphize the woods that in "Correspondances" remained purely symbolic. "The claim to verbality in the equivalent line from 'Correspondences,'" de Man writes, "'Les parfums, les couleurs, et les sons se répondent' seems fantastic by comparison. The omnipresent metaphor of interiorization, of which this is a striking example, here travels initially by ways of the ear alone" (256). If the lyric is, as de Man claimed, the instance of represented voice, then the later poem's naturalization of voice is a lyricization of voice. But what travels where how? De Man's use of the English idiom slips just slightly in its own "claim to verbality." Few English speakers would *say* "by ways of," but the plural makes an odd textual sense to an ear caught between languages. What is "the omnipresent metaphor of interiorization" that is said to be transported "by" these "ways"? As de Man notes, "no 'comme' could be more orthodox than the two 'commes' in these two lines. The analogy is so perfect that the implied anthropomorphism becomes fully motivated" (255). Yet if anthropomorphism "is not just a trope but an identification on the level of substance," whose internalized, subjective identity is thus "motivated"? Are these lines driven by "a totalizing desire" toward the private interior or by means of (the idiom that must have crossed "by way of" in de Man's ear) a litany of conventional lyric figures? Whose depths—the poet's, the critic's, or the genre's—does this *De profundis* sound?[58]

De Man's answer is contained in one word: "pathos." The experiential subject dispersed in the closing catalogue of "Correspondances" is "retrieved" by the opening swell of "Obsession":

The gain in pathos is such as to make the depth of *De profundis* the explicit theme of the poem. Instead of being the infinite expanse, the openness of "Vaste comme la nuit et comme la clarté," depth is now the enclosed space that, like the sound chamber of a violin, produces the inner vibration of emotion. We retrieve what was conspicuously absent from "Correspondances," the recurrent image of the subject's presence to itself as a

106

spatial enclosure, room, tomb, or crypt in which the voice echoes as in a cave. The image draws its verisimilitude from its own "mise en abyme" in the shape of the body as the *container* of the voice (or soul, heart, breath, consciousness, spirit, etc.) that it exhales. At the cost of much represented agony ("Chambres d'éternel deuil où vibrent de vieux râles["]), "Obsession" asserts its right to say "I" with full authority. (256)

The indictment leveled at the recuperative anthropomorphism of the later poem is palpable in this prose; at the same time, however, there is a recuperation *of* the poem taking place in the critic's rendition of it. The analogies that de Man imports here—"like the sound chamber of a violin" and "the voice echoes as in a cave"—are not derived from the corpus of Baudelaire's lyrics but from the corpus of Paul de Man's readings of the lyric. The first alludes to de Man's comprehensive reading of Rilke in *Allegories of Reading* (1979), at the center of which is an analysis of the figure of the poet as the string of a violin (from Rilke's "Am Rande der Nacht"). De Man much admired the trope of the violin in Rilke's poems because, he writes, "The metaphorical entity is not selected because its structure corresponds analogically to the inner experience of a subject but because its structure corresponds to that of a linguistic figure: the violin is *like* a metaphor because it transforms an interior content into an outward, sonorous "thing" . . . it is the metaphor of a metaphor."[59]

Whereas in his reading of "Obsession" de Man's analogical use of the violin is meant to evoke "the subject's presence to itself," in his reading of Rilke the violin "corresponds" to a linguistic figure; on one hand the metaphor is said to evoke "emotion" but on the other merely to mime a "structure." When a comparison of de Man's own figures reveals is that it is not the figures themselves that evoke "the inner experience of a subject" that de Man identifies as lyric; instead lyric reading produces the effect of that subject.

It is evident in both passages that de Man wants to oppose subjective experience to pure figuration; as in his comparison between "Correspondances" and "Obsession," however, a comparison of de Man's own figures tends to collapse the very opposition that sustains his analyses. Yet perhaps that was de Man's point all along. In several earlier essays de Man had invoked the notion of the poem as a "spatial enclosure" ("room, tomb, or crypt . . . cave") that figures the illusion of an interior consciousness, and in each his central move had been to turn that illusion inside out so that the enclosure was itself transformed from the subject's protective "shelter" (a favorite de Manian charge) into a device for its production.[60] Yet in his passage on "Obsession," de Man employed these analogies accumulated from his reading of other lyrics in order to mimetically enclose an analogy *to* the lyric. Baudelaire's "Chambres d'éternel deuil" are echo chambers not so unlike those "de longs échos" of "Correspondances," and what they echo is a lyric convention (*De profundis*) rather than an unmediated personal cry of anguish. Certainly this is *"represented* agony" at least as expansive as the sensations of the earlier poem, dispersed as it is among several figures ("bois," "cathédrales," "l'orgue") and several persons (*"nos* cœurs maudits") as well as transferred to an explicitly literary and textual register by the Latin phrase. It is hard to understand how that dispersion allowed de Man to assert that "'Obsession' asserts its right to say 'I' with full authority," since the subjective form of the first-person singular pronoun appears nowhere in the stanza itself. Perhaps—as the accidental omission (bracketed in our text) of the closing set of quotation marks in de Man's closing citation of "Obsession" in parentheses ironically suggests—it is the critic's rather than the poet's "I" that emerges here "with full authority," an authority derived from the pathos of his own elegy for the genre that is his subject.[61]

This is to say that if, as de Man wrote in an earlier essay on the formalist interpretation of the lyric, "poetry is the foreknowledge of criticism," the reverse must also be true.[62] Criticism that knows its object as poetry (as a "canonical and programmatic sonnet") sustains that generic identification even (or perhaps especially) in its negation. Indeed, in the vehemence of his rejection of the term, de Man ends by reviving a more idealized sense of the lyric than most readers would have had at the start of his essay. "In the paraphernalia of literary terminology," de Man concludes, "there is no term available to tell us what 'Correspondances' might be. All we know is that it is, emphatically, *not* a lyric. Yet it, and it alone, contains, implies, produces, generates, permits (or whatever aberrant verbal metaphor one wishes to choose) the entire possibility of the lyric" (261–62). "It and it *alone*"? "The *entire* possibility of the lyric"? De Man's concluding declarations are so excessive that one is tempted to call them, indeed, *obsessive. The claim that "Obsession" embraces the lyric experience artfully repressed by "Correspondances" has shifted from the declarative assurance of the details of de Man's rhetorical reading into the affective register of a performative attachment to just what those statements deny—into an expressive attachment, that is, to the lyric.

This structure of highly emotionally inversed attraction and denial actually rather suggestively parallels Freud's structural description of obsession, in which "the symptoms acquire, in addition to their original meaning, a directly contrary one. This is a tribute to the power of ambivalence, which, for some unknown reason, plays such a large part in obsessional neuroses. In the crudest instance the symptom is diphasic: an action which carries out a certain injunction is immediately succeeded by another action which stops or undoes the first one even if it does not go quite so far as to carry out its opposite."[63] *Ambivalenz*, a word coined by Freud in his analysis of obsession, certainly characterizes de Man's "specular" coupling of Baudelaire's lyrics, as its power saturates the "aberrant verbal" qualifications which attend the "Yet . . ." syntax that undoes his reiterated injunction against the lyric. The strategy of taking away with one hand what has been given by the other is, of course, a typical feature of deconstructive reading—yet in this passage the usual order is reversed: de Man's essay ends by restoring (albeit ambivalently) "the entire possibility" it has worked to undo.[64] By generating a string of approximations of what the lyric *would* be if it had not been so "emphatically" negated by the previous statement, de Man ends by pushing "the lyric" just outside the field of representation. Thus the pathos of his elegy for the subject with which the criticism that obsessed de Man was obsessed also makes of the lyric a subject for obsessional elegy, for in the last lines of his essay "the lyric" is no longer a proposition but a proper name.[65]

Still, as Freud would have it, the name that de Man gives to the extrametaphoric, uncanny "possibility" of the postlyrical "does not go quite so far as to carry out its opposite": what "the desired consciousness of eternity and of temporal harmony as voice and as song" (the "chambres d'éternel deuil où vibrent de vieux râles") is opposed to at the end of the essay is, we recall, "the materiality of actual history" (262). Presumably, the former would be the property of "generic terms such as 'lyric,'" while the latter would escape the "resistance and nostalgia" that de Man has associated with "the defensive motion of the understanding, the possibility of a future hermeneutics" (261). My point is that the hermeneutic practice of "Anthropomorphism and Trope in the Lyric" had already comprehended, despite itself, a contrary meaning of "*historical* modes of language power" (262). According to de Man's own (Nietzschean) logic, "language power" should read as an oxymoron, since the "unintelligible" force of extreme materiality is what the language closely read as lyric, in its "defensive" or purely aesthetic aspect, cannot admit. That is as far as de Man got, and it is a long way. But when de Man wrote, elegiacally, that lyric pathos cannot allow for "*historical* modes of language power," modes he characterized as "non-anthropomorphic, non-elegiac, non-celebratory, non-lyrical, non-poetic" (262), he was not allowing that before modern lyric reading became a form of critical power, poetry itself may have been such a mode.

Against (Lyric) Theory

Although I have attempted to show that de Man worked very much within the grain of the New Criticism in his adoption of the lyric as a synecdoche for literature and in his construction of the lyric through the practice of close reading, in the profession of literary study built around the lyric, de Man came to stand for the incursion of European literary theory into American practical criticism.[66] De Man personified that incursion, in part because his deeply subjective investment in the dismantling of the lyric made other critical readers uneasy. The reaction against de Man took many forms, and one form it took was to oppose a pragmatist approach based in Anglo-American analytic philosophy to de Man's basis in Continental philosophy. It also took the form of a reaction against the lyric. In the issue of *Critical Inquiry* for Summer 1982, Steven Knapp and Walter Benn Michaels published an essay provocatively entitled "Against Theory," which claimed to argue that "the whole enterprise of critical theory is misguided and should be abandoned."[67] Naturally, several professional critical theorists took up the challenge and responded—thus fulfilling, one assumes, Knapp and Michaels's intention. Despite, that is, the essay's stated aim to put an end to "the theoretical enterprise" (AT 30), its locus of publication and its polemical stance suggested that what Knapp and Michaels were actually out to do was, as W.J.T. Mitchell put it, to "out-theorize the theorists" (AT 9).

By pointing to a discrepancy between the implicit and explicit purposes of the piece—or between the essay's "intention" and its "meaning"—what I have just done is exactly what Knapp and Michaels argued should not be attempted, since "the clearest example of the tendency to generate theoretical problems by splitting apart terms that are in fact inseparable is the persistent debate over the relation between authorial intention and the meaning of texts" (AT 12). Against my consideration of such a tendency on the part of the theorist who was Knapp and Michaels's most prominent unnamed target, I want to consider briefly only one aspect of the argument in "Against Theory" (an argument that, as we shall see, Michaels repeated over twenty years later with explicit reference to Dickinson) that "the meaning of a text is simply identical to the author's intended meaning" (AT 12): namely, that the text central to this contention is a lyric poem.

While the debate that ensued in and around Knapp and Michaels's essay was based entirely on this one small text, neither the authors nor their critics appeared to think that the genre of their example made much of a difference. Yet just as the critical situation of "Against Theory" cast its goal of abolishing its own situation in an ironic aspect, so the situational definition of the lyric may have decided "the persistent debate over the relation between authorial intention and the meaning of texts" in advance. While on one hand Knapp and Michaels argued that "once it is seen that the meaning of a text is simply identical to an author's intended meaning, the project of meaning in intention becomes incoherent," on the other they supported that claim with an instance of the literary genre traditionally devoted to begging the question of first-person coherence. What their essay did not say about the specific structure of lyric reference spoke volumes about the importance that structure held (and still holds) for both the "pragmatic" and the "theoretical" extremes of literary study. Knapp and Michaels's silence on the theory of the genre that served as a condition for their practice suggests, among other things, that whatever the relation between textual meaning and authorial intention may be taken to be, there are no "generic" intentions, or intentions uninfluenced by the conventions of genre. While de Man's theory idealized a pure and practically impossible historical practice removed from the fiction of genre, Knapp and Michaels's practice paradoxically ended by idealizing the very theoretical potential of the genre they adopted to render theory impractical.

That potential became immediately (and excessively) obvious in the anecdote Knapp and Michaels offered as empirical proof that "the moment of imagining intentionless meaning constitutes the theoretical moment itself":

Suppose you're walking along a beach and you come upon a curious sequence of squiggles in the sand. You step back a few paces and notice that they spell out the following words:

> A slumber did my spirit seal;
> I had no human fears:
> She seemed a thing that could not feel
> The touch of earthly years.

This would seem to be a good case of intentionless meaning: you recognize the writing as writing, you understand what the words mean, you may even identify them as constituting a rhymed poetic stanza—and all this without knowing anything about the author and indeed without needing to connect the words to any notion of an author at all. You can do all these things without thinking of anyone's intention. But now suppose that, as you stand gazing at this pattern in the sand, a wave washes up and recedes, leaving in its wake (written below what you now realize was only the first stanza) the following words:

> No motion has she now, no force;
> She neither hears nor sees;
> Rolled round in earth's diurnal course,
>   With rocks, and stones, and trees.
> (AT 15)

According to Knapp and Michaels, the arrival of the second stanza of "the wave poem" makes clear "that what had seemed to be an example of

111

intentionless language was either not intentionless or not language" (AT 16). Why should this be the case? Although they do not say so, the authors seem to assume that the two stanzas together call for an explanation because "you" will recognize them now as *a poem*. Though continuing to call the lyric "the wave poem" rather than "A Slumber Did My Spirit Seal," they even assume that "you" may recognize it as a poem by Wordsworth: "You will now, we suspect, feel compelled to explain what you have just seen. Are these marks mere accidents, produced by the mechanical operation of the waves on the sand (through some subtle and unprecedented process of erosion, percolation, etc.)? Or is the sea alive and striving to express its pantheistic faith? Or has Wordsworth, since his death, become a sort of genius of the shore who inhabits the waves and periodically inscribes on the sand his elegiac sentiments?" (AT 16). The alternative speculations offered above are meant to be mutually exclusive: either the poem has been written by the sea or Wordsworth's ghost or it is the effect of a nonintentional natural process. In the latter case, the marks would not constitute a "poem" at all but would be "accidental likenesses of language." The intent of the anecdote was to make this latter alternative unimaginable, as indeed it is: "you" already knew that this is a poem by Wordsworth, a poem about the loss and potential recuperation of human agency and, since you were reading this hypothetical narrative in the pages of *Critical Inquiry* and not on a beach, you might have also known, as Knapp and Michaels concede in a note (AT 15n5), that the same short lyric had been employed by E. D. Hirsch, P. D. Juhl, J. Hillis Miller, and M. H. Abrams in essays on the question of authorial intention.[68] In fact, from the first line of the poem, the rest of the argument would have seemed more amusing than relevant to you, not only because its citation indicates a receding series of critical citations but because knowledge of the poem's authorship has never decided much about its interpretation.

The ruse in which Knapp and Michaels left the question of authorship open until "you notice, rising out of the sea some distance from the shore, a small submarine, out of which clamber a half dozen figures in white lab coats" (AT 17), made possible a deus ex machina of empiricism that was never suspended in the first place. This "new evidence of an author" emerging from the submarine and shouting " 'It worked! It worked! Let's go down and try it again' " was, of course, a better allegory for the strategy of the essay than for any possible reading of the poem. If, as Knapp and Michaels conclude, "the question of authorship is and always was an empirical question; it has now received a new empirical answer," we might concede the point only in the sense that the old empirical answer—that "A Slumber Did My Spirit Seal" was a lyric written by Wordsworth in 1799 in

Germany—had to be forgotten in order to make us believe that we were remembering that this "theoretical moment" had been a set-up.

The fallacy of the anecdote established in order to prove the fallacy of "doing theory" drew much immediate fire from critics on both sides of the "intentionalist" debate, and it is not my purpose to recount the details of that debate here. I sketch its outlines merely in order to notice that this particular discourse "for" and "against" the "theoretical enterprise" depended upon certain unstated assumptions about lyric reading which it therefore ended by exemplifying. In one of the most pointed responses to Knapp and Michaels, Jonathan Crewe found their style characterized by a "maneuver in which the authors disqualify a distinction only to appropriate its effects," a maneuver Crewe felicitously labeled "smash and grab, or S. & G. for short" (AT 59). The "wave poem" was, according to Crewe, a signal instance of S. & G., since "the wave poem does not *resemble* a poem by Wordsworth but is actually identical to one. What the authors have, whether they like it or not, is a wave *poem* that happens not to lend itself to pragmatic interpretation" (AT 61–62).[69]

Crewe did not insist on the genre of the linguistic conventions smashed and grabbed by the wave-poem narrative, but his description helps me to do so. Suppose you are walking along a beach and you come upon a curious sequence of squiggles in the sand. You step back a few paces and notice that they spell out the following words:

> Who that cares much to know the history of man, and how the mysterious mixture behaves under the varying experiments of Time, has not dwelt, at least briefly, on the life of Saint Theresa, has not smiled with some gentleness at the thought of the little girl walking forth one morning hand-in-hand with her still smaller brother, to go and seek martyrdom in the country of the Moors?

It is fair to say that the distinction between authorial intention and textual meaning disqualified and then reappropriated in the story of finding the Wordsworth poem would have to be made in a very different way for the Prelude to *Middlemarch*. Whether or not you recognize this prose as George Eliot's, chances are that it would not occur to you that in order to understand what this sentence means you would first need to determine the author's intention; even if the sentence washed up in two stages (and therefore could not have been etched with a stick by some previous beach-walker), wondering how these words appeared in this place and wondering what the words say would remain two distinct questions. In the imaginary context of the sand, the question the sentence poses might seem to have more to do with Saint Theresa or the nature of belief than it does in the context of the novel, but that belief is not contingent on finding out whether this is one of "the varying experiments of Time" or whether ghosts or the sea are capable of writing. In "A Slumber Did My Spirit Seal," however, one does want to know something more about the identity of the "I" who "had no human fears" (when? of what?) and about this person's relationship to the "she" who "seemed" (like a poem?) an object of contemplation. Without thinking along these lines, neither the reader of the sand nor the reader of the book can make much sense of the two sentences of Wordsworth's lyric.

The problem raised by the "found" poem is a smashed version of the problem grabbed from the moment embedded within the poem as-it-is-received-as-a-lyric—that is, as it becomes accessible to lyric reading. As Lukács wrote in 1914 (echoing Hegel's and anticipating Adorno's and Heidegger's lyrical notions), "such moments are constitutive and form-determining only for lyric poetry; only in lyric poetry do these direct, sudden flashes of the substance become like lost original manuscripts suddenly made legible; only in lyric poetry is the subject, the vehicle of such experiences, transformed into the sole carrier of meaning, the only true reality.[70]

We may notice just how much the beachwalker's failure to imagine "intentionless language" owes to this notion of the lyric's revelation of language *as* intentional. One's entrance into a lyric often delivers this very Wordsworthian "shock of mild surprise," since to come upon such lines as "phainetai moi kenos theosin" or "voi ch'ascoltaie in rime sparse il suono" or "Mine eye and heart are at a mortal war" or "Jezt komme, Feuer!" or "When I have fears that I may cease to be / Before my pen has gleaned my teeming brain," is to be privy to an experience for which we have no immediate context. In order to establish a context, we will inevitably have recourse to what we know about Sappho's fragments or to the sonnet sequences of Petrarch and Shakespeare or to Hölderlin's hymns or to Keats's occasional sonnets. Which is to say that in order to interpret these lines we will immediately ask a double-sided question concerning the intentions of the author and the intentions of the form. Both the correlation and the difference between these two sides of the question will depend (as they do in the Wordsworth poem and in Knapp and Michaels's allegorical version of it) on the relation between an irrecoverable past ("like lost original manuscripts") and an isolated moment of illumination in the present ("suddenly made legible"). The question is how we get from past to present— or how a text read as lyric is "suddenly" discovered *as* a lyric, since it is unlikely that one will encounter it on a beach.

Indeed, alas, these days it is much more likely that one will encounter the transformation of lyric into "the sole carrier of meaning, the only true reality" in literary criticism than anywhere else. In 2004, over twenty years after the publication and reception of "Against Theory," Michaels returned to the question of literary intention by creating a complex conversation between Dickinson, Susan Howe—one of Dickinson's most prominent lyric readers—and Paul de Man. Although Michaels still does not raise the question of the lyric explicitly, all of his questions about literary meaning in *The Shape of the Signifier* revolve around lyric poets such as Dickinson and Wordsworth or lyric readers such as Howe and the New Critics and de Man. Thus Howe's deeply invested lyrical reading of the details of Dickinson's manuscripts in *My Emily Dickinson* and *The Birthmark* become for Michaels instances of a "commitment to the materiality of the signifier" that aligns her reading of Dickinson with de Man's opposition between "the materiality of actual history" and aesthetic ideology.[71] The fact that both Howe and de Man would be horrified by such a comparison, since Howe's version of textual materialism has everything to do with Dickinson's original poetic intentions and de Man's utopian view of "*historical* modes of language power" would by definition escape poetic intention, is part of Michaels's logic. His point in taking up the recent materialist interest in Dickinson's manuscripts and comparing it to de Man's interest in an illegible materiality is to return to the argument in "Against Theory" that "texts mean what their authors intend" (11). By making Howe and de Man say the same thing when they had intended to disagree, Michaels wants to raise the question "of what a text is—of what is in it and what isn't, what counts as part of it and what doesn't" (11). It is one thing to raise that question in relation to the relatively recent work of literary critics. In those cases, Michaels's conclusion that the answer to what a text is will always depend on the position of the reader, on "what's there to you, a question about what you see" (11) makes sense. Interpreters of literature do (sometimes despite themselves) offer their own perspectives. But how would we know what we are seeing when we already know that we are reading a lyric; if, say, a poem was written in 1799 or 1862, and we encounter it neither on a beach nor in a lost manuscript, but in a book or on the Web in the twenty-first century?

My point has been that we would only know that a poem intended (if poems could intend) to be a lyric once it has been critically rendered as such at various moments before the moment in which you encounter it. As in the instances of de Man's reading of Baudelaire's by then paradigmatic modern sonnet or Knapp and Michaels's reading of Wordsworth's iconic romantic lyric, or Howe's reading of Dickinson's every blot, dash, and swerve as poetry, what every literary interpreter must assume about such texts is that they are poetic texts. Further, since for twentieth- and twenty-first-century literary critics, all poetic texts are lyrics, all of these readers—

including Michaels—must assume some of the protocols of lyric reading in order to read them at all. In his latter-day version of an apparently innocent encounter with Wordsworth's poem, it is telling that this time Michaels situates that fantasy not on a beach but on Mars, within the genre of science fiction. Whereas in "Against Theory" Knapp and Michaels had to allow for the possibility that someone had written the words that you encounter on the beach, in *The Shape of the Signifier* (or on Mars) "where there are no other persons, you know right away that the marks have not been made by anyone and that if what you're looking at is a poem (a poem apparently about Earth), it is the planet itself that produced it" (57). "*If what you're looking at is a poem*"?

How would you know? It is by now apparent that the opening paragraph of *Dickinson's Misery* is a smashed & grabbed version of the literary theoretical problem of how to recognize a poem when we see one—not in a possible world but in the one in which we find ourselves at the moment. In the chapters that follow, I will argue that neither a purely theoretical nor a purely pragmatic answer can adequately address that problem, since the question of how to get from past to present—from lyric history to lyric theory and back again—requires a combination of the two. It requires us to think both historically and theoretically: in Dickinson's case, to think through the differences between what Dickinson's texts might have been at other moments (notes of consolation, say, or newspaper verse, or commentary on enclosed flowers, elegies for soldiers or a dog or a culture or a season, or thank-yous, or appeals for publication, or scandalous secret winks, or language surrounding a dead insect) and the lyrics they have become. Because we cannot go back to a moment before they became lyrics, or back to a moment before lyric reading was the only way to apprehend a poem, we must try to keep both their material and contingent as well as their abstract and transcendent aspects in view at the same time. As the history of lyric reading attests, that is not easy to do.

As we have seen in New Criticism and in de Man and in Knapp and Michaels and, again, in Michaels, one reason such double vision is so difficult is that what is at stake in it has come to be not only the definition of the lyric, but the definition of texts and even of persons and the worlds in which they encounter texts and make them into lyrics. In a recent impassioned plea for the understanding of poetry as "an anthropomorphic project," Susan Stewart has ventured one solution to the problem of how to mediate between the abstraction of the lyric available to all interpretation and its historical and material contingency.[72] "The cultural work of lyric," Stewart writes, is the "work of individuation under intersubjective terms" (13). Against the tendency in literary theory to imagine texts on other theoretical planets, or to imagine that history is what poetry leaves out, Stewart emphasizes "the human image as a consequence of representational practices rather than a prior referent. Only in this way can human subjectivity be viewed in historical terms" (342 n. 107). In the pages that follow, I will suggest that Dickinson's work accomplishes exactly what Stewart's humanist reading of the lyric would find there, but that it does so precisely because it so strenuously resists substituting the alienated lyric image of the human—the very image the modern reading of the lyric has created—for the exchange between historical persons between whom the barriers of space and time had not fallen.

Dickinson's Figure of Address

"The only poets"

I<small>N HER TRANSLATION</small> of Sappho, Anne Carson asks her reader to compare a fragment that begins,

>]Sardis
>   Often turning her thoughts here
>]
> you like a goddess
>   And in your song most of all she rejoiced.
>
> But now she is conspicuous among Lydian women
>   as sometimes at sunset
>   The rosyfingered moon
>
> surpasses all the stars . . .

to a letter that Emily Dickinson wrote to Susan Gilbert in 1851:

> I wept a tear here, Susie, on purpose for *you*—because this "sweet silver moon" smiles in on me and Vinnie, and then it goes so far before it gets to you—and then you never told me if there *was* any moon in Baltimore— and how do *I* know Susie—that you see her sweet face at all? She looks like a fairy tonight, sailing around the sky in a little silver gondola with stars for gondoliers. I asked her to let me ride a little while ago—and told her I would *get out* when she got as far as Baltimore, but she only smiled to herself and went sailing on.
>
> I think she was quite ungenerous—but I have learned the lesson and shant ever ask her again. To day it rained at home—sometimes it rained so hard that I fancied you could hear it's patter—patter, patter, as it fell upon the leaves—and the fancy pleased me so, that I sat and listened to it—and watched it earnestly. *Did* you hear it—or was it *only* fancy? Bye and bye the sun came out—just in time to bid us goodnight, and as I told you sometime, the moon is shining now.
>
> It is such an evening Susie, as you and I would walk and have such pleasant musings, if you were only here—perhaps we would have a "Reverie" after the form of "Ik Marvel," indeed I do not know why it

wouldn't be just as charming as that of that lonely Bachelor, smoking his cigar—and it would be far more profitable as "Marvel" *only* marvelled, and you and I would *try* to make a little destiny to have for our own.[1]

Carson points out that "more explicitly than Sappho, Emily Dickinson evokes the dripping fecundity of daylight as foil for the mind's voyaging at night. Almost comically, she personifies the moon as chief navigator of the liquid thoughts that women like to share in the dark, in writing" (371n). It is a long, odd, suggestive comparison, especially since the Dickinson passage seems on the face of it to have so little to do with the Sapphic fragment. The equation of Sappho and Dickinson as types of feminine lyricism is an old one—or rather, it is a specifically dated association, since as Yopie Prins has shown, "what we now call 'Sappho' is, in many ways, an artifact of Victorian poetics" and, as we have begun to see, what we now call "Dickinson" is certainly an artifact of Victorian and modern poetics.[2] Thus Carson's note may associate Sappho and Dickinson on the basis of their exemplary lyrical status, or in order to attribute to Sappho a familiar modernity and to Dickinson an archaic Sapphism that would be simultaneously the desire for a woman and the desire for writing. Yet despite all the forms of literary and personal desire that align these texts with one another, one difference is obvious: Sappho's is a lyric and Dickinson's is a letter. Wherever or whoever or whenever Sappho's "you" was meant to be, Dickinson's "you" was Susan, and she was not there.

This is to say that where or who "you" are makes a difference in, among other things, historical questions of genre. If we thought that Sappho's object of address was sitting before her as she played this particular song on her lyre, we would still think of her fragment as a lyric. But if we thought that Dickinson's object of address was sitting before her as she spoke these words, we would not think of her letter as a letter. And if we thought that the "you" of and to whom Dickinson wrote was a fictive person, an object of imagination, and we printed her lines like this:

> She looks like a Fairy tonight,
> Sailing around the sky—
> In a little silver
> Gondola, with Stars for—
> Gondoliers—

we would think that she had written a lyric poem.[3] Yet if we thought that Sappho had written her lyric first as a letter, it would not be a lyric in the strict sense for her place and time—though, of course, such enticing printing as Carson's is how Sappho's letters have survived as lyrics, or as evidence of the "artifact" she has become. The difference between Sappho's lyric and Dickinson's lyric would then also be a difference in genre, since as Carson puts it, "Sappho was a musician," whose verse was (or so the story goes) meant to be heard in performance, and Dickinson was a writer, whose verse was intended for performance by a reader.[4] But what sort of performance by what sort of reader? The Dickinson letter cited by Carson is not a lyric, yet in it Dickinson worries over and over that it will be read as if it were. Why would Dickinson *not* want to be read as if she were writing lyrics?

Dickinson's letter begins by lamenting that she cannot offer Susan a particular lyric, "this 'sweet silver moon.'" Since the letter goes on to invoke other publications that were all the rage in 1850, a likely candidate for the allusion is a song that Tennyson added to *The Princess* (1847) in 1850. *The Princess*, a poem in several genres that Tennyson called "A Medley" and that Isobel Armstrong has succinctly described as "a burlesque and a feminist tract," was read by both young women in 1848, and by Susan with particular interest.[5] Yet Dickinson's letter does not allude explicitly to the poem's vexed treatment (and elaborate story) of the issues of female education and equal rights (issues that formed so much of the exchange between Dickinson and Gilbert at the time), invoking instead one of the interpellated songs that seems to have little to do with the narrative parts of the poem—except that it insists on affectionate attachment, which in Tennyson is woman's proper sphere. The song is a lullaby, and it begins with the line "Sweet and low, sweet and low" (which later became the song's title), and ends with the lines,

> Father will come to his babe in the nest,
> Silver sails out of the west
>   Under the silver moon:
> Sleep, my little one, sleep, my pretty one, sleep.[6]

Tennyson's song may have been influenced by an English folk song, "Roll on Silver Moon" (often called just "Silver Moon"), that was published as sheet music for the piano in both England and the United States in 1847. The song begins,

> Roll on silver moon, point the trav'ler this way
> While the nightingale's song is in tune . . .[7]

Given Dickinson's reputation as a pianist, and her home's collection of popular sheet music, "Silver Moon" is just the sort of thing she would have played—and, given her reputation for musical improvisation, may have played variations on. In any case, the slight mention of "the 'sweet silver moon'" at the beginning of the letter summons a lyrical presence (of the moon, of domestic tranquility, of literate conversation, of music, of poetry) that the letter quickly (and rather pathetically) forswears. Unlike the moon in Tennyson or in the folk song, the presence of the moon over the heads of the separated friends marks distance rather than union: "it goes so far before it gets to you . . . you never told me if there *was* any moon in Baltimore." The reassuring personification of the moon's "sweet face" that *would* be apparent to Susan if such a lyrical illusion of presence were possible is in doubt in Dickinson's letter, though for it she substitutes another fanciful personification, an extended simile. The pathos of the simile is that a fairy moon "with stars for gondoliers" cannot, of course, give Dickinson a lift to Baltimore, so although the moon "smiled to herself" and thus finally did assume an imaginary face, she "went sailing on" away from both writer and reader rather than, as in the songs, sailing or rolling "this way."

The distance between Dickinson and Baltimore surely required no further elaboration, so why does the letter keep returning to it? In the second paragraph, what Carson dubs "daylight's fecundity" takes another fanciful form, the "patter—patter, patter" of the rain on the leaves. Unlike the moon's face, the sound of the rain is not a wishful or imaginary effect; this time, the trope is not prosopoeia but onomotopoeia, and it represents, in cliché (or perhaps in a variation on Longfellow's "pitter-patter"), what Dickinson heard, not what she could not pretend Susan heard or saw, or what she pretended to see. Yet the letter is still anxious: "*Did* you hear it, Susie—or was it *only* fancy?" The question is rhetorical, and banal; if it rained in Baltimore at the same time that it rained in Amherst, then the answer would be yes, and if not, no. There is no poetry here. The shift, then, to the 1850 bestseller *Reveries of a Bachelor* by "Ik Marvel" (Donald Grant Mitchell) may be a way of putting fiction in its proper place, between the covers of a book. Indeed, Marvel's (or Mitchell's) book is all about the difference between imagining and living, and especially about the difference between fantasizing about the desired other and touching her. In the book's first three chapters, the Bachelor thinks of the reasons not to marry, then imagines the sort of woman he *would* marry if he were to do so, and then laments the death of the woman he ends by being glad he did not marry after all (all the while "smoking his cigar").[8] Against such fireside fancy, Dickinson places the "far more profitable" intimacy that she and Susan "would *try* to make" between them, "if you were only here." That intimacy is not only something that Dickinson cannot write about because it is queer, or can only share, as Carson puts it, "in the dark," but something that she wants, for some reason, not to turn into literature.[9]

The fact that Dickinson's letter itself *is* now literature—a footnote to a famous poet's translation of a famous poet, several pages in this and several other books of literary criticism—makes Dickinson's distinction between her writing and at least some kinds of literature harder for us to see, or to read. But in passages not cited by Carson, the letter goes on to insist upon that distinction:

> Longfellow's "golden Legend" has come to town I hear—and may be seen *in state* on Mr. Adams'[s] bookshelves. It always makes me think of "Pegasus in the pound"—when I find a gracious author sitting side by side with "Murray" and "Wells" and "Walker" in that renowned store— and like *him* I half expect to hear that they have *"flown"* some morning and in their native ether revel all the day; but for our sakes dear Susie, who please ourselves with the fancy that we are the only poets, and everyone else is *prose*, let us hope they will yet be willing to share our humble world and feed upon such aliment as *we* consent to do! You thank me for the Rice cake—you tell me Susie, you have just been tasting it . . .

The letter's rehearsal of the women's exchange over and through books (their own version of Tennyson's ill-fated women's college in *The Princess*) takes an interesting turn here, not accidentally when it gets to Longfellow. If "Marvel" was popular romance (what Dickinson's upstanding father later called, as she phrased the condemnation, " 'somebody's *rev-e-ries*,' he didn't know whose they were, that he thought were very ridiculous"), Harvard's Professor Longfellow was the modern classic.[10] His translation of *The Golden Legend*, or *Lives of the Saints* (Jacobus de Voragine, 1260) was offered to the American reading public in 1850 as a sort of crash course on medieval European culture (crash courses on European culture being Longfellow's specialty). Dickinson's use of the phrase *"in state"* to describe the book's appearance as if it were a dead body parodies the consequences of admission to the print public sphere, a condition in which the display of the body (or book) is also a kind of disembodiment, or self-abstraction.[11] Since such abstracted disembodiment was also the fate of the saints, the joke may seem to elevate Longfellow, but cultural elevation, especially as disembodied transcendence, itself turns out to be the joke.

Dickinson's invocation of "Pegasus in Pound," the proem to *The Estray* (1847), associates Longfellow's allegory of the visit of "the poet's winged steed" to " a quiet village" with the book's visit to the bookstore in Amherst. In the proem, "the school-boys" find Pegasus "upon the village common," and "the wise men, in their wisdom, / Put him straightway into pound." In Dickinson's letter, the book's analogous captivity is represented by its place on the shelf alongside Murray's *English Grammar* (1795), Wells's *A Grammar of the English Language* (1846), and Walker's *A Critical Pronouncing Dictionary, and Expositor of the English Language* (1827).[12] Between quotation marks, the names of the lexicographers are

personified "sitting side by side" with Longfellow, as if to imprison literature in a lesson on grammar (a relevant issue, not only because of the
theme of imaginative or imaginary education that runs through the letter,
but also because Susan was in Baltimore to teach grammar school). The
sense of the rest of the sentence must be that "a gracious author" can, like
Pegasus, break free of such mundane constraint, but "Murray" and "Wells"
and "Walker" would not approve of the grammar of the analogy. "Like
him [Pegasus? Longfellow?] I half expect [I and he both expect? I expect
that they will be like him?] to hear that they [the grammarians? Pegasus
and Longfellow?] have *'flown'* some morning and in their [whose?] native
ether revel all the day." The confusion between pronouns probably will
not bear too much scrutiny, which may be one of the problems with reading a twenty-year-old's personal letter to her girlfriend as if it were a literary text.[13] But it is a letter *about* reading literary texts, and finally about not
wanting to be read in the ways those were read. For we "who please ourselves with the fancy that we are the only poets, and everyone else is
prose," know the difference, and know, too, that the fancy cannot cheat so
well that one should be mistaken for the other, or that the moon could take
someone from Amherst to Baltimore, that sexual fantasy is as good as sex,
or that rice cakes are available in print.

The elaborate relation between the pleasures of private embodiment
and the perils of public disembodiment could also be the stuff of lyric, as
we shall see in the last chapter of this book when we turn to Dickinson's
relation to nineteenth-century female lyric sentimentalism. But in the
early letter to Susan, which is so often cited as evidence of the young
poet's literary aspirations, the allusions point beyond the letter's text toward readings or conversations or jokes or songs the correspondents had
shared in what is ordinarily referred to as private life. That is a generic
convention, of course, but Dickinson seems particularly anxious to call attention to it. Like the leaf attached to the early letter to Austin or the dead
cricket folded within the square of paper within the letter to Mabel Todd,
or the flowers sent with her notes to everybody, the "you" addressed by
Dickinson's letter has more in common with Baltimore and rice cakes than
with the moon or fairies or gondolas or reveries or flying horses—or lyric
poetry. Perhaps this is because as long as the addressee is elsewhere, she is
not like the fading leaf or disintegrating cricket or dying flowers *or* "Pegasus in Pound." In order to keep the pathos of life's appropriation by literature from becoming the pathos *of* literature, Dickinson makes it into
something else. But what *is* that something else—a letter or a poem? Poetry or prose? Like Sappho's fragment, Dickinson's letter to Susan is missing its last page so, like the genre of the Sapphic fragment, the genre of
Dickinson's fragmentary letter may now be up to us. Yet unlike Sappho's

fragment, in which the "you" is tantalizingly indeterminate, Dickinson's letter's address is historically determined, with a vengeance: this letter is for Susan and no one else. Thus the generic poles with which this comparison began—Sappho performed her own lyrics, Dickinson's writing is performed by a reader—can now be reversed: when we now read Sappho, we can (like Marvel's Bachelor) imagine "you" as anyone we like (usually ourselves), but only Susan knew what to make of most of Dickinson's letter, and she is not the one who made it into poetry.

Or prose. Since the time of Dickinson's publication, the distinction between the two has been at issue, as has the distinction between poems and letters, life and literature, privacy and publicity. As we have seen, Dickinson's early editors claimed to know the difference, as does the most recent editor of the two three-volume Harvard sets of the *Poems* and *Letters*. But lots of readers in between, especially readers of Dickinson's manuscripts, have been more confused. Reviewing Johnson's 1955 variorum edition of the *Poems*, John L. Spicer commented in 1956 that

> one of the most difficult problems of the editor has been the separation of prose from poetry. This may come as a surprise to some readers. The only surviving prose Emily Dickinson wrote occurs in her letters, and, in their published form, the poetry in them is always neatly set off from the prose. In her manuscripts, however, things are not so simple. She would often spread out her poetry on the page as if it were prose and even, at times, indent her prose as poetry. . . . Assuming that what Emily meant as poetry must be taken out of the letters, how does one go about it? Should one only print variants of lines which she has used somewhere else in her poems? Should one set up a standard for indentation, rhyme, or meter? Or should one merely do again what Mrs. Todd tried to do and divide the poetry from the prose by guessing the poet's intentions?[14]

Pointing out that "Johnson seems to have chosen this last solution," Spicer concludes instead that "the reason for the difficulty of drawing a line between the poetry and prose in Emily Dickinson's letters may be that she did not wish such a line to be drawn. If large portions of her correspondence are considered not as mere letters—and, indeed, they seldom communicate information, or have much to do with the person to whom they were written—but as experiments in a heightened prose combined with poetry, a new approach to both her letters and her poetry opens up" (140). Since "John L. Spicer" was otherwise known as the avant-garde California poet Jack Spicer, his suggestion that Dickinson's writing be read as experimental prose-poetry was a way of making Dickinson avant-garde, of recasting old manuscripts as modern literature.

As we have seen, as novel as Spicer's suggestion was (and, as we shall see, prescient of contemporary approaches such as Susan Howe's and Marta Werner's), he followed in what was already an established tradition. If Todd and Higginson, in the 1890s, drew a line between poetry and prose in order to make Dickinson's poetry into late Victorian literature and her letters into the story of the Victorian Poetess, and Susan Gilbert Dickinson's daughter, Martha Dickinson Bianchi, published, in 1914, the verse Dickinson sent to her mother as a series of Imagist poems, and Johnson, in 1955, separated poetry and prose according to a New Critical idea of the poem as divorced from its maker, then Spicer's idea of Dickinson's letters "as experiments in a heightened prose" made Dickinson into the precursor of L=A=N=G=U=A=G=E poetry, a position occupied by Spicer himself. Yet Dickinson's private letter took several nineteenth-century literary genres in and spit them out before the history of her publication and reception began. The difference between "the only poets" and "*prose*" in that letter is not a difference in genre but a difference between us and everyone else, between personal and personified address.

As I began by suggesting, a difference in address can become a difference in genre as the public transmission of a text makes it so, but that historical process does not mean that the writer originally intended that form of address to make such a difference. Many of the debates in recent Dickinson scholarship have taken place over the question of whether Dickinson intended to write poems or letters, or letter-poems, or poem-letters. When, in 1995, Ellen Hart followed in Spicer's wake by suggesting that "the relationship between poetry and prose is so complex in Dickinson's writing that lineating poetry but not prose [in print] sets up artificial genre distinctions," Domhnall Mitchell responded in 1998 by measuring various lines of "prose" and "poetry" in the manuscripts in tenths of centimeters, concluding that "contrary to Hart's view . . . there does seem to be *some* visual indication of a generic shift" in some letters.[15]

If Mitchell went to an extreme to prove that the difference in genre that Hart claimed was "artificial" *might* be inherent after all (and thus, ultimately, might justify Franklin's editorial procedure in the 1998 *Poems*) that may be because what is at stake in such fine distinctions is not the existence of Dickinson's writing as either poetic or epistolary but the existence of literary criticism. The reason that the distinction between genres seems an important point of debate for literary critics is that once the genre of a text is established, then, as we saw in the last chapter on lyric reading, protocols of interpretation will follow. In other words, what is at stake in establishing the genre of Dickinson's writing is nothing less than its literary afterlife. Even Hart and Martha Nell Smith, whose work on the Dickinson Electronic Archives and in *Open Me Carefully* seeks to deconstruct "genre distinctions as the dominant way of organizing Dickinson's writings" by posting those writings on the Web as various "Correspondences" and by making a volume that does not distinguish between poems and letters, suggest that "Dickinson's blending of poetry with prose, making poems of letters and letters of poems, [was] a deliberate artistic strategy."[16]

But to motivate generic confusion by attributing it to an "artistic strategy" is to emphasize generic distinctions once again, and especially to emphasize Dickinson's authority as a poet. As I have suggested in the previous chapters, that authority is an effect of lyric reading, or of the sort of interpretation Dickinson's early letter to Susan is so anxious not to attract. Dickinson's early letter is careful not to turn her reader into a personification rather than a person, yet that is exactly the change that a history of lyric reading has worked on Dickinson. Rather than try to decide whether Dickinson wrote poems or letters, or letters as poems, or poems in letters, I want to focus on the figures of address in her writing, on how and why and where Dickinson invokes "you." Rather than measure the length of her lines or isolate metrical passages or concentrate on texts in the fascicles not included (as far as we know) in letters, we might want to notice how Dickinson's figures of address tend to insist that we not make about her writing the very generic decisions we have made.

Lyric Media

We have already noticed that in his preface to the first publication of Dickinson's poems in 1890, Higginson began by warning his readers that "the verses of Emily Dickinson belong emphatically to what Emerson long since called 'the Poetry of the Portfolio,'—something produced absolutely without the thought of publication, and solely by way of expression of the writer's own mind." Dickinson herself could not be "persuaded to print," Higginson continued, because although the daughter of "the leading lawyer of Amherst," she "habitually concealed her mind, like her person, from all but a very few friends . . . she was as invisible to the world as if she had dwelt in a nunnery." The Dickinson that Higginson thus introduced is "emphatically," "absolutely," "solely" private, a creature of privilege (one of her own favorite words), a law unto herself. Modern readers have often complained of Higginson's apologetic presentation of the poet whose fame would so far outstrip his own, and many have sought to qualify his notion of Dickinson's isolation. Higginson's placement of Dickinson's audience has gone largely unchallenged, however, and it is worth asking why we have been so content to stay in the position he bequeathed to us. What his introduction made sure of was that those first readers of the poems in "print" knew that what they were being allowed to read was not intended to be read by *them*. As we have seen, the response in the 1890s was immediate and popular interest: Dickinson's *Poems* became a sensation, a bestseller, a "fad."[17] If the notion of a published privacy—a privacy that circulates—has proven immensely attractive ever since, perhaps this is not because of the way we read Emily Dickinson, but because of the way we read lyrics.

Nowhere is the definition of lyric poetry as privacy gone public more striking than in the publisher's advertisement for the second volume of the *Poems* in 1891 (Buckingham 387). Beside several citations from reviews proclaiming Dickinson's "original genius," Roberts Brothers chose to include this perplexing notice:

> Here surely is the record of a soul that suffered from isolation, and the stress of dumb emotion, and the desire to make itself understood by means of a voice so long unused that the sound was strange even to her own ears.—Literary World

> 16mo, cloth, $1.25 each; white and gold, $1.50 each; two volumes in one, $2.00

How could such a comment be expected to sell books? The publisher's motive becomes even more difficult to assign when we take into account the context of this citation, for it is drawn from Dickinson's first bad review. Reacting against Dickinson's sudden popularity in 1890, the reviewer for Boston's *Literary World* compared Dickinson to the first deaf-mute to be educated, called her "a case of arrested development," and commended "this strange book of verse—with its sober, old-maidenly binding, on which is a silver Indian pipe, half fungus, half flower—to pitying and kindly regard" (Buckingham 48). The publisher, having reduced the price of the first edition of the *Poems*, seems to have anticipated what is only clear now, in retrospect: even this extremity of condescension merely exaggerated the appetite of the reading public. The "old-maidenly" pathos of Dickinson's isolation (here notably, as in Higginson's preface, transferred from person to book) answered to an idea that what the poetic voice registered *was* "the record of a soul that suffered" from an exemplary self-enclosure. The reviewer's comment on the book's ornament ("half fungus, half flower") also slips curiously across the border between writer and text, and while it is certainly meant to sound disparaging, it partakes as well of the idea that darkness and deprivation produce a lyric beauty.

This sort of transference from person to text to symbol of poetic inspiration goes on frequently in the early reviews, and always in the interest of opposing a valued and implicitly feminized lyric quality to public convention. "It is a rare thing in these days of universal print to find a poet who is averse to seeing his or her work before the public," wrote a reviewer for the Boston *Daily Traveller*. "The freedom and fullness of verse written only as expression of the inward thought, without heed of criticism or regard for praise, has a charm as indefinable as the song of a wild bird that sings out of the fullness of its heart" (Buckingham 23). Wittingly or unwittingly, the reviewer was glossing his own echo of Higginson by echoing Shelley's classic description of the poet as "a nightingale, who sits in darkness and sings to cheer its own solitude with sweet sounds; his auditors are as men entranced by the melody of an unseen musician, who feel that they are moved and softened, yet know not whence or why."[18] Entranced by Higginson's revelation of the invisibility of the source, the readers to whom Dickinson's first editor addressed her poems responded by understanding that his portrait of a wealthy white woman shut up in her house made Dickinson the perfect figure of the lyric poet.[19] In order to grasp in detail the relation between Higginson's Dickinson and later versions of lyric isolation, we would need to trace the reception history that transformed Dickinson's lyricism from unseen birdsong to the alienated personal voice essential to the New Critical reception of Dickinson. Along the way, we would want to stop to notice that one moment in that transformation was the modernist version of Dickinson's voice as distinct from the public voice of mass culture. As Percy Lubbock phrased that view (in a review of Conrad Aiken's landmark modernist edition of *Selected Poems of Emily Dickinson*) in 1924, "her voice was unique, and she flung out the short cry of her joy or pain or mockery with a note that cannot be forgotten. It is much to say in a world where voices are so many."[20] The few decades that separate Higginson's Dickinson from Lubbock's had already made a difference in the interpretation of Dickinson's figure of lyric address, and a careful study of those decades would give us a better idea of the figure we have inherited.

But this is not such a reception study, and what I want to pursue here instead is the structure of address supposed by the consistent postpublication definition of Dickinson's as a private—and therefore transcendent—lyric voice. If her old-maidenly strangeness, her nunlike privacy worked (and still works) to make her poetry seem to readers like the voice that speaks to no one and therefore to all of us, this must be because from the moment that Dickinson's writing was published and received as lyric poetry has devolved a history of reading a particular structure of address into the poems. This structure is one in which saying "I" can stand for saying "you," in which the poet's solitude stands in for the solitude of the individual reader—a self-address so absolute that every self can identify it as his own. The fact that it was *her* own seems in effect to have made Dickinson a clearer mirror for the poetics of the single ego. Already consigned to the private sphere by reason of gender (and kept comfortably there by benefit of class), Dickinson could represent in person and in poem (the two so quickly becoming indistinguishable) the prerogative of the private individual—namely, the privilege to gain public power by means of a well-protected self-sufficiency.[21] The ease with which "I" can become "you," "she" becomes "he," and the private self is coined as public property in a poetics of individualism was aptly exemplified by William Dean Howells's influential literary championship of Dickinson in her first year of publication: "The strange *Poems of Emily Dickinson* we think will form something of an intrinsic experience with the understanding reader of them," Howells began. Just how "intrinsic" that experience was for Howells he reveals at the end of his essay: "this poetry is as characteristic of our life as our business enterprise, our political turmoil, our demagogism, our millionarism."[22] The poetry Higginson was so careful to cast "emphatically" as the "expression of the writer's own mind" immediately became the expression of the reader's own identity. What Howells so explicitly says—and he says it not just for himself but for each of "us"—is "Emily Dickinson, *c'est moi.*" It is as much as to say, as has so often been said since and in so many ways, "Emily Dickinson, *c'est le moi.*"

To say that in remaining closed upon herself Dickinson managed to represent the self and therefore to become "characteristic of *our* life" is to trace in her poetry the syllogistic logic of address that, as we have seen, dominates postromantic theories of lyric reading. Put simply, that logic converts the isolated "I" into the universal "we" by bypassing the mediation of any particular "you." This bypass or evasion serves the purpose of what Herbert Tucker has called "the thirst for intersubjective confirmation of the self, which has made the overhearing of a persona our principal means of understanding a poem."[23] The key term here is "*over*hearing": the "intersubjective confirmation of the self" performed by a reading of lyric based upon the identity between poet and reader must be achieved by denying to the poem any intersubjective economy of its own. On this view, in order to have an audience the lyric must not have one. The paradox is audible in Shelley's 1821 "Defence," and is fixed into definition by John Stuart Mill in 1833 in a moment to which reference was made in the first chapter on lyric discourse, though Tucker's self-conscious repetition of that moment makes it worth repeating here. "Eloquence is *heard*, poetry is *overheard*," Mill writes, "Eloquence supposes an audience; the peculiarity of poetry appears to us to lie in the poet's utter unconsciousness of a listener. Poetry is feeling confessing itself to itself, in moments of solitude."[24] In order to overhear such a radically internalized solitude, the reader is supposed to partake of a parallel—that is, identical—seclusion.

Mill's later figure for this parallelism is striking: lyric "song," he continues, "has always seemed to us like the lament of a prisoner in a solitary cell, ourselves listening, unseen in the next."[25] Cell to cell, one prisoner to another, this form of address is sustained by the pathos of solitary confinement—but who or what has imposed the sentence?

When, in 1957, Northrop Frye repeated without alteration Mill's version of lyric as "preeminently the utterance that is overheard," he went so far as to say that there is "no word for the audience of the lyric" because "the poet, so to speak, turns his back on his listeners."[26] In Frye's repetition of Mill, "the lament of the prisoner" has become the individual poet's choice; the poet "turns his back" on a real, historical audience in order to create ("so to speak") a fictive one. In Frye's words, "the lyric poet normally pretends to be talking to himself or to someone else: a spirit of nature, a Muse . . . a personal friend, a lover, a god, a personified abstraction, or a natural object."[27] As the range of Frye's list suggests, by not addressing anyone in particular the poet "pretends" to address everything in general—to achieve a form of transcendentally apostrophic address. But Mill's prison scene poses questions that haunt Frye's modern lyric inwardness: why should the poet pretend? What are the conditions of such isolation? Is all lyric, then, imaginary address? Is there no difference between an apostrophe to a natural object and an intimation to a personal friend? Does the poet choose to turn his back or is he somehow constrained to do so—by history, by circumstance, or by the very theory of reading that defines lyric address as the subject's self-address, as not directed toward any specific destination and therefore universally applicable to objects of imagination, objects of tradition, objects of desire, objects of worship, objects of thought, and objects of perception alike?

It is worth noticing Mill's own shift in metaphors for lyric self-address in order to begin to answer these questions, especially since later lyric theorists in the Anglo-American tradition like Frye and Tucker tend to invoke the same metaphors almost word for word. In his 1833 essay "What is Poetry?" Mill begins by dismissing what he calls the "vulgarest" of the many answers to the title's question, "that which confounds poetry with metrical composition." He thus does away with neoclassical distinctions between genres, preferring to emphasize that "the object of poetry is confessedly to act upon the emotions." Yet that ambition (which he attributes to Wordsworth) is not sufficient for Mill, since novels, for example, also act upon the emotions, and yet "there is a radical distinction between the interest felt in novels as such, and the interest excited by poetry." Committed to a definition of poetry based on affective response, Mill's will to lyricize then takes a long turn through narrative and descriptive forms, which he finally finds insufficiently direct in their address to the "human soul." It is this further narrowing of what is "essential" in poetry to a form of direct address that necessitates Mill's famous distinction between poetry and eloquence.

In insisting upon address as the defining feature of the poetic, Mill risks making lyric into personally interested discourse. The metaphor of the "soliloquy" is a way for Mill to emphasize the effect of poetic address on its reader and at the same time insist that such an effect is unintentional. But is it? Mill's extension of the metaphor makes his double bind clearer: "it may be said that poetry, which is printed on hot-pressed paper, and sold at a bookseller's shop, is a soliloquy in full dress, and upon the stage. But there is nothing absurd in the idea of such a mode of soliloquizing. . . . The actor knows that there is an audience present; but if he act as though he knew it, he acts ill." Of course, an actor *does* intend to produce an effect in his audience, so while the theatrical metaphor allows Mill to distinguish lyric from public or persuasive rhetoric, it also breaks down the distinction he wants to maintain: it makes lyric into a public performance that only pretends to be self-addressed.

It is this rhetorical predicament that may prompt Mill to alter or intensify the metaphor when he writes of the lyrical effect of music on its listeners. "Who can hear these words," Mill writes, "which speak so touchingly the sorrows of a mountaineer in exile:

> My heart's in the Highlands—my heart is not here;
> My heart's in the Highlands, a-chasing the deer,
> A-chasing the wild deer, and following the roe—
> My heart's in the Highlands. Wherever I go.

Who can hear those affecting words, married to as affecting an air, and fancy that he sees the singer? That song has always seemed to us like the lament of a prisoner in a solitary cell, ourselves listening, unseen, in the next."[28]

Mill's substitution of the performance of a song (by Burns) for the performance of an actor's soliloquy, of "unseen" voice for stagelit speech, speaks volumes about the complexity of the figure of address he wanted to claim as the special object of the lyric. In 1833, Mill's definition of poetry as essentially lyric still needed to negotiate several genres, and not accidentally, he found what he was looking for in a genre that may be literally overheard rather than figuratively "overheard," in an archaic version of lyric as song rather than in modern "poetry, which is printed on hot-pressed paper, and sold at a bookseller's shop."

This is to say that Mill's answers to the questions raised by what has become his definitive emphasis on lyric isolation were, in 1833, still enmeshed in the complexity of various genres of address, especially in written verse. Yet later critics of the lyric have often taken up Mill's influential metaphors for lyric address while ignoring both their generic complication and their concern about the relation between writing and voice. Helen Vendler, for example, introduced her 1997 book on Shakespeare's sonnets by explaining that "lyric, though it may *refer* to the social, remains the genre that directs its *mimesis* toward the performance of the mind in *solitary* speech. Because lyric is intended to be voiceable by anyone reading it. . . . The act of the lyric is to offer its reader a script to say. . . . The lyric . . . gives us the mind alone with itself. Lyric can present no 'other' as alive and listening or responding in the same room as the solitary speaker."[29] Vendler includes at the back of her book a CD recording of herself reading the sonnets. By the late twentieth century, then, the normative reading of the lyric as normative poetic genre had collapsed Mill's fine distinctions into the reader's soliloquy, the reader's isolation, the reader's expression. That collapse was enabled by Vendler's complete erasure of the "other" Mill kept marginally alive, out of sight. Mill's fantasy that the reader of lyric is an unseen listener to distant music turns into Vendler's fantasy that her reader will, thanks to a medium unavailable to Mill, listen to the literary critic's voice reading the poet's script "in person" in the solitude created by Walkman or stereo.

The literary critical interpretation of Dickinson's writing as lyric has often veered perilously close to the scene of reading suggested by Mill and personified by Vendler. As Higginson and his contemporaries were the first to notice, Dickinson herself seemed to have made literal the seclusion of the lyric self in its solitary cell.[30] Those readers were also the first to read that literal confinement back into metaphor, so that the listeners in the next cell become Mill's "ourselves." The metaphor that supports such a reading is *the* lyric metaphor: the figure of the speaking voice. If we think of the lyric as "the lament of a prisoner in a solitary cell," or as "the performance of the mind in *solitary* speech," then we must position ourselves as readers who are hearers or performers "unseen." The metaphor of voice bridges the otherwise incommutable distance between one "solitary cell" and another, between two otherwise mutually exclusive individuals, two "soliloquies." Most importantly, it does so by claiming to transcend the historical circumstances of those individuals or performances, by placing "us" in the same metaphorical moment with the "speaker" ("listening . . . in the next" solitude, or becoming that speaker ourselves).

I would like to suggest another way of placing ourselves in relation to Dickinson's structures of address. Rather than consider the lyric "I" as a "speaker" or, as Tucker puts it, a "persona" who talks to herself and so speaks for all of us, I want to examine what happens when Dickinson's writing directly addresses a "you," when that writing attempts to turn toward rather than away from a specific audience. In turning from "I" to "you," and from the metaphor of speech to the act of writing, Dickinson's writing traced an economy of reading very different than the one that Higginson and Mill and Vendler projected for the lyric and most readers of Dickinson as a lyric poet have imagined: a circuit of exchange in which the subjective self-address of the speaker is replaced by the intersubjective practice of the writer, in which the writer's seclusion might be mediated by something (or someone) other than ourselves.

"THE MAN WHO MAKES SHEETS OF PAPER"

The way in which I address you depends upon where you are. If you are very near, I can whisper. If you are across the table, I can speak. If you are upstairs or just outside, I can shout. If you are too distant to hear (even to overhear) my voice, I can write. And in the illusion peculiar to written address, the condition of your absence (the condition of my writing) conjures a presence more intimate than the whisper—more intimate, that is, than the metaphor of the voice, of a speaking presence, would allow.[31] Dickinson acknowledges this property of writing often in her letters, as we noticed in the early letter to Susan with which we began. A little over a year later, she wrote to Susan that "as I sit here Susie, alone with the winds and you, I have the old *king feeling* even more than before, for I know not even the *cracker man* will invade *this* solitude, this Sweet Sabbath of our's" (L 1:77). As Dickinson writes, "*this* solitude" becomes an intersubjective space in which the deictics "here" and "this" can point away from what it is to be alone toward a moment in which, in writing, the writer is "alone with." As Dickinson's emphasis suggests, it is the page itself that offers a communion that displaces in that moment what earlier in the letter she has called "*their* meeting." Their meeting takes place in church; our meeting takes place in "the church within our hearts."

And as she writes, the transmutation of church building to mutual sympathetic investment comes to depend upon the very transit that both threatens and enables such investment "within." Within a sublime solitude ("the old *king feeling*") uncompromised by public commerce (the comical "*cracker man*") Dickinson's letter goes on to imagine a private commerce that does not oppose privacy to community or inside to outside but instead makes the first term inclusive of the second, turning the terms of solitude inside out. This reversal of the normal order (the order in which the public space would include the private, outside would contain inside) takes place not through a logic of identity but by means of the difference which is the very medium of written address:

> I mourn this morning, Susie, that I have no sweet sunset to gild a page for *you*, nor any bay so blue—not even a chamber way up in the sky, as your's is, to give me thoughts of heaven, which I would give to you. You know how I must write you, down, down, in the terrestrial; no sunset here, no stars; not even a bit of *twilight* which I may poeticize—and send you! Yet Susie, there will be romance in the letter's ride to you—think of the hills and the dales, and the rivers it will pass over, and the drivers and conductors who will hurry it on to you; and wont that make a poem such as can ne'er be written?

What the movement of this letter makes explicit—and I want to maintain that it is very much what is implicit in the movement of several of Dickinson's texts that we now know as lyrics and that, like the letters to Susan, take the direction and destination of address as their subject—is that "*this* solitude" in which I am not alone but "alone with" has everything to do with the material circumstances of writing and little to do with what that writing will be taken to (figuratively) represent. Representation as mimesis, especially in the ideal terms that "I may poeticize," would be inevitably elegiac (in Dickinson's pun, "I mourn this morning," its distance from the "sweet sunset" of which Susan may have written). Rather than send a metaphorical "here" there, Dickinson asks her reader to imagine the "romance in the letter's ride"—that is, to retrace the deferral of the letter that Susan now holds in her hands. From Dickinson's hand through the hands of "the drivers and conductors" to Susan's hand, the letter becomes "a poem such as can ne'er be written." It does so, paradoxically, because rather than "poeticize" the celestial it remains "down, down, in the terrestrial" within an economy of hands, hills, dales, rivers, drivers, conductors, and literal letters rather than within an idealized universe of gilded pages, "thoughts of heaven," sunset, stars, "a bit of *twilight*."

The intimacy established in the physical exchange of the letter, the intimacy that makes of its transfer a "romance," is a privacy encompassing the public circle already inscribed upon it with the writer's admission of what makes "*this* solitude" of the written page something of our's. What writer and reader mutually possess are not identical solitudes (my sunset like your sunset, my stars like your stars, my little "chamber way up in the sky, as your's is") but is rather the letter itself. That letter substantiates the otherwise purely metaphorical relation between writer and reader. It embodies the separation between their two bodies. But since it is not a metaphor, this third, literal body is also always insufficient, radically contingent. As Dickinson writes at the end of her letter, "Susie, what shall I do—there is'nt room enough; not *half* enough, to hold what I was going to say. Wont you tell the man who makes sheets of paper, that I hav'nt the *slightest respect* for him!" The epistolary convention of complaining that one's time to write has run out has turned here to a mock protest against the page that will not "hold what I was going to say." What the page does hold, however, is what Susan holds and is (thanks nevertheless to "the man who makes sheets of paper" and, like the "drivers and conductors," adds another pair of hands to the letter's history) held within it. The object of address has become its subject, as the letter has implicated everyone "outside" the writer's solitude within the "sheets of paper" that hold not "what I was going to say" but only what can be written, read, held.

The early letters to Susan allow Dickinson to displace the plane geography of here and there, outside and inside, self and other, with the more complex discursive field available to reading and writing because they begin in a pathos of distance or isolation that they then revise by revising the very conditions or media of address. In both letters, the conditions of intimate address are explicitly opposed to the conditions imagined as "poetic." The earnest wit of those letters makes the desire for such revision and the imagery of such opposition especially graphic, but it is a desire evident in almost everything Dickinson wrote. About ten years after the letters to Susan, in 1861, Dickinson sent a note to Samuel Bowles, editor of the *Springfield Republican*, and pinned it around the stub of a pencil (fig. 18):

> If it had no pencil,
> Would it try mine—
> Worn—now—and *dull*—sweet,
> Writing much to thee—
> If it had no word—
> Would it make the Daisy,
> Most as big as I was—
> When it plucked me?

> Emily

The note was printed as poem 654 in 1945 in *Bolts of Melody*, under the heading, "Poems Personal and Occasional." It was then included in Johnson's 1955 edition of the *Poems* as number 921 and in Franklin's 1998 edition of the *Poems* as number 184. None of these twentieth-century publications of the letter as a lyric could, of course, include the pencil—but in any event that was for Bowles's and not for later readers' use. He was meant to write back, or if he could not write (Bowles was ill at the time), at least

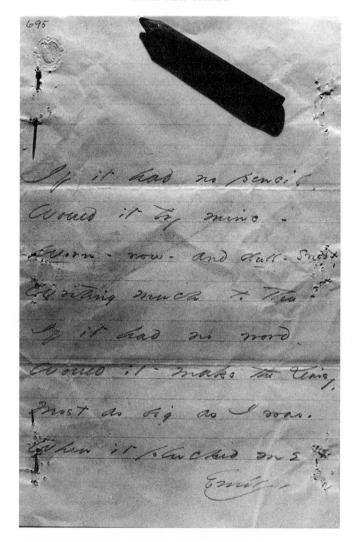

Figure 18. Emily Dickinson to Samuel or Mary Bowles, 1861. The pin marks where the pencil was fastened are visible to the right of the pencil. Courtesy of Amherst College Archives and Special Collections (ED, ms. 695, with enclosure).

draw in response to the direct address of a personal code in which Dickinson sometimes signed herself "Daisy." The "it" with which Dickinson addressed Bowles in this note is grammatically impersonal but rhetorically intimate in the context of their exchange, and a later reader like Vendler would have a hard time identifying herself as the "speaker" of that pronoun. This note is not an overheard soliloquy or "a script to say," but an invitation to written exchange. It is not self-addressed and therefore addressed to all of us; it is—or was—addressed to Samuel (or perhaps Mary)

Bowles. Now, that address may be why Todd and Higginson did not publish the note as a lyric, and Mill and Vendler might also argue that it does not qualify for their definition of the genre. Yet as we have seen, once printed by Bingham and Johnson and Franklin as a lyric, the text is likely to be read as if it were intended for performance by an anonymous reader, difficult as that performance might be to imagine.[32]

Between Bowles and Dickinson, on the other hand, the relation between personal and public address, between writing letters and reading poems, between genre and medium, between poetry and the paper it is written on, was already an old joke by 1861, at least since Bowles published Dickinson's first poem in the Springfield *Daily Republican* in February 1852, just days before Dickinson's letter to Susan about the "poem such as can n'er be written." The editor prefaced the valentine that Dickinson had originally addressed to William Howland with a playfully impersonal address to Dickinson, and an invitation to inaugurate a "more direct" correspondence with the print public sphere:

The hand that wrote the following amusing medley to a friend of ours, as "a valentine," is capable of writing very fine things, and there is certainly no presumption in entertaining a private wish that a correspondence, more direct than this, may be established between it and the *Republican*:

> "Sic transit gloria mundi,"
> "How doth the busy bee,"
> "Dum vivimus vivamus,"
> I stay mine enemy!
>
> Oh "veni, vidi, vici!"
> Oh caput cap-a-pie!
> And oh "memento mori"
> When I am *far* from thee!
>
> Hurrah for Peter Parley!
> Hurrah for Daniel Boon!
> Three cheers, sir, for the gentleman
> Who first observed the moon!
>
> Peter, put up the sunshine;
> Pattie, arrange the stars;
> Tell Luna, *tea* is waiting,
> And call your brother Mars!
>
> Put down the apple, Adam,
> And come away with me,

So shalt thou have a *pippin*
　　From off my father's tree!

I climb the "Hill of Science,"
　　I "view the landscape o'er;"
Such transcendental prospect,
　　I ne'er beheld before!

Unto the Legislature
　　My country bids me go;
I'll take my *india rubbers*,
　　In case the wind should blow!

During my education,
　　It was announced to me
That *gravitation, stumbling*,
　　Fell from an *apple* tree!

The earth upon an axis
　　Was once supposed to turn,
By way of a *gymnastic*
　　In honor of the sun!

It *was* the brave Columbus,
　　A sailing o'er the tide,
Who notified the nations
　　Of where I would reside!

Mortality is fatal—
　　Gentility is fine,
Rascality, heroic,
　　Insolvency, sublime!

Our Fathers being weary,
　　Laid down on Bunker Hill;
And tho' full many a morning,
　　Yet they are sleeping still,—

The trumpet, sir, shall wake them,
　　In dreams I see them rise,
Each with a solemn musket
　　A marching to the skies!

A coward will remain, Sir,
　　Until the fight is done;
But an *immortal hero*
　　Will take his hat, and run!

Good-bye, Sir, I am going;
   My country calleth me;
Allow me, Sir, at parting,
   To wipe my weeping e'e.

In token of our friendship
   Accept this "Bonnie Doon,"
And when the hand that plucked it
   Hath passed beyond the moon,

The memory of my ashes
   Will consolation be;
Then, farewell, Tuscarora,
   And farewell, Sir, to thee! (F 2)

Whatever we make of these lines, it would be difficult to make them a lyric. Bowles uses the Tennysonian term "medley," and that seems about right, combined with the "valentine" that provided the lines' occasion. There are too many lines and they move in too many directions for me to have cited them all, and yet I have done so in order to make just that point: they do not conform to the protocols of critical citation, lyric reprinting, or lyric reading (it would be virtually impossible to offer a reading of them along the lines of de Man's reading of Baudelaire's sonnet). Though they fall into the alternating tetrameter/trimeter measure by which Dickinson's poems would become known, they do not *sound* like "Dickinson." They appear to be what they probably were: a pastiche from various sources, most of them textbooks, one of them Shakespeare, and most of them fairly unmediated by anything we would recognize as a "lyric" perspective. This may in fact be Dickinson's earliest juvenilia.[33] Unlike the letters to Susan, the valentine begins in a pathos of distance or isolation ("When I am *far* from thee!") that is mediated by many, many things that are not the writer or the reader. But unlike the exfoliating allusions in the letter to Susan cited by Carson with which this chapter began, those allusions are not in-jokes between the writer and a particular reader (though Howland was a tutor at Amherst from 1849 to 1851, so some of them may be); they are a cultural grab bag of languages, texts, stories, myths, aphorisms, and bons mots. That is what makes them so *printable* in a daily paper, if not susceptible to the sort of close reading usually performed in a book of literary criticism. Yet the valentine that Bowles printed as newspaper copy may not have been so printable in another sense—or rather, the parts that the *Republican* could not print may already have been cut out of a paper or a book and turned into a material pastiche that accompanied the linguistic pastiche.

Or so one might imagine; there is no surviving manuscript of the valentine to Howland, but the specificity of its wild range of allusions invites the speculation that the copy sent to Howland may have looked very different than the *Republican* version, perhaps something like the valentine that Dickinson sent to William Cowper Dickinson at the same time (fig. 19). Unlike the valentine sent to Howland, the spare text on the valentine sent to Cowper Dickinson borrows from one old ballad called "The Batchelor's Delight," which begins,

> The world's a blister sweld with care,
> > much like unto a bubble,
> Wherein poor men tormented are
> > with women and with trouble,
> And every one that takes a wife
> > Adds [toil and] sorrow to his life,
> and makes his burden double.[34]

But like the valentine published in the *Republican*, the valentine Dickinson sent to Cowper Dickinson incorporated the materials of the schoolroom, this time actual printed materials intended to imprint the student. The small cut-out of the sleeping king, for example, was excised from Dickinson's family's copy of *The New England Primer*, and the other pictures (the man with a stick and the woman with a broom beating dogs, the boys and girls making bubbles, the little boat) were probably taken from primers as well. As Patrica Crain has argued, the domestic dissemination of such animated literacy characterized nineteenth-century American culture, installing the letters of the alphabet "as participants in the doings of everyday life, as players within or even generators of social and intimate life. Agents of action, affiliated with consumption, aligned with money and capital, the alphabetic letters had become ubiquitous [by the nineteenth century]. Bound with the passions and incorporated into personality, such letters produced a form of literacy in which the self is both mirrored and created through silent, solitary reading."[35]

In Crain's lovely description of the child's—and the culture's—disciplinary incorporation of the *ABC*s, she evokes a lyric moment of alphabetic mimesis, a moment in which printed letters themselves furnish (in all sorts of lifelike postures) the intersubjective confirmation of the self. Further, Dickinson's pastiche of fragments of ballad and fragments of hot-pressed paper mimes rather exactly Mill's lyric media. Dickinson's valentines to Howland and Cowper Dickinson use the materials of her culture's invitation to lyric imprinting to keep that genre of intersubjective confirmation at a distance. Instead, they invite the reader to share their resistance to popular song's romance as well as the *ABC*'s disciplinary tutelage

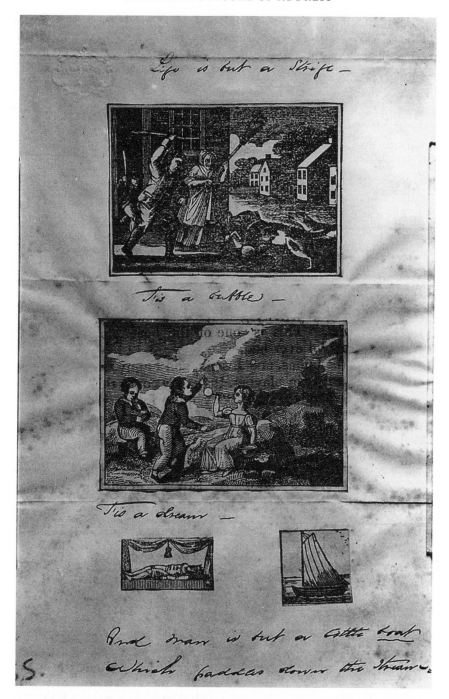

Figure 19. Emily Dickinson to William Cowper Dickinson, around 1852. Courtesy Yale University Library, Manuscripts and Archives.

(thus the calls to arms in the Howland valentine), literally constructing the fantasy of a conspiratorial counterliteracy mediated by sheets of paper converted to purposes that were not intended by the man who made them.

Martha Nell Smith has suggested that we regard Dickinson's cut-outs, occasional sketches, and collages as "cartoons," or send-ups of and challenges to "the literary, political, and family institutions that have helped to reproduce the cartoon-like image of a woman poet commodified."[36] Yet that restrospective view of the poetess in white (or, more recently, in leather) has more to do with the cultural caricature of Emily Dickinson after her publication as a lyric poet in the twentieth century than it does with Dickinson's use of the nineteenth-century materials of literate circulation—or of the transmission of various literacies.[37] Smith is surely right that recent exposure (for which Smith herself is largely responsible) of what at least some of Dickinson's poems "really looked like" will change popular views of the sort of poetry she wrote, or the kind of poet people think that Dickinson was. But most readers will still think that such youthful pieces of ephemera have little to do with Dickinson's mature lyrics. That may be why the first edition of Dickinson's *Poems* in which the valentine to Howland appeared was Johnson's 1955 scholarly edition, and the valentine to Cowper Dickinson has never been published as a poem at all. As Austin Warren complained at the time of Johnson's edition, "many of [Dickinson's] poems are exercises, or autobiographical notes, or letters in verse, or occasional verses. . . . But the business of the scholar is to publish all the 'literary remains.'"[38] We could, like Warren, dismiss such contingent phenomena as of interest only to scholars in order to be *readers* of Dickinson's lyrics, but to do so would mean ignoring the fact that the distinction between poems (in more than one sense) and letters (in more than one sense) was not an issue that simply arose for Dickinson's editors and critics after her "literary remains" were recovered; it was a distinction present to Dickinson and her readers throughout her writing life, from the early gushing letters and occasional verse to the later gushing letters and occasional verse. It was also an issue often agonizingly rather than comically at stake in the verse that has come to be considered not cartoonish or occasional but, above all, lyrical.

"You—there—I—here"

In fascicle 33, three sides of two folded sheets of laid, cream, faintly ruled stationery are taken up by the lines that are now Poem 706 in Franklin's edition (figs. 20a, 20b). These lines were among the poems published in

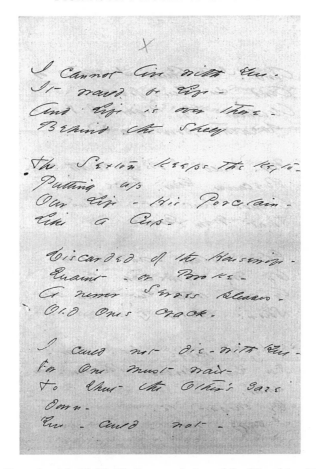

Figure 20a. From fascicle 33 (H 41). By permission of the Houghton Library, Harvard University.

the first edition of 1890 (under the title "In Vain"), and they have often been read since as testimony of Dickinson's isolation. Even more often, their invocation of a pathos of literal seclusion has been identified with a pathos of figurative seclusion—that is, with Dickinson's lyric self-address. As far as we know, the lines were not also sent as a letter, and the only manuscript copy of them that has survived is included in the fascicle.[39] If, however, "I cannot live with You—" tells us, as Cynthia Griffin Wolff has suggested, "more about Emily Dickinson herself than any other single work," it is remarkable that it should say "I" by saying "you" so often (more often than does any other published Dickinson lyric).[40] As Sharon Cameron has written, "we must scrutinize the poem carefully to see how renunciation can be so resonant with the presence of what has been given up" (LT 78):

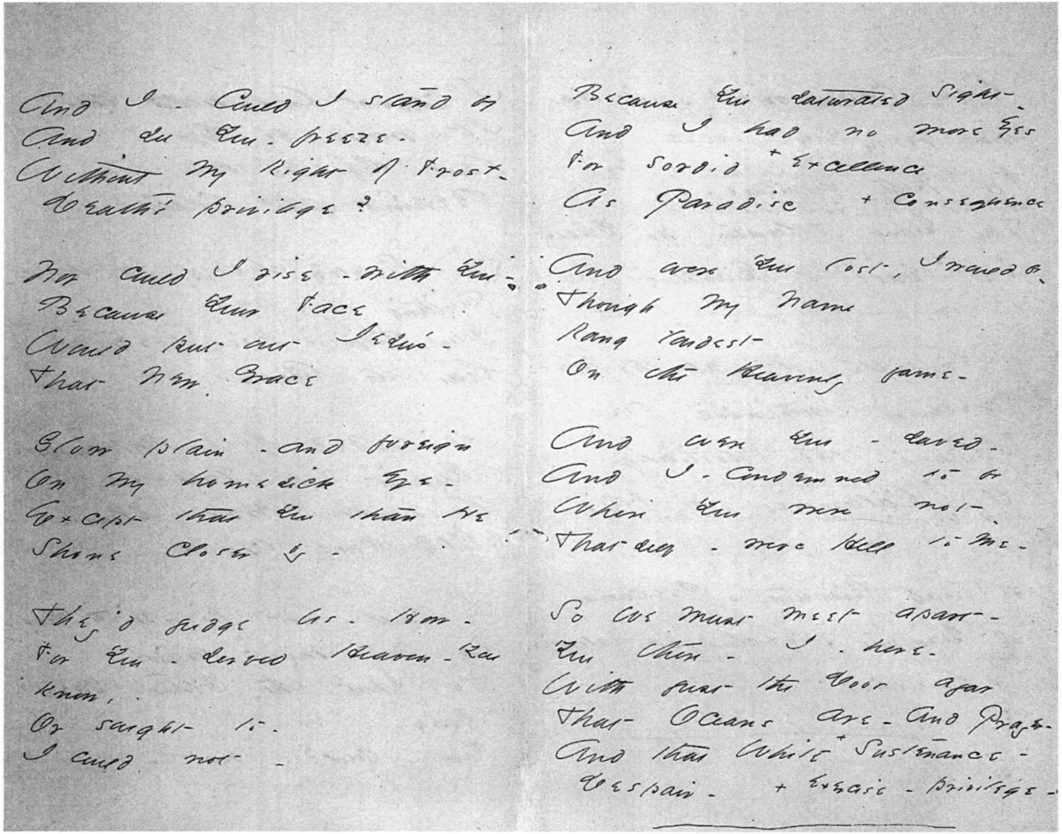

Figure 20b. From fascicle 33 (H 41). By permission of the Houghton Library, Harvard University.

I cannot live with You—
It would be Life—
And Life is over there—
Behind the Shelf
The Sexton keeps the Key to—
Putting up
Our Life—His Porcelain—
Like a Cup—

Discarded of the Housewife—
Quaint—or Broke—
A newer Sevres pleases—
Old Ones crack—

I could not die—with You—
For one must wait
To shut the Other's Gaze down—
You—could not—

And I—Could I stand by
And see You—freeze—
Without my Right of Frost—
Death's Privilege?

Nor could I rise—with You—
Because Your Face
Would put out Jesus'—
That New Grace

Glow plain—and foreign
On my homesick eye—
Except that You than He
Shone closer by—

They'd judge Us—How—
For You—served Heaven—You know,
Or sought to—
I could not—

Because You saturated sight—
And I had no more eyes
For sordid excellence
As Paradise

And were you lost, I would be—
Though my name

Rang loudest
On the Heavenly fame—

And were You—saved—
And I—condemned to be
Where You were not
That self—were Hell to me—

So we must meet apart—
You there—I—here—
With just the Door ajar
That Oceans are—and Prayer—

And that White ˣSustenance—
Despair— ˣ Exercise—Privilege—

These lines are indeed resonant with the presence of what is absent, though perhaps this is because it is not the object of address—the phenomenal "You" her or himself—that is here renounced but instead a figure for "you" (the first of what will be a series of such figures) that is considered and found wanting. What is strategically renounced, in other words, is not the presence of the other but the way in which figurative language works to replace that other with an illusion of presence that would mean the other's death. It is this illusion that the lines try hard not to forget. The results of forgetting are abruptly enacted in the oddly extended initial comparison of "Our Life" to "a Cup // Discarded of the Housewife—" and locked away by the "Sexton." When what "would be Life"—that is, the full presence that would cancel language, that would make writing unnecessary—leaves "Our" hands it becomes reified into figure. In Dickinson's stunningly contracted line, the passage from redundant presence to figurative absence is a matter of shifting pronouns: "Our Life—His Porcelain—." Like the *cracker man* and "the man who makes sheets of paper" in Dickinson's letter to Susan, the Sexton who "keeps the Key" seems at first an agent of invasion and constraint, the representative of the (notably masculine) public world imposing his law upon "Our Life." But what a Sexton does, we recall, is, according to Dickinson's dictionary, "to take care of the vessels, vestments, &c., belonging to the church."[41] For the Sexton, sacramental symbols are *things* ("Our Life—His Porcelain—") and so can be handled "Like a Cup," valued or devalued ("Discarded") according to the hands they fall into. The Sexton does not stand for what separates "I" from "You," for a public law to which "Our [private] Life" is opposed; rather, what the Sexton represents is the transformation of "Our Life" into figure. Once that figure is introduced, the simile takes over, intensifying the sense of referential instability signaled by the change in pronouns and by the apparently arbitrary little narrative of the Housewife. The Sexton and the Housewife are thus the antitypes to the "drivers and conductors" of Dickinson's letter: they take the figure of the "Cup" literally and, forgetting that it *is* a figure (as they are figures), they have the potential of delivering it into the wrong hands.

But whose are the right hands? If "Life is over there—" when it becomes a metaphor, where is it if it does not? Is there any alternative to the privative fatality of figuration? These are questions that the lines back away from to then ask over and over with an urgency bordering on obsession. Before considering the litany of responses that make up the body of what is now one of Dickinson's most famous poems, we may better understand what is at stake for Dickinson in the apparent opposition between life as full presence and life as figure by placing these lines beside others from the same period (about 1862) that she wrote (or copied) on the same stationery bound in a very similar, slightly later fascicle (figs. 21a, 21b, from fascicle 34). The lines (now F 757) begin in a parallel worry over the figuration of address:

> I think To Live—may be a
> ×Bliss
> To those ×who dare to try—
> Beyond my limit to conceive—
> My lip—to testify—
>
> I think the Heart I former
> wore
> Could widen—till to me
> The Other, like the little
> Bank
> Appear—unto the Sea—
>
> I think the Days—could every one
> In Ordination stand—
> And Majesty—be easier—
> Than an inferior kind—
>
> No numb alarm—lest Difference
> come—
> No Goblin—on the Bloom—
> No ×start in Apprehension's Ear,
> No ×Bankruptcy—no Doom—
>
> But Certainties of ×Sun—
> ×Midsummer—in the Mind—

147

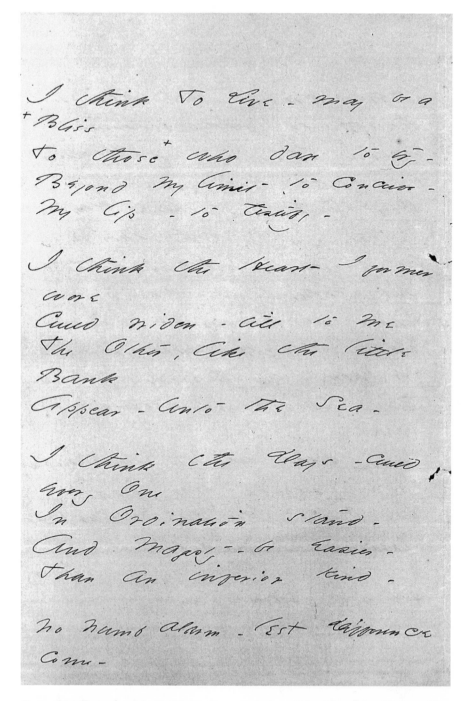

Figure 21a. From fascicle 34 (H 50). By permission of the Houghton Library, Harvard University.

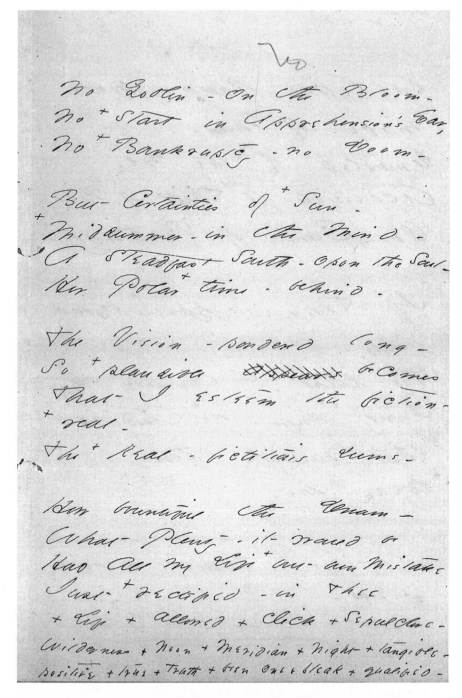

Figure 21b. From fascicle 34 (H 50). By permission of the Houghton Library, Harvard University.

A steadfast South—upon the Soul—
Her Polar ˣtime—behind—

The Vision—pondered long-
So ˣplausible ~~appears~~ becomes
That I esteem the fiction—
ˣreal—
The ˣReal—fictitious seems—

How bountiful the Dream—
What Plenty—it would be—
Had all my Life ˣbut been Mistake
Just ˣrectified—in Thee
ˣLife ˣallowed click ˣSepulchre—
Wilderness ˣNoon ˣMeridian ˣNight ˣtangible—
positive ˣtrue ˣTruth ˣbeen one ˣbleak ˣqualified—

The first of these lines, especially in the variant version, echoes directly the tautology that launches the lines that begin "I cannot live with you—." In this sense, one line may be read as a variant of the other, or the two sets of lines may be read as proliferating variations on the same theme—though what that theme might be it is hard to say, and it is even harder to say why it seems to require so many variations. Cameron, the best reader of Dickinson's variants, has provocatively suggested that "by amplifying the idea of a subject to include its variants as well as variant ways of conceiving it [Dickinson produces] utterances that are extrageneric, even unclassifiable. And (for that reason, in a way that it seems to me no one yet has quite explained) untitled."[42]

These lines, at least in manuscript, are certainly "extrageneric," but are they an "utterance"? Dickinson's lines have often been *read* by literary critics as represented speech, even when readers try to make their graphic, genre-breaking, "untitled" moves more apparent. Mary Jo Salter typifies the assumption that even variant lines represent the properties of voice when she writes that Dickinson's variants "may have represented to her either revisions or . . . overtones: that is, each well-chosen alternative was at least as right as any other, and possibly most beautiful when held in mind with the other(s), like a chord."[43] Yet Cameron's emphasis on the intersubjective, extrageneric quality of the variants also urges one to attend to the words that crowd the bottom of the second page of the manuscript as something other, something stranger, than "utterance," in one or several voices. As Dickinson put it in a letter to Higginson, "a Pen has so many inflections and a Voice but one" (L 2:470). Perhaps so many inflections of the pen riddle the page of "I think To Live—" because to inflect that initial tautology is the lines' problem. What "I think To Live—may be a / ˣBliss [ˣLife]" and "I cannot live with You— / It would be Life—" share as redundant propositions is the implication that were the possibility of presence not foreclosed, all one could say would be "Life—Life—Life—Life—Life" over and over in a blissful stutter. Put another way, the desire that informs these lines is the desire that they need not be written.

But the lines were written, of course, and so inflected with a desire that diverts the crisscrossing hesitations with which they begin by almost ending. They do proceed, but in a direction that is anything but linear. Loop by metric loop, the lines of "I think To Live—" turn back upon that opening line as if locked by the Sexton's key within its syntax. The lines assume the burden of defining an infinitive that has already been defined as indefinable: "Beyond my limit to conceive— / My lip—to testify—." What the rest of the lines bear witness to is the attempt to write the unsayable, to inflect an ideally uninflected—experience? sense-certainty? "Life," as the term appears here, is an ontological absolute. "Had we the first intimation of the Definition of Life," Dickinson wrote to Elizabeth Holland, "the calmest of us would be Lunatics!" (L 2:492). Not being able (or refusing) to define *what* it is, the lines go on to decline *where* Life "may be" if "it would be." That proleptic "may be" places what follows in the perspective of anticipation, so that what "may be" would be conceivable only in terms of what was: "the Heart I former / wore," "an inferior kind" of time. This entanglement of anticipation and retroaction predicated in the first nine lines by the repetition of "I think" gives way to another anaphora: "No . . . / No . . . / No . . . / No . . . no . . ." We could read the retrograde progression from the ninth to the twelfth lines as a (failing) attempt to extricate thinking from the temporal trap in which the grammatical structure of address has thinking locked. In those lines, "Difference" has already come, the "ˣstart [ˣclick] in Apprehension's Ear" has already been registered. The "click" (of the key?) in the variant interrupts the first lines' grasp (apprehension) of what it "may be" "To Live" and marks their suspicion (apprehensiveness) that that *what* is outside the reach of language—or of writing. When the fifth stanza then seeks to deny the denial of the fourth, its "Certainties" are made less certain by the differential (that is, written) framework that they claim to transcend. While the alliteration and subtle assonance of the lines strive to give the impression of sameness (an impression located in their acoustic effects: "Certainties . . . Sun" / "Midsummer . . . Mind" / ". . . steadfast South . . . Soul") "Sun," "Midsummer," and "South" are themselves only articulable in their difference from the ". . . Polar time—behind—." The address, still enmeshed in the tragic temporality of a retroactive anticipation, cannot name the place beyond this predicament until its last two spare monosyllables: "in Thee." The figure of address is revealed in the end to have been the "what," the subject, that the lines have anticipated all along. In Helen McNeil's reading, " 'Thee' is whatever would give the mind whatever the mind desires."[44]

At the end of "I think To Live—," the deferred designation of "Thee" is not, however, merely the vehicle of desire's fulfillment; "Thee" is the name *of* desire, its unlocatable location. Or perhaps we should say its suspended location, for it is in the end at the dead center of the chiasmus between "the fiction— / ˣreal—[ˣtrue]" and "The ˣReal [ˣTruth]—fictitious . . ." When desire's prolepsis "So ˣplausible [ˣtangible—ˣpositive] becomes" that desire "seems" answerable, its object is canceled by the rhetorical crossroads at which that object is sublated in "seems." That suspension is in effect a refusal to sublimate "Thee" by apprehending the other in figure—that is, to forget that its plausibility would be an effect of the apostrophe that the lines defer. Why go to so much trouble to put it off? In a different mood, Dickinson might have mediated desire's life-and-death alternatives by substituting an enclosure or an allusion or, perhaps, a drawing of a tombstone like the one she penciled on the back of a fragment of stationery (figs. 22a, 22b) that reads,

> Soul, take thy risk,
> With Death to be
> Were better than be not
> with thee[45]

But the lines that begin "I think To Live—" just keep doubling back on themselves. Why would Dickinson want to mark and remark, reach toward and away from the object of these lines' address, to stage such a pathetic near-miss? The apostrophe that works retroactively to bring the object of address closer is qualified by its position at the edge of the lines' temporal grasp. Captive of neither the Imaginary "Other" self with which the lines begin nor of the Symbolic register they surround, "Thee" is in the position that Lacan came to name the Real: that point on the horizon of language that sets desire (or language-as-desire) in motion but which language (or the subject constructed from it) cannot (in order to keep desiring) apprehend.[46] To do so would mean to stop desiring, or to stop living—or to stop writing and rewriting.

What this reading of "I think To Live—" allows us to understand about the anxiety of the first lines of "I cannot live with You—" is that that anxiety stems not only from the distance that separates "I" from "You" but from the consequences of the apostrophe that separation invokes. While "I think To Live—" defers its apostrophe until its last word (so that, in effect, the apostrophe cannot become what de Man would identify as the personal abstraction of a prosopopoeia, cannot attribute to "Thee" a face, a

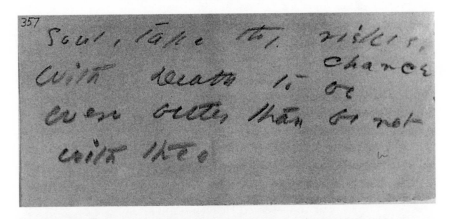

Figure 22a and 22b. Emily Dickinson, about 1867. Courtesy of Amherst College Archives and Special Collections (ED ms. 357).

figure), "I cannot live with You—" begins with the problem of keeping "You" in the Real, outside its own apostrophe's reach. That reach, as the lines demonstrate at length (at fifty lines, this is one of Dickinson's longest published poems) is extensive: it encompasses this life, death, afterlife, heaven, hell, memory, the self:

> I could not die—with You—
> For One must wait
> To shut the Other's Gaze down—
> You—could not—
>
> And I—Could I stand by
> And see You—freeze-
> Without my Right of Frost—
> Death's privilege?

Nor could I rise—with You—
Because Your Face
Would put out Jesus'—
That New Grace

Glow plain—and foreign
On my homesick Eye—
Except that You than He
Shone closer by—

They'd judge Us—How—
For You—served Heaven—You know,
Or sought to—
I could not—

Because You saturated Sight—
And I had no more Eyes
For sordid ˣexcellence ˣconsequence
As Paradise

As Cameron suggests, this "catechism is one of renunciation," but it is important to notice that what is renounced at each stage of this catechism is a face-to-face encounter with "You" (LT 78). In other words, what is renounced is the performative affect of apostrophe, the trope that brings "You" into the moment of speech. In the fourth and fifth stanzas, that renunciation turns on the moment of death (as "I could not die—with You—" follows almost by catechistic rote upon the first line, save for the graphic stutter of the em dash), or the moment a nineteenth-century reader would recognize as the death vigil. Whether one shuts "the Other's Gaze down—" or ". . . I stand by / And see You—freeze—" the emphasis is on envisioning an encounter that the lines do not want to envision, not only because doing so would be an admission of mortality but because seeing the other's face would mean turning "You" into a fiction. That fiction would allow address to transcend the material circumstances of separation, as the abrupt and seamless transition from physical death to life after death insists. If the lines were to admit such transcendence (and this is, after all, the historical moment of Elizabeth Phelps's *The Gates Ajar*, the popular novel in which reunion after death is carried on in vivid, even domestic detail, and to which the last stanza may contain an allusion), "Your Face / Would put out Jesus'."[47] But by not imagining its own apostrophe as transcendent, the lines do not give a "Face" to "You"; what they do instead is to tally the consequences as if they were to do so.

The complexity of this conditional temporality is very much like that of "I think To Live—" and it has, understandably, confused a reader as perceptive as Cameron. "Interestingly enough," Cameron writes, "what prohibits union seems to be the fact that it has already occurred. . . . For although 'Because Your Face / Would put out Jesus'—' seems suppositional, two stanzas later the event is echoed, and located not in the future at all, but rather in the past:

> Because You saturated Sight—
> And I had no more Eyes
> For sordid excellence
> As Paradise." (LT 80)

The problem with this reading is the assumption that the slip into the past tense constitutes the ninth stanza as an "event." As in the first stanzas of "I cannot live with You", in which "Our Life" becomes "his Porcelain" when the figure is taken literally, the shift from the sixth quatrain's "Would" to the seventh stanza's "Shone" happens at the point at which the lines, for the moment, enter into their own fiction. Not incidentally, ". . . I esteem the fiction— / ˣreal [ˣtrue]" at the very moment that the lines turn back upon the I's "Eye," and the effect of that turn is blinding. In the fictive vision that the figure of apostrophe would make plausible, the illusion of a full presence would blind the I/Eye to the fact that "Your Face" would be an illusion, an effect of performative utterance (the variant for the "excellence" of figure's therefore ironically "sordid" Paradise is "consequence"). To mistake the performative dimension of apostrophe for a statement of historical presence would be to become the Sexton, for to imagine that "over there" is already here is to make sure that "You" will dissolve into figment.

As Dickinson wrote in other lines in 1862, also in a fascicle (13), that begin, "You see I cannot see—your lifetime—" (F 313), the representation of desire's object threatens to take the place of that object itself:

> Too vague—the face—
> My own—so patient—covers—
> Too far—the strength—
> My timidness enfolds—
> Haunting the Heart—
> Like her translated faces—
> Teazing the want—
> It—only—can suffice!

When what is now the ninth stanza of "I cannot live with You—" enters into the past tense of ideal union *as if* that union had already occurred, the "translated faces" of desire tease the lines momentarily out of thought. If the lines ended here, we could say that apostrophe (or the fiction of address) had worked its charm. But the three stanzas that issue from this moment deny apostrophe its due, and in so renouncing the "saturated Sight" of figure they must find a way out of its "Haunting" and "Teazing" logic. They must reach toward, in other words, what ". . . only—can suffice!" without appropriating the object in a rhetorical illusion of sufficiency. They must give "You" a figure that is not a "translated face."[48]

As in "I think To Live—," where the inflections of the pen bear witness to what is "Beyond my limit to conceive— / My lip—to testify—," the concluding movement of "I cannot live with You—" sustains an address to a "You" positioned just beyond apostrophe's limit. Stanzas ten and eleven withdraw from the fictive moment of absolute insight to reassert the fallacy of an identity between self and other, here and there. Thus the penultimate stanza sums the danger of a figurative logic of self-projection:

> And were You—saved—
> And I—condemned to be
> Where You were not—
> That self—were Hell to Me—

This last line is inflected by two important literary echoes: Satan's "I Myself am Hell" from *Paradise Lost* and Heathcliff's Satanic address to the dead Catherine in *Wuthering Heights*. The allusion to *Paradise Lost* has often been noticed, but it has not been noticed that Dickinson's Milton has been mediated here by Brontë's Miltonic hero who, "condemned to be" where Catherine is not, invokes her presence in his own tormented apostrophe, an invocation that grows directly from the question, "Where is she?": "Not *there*—*not* in heaven—not perished—where? Oh! . . . Catherine Earnshaw, may you not rest, as long as I am living! . . . Be with me always—take any form—drive me mad! Only *do* not leave me in this abyss, where I cannot find you! Oh, God! it is unutterable! *I cannot* live without my life! I *cannot* live without my soul!"[49] Heathcliff, master of the egotistical sublime that he is, keeps Catherine with him and "Not *there*" in the very form of his address to her. In the novel, the performative force of his utterance actually works: Catherine stays, one of desire's "translated faces." If the pathetic tug beneath the statement "I cannot live with You— / It would be Life—" has been all along "I *cannot* live without my life," that pathos is finally qualified (or "rectified") by the allusion to *Wuthering Heights* and Brontë's ambivalent portrait of her hero's fantastic act of identification through invocation. The concluding stanza of what is now Dickinson's poem suggests an alternative to the sort of romantic selfhood that

Heathcliff—and especially Heathcliff's use of the figure of apostrophe—represents.[50]

That alternative is sketched in lines that offer an appropriately tentative version of a form of address that would not be an act of appropriation and perhaps not even a fiction:

> So We must meet apart—
> You there—I—here—
> With just the Door ajar
> That Oceans are—and Prayer—
> And that White Sustenance— ˣexercise ˣprivilege
> Despair—

These lines are remarkable for what they do not say. They do not say, with Heathcliff, "Be with me always." They do not locate the invoked "You" within the self; they do not claim that your "there" has been transmuted (or, in Dickinson's better word, translated) into my "here." In other words, the lines recognize the threat inherent in the figure of apostrophic address; they register the way in which "this figure," as Jonathan Culler has written, "which seems to establish relations between self and other can in fact be read as an act of radical interiorization and solipsism."[51] In the second chapter, I suggested that the de Manian suspicion of figuration—especially de Man's suspicion of lyric figuration—that Culler invokes is bound up with an idea of the lyric as an ideal, ahistorical genre. The sort of diplomatically erotic "relations" that Dickinson's lines imagine at their close are predicated upon the rejection of such solipsism, as well as such lyric idealization: "You" remain "there—I—"—stranded between dashes—remain "here." And as Cynthia Griffin Wolff has suggested, "what sense can there be in the lines 'So We must meet apart— / You there—I—here—,' unless 'here' refers to the very page on which the poem is printed?"[52] What sense, indeed. If the directly referential function of "here" persuades us that what the deictic points to is the page we hold in our hands (but not exactly *that* page, of course, once the poem "is printed" and many pages are delivered into many hands), what would the referential function of "there" be? Wolff's solution, that "'We,' reader and poet, do indeed 'meet,' but only 'apart,' through the mediating auspices of the Voice and the verse," ignores the problem to which the extended final stanza is the solution.

What Dickinson offers instead in her last two lines is an alternative to the metaphor of the voice of the poet speaking to herself "here" in the poem we are reading. What we are reading is not a voice (or a "Voice"). It is, as Griffin Wolff herself points out, a page. The difference seems important in a poem so preoccupied with the effects of the very figure of opening one's mouth to say "O," to say "You." Whatever "that White Suste-nance—ˣexercise ˣprivilege" may be taken to be, it is manifestly silent. That "White Sustenance," like the white page on which she writes, is all that is left to the poem's I/Eye if the transcendence of figurative address is refused. The poem's "I" and "You" are sustained by that page in the sense that they are both (as pronouns) borne by it and (as subjects) hold it as they write and read, but compared to the imagined vision of Paradise, the slight weight of a page is small compensation. It is, in fact, no compensa-tion at all in the Emersonian sense of an ideal reciprocity in which, as Emerson wrote, "the copula is hidden."[53] The page rather sustains the ten-uous connection between "I" and "You" by materializing that copula, a re-lation as difficult to read as is the grammatical copula of the poem's last lines.

For in some subtle and disturbing sense, the "White Sustenance" of the page is at once a comforting material presence and as blank as the figure of a figure. The (agrammatical) placement of "are," on which the cat-achrestic series of metaphors of the last lines depends, makes the identity between ". . . that White Sustenance—ˣexercise ˣprivilege / Despair—" and the page much more difficult to hold in mind than the simile that I have just ventured can admit. On the basis of this single and singularly awkward copula, "the Door ajar," a metaphor of place that would stabilize the relation of "there" and "here," gives way to "Oceans," a much less sta-ble figure of place, and then to "Prayer," a metaphysical displacement of presence. "Prayer is the little implement," Dickinson wrote,

> Through which Men reach
> Where Presence—is denied them.
> They fling their Speech
>
> By means of it—in God's Ear—(F 623)

Such an ironic apostrophe, a futile "exercise," a pathetic "privilege," presses rather desperately against the "White" page that is itself the trace of apostrophe's ambition. Not I, not you, not here, not there, not this, but "that," if White Sustenance" is a figure for the page then it is a figure with-out a face. It is the historical, as opposed to the fictive, material of address.

"The most pathetic thing I do"

That address's capacity to mediate—to join "I" and "You" as subjects pre-cisely by keeping the pronouns "apart"—depends, of course, on its suc-cessful passage from self to other. To return to the terms of Dickinson's letter to Susan, "the letter's ride to You—" is what allows reading to take place at all. In giving selected lines from the fascicles the sort of attention to grammatical and rhetorical detail known as "close reading," I have made them into the lyrics that they try so hard not to become. Like you, I first read them as lyrics in Johnson's and Franklin's editions, and perhaps like you, I am a literary critic. But Dickinson's highly literate incorporation of just about every literary convention in the book does not make her into a lyric poet—yet, like the white page and its pathetic apostrophe, literal and figurative address are almost impossible to tell apart after a over a century of lyric reading of her writing has rendered them identical. If we knew, for example, that the "you" in the lines "I cannot live with you—" was Susan, and that she would not "overhear" but *respond* to what Dickinson wrote to her, would that mean that the lines are not a lyric?[54] If we knew that the lines were definitely never sent to anyone at all, that they were written to be locked into a box that Dickinson may or may not have intended for "the world" to see after her death, would that mean that the lines *are* a lyric? I have been suggesting that these questions became pressing for the twentieth-century interpretation of lyric poetry in a way that was not at all pressing for Dickinson. The pathos in Dickinson's writing is located elsewhere, in a place so alien to our reading of the genre we have attributed to her work that we have not been able to see it, though it has been there all along. What most of her "extrageneric" compositions worry about is whether they will literally reach the reader, and whether that reader will respond. Although Dickinson's specifically written forms of address mediate between self and other in a much more directed (Dickinson might say "plausible") way than does the metaphor of lyric voice, as the tentativeness (and desperation) of the conclusion of "I cannot live with You—" suggests, in being more specific than the figure of the transcendentally individual voice, the medium of the page is also less sure of its destination. Though a letter or a poem to Susan might imply the historical Susan as its ideal reader, the letters and poems that have come into our hands have, in their passage, implicated us as readers as well. Rather than imagine ourselves voyeurs identified with a privileged lyric solitude or solitary readers of a fragmentary romance novel—that is, rather than worry about whether Dickinson wrote lyrics or letters or letter-poems— we might begin to take account of the way in which a third position has been built into Dickinson's structures of address.

Unlike the reader of a lyric or the reader of (someone else's) personal letter, the reader of the historical materials of Dickinson's various figures of address enjoys no intersubjective confirmation of the self. Far from it. The way in which Dickinson's writing often invites or assumes a reader other than its (often unavailable or out of reach) historical addressee, and other than an imaginary, sympathetic eavesdropper or theatrical audience in the distant future, is difficult to characterize, or at least contemporary literary criticism has no language for it. But it is definitely there, in the writing—or perhaps it would be better to say that it is there *on* and outside the writing, or on the sheets of paper that sustained that writing and that may have passed between other people to whom it no longer refers. On a flyleaf from her father's copy of Washington Irving's *Sketch Book of Geoffrey Crayon*, for example, Dickinson penciled some lines that seem to be directly addressed (fig. 23):

> The most pathetic
> thing I do
> Is play I hear
> from you—
> I make believe
> until my Heart
> Almost believes
>   it too
> But when I
> break it with
>   the news
>   You knew it
>   that
> was not true
> I wish I had
> not broken it—
>   Goliah—so would
>   you—[55]

I suppose that we could read these lines (or we can, now that the flyleaf has been excised from Irving and the lines have been printed) as Mill's "lament of a prisoner in a solitary cell," or as an overheard song, or a soliloquy, or as Vendler's "performance of the mind in *solitary* speech." And I suppose that if we considered them within those received phenomenologies of lyric reading, we might say that it does not matter who or where Dickinson's "Goliah" was, since the address to him or her was obviously so figurative (rather like, say, "Danny Boy" in a Scottish ballad Mill does not invoke), and it does not much matter when or where they were written. Yet if we happen to know that they were written in the early 1870s, and that Dickinson once compared Susan to "Goliah" in a letter in 1854 (L 154), and that in 1869 there was a celebrated discovery (which turned out to be a hoax) in Susan's native upstate New York of "the American Goliah," then we might think that the lines on the flyleaf were the draft of a

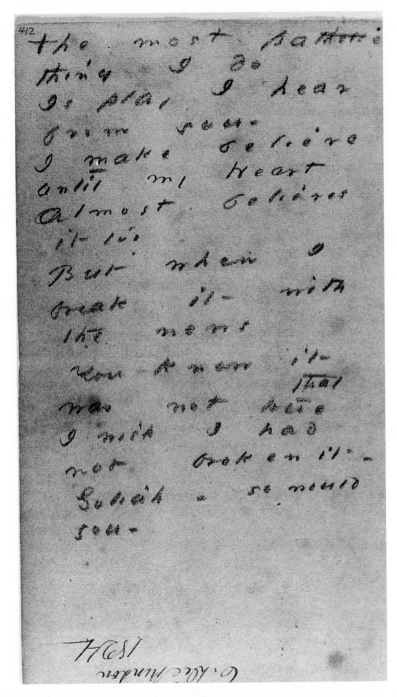

Figure 23. Flyleaf torn from Edward Dickinson's copy of Washington Irving's *Sketch Book of Geoffrey Crayon*. Courtesy of Amherst College Archives and Special Collections (ED ms. 412).

letter-poem to Susan. "The American Goliah" (a story all over the papers, including the Springfield *Republican*, in October 1869) was a ten-foot figure of a man "discovered" near Syracuse, about which there immediately ensued a debate "whether the colossal figure [was] a petrifaction or a piece of statuary." A widely circulated ode entitled "To the Giant of Onondaga" consisted of a direct address to the figure, apostrophizing it to "Speak Out, O Giant! . . . thy story tell," in order to solve the controversy.[56] If the flyleaf lines were the draft of a letter to Susan, we could read "Goliah" as a name for exactly the figure of address I have been attempting to describe, or that Dickinson attempted to resist, the illusion created by apostrophe: the fictive figure with a no longer animate face. On this reading, Susan's lack of personal response in that moment meant that she could only be imagined as a petrified, and mute, figure of address. Yet if the first reading of the flyleaf lines is too indefinitely metaphorical (Emily Dickinson as folk song), the second is perhaps too definitely, or quirkily, historical—though that history does shift toward metaphor, as history tends to do. Between those extremes there is the flyleaf from Dickinson's father's copy of Irving, a piece of paper already part of a printed book that fits into neither account of Dickinson's figure of address. It is even more unreadable, less responsive than the petrified face of "Goliah"; it does not sound or look like us.

In 1914, Susan's daughter and Dickinson's niece, by then named Martha Dickinson Bianchi (because, rather like Margaret Fuller, she had gone to Italy and married an Italian Count, though she came back to Amherst without him), published a small volume of the verse that Dickinson had sent to her mother. In her Preface, Bianchi explained: "The poems here included were written on any chance slip of paper, sometimes the old plaid Quadrille, sometimes a gilt-edged sheet with a Paris mark, often a random scrap of commercial note from her Father's law office. Each of these is folded over, addressed merely 'Sue,' and sent by the first available hand."[57] Susan had not given her cache of Dickinson manuscripts to Todd and Higginson. Bianchi writes in her preface that she seriously considered burning them, but decided to publish them for the benefit of "the lovers of my Aunt's peculiar genius" (vi). In doing so, she omitted the addresses to "Sue" and printed each of them alone on a separate white page, untitled, as if she had brought her aunt back with her from Europe as a new *Imagiste*. The last poem in her volume evokes in its placement the pathos of what Bianchi calls "the romantic friendship" between her aunt and her mother. One can see why she chose it, since the temporal confusion that we have noticed in the lines that begin "I think to Live—" and "I cannot live with You—" also informs Bianchi's last poem, but this time it is the time of reading itself that proves difficult if not impossible to locate:

I did not reach Thee
But my feet slip nearer every day
Three Rivers and a Hill to cross
One Desert and a Sea
I shall not count the journey one
When I am telling thee.

Like the other opening lines of those other forms of address, this stanza opens by closing a possibility to which it must then attempt a different approach. But how can one approach a destination that has already been canceled *as* destination? How can one get from here to there when (to paraphrase Gertrude Stein) there is no there there? The second line's assertion that "my feet slip nearer every day" is logically baffling in its apparently willful denial of the situation that the first line has already stated as fact. In slipping from past to present tense, the line is not progressing but backing up—or, in Robert Weisbuch's phrase for such moves in Dickinson's poems, the lines are "retreating forward."[58] They do so in order to recount in the fictive present a time the sixth line explicitly identifies as the time of " telling," an encounter that can take place "When" I reach what "I did not reach." As in "I think To Live—," the line between history and fiction is here a treacherous one to tread, and yet for four more stanzas it is literally the line that the "I" does tread, her poetic "feet" (in Dickinson's usage, almost always a pun on metric writing) traversing "Three Rivers and a Hill . . . / One Desert and a Sea." The lines' geography is reminiscent of "the hills and the dales, and the rivers" that Dickinson imagines in the early letter to Susan as the "romance in the letter's ride to you—." In the letter, we recall, Dickinson compares that romance to "a poem such as can ne'er be written." Such a poem, however, was written: it is Poem 1708 in the Franklin edition—although in more than one sense, the poem slipped near its destination.

The text of these lines is available to us only by virtue of a transcript made by Susan herself. There is no manuscript version of this poem in Emily Dickinson's hand, no flyleaf, no slip of paper, no Quadrille, no Paris mark, no ad, no cut-out; the hand from which the published poem was taken is Susan's. If the hand-to-hand economy of written correspondence is to mediate our future reception of Dickinson's writing (as I have been arguing that both the historical form and figurative content of Dickinson's writing suggest that it should), then another message sent to Susan around 1864 acquires an uncanny sense for us (fig. 24): "for the Woman whom I prefer," Dickinson wrote, "Here is Festival—Where my Hands are cut, Her fingers will be found inside—" (L 288). Removed from the "Festival" of Dickinson's "Here," from the time and place of her writing, not the

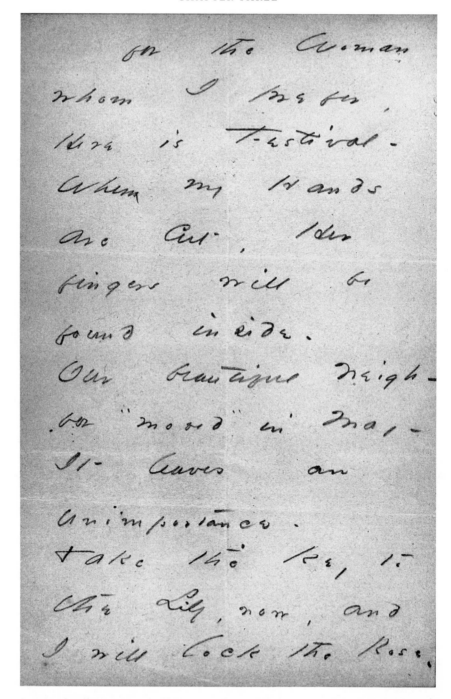

Figure 24. Emily Dickinson to Susan Gilbert Dickinson, around 1864. By permission of the Houghton Library, Harvard University.

preferred reader of that writing but the readers deferred, future critics of Emily Dickinson would do well to notice that there are more than two pairs of hands complicit in this startling figure of address. Reading Emily Dickinson here and now, ours are the unseen hands most deeply "committed": they are doing the cutting. Whether a literary text always reaches its destination or whether it has always already gone astray, whether Dickinson wrote letters or Dickinson wrote poems, it is worth returning to her forms of address with an eye to the way in which they have anticipated both alternatives and to the corrective they offer retroactively to Higginson's still influential version of Dickinson's writing as privileged self-address—or as a private language addressed, lyrically, to all of us.[59] At least it is time that we cut more carefully, that we learned to tell the difference.

"Faith in Anatomy"

Achilles' Head

Jay Leyda thought that it was a reminder to place a book order. David Porter thought that it was "a postage stamp with paper arms glued on."[1] My students usually think that it is an avant-garde collage. The three-cent stamp with a picture of a steam engine on it stuck to clippings from *Harper's Weekly* that read "GEORGE SAND" and "Mauprat" (figs. 25a, 25b) seems to have little to do with the lines Dickinson wrote around it. It would be difficult to print the lines in the patterns they assume to make way for the bits of print stuck between them. I will reprint them here *almost* as they appear in the Franklin edition (F 1174), taking the liberty of adding the variants in approximately the places they occupy on Dickinson's pages:

Alone and in a Circumstance

Reluctant to be told

A spider on my reticence

Assiduously crawled
deliberately
determinately
impertinently

And so   much more at home than I

Immediately   grew
I felt   myself a
                the
And hurriedly withdrew—
          hastily

Revisiting my late abode

with articles of claim

I found it quietly assumed

as a Gymnasium
for

where tax asleep and title off
                    peasants
Perpetual presumption took
                    complacence

                    lawful
As each were special Heir—
                    only
A If any strike me in the street

I can return the Blow,

If any take my property
                    seize
According to the Law

The Statute is my Learned friend

But what redress can be

For an offence not here nor there
          not   anywhere
So not in Equity—

That Larceny of time and mind

The marrow of the Day

By spider, or forbid it Lord

that I should specify—

Whatever these lines may be about, they are not (except in the most literal sense) about the stamp and clippings. Here, the objective enclosure or paste-on does not fill in the "omitted center" or restore the lines' "revoked . . . referentiality" or explain their "strategies of limitation."[2] Porter, one of the few critics to attend to these lines at all, has suggested that the reason that the "circumstance" of the text is withheld is that "it chronicles, in fact, the visit of a spider to a privy and particularly to an unmentionable part of the occupant's anatomy" (17). Jeanne Holland has taken up Porter's suggestion and expanded its reference to the larger domestic economy in which Dickinson made manuscripts like this one out of "household detritus," incorporating her brother's and father's legal rhetoric into her "woman's work . . . progressively refin[ing] her own domestic technologies of publication" against the masculine public sphere.[3] Both readers, understandably, want to domesticate the strangeness of the lines and their contingent circumstances, and it is worth noting that they do so by arguing that Dickinson blurs her culture's line between usefulness and waste, poetry and shit, a distinction

167

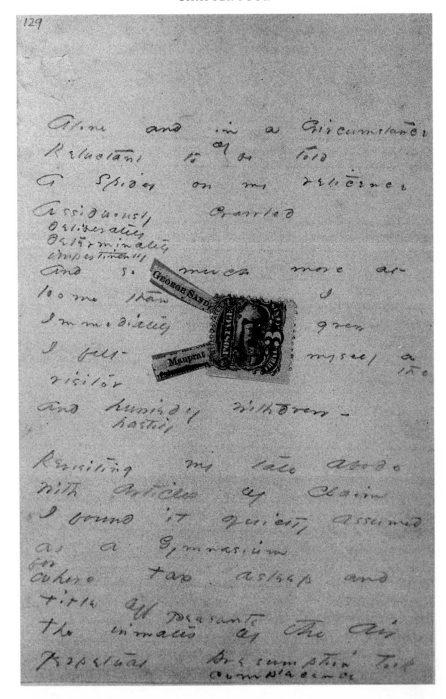

Figure 25a. Emily Dickinson, around 1870. Courtesy of Amherst College Archives and Special Collections (ED ms. 129).

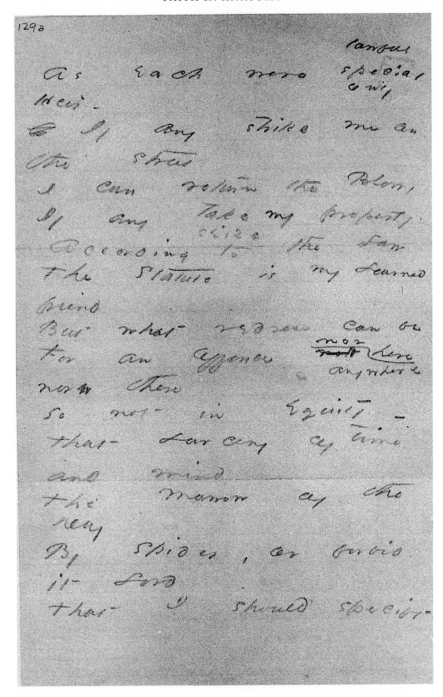

Figure 25b. Emily Dickinson, around 1870. Courtesy of Amherst College Archives and Special Collections (ED ms. 129).

made and unmade with reference to gender and the body. Both readers also identify the objects on the text with or as the subject in the text ("paper arms," "her own domestic technologies"). But what *is* (or *was*) the relation between these lines, anatomy, gender, privacy, publicity, intellectual and material property, technology, circulation, social economy, and the blue-and-white stamp gluing together an author's name and the title of a novel? Is that relation legible or illegible in Dickinson's manuscript?

In order to answer that question, we might begin by posing another. Do the eccentric materials sometimes pasted on or enclosed within Dickinson's writing really *matter* to the poetry that has been read off of them? In some ways, no. The pencil draft of "After a hundred years" (F 1,149), for example, could not be said to refer to the domestic list on the back of the page on which it was written (figs. 26a, 26b):

After a hundred years

Nobody knows the place
knew
Agony that enacted there

Motionless as Peace

———————

Weeds triumphant ranged

Strangers strolled and spelled

At the lone Orthography
Of the Elder Dead

———————

Winds of Summer Fields

Recollect the way—

Instinct picking up the Key

Dropped by memory—

verso:

Prunes—

Apple—

Graham Bread

Conservatory

Dough nuts

All that these two texts have in common is paper. After a hundred years, the poem has passed into the cultural memory instituted by literature; the miscellany has been consigned to the scholar's documentary interest. Yet precisely for that reason, it is the latter that may affect us now with some of the uncanny power contained in the lines' central pun on reading. The "Strangers" who discover the traces of the dead in Dickinson's version of the country churchyard are "spelled" from their stroll by stopping to read them; in order to do so, they must "spell" out "the lone Orthography" that indicates the dead's now "Motionless" presence; so spelling, these strollers may fall under the spell of the dead's strangeness. That effect depends on an act of deciphering that is epistemologically incomplete, since it cannot grant the dead new life: these are strangers after all, with no direct experience of the past and the "lone Orthography" does not, in the poem, eventuate in the proper names of "the Elder Dead" (except, perhaps, in the initials E. D.). The readers in and of these lines thus speculate in specular fashion, doubly identified and doubly self-estranged by their interruption by the spirits of "the place." In this place, the pathos of history ("Agony that enacted there") has been reduced to an inscription only "Winds" know how to read—which is to say that no one does. The habits of "memory"—received modes of identifying writing and reference in the person of a living subject—have been displaced by an "Instinct" that hovers between perception and cognition, between the musical "Key" one might hear on the wind and the "Key" to a foreclosed interpretation.

In both of these examples—in attempts to read the blue stamp stuck to printed proper names and in Dickinson's fiction of the no-longer-legible—what is missing is the established literary character that will inevitably influence actual readers who encounter Dickinson's work not in these conjured places but in classrooms, anthologies, and editions. The truth is that we know too much about "Emily Dickinson"—poet, recluse, Myth of Amherst—to be able to imagine her "Orthography" as anything stranger (or more historically distant) than the traces of a subject who will already have been remembered. As Randall Jarrell wrote fifty years ago, "after a few decades or centuries almost everyone will be able to see through Dickinson to her poems."[4] But maybe it works the other way around: after a few decades or centuries almost everyone will be able to see through the poems to Dickinson. That would be remarkable, since for over a hundred years, it is poetry that has been successively personified by versions of Dickinson: by the isolated private genius composing only for herself; by the neglected protomodernist writing for an audience she had yet to create; by the artist crafting gems of timeless hermetic verse; by the renegade subverting the precepts of her society; by the woman working against the grain of patriarchy; by the writer taking up and forging a women's literary

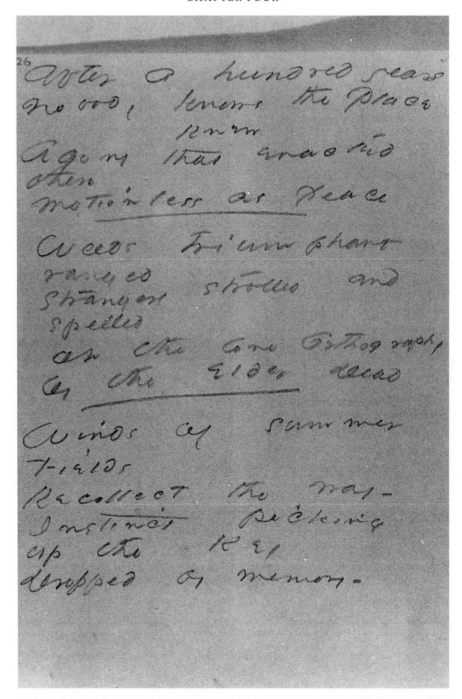

Figure 26a. Emily Dickinson, about 1868. Courtesy of Amherst College Archives and Special Collections (ED ms. 126, 126a).

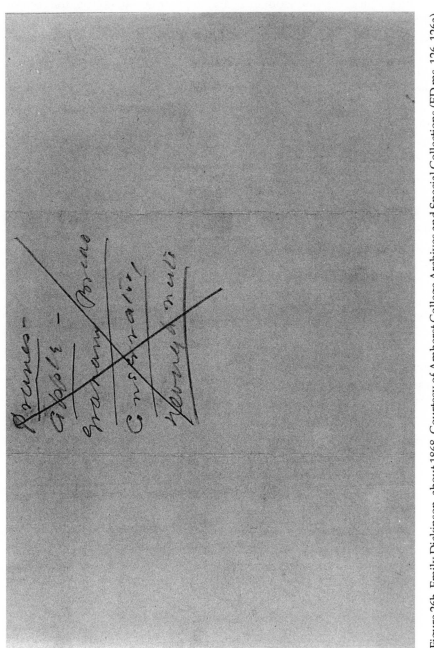

Figure 26b. Emily Dickinson, about 1868. Courtesy of Amherst College Archives and Special Collections (ED ms. 126, 126a).

tradition; by the lesbian retreating from and challenging straight norms; by the privileged white woman addressing her familiars from the comfort of her big house; by the one-woman avant-garde small press. The recursive logics of the lyric genre in which Dickinson's work has been received and of the gendered identity that has served to narrate her relation to that genre inevitably implicate the person in the poems.[5] Even if one were to show that Dickinson's writing was largely citational, thoroughly textual, intricately dialogic, and historically material, its subject would still "spell" Emily Dickinson.

Feminist theory has been vitally concerned with the forms of personal survival available in women's writing—"vitally" so since the rationale of feminist literary studies is at stake in them.[6] At least since the 1970s, Emily Dickinson has personified American feminism's investment in personal reference, and her writing has personified "a genre," as Sandra Gilbert and Susan Gubar put it, "that has traditionally been the most . . . assertive, daring, and therefore precarious of literary modes for women: lyric poetry."[7] Gilbert and Gubar's view of the lyric as self-referential had, as we have seen, a long history, but their view of the genre as "assertive" was their version of that history, and it followed from their Bloomian argument that the Anglo-American literary tradition is agonistic, and that to enter the literary field is, for a woman, a personal battle. On this logic, the more personal the genre, the braver the battle. Thus the conclusion of their argument took place over the body of Emily Dickinson, a body they identified not only with definitions of gender and genre (and gender in genre), but with a strangely anatomized version of writing itself. In their reading of the well-known lines that begin "A Word dropped / careless on a Page" (fig. 27; F 1268)—

A Word dropped

Careless on a Page

May stimulate an Eye
　　　Consecrate
When folded in perpetual seam

the Wrinkled Maker lie
　　　Author

Infection in the sentence breeds

~~And~~ we ~~may~~ inhale Despair

At distances of Centuries

From the malaria—[8]

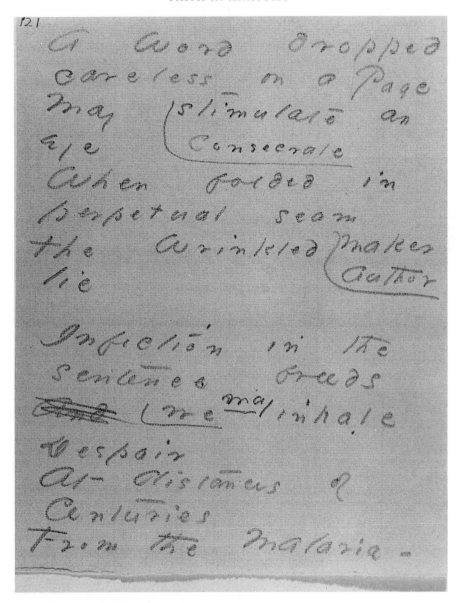

Figure 27. Emily Dickinson, about 1872. Courtesy of Amherst College Archives and Special Collections (ED ms. 121).

—for example, Gilbert and Gubar suggest that

for any reader, but especially for a reader who is also a writer, every text can become a "sentence" or weapon in a kind of metaphorical germ warfare. Beyond this, however, the fact that "infection in the sentence *breeds*" suggests Dickinson's recognition that literary texts are imprisoning, fever-inducing; that, since literature usurps a reader's interiority, it is an invasion of privacy. Moreover, given Dickinson's own gender definition, the sexual ambiguity of the poem's "Wrinkled Maker" is significant . . . even the maker of a text, when she is a woman, may feel imprisoned within texts—folded and "wrinkled" by their pages and thus trapped in their "perpetual seam[s]" which perpetually tell her how she *seems*.[9]

If Porter imagined the "invasion of privacy" described by the lines that begin "Alone and in a Circumstance" rather literally as a bug on the poet's privates, Gilbert and Gubar imagined literature as a figurative bug *in* the poet's privates. The stunning idea that "literature usurps a reader's interiority" exaggerates the phenomenology of the intersubjective confirmation of the self that we have noticed in nineteenth- and twentieth-century lyric reading; what is fascinating here is that overhearing a lyric voice or performing a lyric script has modulated into catching a lyric disease. Further, the critics' vocabulary of agency ("weapon," "warfare," "coercive," "imprisoning," "fever-inducing," "usurps," "invasion") overwhelms Dickinson's metaphor of disease and its pathos of indeterminate agency, turning a condition passed accidentally from one body to another into a narrative of the subjection of one body to another.[10] The body that is not Emily Dickinson's in this lurid scenario is the body of *literature.* But literature has no body. That may be why in another curious turn, Gilbert and Gubar stopped making literature an organic agent of violation, instead turning the poet into "wrinkled" paper, subjectively mirrored and "trapped" by pages that "perpetually tell her" about—of all things—herself. In literature, intersubjective confirmation seems to work both ways.

Dickinson would be happy to hear that, since in her scenario of "Infection in the sentence" the transmission of a page from one subject to another is, as we saw in the last chapter, much less sure of its destination. Indeed, the "Despair" on Dickinson's manuscript page is literally predicated by the most tentative part of the manuscript: an "And" that is crossed out, a bracket before "we," and a superscripted "may" that is underlined, either for emphasis or perhaps, like the bracket, to show that it is part of the line that ends with "inhale." Gilbert and Gubar used Johnson's 1955 edition for their reading, so that the line on their page read "We may inhale Despair" (J 1261). It is possible that if Johnson had printed Dickinson's underlining, feminist critics at the distance of a century *may* have allowed Dickinson's pathos of indeterminate literacy to infect their theory of "the woman writer and the anxiety of authorship," but it is also possible that it would have made no difference. It will certainly make no difference to future readers of Franklin's edition, since he prints the line as "And we inhale Despair," restoring the crossed-out "And" and deleting the emphasized "may." Apparently, literary transmission is not as tentative a business for Franklin as it may have been for Dickinson—if we are to judge by the words that Franklin intentionally sets on the page, and that Dickinson crossed over, out, and under. Dickinson's misery may not be communicable at distances of centuries because writers and editors and readers may be careful, but words are careless.

Or they *may* be. If the fantasy of an incarnate literary text animates Gilbert and Gubar's reading, a related fantasy has animated the more recent feminist critical turn to Dickinson's manuscripts and the feminist critique of Johnson's and Franklin's editorial choices. That imaginary is visible in the spectacular presentation and interpretation of Dickinson's late fragments by Marta Werner that I discussed in the first chapter, but its most influential expression has been Susan Howe's insistence on a return to the manuscripts as revelations of Dickinson's "visual intentionality," a version of textual materialism I invoked in the second chapter. We cannot experience "the layerings and fragile immediacies of [Dickinson's] multifaceted visual and verbal productions," Howe argues, in the "authoritative editions [that] freeze poems into artifacts."[11] How can we read, critique, construct and deconstruct Dickinson's intention, Howe asks, "before we have been allowed to even see what *she, Emily Dickinson*, reveals of her most profound self in the multiple multilayered scripts, sets, notes, and scraps she left us? I cannot murmur indifferently: 'What matter who's speaking?' I emphatically insist that it does matter who's speaking" (20). The brand of textual indeterminacy Howe takes to task here is Foucault's question in "What is an Author?"—a question that Foucault takes from Beckett. Although her own writing folds text into modern text into modern text, Howe insists that the problem with reducing the creator of the text to an "author function" is that we can no longer hear the poet's voice in her writing when it is reduced to "discourse"—or even when it is transcribed into print. That is, while Howe's reading is often focused on minute textual details (the placement of a dash, an ×, a -, the size of a letter, the space between letters), she reads the smallest aspects of Dickinson's handwriting not just as graphic marks, or even as performances of Dickinson's literary personae but, literally, as *"Emily Dickinson."* "I often wake up in the night," Howe confessed in an interview, "and think, No, I am wrong. She would not agree. She would be angry with me."[12] Because it is hard to imagine that intention is entirely visible in writing at distances of centuries, Howe wakes up worrying that she does not know what the many layers of script "say" after all, and she worries that in not knowing what they *may* say, she has personally violated Emily Dickinson, has made her "angry." Howe's deeply invested, deeply lyrical reading of Dickinson makes writing into personhood, but verges on despair at the prospect of making a person into writing.

The double bind that feminist critics of Emily Dickinson find themselves in is not new. In this chapter, I will suggest that Dickinson has epitomized assumptions about both literary and personal identity not only because those assumptions are always mediated by gender and genre, but because they participate in the notion that writing itself is incarnate. The impulse of the first part of what follows is thus historical, for in it I attempt to trace an arc away from the last hundred years' implicit identification of written letters with living persons. The question this chapter attempts to answer might be phrased, "How does writing come to be read *as* a person?" That is not at all the same thing as asking how writing came to be read as personal expression. In the fantasy of the incarnate letter that emerged in mid-nineteenth-century American thought, reading implicitly became identified with the immediate perception of the human body. If that seems an odd, though familiar idea, perhaps it is so both because of the difference between Dickinson's historical moment and our own *and* because the referential assumptions of that moment still subtend our own. That, in any case, is the implication of the Dickinson texts I will turn to in the second part of the chapter. In one small fascicle text and in the fragment of a private, now public letter, I will explore Dickinson's explicit analogies between writing and embodiment. Since such associations are deeply inscribed in the representative versions of the genre that has defined her practice as well as in representations of the gender that defined her person, my focus on writing will return to the feminist concern with the relation between the woman and the poem, a relation that Dickinson's writing made stranger than her later readers have wanted to admit. If print versions of Dickinson threaten to disarticulate the relation between the woman and the writing by abstracting her personal marks into the unmarked marks of the public sphere, the feminist reading of Dickinson in both print and manuscript has tried to restore the person to the poems, to mark the body that print makes disappear. But given the history of such interpretation, feminists might want to be careful how we do that. If we can neither place ourselves before or after the history of reading Emily Dickinson as a literary subject, in a place "Nobody knows" or *"knew,"* we may still learn to read her with almost as little hermeneutic defensiveness as she read herself. Almost. As Dickinson wrote of another poetic institution, "While Shakespeare remains Literature is firm—An Insect cannot run away with Achilles' Head" (L 368).

THE INTERPRETANT

Two very different thinkers in Dickinson's immediate intellectual culture—
the genteel critic so influential in presenting Dickinson to the public, and
a linguistic philosopher who never knew anything about her—seem to
have shared the strange assumption that the literal characters of the page
were instinct with embodiment. In his collection *Women and the Alphabet*
(assembled in 1900, though several of the essays were written earlier),
Higginson told a story about "the Invisible Lady" who,

> as advertised in all our cities a good many years ago, was a mysterious
> individual who remained unseen, and had apparently no human organs
> except a brain and a tongue. You asked questions of her, and she made in-
> telligent answers; but where she was, you could no more discover than
> you could find the man inside the Automaton Chess-Player. Was she in-
> tended as a satire on womankind, or as a sincere representation of what
> womankind should be? To many men, doubtless, she would have
> seemed the ideal of her sex, could only her brain and tongue have disap-
> peared like the rest of her faculties. Such men would have liked her al-
> most as well as that other mysterious personage on the London sign-
> board, labeled "The Good Woman," and represented by a female figure
> without a head.[13]

Higginson's interest here, as in his initial feminist argument in "Ought
Women to Learn the Alphabet?" forty years earlier, is in the cultural
enfranchisement—the cultural presence—of women.[14] It is in the service
of enfranchisement that he invokes the prejudice of the "many men" who
idealize female obscurity in the public sphere, men who either render
"womankind" incorporeal or who prefer their projected "mysterious personage" as a personification without a head.

Yet which is it to be? To be all mind or to be all body is to be "invisible"
in very different ways. The severed expression of "a brain and a tongue"
exerts an apposite personal agency to that of the obscenely decapitated
"Good Woman"; indeed, one wonders how the Invisible Lady could be
told apart from "the man inside the Automaton Chess Player" except by
the advertiser's label required to identify the person within the machine.
That the men who mythologized her "would have liked her almost as
well" as her exclusively sexualized counterpart reveals less, perhaps, from
our perspective, about the misogyny Higginson condemns than it does
about his own symptomatic confusion over where to locate (or how to
anatomize) the gendered identity for which he assumed advocacy. Talking

head or mute body—which would mark woman's characteristic acquisition of the alphabet, which one admit her to the culture of letters that would confer an identifiable written persona, a *literal* figural visibility?

Higginson's point, of course, is that, for the humanist project he has in mind, neither bisection will do. "Ceasing to be an Invisible Lady," the lettered woman "must become a visible force: there is no middle ground." Yet the force made visible by the disciplinary power of the alphabet remains entrenched in this middle ground in Higginson's feminist writings. In an essay on Sappho in 1871, for example, Higginson sought to endorse Welcker's 1816 article "Sappho Vindicated from a Prevailing Prejudice" by enforcing the distinction between autobiographical and dramatic reference in poetry. In response to another German scholar who emphasized Sappho's lesbian eroticism, Higginson thus writes that "he reads [Sappho's] graceful fragments as the sailors in some forecastle might read Juliet's soliloquies, or as a criminal lawyer reads in court the letters of some warm-hearted woman; the shame lying not in the words, but in the tongue."[15] The "tongue" that tells Sappho's graceful fragments as dirty jokes is in this case a synecdoche for the pejoratively masculinized representative body (a sailor, a criminal lawyer) that commits the vulgar faux pas of taking literature—and especially poetry—literally. "It is as if one were to cite Browning into court and undertake to convict him, on his own confession, of sharing every mental condition he describes."

Yet even as he indicts the becoming-literal of the literary—and the becoming-personal of personae—as a modern corruption more threatening than the sexual "cloud of reproach" it evokes, Higginson ends by displaying Sappho-the-woman as the index of his own civilizing aspirations. Whatever her life may turn out to have been, Higginson writes, "Sappho is gone," and

> modern nations must take up again the problem where Athens failed and Lesbos only pointed the way to the solution—to create a civilization where the highest culture will be extended to woman also. It is not enough that we should dream, with Plato, of a republic where man is free and woman but a serf. The aspirations of modern life culminate, like the greatest of modern poems, in the elevation of womanhood. *Die ewige Weibliche zieht uns hinan.*[16]

Under the sign of modernity, national and gendered identities are married in order to reproduce themselves as "the highest culture," a culture re-embodied by the now elevated—because dead—woman and by the characters of a literary language. The idealizing decorporealization of power that Higginson caricatured in "the Invisible Lady" he reads in a sincere register in his citation of Goethe's *Faust.* Unattributed and untranslated at the end of his essay, Higginson's allusion addresses an imagined community of educated readers of belles lettres, readers who are charged with reversing the errors of the sailors and lawyers, who recognize the ideally transcendent (rather than perversely literal) identity between gender and genre.[17] Yet even in the optative temporality into which the greatest of modern poems projects us (*zieht uns hinan*) Higginson's reiteration of the *grammatical* gender of Goethe's "Eternal Feminine" makes a quite literal slip. While the conceptual referent of *Weibliche* may seem to demand a feminine article, it is in the German language neuter: Goethe's line reads not *Die ewige Weibliche* but *Das ewig-Weibliche.* On the level of the alphabet, then, the difference an article (or three letters) can make enacts the conflation of gender and genre called forth by Higginson's citation. That is, it unwittingly performs the fantasy that grammar, like an anatomy, would be gendered not by arbitrary signs attached to a concatenation of mute bodies but would be subsumed by the eloquent rhetoric of natural law—the law of an embodied writing.

Higginson casts this law as, above all, *literary,* as he goes on to give various examples of the relation between literal and lettered womanhood, including not only Sappho, Faust, and Browning, but the notoriously public literary personae of Margaret Fuller and George Sand. Before turning back to a consideration of writings of the woman poet he introduced into this company in 1890 as one who "habitually concealed her mind, like her person, from all but a very few friends," who "was as invisible to the world as if she had dwelt in a nunnery" (*Poems* 1890, iii), I want instead to turn briefly to an unlikely analogue to the theory of anatomically scripted reference that Higginson's anecdotes and allusions tended to perform. During the 1860s and 1870s, when Higginson was writing his *Atlantic* essays in Cambridge and Dickinson was writing in Amherst, the philosopher Charles Sanders Peirce was developing in his early lectures at Harvard the semiotic logic that became the basis of American pragmatism. According to this logic, reference is always an emphatically empirical matter: as Peirce has it, "Nothing is assumed [in the semiotic] respecting what is thought which cannot be securely inferred from admissions which the thinker will make concerning external facts."[18] As Peirce represents these "facts," however, what is most secure about them is that they are, like Higginson's examples, based on the assumption that identity, in order to be empirically indicative, must be both modeled on the principles of natural law and at the same time susceptible to the abstraction of written representation. Indeed, Peirce's creation of the semiotic appears to have depended upon his presentation of writing as already embodied.

Thus in the lecture entitled "On a Method of Searching for the Categories" (1866), the three aspects of the semiotic—the "ground," the "cor-

relate," and the "interpretant"—all exhibit, in Peirce's illustratively pragmatic examples, the phantasmatic "fact" of the incarnate letter. His remarkable instance of the primary "ground" of referential thought is the
proposition, "Ink is black." "Here," Peirce writes—in one of many uses of
the deictic to express the principle of deixis—"the conception of *ink* is the
more immediate; that of *black* the more mediate, which to be predicated of
the former must be discriminated from it and considered *in itself* not as ap-
plied to an object but simply as embodying a quality, *blackness.* Now this
blackness is a pure *species* or abstraction, and its application is entirely hypothetical."[19] Although Peirce's term for "these conceptions between *being*
and *substance*" is "*accidents,*" there is, I would argue, nothing accidental
about his use of a thematics "embodying" writing to describe the process
of cognition. In the proposition "Ink is black," *ink* is the *substance* of the
proposition. As such, according to Peirce, it has no *being*, for "to say that
substance has being is absurd for it must cease to be substance before being
or non-being are applicable to it." The definition of a substance is, then,
that it can only find "being"—which, for semiosis, must mean *meaning*—
only by embodying an apprehensible "quality"; it is this quality, and not
the mute substance to which it attaches, that serves as the referential basis
for the passage of perception into legibility. "We mean the same thing
when we say 'the ink is black,'" Peirce writes, "as when we say 'there is
blackness in the ink': *embodying blackness* defines *black.*" Because "*embodying blackness* defines *black,*" blackness becomes what Peirce calls a "pure
abstraction," an elementary conception that can "arise only upon the re-
quirement of experience." We experience blackness; ink embodies this experience; ergo, blackness gives meaning to what defines it *as* a referent.
Blackness is what the ink-body means. And it may go without saying that
in the United States in 1866, such a structure of meaning naturally (as it
were) allows particular bodies to be signed into the cultural semantics of
"blackness."[20]

This is to say that the theory of indexical meaning that Peirce developed
turns personified abstractions into persons through the agency of the letter already embedded in the nineteenth-century American unconscious.
The third, synthesizing stage of the semiotic, the stage of "Representation," makes most explicit—and most problematic—the logic that transforms ink into bodies and bodies into ink. Because Peirce sees clearly that
referential meaning depends on the structure of a comparison (this he
calls the "correlate"), it is his articulation of that structure that bears the
weight of his theory. It is also, then, in his representative examples of representation, that we find the most complex and revealing description of
the mutual implication of anatomized letters and literalized anatomies.

Because that mutual implication is best traced not only in the examples themselves but in the way the logic moves *between* them—as Peirce would say, in the elementary conceptions entailed in their comparison—I will cite the passage on representation at some length in order to ask my reader to attend to the analogies through which one substance becomes a quality and again a substance, one letter becomes a body and again a letter:

> Reference to a correlate is clearly justified and made possible solely by comparison. Let us inquire, then, in what comparison consists. Suppose we wish to compare L and Γ; we shall imagine one of these letters to be turned over upon the line on which it is written as an axis; we shall then imagine that it is laid upon the other letter and that it is transparent so that we can see that the two coincide. In this way, we shall form a new image which mediates between the two letters, in as much as it represents one when turned over to be an exact likeness of the other. Suppose, we think of a murderer as being in relation to a murdered person; in this case we conceive the act of the murder, and in this conception it is represented that corresponding to every murderer (as well as to every murder) there is a murdered person; and thus we resort again to a mediating representation which represents the relate as standing for a correlate with which the mediating representation is itself in relation. Suppose, we look out the word *homme* in a French dictionary; we shall find opposite to it the word *man,* which, so placed, represents *homme* as representing the same two-legged creature which *man* itself represents. In a similar way, it will be found that every comparison requires, besides the related thing, the ground and the correlate, also a *mediating representation which represents the relate to be a representation of the same correlate which this mediating representation itself represents.* Such a mediating representation, I call an *interpretant,* because it fulfills the office of an interpreter who says that a foreigner says the same thing which he himself says.[21]

A transparent letter *L*; the act of murder; a two-legged creature; the translation of a foreign language: these are the instances Peirce offers to fulfill "the office" of representation. The story that this sequence itself tells about that office would fill volumes—but let me just point to its cast of characters. First, enter the material letter *L* and its transposition: this character is "material" because it may be manipulated into a mark that can be *seen* but not read. According to Peirce, in order to turn seeing into "reference" (perception into cognition), we must literally translate—or carry over—one typeface to another: Γ becomes "transparent" to *L* in this translation, "so that we can see that the two coincide." What is canny about the instruction is that it mimes the interpretive practice that it also determines, thus making the unconditional agency of imagination (invoked by the passage's reiterated imperative, "*Suppose . . .*") seem "an exact likeness" of a literacy already conditioning these terms. This example makes reading appear an empirical process by challenging the reader not to do it. We are not actually asked to recognize *L* as a letter of the roman alphabet or to interpret Γ as, say, a Greek capital gamma; we are merely asked to superimpose these shapes by lifting them, in the mind, off of the page. The "new image" so lifted "mediates between the two letters" because it seems to simply reflect their anatomy rather than to construct their meaning.

Yet a murderer's relation to a murdered person could hardly be thought analogous to the "transparent" relation between a right-side-up and upside-down letter of the alphabet—or could it? In order to mediate between the terms of this second comparison, "we conceive the act of the murder," an act that acts as the film through which we are to picture—as if empirically—the two as coincidental or the same. The potential violence of the as-if quality of the notion of an empirical identity begins to emerge here as a property not only of the image of murder but of the image of the letter (and even of the *-er* suffix that transliterates one into the other). That potential then underwrites, as it were, Peirce's third example, in which he anthropomorphizes the relation between the imaginary play of the letter and the corpse it may leave in its wake. What unites the French *homme* and the English *man* is not the French dictionary, which merely places one word "opposite" to another, but the idea of a "two-legged creature." The representation produced by the facing-off of the two words in the lexicon (which acts, by the way, like the "new image" in the passage's first example and like the ink in Peirce's earlier proposition, as the mute reflective substance of this apposition, its mirror) has a long history in letters. From Oedipus's riddle to Shakespeare's "bare forked animal," the two-leggedness of the "creature which *man* itself represents" has stood as the problematic figure of the human sacrifice entailed in the semiosis of the human. The potentially tragic consequences of anatomizing *h-o-m-m-e* or *m-a-n as if* the word were not itself the creature of Western strategies of representation—that is, as if an alphabet could be translated into perception as a transparently self-identified body—may cause Peirce to "say the same thing which he himself says," and yet to end up writing something different.

The difference inherent in each of Peirce's suppositions is the subjective agency invoked in and as the very "mediating representation" that is directed to translate them as instances of the same. His description ends up performing exactly the opposite "office" than the one it states as its purpose because he grounds it in the anatomical imaginary his thought implicitly associates with the materiality of writing. Walter Benn Michaels and Michael Fried have argued that such an association characterizes various American texts of the second half of the nineteenth century in which "writing as such becomes an epitome of a notion of identity as difference from itself (in that writing *to be* writing must in some sense be different from the mark that simply materially it is); and that this is important above all because, in those texts and others, the possibility of difference from itself emerges as crucial to a concept of personhood that would distinguish persons from both pure spirit . . . and from pure matter."[22] If indeed Michaels and Fried are right to point to writing as "an epitome" of mid-to-late nineteenth-century versions of subjectivity, even my brief examples from Higginson and Peirce suggest that they may be cutting off (that is, themselves *epitomizing*) half of the analogy's point.

What mediates between spirit and matter, what a letter means and what a letter is? For both Higginson and Peirce, and, I would argue, for Fried and Michaels, the function that Peirce would call the "interpretant" is performed by literature. Literary figures explain the relation between anatomy and letters. In the second half of this chapter, I will turn to some of the ways in which Dickinson associated her culture's rhetorical inscription of personhood with various forms of literary mediation. Because the relation between the ideality and materiality of personhood and the ideality and materiality of writing is, as we have seen, already embedded in the discourse of the genre that has come to define Dickinson's writing, her associations often turn a precise and excruciating focus on the role of the lyric reader who, like Higginson and Peirce and their twentieth-century successors, would suppose that letters could refer—even in their differences—to bodies.

"No Bird—yet rode in Ether—"

Consider what the following short text from one of the unbound sets (fig. 28; set 5), written toward the end of the war in early 1865, does to the notion of subjective—and anatomically inscribed—lyric reference:

> Split the Lark—and
> you'll find the Music—
> Bulb after Bulb, in
> Silver rolled—
> Scantily dealt to the
> Summer Morning
> Saved for your Ear, when
> Lutes be old
>
> Loose the Flood—
> you shall find it patent—

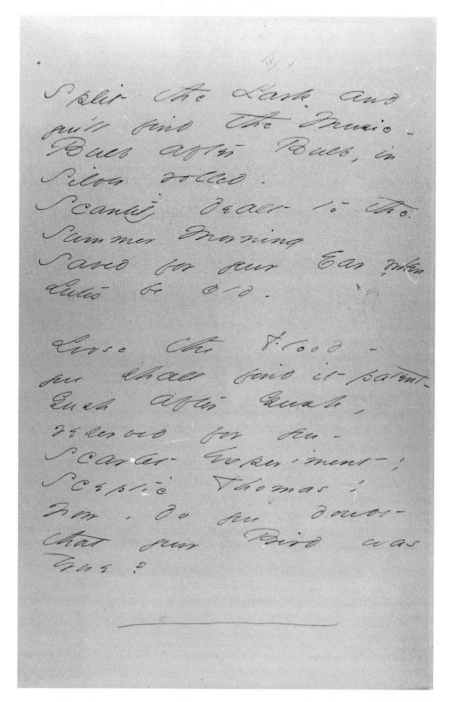

Figure 28. Emily Dickinson, 1865. Courtesy of Amherst College Archives and Special Collections (ED ms. No. 87-3, verso).

Gush after Gush,
reserved for you—
Scarlet Experiment!
Sceptic Thomas!
Now—do you doubt
that your Bird was
true? (F 905)

This text stages the act of its own reading in sadomasochistic terms. What is perhaps less obvious about this rather offensive staging is that its terms are drawn from a nineteenth-century discourse already troubled by the approach to written—and particularly literary—representation that Dickinson here parodies. By "perhaps less obvious," I mean that literary critics since 1896, when these lines were first printed as a lyric, have consistently interpreted it as the poet's lyrical send-up of scientific empiricism. An anonymous reviewer for the 1896 *Boston Beacon* went so far as to suggest that it be read as the bird's dramatic monologue: "Miss Dickinson rarely falls into another's manner," the reviewer remarks, "but could Browning himself have bettered this?" Such an odd aesthetic apprehension of Dickinson's text may be due in part to the rather odd title given the poem by Todd: "Loyalty." The literary framing—genre identification, bound publication, title, critical review—seems to have invited a legacy of the sort of educated response that Higginson (that other reader of Browning) would have counted on. Thus a more recent critic explains that "the poem's real meaning is inverted" so that rather than cooperating with the demand for proof, "this poetic experiment effectively disposes of the empirical approach."[23] One sees the point: poetic trope reverses apparent meaning, whether in the Victorian personage of a dramatic speaker, or in the New Critical understanding of the artistic function of irony. Either way, the image that mediates between the letters on the page and their "real" meaningful inversion is Literature (and especially lyric) with a capital *L*. Yet lyric—or, specifically, the reading of it as indexical cultural identity— may itself be the object of Dickinson's perverse anatomy lesson.

For, suppose you split a lark: what you will find, at least in Dickinson's first stanza, is poetry. Birdsong is Dickinson's figure for poetic writing in (by my last count) over three hundred texts, and it is the subject of her elegies for several women poets, notably Charlotte Brontë and Elizabeth Barrett Browning. In the beautiful elegy for Brontë (F 146; fascicle 7), the death of the woman is conflated with the death of the literary pseudonym "Currer Bell," which is said to migrate as

This Bird—observing others
When frosts too sharp became

187

> Retire to other latitudes—
> Quietly did the same—
>
> But differed in returning—

The place to which "Currer Bell" differed in returning is, of course, the grave, but it is also the locus of lyric,

> Since Yorkshire hills are green—
> Yet not in all the nests I meet—
> Can Nightingale be seen—[24]

The invisible location of the embodied source of lyric song is the familiar topos of romantic poetics that Dickinson evokes here, for, as we remember from Shelley's figuration of it, the poet is "a nightingale, who sits in darkness and sings to cheer its own solitude with sweet sounds; his auditors are as men entranced by the melody of an unseen musician, who feel that they are moved and softened, but know not whence or why." In the romantic ideal of lyric affect, bird-poets would have no bodies. In Shelley's "To a Sky-Lark," the object of poetic address is actually the literary dissolution of the body:

> Hail to thee, blithe Spirit!
> Bird thou never wert—
> That from Heaven, or near it,
> Pourest thy full heart
> In profuse strains of unpremeditated art.

"Like an unbodied joy," Shelley's lark bleeds only music. Dickinson's lark, however, produces a bizarrely literal (or "Scarlet") version of Shelley's "profuse strains." Her parody is too strong *not* to be of Shelley, but it is also mediated by yet another nineteenth-century poetic treatment of the Shelleyan lyric ideal, a rather incidental passage in Barrett Browning's *Aurora Leigh* in which the poet Aurora reflects that

> The music soars within the little lark,
> And the lark soars. It is not thus with men.
> We do not make our places with our strains,
> Content, while they rise, to remain behind
> Alone on earth instead of so in heaven.[25]

That the difference between real and metaphorical identities should be remarked by allusion to a poem about the career of a woman poet who is here writing a poem alluding to Shelley goes some way toward indicating how intimately sexual difference is associated with literary anatomies in the several birds Dickinson's text (with such violence toward the letter of its sources) begins to splinter. The "Bulb after Bulb, in / Silver rolled—" revealed in the fascicle lines echoes her elegy for Barrett Browning in which "Silver—perished—with her Tongue—" (F 600).[26] In the elegy, written perhaps two years earlier than "Split the Lark—," the relation between the poet and her aesthetic trace is also cast as consubstantial, nature and artifice having become impossible to tell apart:

> Not on Record bubbled other,
> Flute, or Woman, so divine—

Yet whereas the elegy mourns the mutual passing of "Silver" and Tongue," "Flute, or Woman," its conclusion also plays upon a way in which writing might alter personhood, and particularly sexual identity, as well as already be inscribed within it:

> What, and if, Ourself a Bridegroom—
> Put her down—in Italy?

The place in which Barrett Browning made her last strains is here imagined, if only in hesitation, as a land in which lyric strains would make "our places" different. In the lines that begin "Split the Lark," however, such a utopian possibility is checked by the incorporation of a reader who will insist that the lyric subject, in its very ethereal character, remain identifiably corporeal.[27]

To return for a moment, then, in a different strain, to the structure of Peirce's literally anatomized semiotic, what Dickinson's writing tends to do is to expose the "ground" of lyric reference as the oxymoron of an embodied abstraction. While Shelley's poem, bent on abstracting embodiment, is addressed to the lark, and Barrett Browning's is addressed to the pathos of such abstraction, Dickinson addresses "Sceptic Thomas," the type par excellence of the interpreter who demands that cognitive apprehension be secured by the evidence and pathos of physical fact. Christ, we recall, admonishes Thomas for his need for substantiation, but the story of Thomas, told at the end of John, is also the occasion for one of the paradigmatic teachings of the incarnation:

> Now Thomas, one of the twelve, called the Twin, was not with them when Jesus came. So the other disciples told him, "We have seen the Lord." But he said to them, "Unless I see in his hands the print of the nails, and place my finger in the mark of the nails, and place my hand in his side, I will not believe."
> Eight days later, his disciples were again in the house, and Thomas was

with them. The doors were shut, but Jesus came and stood among them, and said "Peace be with you." Then he said to Thomas, "Put your finger here, and see my hands; and put out your hand, and place it in my side; do not be faithless, but believing." (John 20:24–29)

Perhaps Thomas should not want to touch Christ's wounds, but as Elaine Scarry has read this passage, what Thomas finds in Christ's flesh is that "the Word of God materializes itself in the body of God, thereby locating voice and body, creator and created, in the same site, no longer stranded from one another as separate categories, thus also inviting humanity to recognize themselves as, although created, simultaneously creators."[28] Thomas's function is thus not only that of the interpreter but, in Peirce's terms, of the *interpretant:* he is himself a "mediating representation." As such, he performs the creative office of mirroring the spiritual materiality of the embodied God—yet Dickinson's version of that reflection is rather more disturbing than Scarry's. As Christopher Benfey has pointed out, Dickinson's "Thomas's doubt and his demand for proof are as faithless and murderous as the demands of the crucifiers."[29] Murderous, yes. But perhaps Thomas's "demand for proof" has such tragic consequences in Dickinson's lines not because of his scepticism but because he represents the cultural belief that the "patent" poetic subject—both opened or dilated and published, or officially sealed—is not composed of separate categories but is materialized in and as writing.

That, at least, is the suggestion of another of Dickinson's texts in which Thomas's demand to touch the word effects a dismemberment of the identities ascribed to both gender and genre. This text (fig. 29) is from one of Dickinson's infamous "Master" letters, the letters "patent," we might say, of Dickinson studies, the manuscripts that have seemed to Dickinson scholars to offer the most enticing clues to the identity of the woman behind the poems and therefore to officiate most authoritatively in their interpretation. Preserved in their unaddressed envelopes (they appear to be fair copies), and left unpublished in their entirety for almost a century, these letters have come to bear "the burden of proof" for the shelves of narratives generated by Dickinson's writing[30]: her attachment to a married clergyman, her fantasies about a married journalist, her passion for her father's best friend, her schizophrenia, her abortion, her lesbian desire.[31] The creative recognition that these private letters have invited has indeed located voice and body "in the same site." The following letter, however, seems, in light of the present discussion to hint at what remains dangerous about such mutual locations—not only when, as Higginson would have it, the literal takes the place of the literary, but when the literary assumes the status of the literal.

190

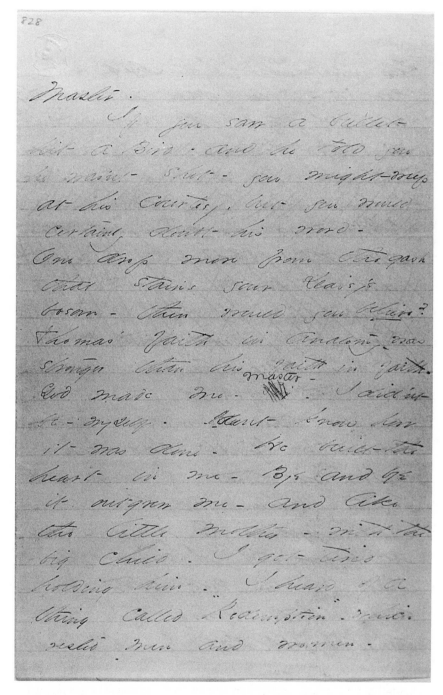

Figure 29. Emily Dickinson to "Master," around 1861. Courtesy of Amherst College Archives and Special Collections (ED ms. 828).

Here is the opening of the letter:

> Master—
>
> If you saw a bullet hit a Bird—and he told you he wasn't shot—you might weep at his courtesy, but you would certainly doubt his word—
>
> One drop more from the gash that stains your Daisy's bosom—then would you *believe?* Thomas' faith in anatomy—was stronger than his faith in faith.[32]

Three discrete representations of the relation between body and voice, sentience and written expression make up this appeal. The first is hypothetical: imagine, reader that a bird who could talk (a poetic text?) "told you he wasn't shot" when you had seen the wound with your own eyes. As in "Split the Lark—," the assumption here is that the wounded body will make the more compelling claim on the imagination. Bullets don't lie. ("Suppose, we think of a murderer as being in relation to a murdered person; in this case we conceive of the act of murder"). But this is a version of substantiation in the frankly fictive conditional. When the representation of the wounded body shifts, so does the *tense* of representation: now witness, reader, "One drop more from the gash that stains your Daisy's bosom." The shift in tense can only be made on the basis of a shift in reference, from fictional "Bird" to a differently fictional "Daisy." The more intimate address of the second figure also depends on a pseudonym, but here it is a more explicitly literary one, since this is the name Dickinson uses for the subject of the Master letters as well as for the subject of many verses on romantic love.[33] The "Daisy," then, bleeds (in catachresis) in the present tense but the question to the reader ("then would you *believe?*") must be phrased in a deictic indicating another conditional: the deferred time of reading. "Thomas' faith in anatomy" is by this point quite explicitly a faith in the written letter *as* an anatomy, a conviction that the "one drop more . . . that stains your Daisy's bosom" is made of ink and that this ink embodies the quality of an identity. Thus this Thomas is said to believe not simply that the imagery of the wounded body may be used to substantiate writing—i.e., if I bleed, *then* would you believe me?—but that the materiality of writing may substantiate a body historically subject to the inversions and perversions of reading (i.e., "put your finger here, and see my hands"). Curiously, it seems to be precisely this latter conviction—so satirically indicted in the lines that begin "Split the Lark—" and rather more painfully and intimately exposed in the "Master" letter—that has informed the feminist reconstruction of Dickinson as a literary subject.

While Dickinson's writing often aggressively invites such readings, we should attend to the address on the invitation. Just after the lines in the letter on "Thomas's faith in anatomy" we may read (or barely discern, so much of the letter is crossed out, the words typographically bracketed here partially concealed from view [fig. 30]):

> God made me—Sir—/Master—/I didn't
> be—myself—[He?] I don't know how
> it was done—He built the
> heart in me—and like
> the little mother—With the
> big child—I got tired
> holding him—I heard of a
> thing called "Redemption"—which
> rested men and women—
> You remember I asked you
> for it—you gave me something
> else—I forgot the Redemption
> ~~in the Redeemed—I didn't~~
> ~~tell you for a long time—but~~
> ~~I knew you had altered me—I~~
> [in the Redeemed—I didn't
> tell you for a long time—but
> I knew you had altered me—I]
> /and/ was tired—no more[x]

> [x]No Rose, yet felt myself a'bloom,
> No Bird—yet rode in Ether—[34]

Having made the reader complicit in the construction of the subject, and having made jarringly explicit how that complicity shifts the place of the subject from wounded Bird to wounded Daisy to the wounded and risen Christ, the letter now reveals that the wound in identity is the wound *of* identity—a letter already written there. This inscription intensifies as well as undermines Gilbert and Gubar's claim that in the way Dickinson wrote "the fiction of her life, a wound has become Dickinson's ontological home."[35] What they aptly term the "hectic rhetoric" of the "Master" letter suggests that the wound is more intimate than feminist criticism generally has imagined: it is not just a theme in the writer's "fiction," but the very condition of ontology, the way the subject is "made" or "built"—or written. This is why the costs of opening it to view may also split it apart. Thus the childishly agrammatical "I didn't be—myself—" may mean both "I did not bring myself into being" and "What I am is not myself" (a pun that would make the line anything but the utterance of a childish per-

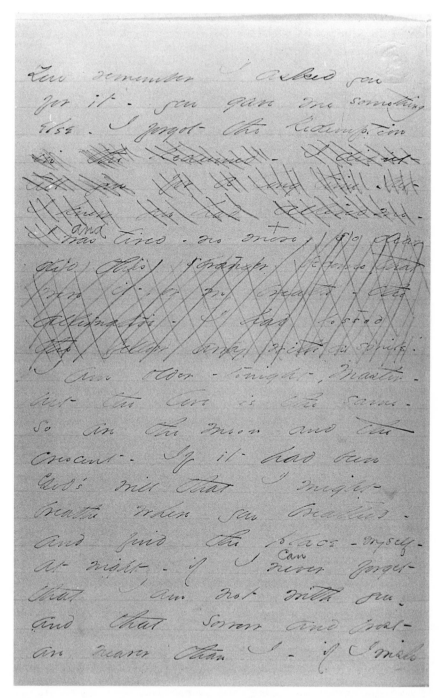

Figure 30. Emily Dickinson to "Master," second page of fig. 29. Courtesy of Amherst College Archives and Special Collections (ED ms. 828).

sona). In effect, the distance between these two possibilities closes dramatically when "the / heart" which is not "my heart" but "the / heart in me" acquires its own agency, dwarfing the self of which it becomes much more than a part: "It outgrew me—and like the little mother—with the big child—I got tired holding him." What is built into the self turns out to have been inseminated: as this script is increasingly determined by the reader's "faith in anatomy," the body begins to be placed outside itself, assuming not only disproportionate size but a disproportionate gender. The "thing called 'Redemption'" would, presumably, if it were not in quotation marks, restore the writer to herself, but marked as the word is by its own iteration, it cannot ransom her. She receives instead "something else," is "altered" yet again, and in a way that this time occasions not a switch in gender but in genre: here the only lines of verse that punctuate the "Master" letters are keyed for insertion.[36] "No Rose," and yet "a'bloom," "No Bird," yet "in Ether," the writer momentarily makes her places with her strains. There is another text that these lines literally repress, however, written in ink and crosshatched in the same pencil with which the verse was written in. After "[I] / [and], was tired—no more," we *may* read,

~~so dear~~

~~did this stranger become, that~~

~~were it, or my breath—the~~

~~alternative—I had tossed~~

~~the fellow away with a smile,~~

[—so dear
did this stranger become, that
were it, or my breath—the
alternative—I had tossed
the fellow away with a smile,]

This version of redemption differs significantly from that of the lovely verse interpolation. "This stranger" is more closely related to "the big child" grown out of the built-in heart, but it is also the "something else" offered as "Redemption" for the burden of written otherness, the effect of what the addressee reclaims, "the Redeemed." The "it" that has haunted self-inscription from the beginning is at once "dear" and a "stranger," and the strangeness of its dearness becomes evident when "the alternative" of a choice between the two is posed: "were it, or my breath—the / alternative—I had tossed / the fellow away with a smile." Does "the fellow" refer to "this stranger" or to "my breath"? The slip of the pen both parallels and unravels the optative verse alternative: the "No . . . yet" syntax occasioned by the shift in genre is an echo of the confusion of desire briefly exposed by the letter's grammatical confusion of gender. The verse lines do not

195

transcend the anatomical imaginary but repeat it in another key. Even in her inadvertantly transgressive moment, the writer finds that both sexual and literary identity have already arisen from the act of writing, that she has invoked the strains of "something else" in her place.

THE QUEEN'S PLACE

In the "Master" letter such textual displacements seem both tragic and inevitable (or tragic because inevitable), as in part, in the pathos of self-experience the letter represents, they must be. The mock-pathos and mock-tragedy of the lines that begin "Split the Lark—" suggest that irony may provide a wedge between the demands of "Sceptic Thomas" and the subject of those demands, and yet the exhibition and dissection of the poetic figure are the costs of addressing the lyric reader's "doubt" as well as his "faith." How might we begin to read Dickinson differently, against rather than in the grain of these appeals? Can Dickinson's writing be said to alter cultural assumptions about the inscription of personal and literary reference in any way other than the performance of their costs?[37] The examples I have chosen in this and other chapters have been intended as invitations to my reader to entertain the possibility that other "interpretants," other forms of referential mediation, are indeed central to the conditions of Dickinson's writing—though how the material history of that writing affects interpretation we may yet be too indebted to nineteenth-century Thomases to see.

In his reading of Whitman's multiple revisions of *Leaves of Grass*, Michael Moon has taken a giant step away from the Thomases by suggesting that

> in an attempt to exceed or "go beyond" the modes of representing human embodiment in the discourse of his age, Whitman set himself the problem of attempting to project actual physical presence in a literary text. At the heart of this problem was the impossibility of doing so literally, of successfully disseminating the author's literal bodily presence through the medium of a book. As a consequence of this impossibility, Whitman found it necessary to undertake the project of producing metonymic substitutes for the author's literal corporeal presence in the text. Out of this difficulty arises the generative contradiction in the text of *Leaves of Grass* as I read it: that which exists between Whitman's repeated assertions that he provides loving physical presence in the text and his awareness of the frustrating but ultimately incontrovertible conditions of writing and embodiment that actually render it impossible for him to produce in his writing more than metonymic substitutes for such contact.[38]

Now, Moon is writing about Whitman, and in some ways that makes all the difference between his revisionary critical project and this one—since, pace a tradition of criticism that pairs them as the great protomodernist, experimental American poets of the nineteenth century, there have never been two writers less like one another than Whitman and Dickinson. One thing they do have in common is the discourse of embodiment to which Moon refers—but whereas he reads Whitman's writing as an attempt to put the (especially male, queer) body into a nineteenth-century discourse that had excised it, I read Dickinson's writing as an attempt to extricate the (especially female, queer) body from a nineteenth-century discourse that had incorporated it.

The reception of Whitman and Dickinson has conflated their very different, even opposed relation to discourses of embodiment because that reception has so essentially lyricized both writers. Both Whitman and Dickinson have become the great American poets of the self, but that is certainly not what they *were*. They both understood the lyric as one of the genres of personified identification that they sought to revise, or redeem. As Moon points out, Whitman did so by revising, over and over, the form of his writing's circulation—by revising, over and over, the same "book." And as Michael Warner has pointed out, part of the contradiction of that insistent revision is "its own perverse publicity . . . its use of a print public-sphere mode of address" at the same time that Whitman keeps coming on to us, keeps beckoning, "Come closer to me."[39] Many feminist critics would claim that Dickinson also revised the form of her writing's circulation, and that rather than cultivate the contradiction of print public-sphere address, she cultivated the contradiction of scribal private-sphere address. On this view, what is perverse about Dickinson's attempt to circulate the "author's literal corporeal presence in the text" is that the manuscript forms in which she chose to do so can no longer circulate, or could just possibly still almost do so in less corporeal fashion in images on the Web or in what Susan Howe and the Dickinson Electronic Archive imagine as a facsimile edition of all the extant manuscripts.[40] But as we have seen, the cultivated perversity of Dickinson's mode of circulation consisted in disentangling rather than extenuating the cultural identification of personhood with writing. Like Whitman, she did so with what Moon calls metonyms, but unlike Whitman, Dickinson did not spin off substitutes for personal affectionate presence in print. Instead, she enclosed things in or stuck things to her writing. She distracted Thomas's gaze by giving him something else to touch.

Yet most of those things are gone. The dead cricket, various flowers or pieces of flowers, some clippings, a stamp, a few bits of fabric have survived in the archive, but the point of Dickinson's familiar circulation of these enclosures was not their survival but their ephemeral recognition. That everyday recognition, that exchange of ephemera, was not, as Howe and other feminist readers of the manuscripts have argued, opposed to the conditions of print. As we have seen, Dickinson (often literally) enfolded print into her writing; I have been suggesting that if Emily Dickinson does not live and breathe in her writing, she *did* live and breathe print culture. As we have also seen, various pages and marks of that print culture not only made their way into her writing, but provided the pages on which she wrote. For Dickinson, print literally did precede handwriting, and part of the effect of its doing so is often to decorporealize and yet personalize that writing. Sometimes it is difficult to say whether the words that Dickinson then "dropped" onto those printed pages are "careless" or intentional, though the lines Dickinson wrote around 1867 on the verso of an advertising flier for "Orr's Boneset Bitters and Lavender Cordial" (figs. 31a, 31b), are at the very least suggestive, at least at the distance of over a century:

> The Merchant of the Picturesque
> A Counter has and sales
> But is within or negative
> Precisely as the calls—
> To Children he is small in price
> And large in courtesy—
> It suits him better than a check
> Their artless currency—
> Of Counterfeits he is so shy
> Do one advance so near
> As to behold his ample flight—
> (F 1134)[41]

Given the elaborate ad, it is hard not to read "The Merchant of the Picturesque" as counterpart to Orr himself, or to read the print representation of Dr. Orr's "sales" as Dickinson's "Counter." While Samuel K. Orr promises to set your bones, to anatomize you, "the Merchant of the Picturesque" is not available on demand. Yet we do not know if Dickinson's joke (if that's what it was) was addressed to anyone but herself. This is the only manuscript version of the lines, and they are barely legible at this distance.

And the situation of most of Dickinson's manuscripts is even more pathetic. So how would we have any idea what or who or where they may have pointed, other than to "Emily Dickinson"? The fragment of the lines that begin "'Lethe' in my flower" (fig. 32), for example, is all that is left of the fascicle manuscript that Todd transcribed before she or someone else crossed out and cut up the lines that begin "One Sister have I in the house—" (F 5; fascicle 2) to which the now fragmentary lines were attached. Another copy of the canceled lines was sent to Susan Dickinson in 1858, and her daughter, later Martha Dickinson Bianchi, pasted that manuscript into her copy of *The Single Hound*, her 1914 print edition of verse that Dickinson sent to her mother, a copy now kept at Harvard. The lines read:

> "Lethe" in my flower,
> Of which they who drink
> In the fadeless Orchards
> Hear the bobolink!
>
> Merely flake or petal
> As the Eye beholds
> Jupiter! My father!
> I perceive the rose!
> (F 54)

If it is clear that the lines attached to these lines in manuscript were directly addressed to Susan (perhaps as a birthday present), there is no historical provenance for the lines Todd transcribed, no evidence of a metonymic enclosure that would attract our attention away from the lines themselves—and yet such a principle of distracted literary perception is what the lines are about. The first four lines are a stunning condensation of Keats's Nightingale Ode (hence the citation of "Lethe" in Dickinson's first line from Keats's fourth), a variation on the play of identification with a romantic lyric figure that we noticed in the lines that begin "Split the Lark—." Yet the substitution of the homely American "bobolink" for the nightingale's "full-throated ease" and the transference of Keats's "vintage" to the lines themselves allow an astonishing shift in the referential layers intrinsic to lyric reading dissected in "Split the Lark—." The alien corn in which Keats's subject must stand in relation to the "immortal Bird" has been replaced by what "the Eye beholds" in Dickinson's. In Keats's address to the nightingale, "thy plaintive anthem fades" because it cannot be kept physically near; in Dickinson's poem, "my flower" contains "fadeless orchards" because, though "merely flake or petal," it appears to be *there* to point to. Whether "Jupiter" names the masculine addressee (a sort of apotheosis of the "Master" or Thomas) or a patriarchal principle that collapses myth into immediate perception is anyone's guess. And it is anyone's guess whether the rose was there to perceive (though my educated guess is that it was). These lines do not finally point toward "Dickinson" but toward something lost and now unnamed and unnameable—toward a less metaphorical context now faded from view.

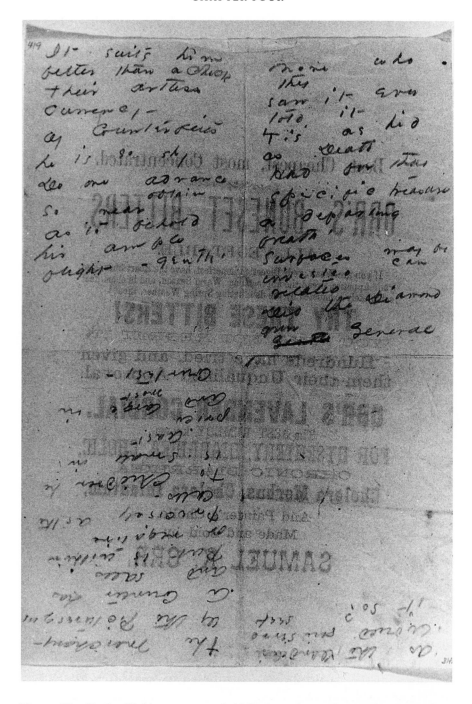

Figure 31a. Emily Dickinson, around 1867. In order to begin the "poem" as reprinted here, the photograph above must be turned upside down. Courtesy of Amherst College Archives and Special Collections (ED ms. 4190).

Figure 31b. Verso of manuscript in fig. 31a. Orr was both the druggist advertised by and the printer of the flier. Courtesy of Amherst College Archives and Special Collections.

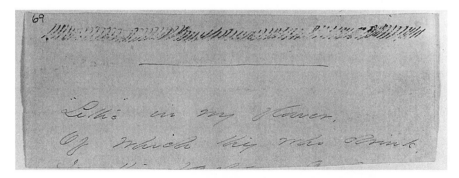

Figure 32. Courtesy of Amherst College Archives and Special Collections (ED ms. 69).

We can (and inevitably will) keep reading Emily Dickinson as one of the great examples of a subjectivity committed to the page. Yet the very insistence of that commitment urges us to reconsider our placement of the subject on the page, or within the identifying loops of reading through which she predicted her writing would be mastered.[42] In order to avoid simply repeating the interpretation foretold by that writing, perhaps we need to begin by imagining letters as something stranger than anatomies. One final detail of the "Master" letter manuscript is so strange that I hesitate to call attention to it—and yet I will do so because such hesitations are also telling. In the section of the letter that just follows the passage cited above, Dickinson writes, "if I wish with a might I cannot repress—that mine were the Queen's place—the love of the—Plantagenet is my only apology." What "the Queen's place" might be is not specified, and in any case it is not much of an apology. The referent might be part of a discourse familiar to the addressee, or it might be part of the letter's ongoing struggle over the writer's "place." If we were to speculate on the image lyrically along these lines, we could refer it to the writer's depiction of herself as "The Queen of Cavalry—" (F 347) and to the desire for a queenly sovereignty that she either refuses or fails to obtain in such poems as "Of Bronze—and Blaze—" (F 319), "I'm ceded—I've stopped being Their's" (F 353), "Title divine, is mine" (F 1072) or "Like Eyes that looked on Wastes—" (F 693). In other words, we could make the image into another poem.

But there is another detail of this letter that, once noticed, might prove distracting to such a lyric reading—a detail we cannot help but perceive, once we see it, as at once inside and outside the lines, rather like the stamp and clippings with which this chapter began. In a tiny frame in the left-hand corner of the stationery on which the letter is written there is the embossed head of a queen poised over the capital letter *L* (fig. 33). The first stroke of the "*w*" in "with" ("with a might I cannot repress") just brushes the edge of the boss's frame. The resistance that most readers will feel to any connection

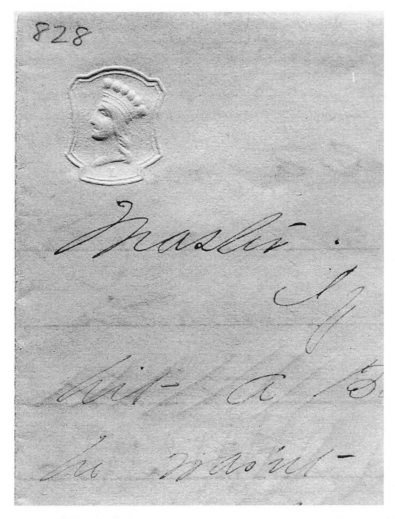

Figure 33. Detail of letter in fig. 29. Courtesy of Amherst College Archives and Special Collections.

between the place of the queen's seal (the Queen of the *L*, we might say, the Queen of the Letter) and the place to which the writer's desire points may be taken as a measure of just how deeply repressed the historical scene of writing must be when the identity of the writer is prescribed in advance. In order to redeem a version of written identity from the transparency effected by the civilizing aspirations of the nineteenth-century legacy of a faith in anatomy, an "Orthography" imaged as neither warm and capable of earnest grasping nor as a dissected and speech-producing body should be brought into view:—See here it is—I hold it towards you.

Dickinson's Misery

"Misery, how fair"

I HAVE NOT BEEN arguing so far that Dickinson did not write lyrics. I have shown that she did not write the lyrics we have read: since the lyric is a creature of modern interpretation, I have suggested that we have made her writing *into* the genre we have read. In some ways, that is a story with a happy ending: as her sister Lavinia wrote in 1890, in gratitude to the editors who first made Dickinson's writing into a book, "the 'poems' would die in the box where they were found" had they not been published and received as lyrics.[1] The many historical versions of those lyrics, the many ways in which they have reflected public interest, have made them a collective enterprise, vehicles for over a century of cultural expression. Yet as I have suggested, that collective identification of and with Emily Dickinson has depended on our construction of her lyrics as private utterances. Her poems can speak for all of us because they do not speak *to* any of us—or so readers have seemed to believe. The persistence of that belief is curious, given what we have noticed about Dickinson's forms and habits of address as well as about her writing's acute concern with—even paranoia about—the ways in which what she wrote would or would not be read, who would read her, when and where. Yet that concern, too, has become part of our definition of the lyric in modernity, as the interpretation of privacy has become one way to understand public life, and as the interpretation of the lyric has come to depend on reflexivity, on formal and rhetorical self-awareness. As the lyric has been taken to represent individual expression, it has also become representative of *our* individual expression—whoever we are. Susan Stewart has recently made an impassioned plea for poetry as "a force against effacement—not merely for individuals but for communities through time as well."[2] But how have we reached the point of supposing that lyric expression represents a struggle against the threat of identity's loss? And how and why has the reading of Emily Dickinson identified her as the figure who represents as well as resists that loss? In the first and second chapters, I suggested some answers to that question from the perspectives of twentieth- and twenty-first-century American lyric editing and theories of lyric reading, and in the third and fourth chapters, I suggested that those answers were derived in part from notions about reference to others and reference to oneself. In this final chapter, I would like to suggest a very different answer from the perspective of a very different version of nineteenth-century American lyric reading, publication, address, and self-reference, a version that also found (and still seems to be finding) its personification in Dickinson.

Perhaps around 1870, Dickinson penciled on a vivid blue sheet twelve lines which may or may not have been copied and sent in her lifetime, which were first published in 1945, and on which none of her later critics has commented (fig. 34). The lines are directly addressed, though to whom no one could say:

> On the World you colored
>
> Morning painted
>
> rose—
>
> Idle his
>
> Vermillion
>
> Aimless crept
> > Stole
> the Glows
>
> Over Realms
>
> Of Orchards
>
> I the Day
>
> before
>
> Conquered
>
> with the Robin—
>
> Misery, how fair
>
> Till your
>
> wrinkled Finger
>
> shored the
> > pushed
> sun away
>
> Midnight's awful Pattern
>
> In the Goods
>
> of Day—
> > (F 1203)

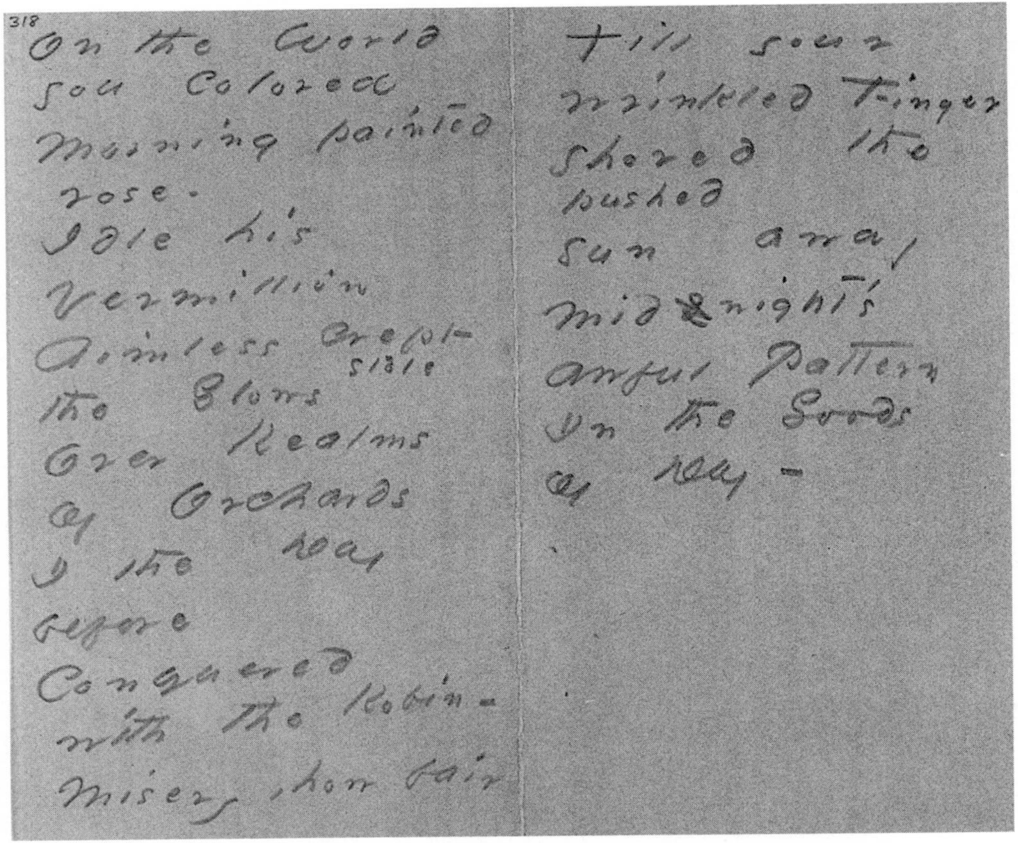

Figure 34. Emily Dickinson, around 1870. Courtesy of Amherst College Archives and Special Collections (ED ms. 318).

These lines repeat, delicately, in variation, the outlines of the problem we have noticed in the previous chapters: in them historical determination appears indistinguishable from figurative power—and yet the subject of these lines cannot help but tell the difference between the two. The imagery of consubstantiality that our reading of "Split the Lark—" and the "Master" letter made explicit in the previous chapter is implicit in these lines, here as there confusing the scene of writing with a figure of direct address in the form of a sentimentally potent but comparatively powerless pathos. In the lines' terms, the "you" to whom the address is directed has prescribed (or "colored") a "Pattern" that renders the personified Morning "Idle" and "Aimless." The anthropomorphized description of the new day's loss of agency serves as background for the memory of the self's former anthropomorphic power "Over Realms / of Orchards," yet the loss is depicted as representational foreground: as a "Vermillion" pentimento ineffectually concealing an unidentified experience that has intervened between one day and another. In the eighth line, the event that has made such a difference between what is seen and what is felt, between a powerful personification and what underlies it, achieves a curious identity: its name is "Misery."

Now in one sense "Misery, how fair" may be read as a synthetic description of what the dawn looks like and how it feels, one way of aligning the contradictory claims of perception and sensibility. But what is the referent of this "Misery"? Is it the elegiac strain of "the Day / before"? Is it the ineffectual beauty of the dawn? Or is "Misery" here a figure of address, another name for "you"? If read as the latter, then this "you" has slipped from cause to effect or, like the morning, partakes of the qualities of both. Like the other apostrophes we have remarked in Dickinson's poems, the apostrophe to "Misery" performatively brings before and after into the present tense, overdetermining the ninth line's "Till" in the same way that "your / wrinkled Finger" appears excessively determinate in the poem's last lines. Like the "Wrinkled Maker" in the lines that begin "A Word / dropped Careless," this authorial finger embodies "you" and "I," writer and reader in the strangely amputated corporation addressed as "Misery." This hovering "Pattern" may be sublimely "awful" but it is not, at a temporal remove, easy to read—in fact, it is its very obscurity that seems to lend it a paternal, patronizing authority. Unlike the "fingers" of "the Woman whom I prefer," this "wrinkled Finger" destines without enabling the writer's hand; its "Midnight" spectral figure is more like that of Hamlet's pointing ghost than like the sponsoring presence revealed "where my Hands are cut" in Dickinson's early letter to Susan. On this view—an admittedly elaborate and retrospective view, possible only in this final chapter—"Misery" is such an apt descriptive address in these lines because it is the best word for Dickinson's equivocal emphasis on the implicit historicity of textual intention, a pathos of transmission that has been realized beyond her wildest dreams.

As we have seen, twentieth-century versions of Dickinson have tended to characterize her lyrics as testimonial, at the same time that the modern construction of Dickinson's authorship has tended to identify all of her written testimony (prose fragments and familiar letters, recipes and responses) as "lyric." As I suggested in the second chapter, twentieth-century theorists of the genre verged toward extremes in response to such a hermeneutic circle, staking claim either to the pole at which the lyric may be viewed as pure figurative vehicle detached from any historical intention or to the opposite pole at which the lyric is so identified with the poet's historical intention that all of its figures may only be read in reference to it. Feminist criticism has had a special interest in mediating between these extremes, and for American feminism Dickinson has consistently proven the exemplary mediatrix. As Jane Gallop suggested, the academic feminist critic "needed Dickinson" in the 1970s because she needed "a woman who is beyond question a great poet, who can hold her own in academic circles, which, under the sway of modernism and New Criticism, valued the poet much more than the novelist, valued the poet not as a writer but as an artist."[3] By the mid-1980s when, according to Gallop, "the literary academy [was] post-structuralist and the reigning values [were] theoretical," the academic feminist literary critic needed Dickinson to testify to the theoretical disruption of New Critical aesthetics, a testimony available in Homans's and Loeffelholz's readings of Dickinson as well as in many later poststructuralisms, including my own. Since the 1980s, as we have seen, the emergence of queer theory, "body criticism," and, at the same time, the emergence of Dickinson's manuscripts into public view (first in Franklin's facsimile edition in 1981 and now on the Web) have encouraged revisionary interpretation and revisionary editions such as those of Smith, Howe, Werner, the Dickinson Editorial Collective, as well as the book you now hold in your hand. For all of these different and evolving feminisms, however, one central pathos remains: Dickinson is the type of the woman poet who struggles to write "I" and mean it.[4] For all, historical determination and figurative power must not pull so far apart that the woman's agency may not be discerned as always figuratively or even literally alive within the poems; whatever the lyrics are said to testify *to* it is always to "Dickinson." For all, the already determined pattern (or signature) of Dickinson-the-poet must ultimately authorize the goods circulated in her name.

In this chapter I will suggest that the enduring pathos of feminist criticism, the readerly pathos so successfully and successively personified by

Dickinson, is not only evident in the shifting lyric ideals that have governed her posthumous reception. It may also be traced to a competing poetic model in her own lifetime, a contemporary discourse from which reception severed her for most of the twentieth century, but which feminist critics have lately tried to restore: the nineteenth-century poetics of misery, or lyric sentimentalism. While twentieth-century versions of Dickinson's verse as personal testimony were frequently, even unabashedly invested in Dickinson's lyric identity, most aligned themselves with modernist canons of taste specifically against the taint of nineteenth-century sentimental excess. Joanne Feit Diehl followed this critical tradition when she attributed to Dickinson a "feminist poetics" which "emerges as an experimental project that approaches modernist theories of art" and even David Reynolds, a critic interested in placing Dickinson in the context of the feminization of nineteenth-century American popular culture, cast that culture as a set of "woman's stereotypes" that for Dickinson became "matters of literary theater and metaphorical play."[5] Cheryl Walker, whose groundbreaking book *The Nightingale's Burden: Women Poets and American Culture Before 1900* (1982) and anthology of *American Poets of the Nineteenth Century* (1992) inaugurated the recovery of women's popular verse of the period, thought that "the more one reads Emily Dickinson the less like her contemporaries she seems."[6] Betsy Erkkila went so far as to suggest that Dickinson "set herself against not only the new commercialization and democratization of literature but also the sentimental women writers who had gained money and fame in the American literary marketplace."[7] Elizabeth Petrino concluded that Dickinson's poetry "far excelled other poets of her age," since other poetesses "agreed to conform their verse to the publishing dictates for women," while Dickinson refused to do so.[8] Yet such attempts to characterize Dickinson as either more aesthetically and politically avant-garde, more aesthetically and politically self-conscious or selective or, against those trends, as more aesthetically and politically reactionary than other "sentimental women writers" of the period all simplified the discourse of mid-nineteenth-century sentimentalism, and especially simplified or even ignored the discourse of nineteenth-century American *lyric* sentimentalism, (or, as I will go on to argue, of sentimentalism as one of the discourses informing modern lyric reading) as emerging work on nineteenth-century American poetry is beginning to make abundantly clear.

As Yopie Prins and I have argued elsewhere, the category of the sentimental Poetess circulated widely from the eighteenth century onward, but 1848 was a peak year in that construction. Four anthologies of "female poets" were published in England and America in that year, evidence that the figure of the woman poet could become a brand name, even if individual poets' names rarely survived the anthologies.[9] As Tricia Lootens has argued so eloquently in *Lost Saints: Silence, Gender and Victorian Literary Canonization*, much of the nineteenth century is devoted to canonizing poetesses who are, as they were, ironically forgotten in the very process of being remembered. Prins and I have suggested that one reason for the reiterated forgetting of the Poetess is that she is not the content of her own generic representation: not a speaker, not an "I," not a consciousness, not a subjectivity, not a voice, not a persona, not a self. Thus she is "generic" in at least two senses, an essentially empty figure that circulates in lyrics as a vehicle of cultural transmission. There is now a wealth of emerging scholarship on both sides of the Atlantic on the many cultural outlines of that figure and the many cultures she transmits. On the American side, Paula Bennett's *Poets in the Public Sphere*, Mary Loeffelholz's *From School to Salon*, and Eliza Richards's *Gender and the Poetics of Reception in Poe's Circle* have all emerged from the fruitful conversation about the Poetess in the last two years.[10] Bennett's emphasis on women poets' participation in the public sphere, Loeffelholz's emphasis on the way women poets moved "from school to salon," from domesticity to publicity to the canon, and Richards's emphasis on poetesses as figures of transference who "share a deep engagement with the mimic functions of the lyric" will create a rich field of study all at once. With that work, it becomes possible to ask anew what Dickinson's relation to the cultural figure of the poetess might be, or might have been. It becomes possible to use the new conversation among scholars of nineteenth-century women's verse to discern more of an old conversation among nineteenth-century women poets and their readers.[11]

Between approximately 1840 and 1880, or the decades central to Dickinson's writing, but before the publication of the first volumes of her work, that conversation was centrally concerned with discerning the differences and similarities between historical and figurative testimony, with defining the relationship between the one giving that testimony and the one to whom it would be directed, and with the gendered and sexualized associations attached to both. Further, as in Dickinson's lines that begin "On the World you colored," the subject of spectacular suffering in nineteenth-century lyric sentimentalism was most often the subject of what Cheryl Walker dubbed "the secret sorrow," an "I" forced—by circumstance or by her own modesty—to bear her burden of affection and pain in a private world.[12] Yet what Walker did not point out is that since this burden is also the occasion for the poem, "the secret sorrow" is an open secret. "Misery, how fair": pain may define the experience of the sentimental subject, but it is also the basis on which she becomes the subject of exchange—even, from our belated perspective, of tradition.

While private feeling may seem the point of first-person affective expression, then, the popularity of the genre in the nineteenth century also indicates that sentiment was a public interest, and it is that interest itself that may account for the surcharge of the "sentimental." As Eve Kosofsky Sedgwick has put it,

> It would be hard to overestimate the importance of vicariousness in defining the sentimental. The strange career of "sentimentality," from the later eighteenth century when it was a term of high ethical and aesthetic praise, to the twentieth when it can be used to connote, beyond pathetic weakness, an actual principle of evil . . . is a career that displays few easily articulable consistencies; and those are not . . . consistencies of subject matter. Rather, they seem to inhere in the nature of the investment by a viewer *in* a subject matter.[13]

The popular investment by readers in the subject matter of first-person feminine suffering had its roots in a "double logic of power and powerlessness" that most scholars of nineteenth-century America now attribute to the period's culture as a whole.[14] Rather than attempt to give a patchwork version of that whole (a cultural archaeology already available, in any case, in the work of those scholars), I want here to reconstruct just a small part of its logic, to translate just a few phrases from a vocabulary that has been on the whole ignored by scholarship on the nineteenth-century preoccupation with the intersection between relations of sympathy and relations of power.[15] If, as Sedgwick argues, "the investment of a viewer *in* a subject matter" also amounts to the investment of a spectator (or reader) in a subject (what Sedgwick also calls "identification through a spectatorial route"), then the genre of lyric poetry occupies a privileged situation in the discursive context of sentimentality since one of its generic features is—or at least has been thought to be—the rhetorical performance of a circuit of vicarious identification. Yet the privileged situation of the lyric in literary studies has also kept it at a remove from historical critiques of "the culture of sentiment" or "the feminization of American culture"— ironically, it has seemed too personal to be included as a type of "cultural work."[16] The oversight seems especially odd when one considers the fulcrum of the sentimental as the principle of vicarious identification. There is nothing more sentimental than sentimental poetry. There is therefore no symbolic production more symptomatic of nineteenth-century America's double logic of power and victimization than the poems widely considered, then as now, too full of personal feeling to testify to anything more important than themselves.

Yet even if a case could be made for the crucial significance of sentimental poetry for an understanding of nineteenth-century public discourse, what would Dickinson's role be in such a case? Given my argument so far about Dickinson's relation to historical generic figures, my reader will probably guess that I will argue that Dickinson worked against the grain of the sentimental lyric genre, or that she modified it, or resisted it, or tried to make sure that her reader did not confuse her writing with it. But that is not what I think. I will suggest instead that Dickinson's writing is immersed in female sentimental lyricism, and especially in the discourse of vicarious feeling—of sentimental lyric reading—that developed around that genre. If, as I have argued, lyric reading is a modern critical fiction, then sentimental lyric reading was one chapter in that fiction. Dickinson may only have become a lyric poet through the posthumous transmission and reception of her writing as lyric, but she was already a Poetess.

"THE LITERATURE OF MISERY"

In the preface to his 1848 edition of *The Female Poets of America*, Rufus Wilmot Griswold began by warning his readers that

> It is less easy to be assured of the genuineness of literary ability in women than in men. The moral nature of women, in its finest and richest development, partakes of some of the qualities of genius; it assumes, at least, the similitude of that which in men is the characteristic or accompaniment of the highest grade of mental inspiration. We are in danger, therefore, of mistaking for the effervescent energy of creative intelligence, that which is only the exuberance of personal "feelings unemployed." We may confound the vivid dreamings of an unsatisfied heart, with the aspirations of a mind impatient of the fetters of time, and matter, and mortality. That may seem to us the abstract imagining of a soul rapt into sympathy with a purer beauty and a higher truth than earth and space exhibit, which in fact shall be only the natural craving of affections, undefined and wandering. The most exquisite susceptibility of the spirit, and the capacity to mirror in dazzling variety the effects which circumstances or surrounding minds work upon it, may be accompanied by no power to originate, nor even, in any proper sense, to reproduce.[17]

Of the many aspects worth remarking in Griswold's attitude here, his counsel that the subject matter of his volume be approached with a hermeneutics of suspicion (he calls it an "antecedent skepticism") is most so. Although on the surface his preface takes the form of a patronizing editorial apology, not very far below that surface Griswold's language worries over the source of that apology. Why should the question of "the genuineness of literary ability" be at stake in the first place? The reason it matters, it seems, is that women may simulate a valued literary quality precisely because that quality comes to them naturally. What is at stake for a reader of this poetry, in other words, is the value of "genuineness" itself, especially in its relation to its visual off-rhyme, "genius." Apparently, "genius" may look "genuine" but not be, because Griswold assumes that his readers will assume that genius is associated with "effervescent energy," "sympathy," intellectual impatience, "exquisite susceptibility," and, most strikingly, with "the capacity to mirror" others. Such intimate semiotic relations between genius and the characteristic symptoms of sentimentalism poise Griswold's descriptions between the eighteenth-century honorific and the later nineteenth- and twentieth-century queasy valorization of literary affect.[18] They also go some way toward explaining that shift in sentiment's career, since Griswold's is not yet a discomfort with the rapt effects of heightened subjective affect but with the gendered and sexualized "power to originate" those effects.

Thus at the end of this passage the editor's concern with the authenticity of represented feelings takes the disturbing form of a derogation of the classical sexual anatomy of the hysterical woman: "the natural craving of the affections, undefined and wandering" is like a roving womb stirring up trouble, impotent to creatively inseminate itself "in any proper sense." The unlikely key term here is "proper." Would the power to reproduce "in any proper sense" be a decorous reproductive power, female feelings wedded to "literary ability" not the simulacrum of male genius but somehow authentically masculine? In what sense would such a power then be "proper"? If, as Griswold goes on to write, "it does not follow, because the most essential genius in men is marked by qualities which we may call feminine, that such qualities when found in female writers have any certain or just relation to female superiority," then what does "feminine" mean? Griswold's attempt to establish an analytical perspective on women's poetry purchases its critical value at the expense of the women poets themselves, since if one can't discern the difference between "effervescent energy" and "creative intelligence," one may be in danger of uncritical reading.

Griswold may have been especially reactionary, but the danger of mistaking sentimental women for creative geniuses seems to have been an open secret in nineteenth-century literary magazines. In a sketch entitled "My Garden" that appeared in the *Atlantic Monthly* in 1862, "Gail Hamilton" (the pen name of Mary Abigail Dodge) began, despite the disguise of her androgynous authorial signature, by asserting,

I am a woman. You may have inferred this before; but now I desire to state it distinctly, because I like to do as I would be done by, when I can just as well as not. . . . The two sexes awaken two entirely distinct sets of feelings, and you would no more use the one for the other than you would put on your tiny teacups at breakfast, or lay the carving-knife by the butter-plate. Consequently it is very exasperating to sit, open-eyed and expectant, watching the removal of the successive swathings which hide from you the dusky glories of an old-time princess, and, when the unrolling is over, to find it is nothing, after all, but a great lubberly boy. Equally trying is it to feel your interest clustering round a narrator's manhood, all your individuality merging in his, till, of a sudden, by the merest chance, you catch the swell of crinoline, and there you are. Away with such clumsiness! Let us have everybody christened before we begin.[19]

The comic "clumsiness" of this scenario (which will have nothing to do with the subject of the sketch, the city dweller's disillusionment with "country living") is due less to its stated preoccupation with undisguised self-representation than to its performative parody of the transferential identifications occasioned by stylistic fictions of gender. Although the plain-dealing opening declarations attempt the impression of gender-neutrality, the implied reader is immediately cast as feminine—or at least as someone domestically knowledgeable enough to understand place-setting decorum. If "the two sexes awaken two entirely distinct sets of feelings," do they awaken those feelings distinctly for the two sexes? That would depend, according to the passage, on where or how you "feel your interest clustering." The strip-tease removal of "the successive swathings" which conceal "a great lubberly boy" (not very interesting) is set against the temptation to merge "all your individuality" in a narrator's manhood, only to be interrupted by "the swell of crinoline" (very frustrating).

The spectacles of identification are so shifting in this passage that the shifty relation between authentic and simulated genders and between a critical and sentimental reading emerges as the passage's point. The more often the narrator reiterates the phrase "I am a woman," the more elaborate her subsequent rhetorical performances become, until she strikes the unmistakable pose of the sentimental Poetess: "A very agony of self-abasement will be no armor against the poisoned shafts which assumed superiority will hurl against me. Yet I press the arrow to my bleeding heart, and calmly reiterate, I am a woman." In the guise of the most authentic possible testimony—the personal statement that demands a masochistic price—"Hamilton" offers the most affected possible performance, a melodrama quickly upstaged when she begins the next paragraph by stating that "the full magnanimity of which reiteration can be perceived only when I inform you that I could easily deceive you, if I chose." Of course the point is that what is most genuine is already most deceptive, since the performativity of literary identity is its least genuine (and most defining) aspect. As in Griswold's preface, the qualities considered natural or essential in the woman consist of such simulated affects, and it is that veneer of simulation over the first-person "proper" claim of authenticity that makes "My Garden" into a parody of the vicarious identities at stake in the "sentimental."

These brief glimpses into two nineteenth-century versions of gendered "identification through a spectatorial route" begin to contextually frame my reading of Dickinson's "Master" letter in the last chapter. Another portrait of the Poetess may have preoccupied Dickinson more directly. The article, which appeared in the *Springfield Daily Republican* for July 7, 1860, was entitled "When Should We Write," and was probably written by Dickinson's friend Samuel Bowles. The article has been linked to Dickinson's personal concerns by several of her critics, but in view of Griswold's and Hamilton's concerns over the performative force of women's claims to authentic self-expression, and especially over the reading that performance might produce, Bowles's commentary on "a kind of writing only too common, appealing to the sympathies of the reader without recommending itself to his subject" is worth considering in more detail, especially since the article gives the subgenre a name:

> It may be called the literature of misery. The writers are chiefly women, gifted women may be, full of thought and feeling and fancy, but poor, lonely and unhappy. Also that suffering is so seldom healthful. It may be a valuable discipline in the end, but for the time being it too often clouds, withers, distorts. It is so difficult to see objects distinctly through a mist of tears. The sketch or poem is usually the writer's photograph in miniature. It reveals a countenance we would gladly brighten, but not by exposing it to the gaze of a worthless world. We know that grief enriches the soul, but seldom is this manifest until after its first intensity is past. We should say to our suffering friends, write not from the fullness of a present sorrow. It is in most cases only after the storm is passed that we may look for those peaceable fruits that nourished by showers, grow ripe and luscious in the sun. There are those indeed who so far triumph over their own personal experiences as to mould them into priceless gifts to the world of literature and art. Like the eider duck bending over her famished young, they give us their heart's blood and we find it then a refreshing drought. But there are marked exceptions. Ordinarily the lacerated bosom must be healed, 'ere it can gladden other natures with the overflowings of a healthful life.[20]

Here Bowles shares with Griswold the concern that female literary sentimental performances may be too genuine for "the world of literature and art"; at the same time, the editorial shares with Hamilton the anxiety that the appearance of first-person literary representation may—in the hands of "poor, lonely and unhappy" women—prove deceptive. For Bowles, however, the reader should beware of these writing women's tendency to take one in not primarily because (as for Griswold) female sentimentalism may mimic the attainments of male sensibility or (as for Hamilton) because the most sincere protestations may turn out to be "exasperating" special effects, but because such "suffering is so seldom healthful." The adjective is intriguing, especially as it initially seems to apply to the "gifted women" themselves but then shifts to characterize the rationale for limiting the publication of their effusions. Bowles's main caution, it turns out, is that "other natures" may be infected by the un-"healthful life" of "our suffering friends." The familiar tone betrays a paternal sympathy for these writers' "personal experiences" yet erupts into a family scene that betrays that the editor's desire to distance himself from female bleeding hearts is also a perverse attraction: the vampiric young at the mother eider duck's breast are, oddly, figures for readers receiving "priceless gifts" from exceptionally successful sentimentalists who "give us their heart's blood and we find it then a refreshing drought." It is at the least a disturbing scene of instruction, partially due to its appropriation of imagery that was the stock in trade of female lyric sentimentalism and partially due to the "then" that should refer to the previous sentence's distinction between "personal experiences" and "triumphant" artistic craft but that instead directly follows a portrayal of "our" relation to that craft as an extreme version of natural appetite. Does "the literature of misery" not recommend itself to the editor's subject because he wishes to protect its writers from "the gaze of a worthless world" or because that world needs to be protected from its own prurient interest in representations of female suffering?

The question is not strictly rhetorical, since the precedence gained by the latter concern in the course of Bowles's article stems not only from the suspicious gender of "our suffering friends" but from contemporary suspicions about the proper subjects of the lyric genre. The most immediate subtext for Bowles's concerns over the "healthful" relation of "personal experiences" to poetic representation may have been Matthew Arnold's preface to the 1853 Edition of *Poems*, since Arnold's argument is audible in the prose of "When Should We Write." By way of explaining why his dramatic poem "Empedocles on Etna" has been omitted from his new edition, Arnold claims that the "class of situation" to which his Empedocles belongs is one "from the representation of which, though accurate, no poetical enjoyment can be derived." Such situations, Arnold writes, "are those in which the suffering finds no vent in action; in which a continuous state of mental distress is prolonged, unrelieved by incident, hope, or resistance; in which there is everything to be endured, nothing to be done. In such situations there is inevitably something morbid, in the description of them something monotonous. When they occur in actual life, they are painful, not tragic; the representation of them in poetry is painful also."[21] "Nothing to be done": for Arnold, "if the representation be a poetical one . . . it is demanded, not only that it shall interest, but also that it shall inspirit and rejoice the reader: that it shall convey a charm, and infuse delight." One can hear Arnold's prescription in Bowles's injunction that "the lacerated bosom must be healed, 'ere it can *gladden* other natures with the overflowings of a healthful life," but the change that Bowles works on Arnold's argument is equally remarkable. Arnold's preface proceeds from the occasion of his self-censorship to a more general case for the cultural work of poetry; his call for an inspiriting poetic representation issues from his conviction that "it is impossible for us, under the circumstances amidst which we live, to think clearly, to feel nobly, and to delineate firmly. If we cannot attain to the mastery of the great artists—let us, at least, have so much respect for our art as to prefer it to ourselves. Let us not bewilder our successors." The transcendence of personal experience in view of the aims of art, in view of the *transmission* of that art to "our successors," serves the purpose for Arnold of both a self-overcoming and a redemption of a decadent age. Implicitly, the lyric-as-personal-testimony is a distinct symptom of that decadence and the lyric-as-vehicle-of-the-tradition might repair the damage. What is arresting about Bowles's use of Arnold is that the politics of "poetical enjoyment" have come to rest in the bosoms of women who "give us their heart's blood"—a maternal inheritance bound to bewilder "our" successors and likely to bring out the worst in "ourselves."[22]

It is now more evident that the recurrent nineteenth-century complaint about women's writing as "too much nature and not enough art" was the symptom of a more general unease with the inevitable proximity between personal and literary testimony in the lyric and especially with the difficulty of distinguishing between them. Further, Bowles's translation of Arnold's worries over the fit representational place of personal pain into a worry over the fit place of women's writing aligns private suffering with a simultaneously feminized and infantilized version of the masculine self (the article is, after all, entitled not "When Should *She*" but "When Should *We* Write"). What sentimental women poets need to do, according to Bowles, is to grow up. He adds to Arnold a Wordsworthian counsel that powerful feelings be "recollected in tranquility" and thus, presumably, transformed from mere photographic miniatures into the larger masterpieces to which Arnold lamented "we" could no longer attain. If women can overcome their "suffering" natures for the sake of culture, in other words, that is a representative way for modern culture to overcome itself. Griswold had, in fact, said as much when introducing his *Female Poets:*

> It has been suggested by foreign critics, that our [American] citizens are too much devoted to business and politics to feel interest in pursuits which adorn but do not profit, and which beautify existence but do not consolidate power: feminine genius is perhaps destined to retrieve our public character in this respect, and our shores may yet be far resplendent with a temple of art which, while it is a glory of our land, may be a monument to the honor of the sex.[23]

Precisely because women are sheltered from "business and politics" they may "retrieve" the spirit of the age; precisely because of the antithetical relation of "feminine genius" to "profit" and the consolidation of "power" it becomes an ideal (even sacred) sign for artistic profit and cultural power. We might recall here William Dean Howells's later remark on Dickinson: "this poetry is as characteristic of our life as our business enterprise, our political turmoil, our demagogism, our millionarism."[24] The woman poet is the perfect vehicle for cultural transference. We recall that Higginson put the logic succinctly in an 1871 essay on Sappho: "The aspirations of modern life culminate, like the greatest of modern poems, in the elevation of womanhood. *Die ewige Weibliche zieht uns hinan.*"[25] Given Griswold's earlier remarks in the same preface on the several ways in which "we are in danger" of crediting as genius a woman's poetry that may be "only the exuberance of 'feelings unemployed,'" and given that Higginson's essay on Sappho consists almost entirely of an elaborate defense of Sappho's art from charges of suicidal self-pity and lesbianism, it is not hard to see that the period's discomfiture with feminine lyric sentimental excess was only one half of a dimorphism, or two distinct forms of the same parts. Those parts fused at one level into the figure of a woman poet who was dangerously and deceptively testimonial; at the other, they combined to form the flower of civilization, of tradition. The value of the latter was guaranteed by the "unhealthy" presence of the former.

In the terms of the Dickinson lines with which we began, the period's nagging question was how to turn the indelible pattern of feminized personal suffering into "the Goods / of Day" (Bowles's "priceless gifts to the world of literature and art"). In Dickinson's lines, the charm and delight (to use Arnold's words) of Morning's artistic representation cannot be extricated from the determining pain of personal experience; the subject of Dickinson's poem cannot, as Bowles would have it, put the distorting affect of the "first intensity" of grief behind her. Instead, midnight collapses into dawn, suffering into representation, morbid reaction into diurnal action, and self into text: "Misery, how fair." The line that hovers grammatically over Dickinson's lines derives part of its rhetorical force from its very Dickinsonian condensation of two aspects of the cultural situation of nineteenth-century women's sentimental lyric, a situation that still informs modern critical reading.

"This Chasm"

The attempt to lift subjective representation free of the perspectival limitations of the merely personal, to lift it away from the tangle of gendered and sexualized interest, to elevate it from the basis of a primitive or natural to the transcendence of an aesthetically crafted performance is also the desire to extricate first-person expression from the referential claims of singular bodies. Again and again, Griswold's, Hamilton's, Arnold's, and Bowles's accounts of the vexed relation between personal and literary identity circle back to the question of bodily identity and its discontents. Karen Sanchez-Eppler has argued that "the extent to which the condition of the human body designates identity is a question of [antebellum] American culture and consciousness as well as politics, and so it is a question whose answers can be sought not only in political speeches but also in a variety of more ostensibly aesthetic forms, from sentimental fiction and personal narratives to those conventionally most ahistorical of texts, lyric poems."[26] The "question," as Sanchez-Eppler sees it, is embedded in abolitionist and feminist rhetoric of the period, but also in the "radical privacy" of Dickinson's lyrics, which "lay bare the contradictory connections between embodiment and representation."[27]

In view of our entrance into the conversation surrounding such contradictory connections in the sentimental lyric, we might extend Sanchez-Eppler's view to include the scope of the identity politics at stake in both the writing and reading of the lyric, and especially to include what I will argue is sentimental poetry's stress on an unrepresentable embodiment, on a historicity threatened by the elevating aims of figuration. Thus the "misery" in "the literature of misery" may be a symptom less of the experiences of "poor, lonely and unhappy" women than of the rhetorical difficulty of pointing to an experience (or an identity) before it becomes a metaphor. On this view, the "ahistorical" situation of the lyric—its association with extreme privacy as well as it aspiration to the more than merely *personal*—is exactly the problem for writers of sentimental verse. It is also, as I have argued in previous chapters, a central problem for Dickinson. Not only does her exposure of "the contradictory connections between embodiment and representation" affiliate her work with the currents of mid-nineteenth-century discourses on identity, but Dickinson's emphasis on the material trace of written (and unwritten) intention may itself be traced past the modern idealization of Dickinson's lyric voice to a moment at which the gendered (that is, bodily) cost of such an idealization was very much at issue. Thus my contention in the previous chapter that "the materiality of writing ends by substantiating the claims of a body historically subject to the inversions (and perversions) of reading" may now be placed within a lyric discourse that brought specific pressures to bear on such claims.

Consider some lines that seem to enfold within themselves the central writerly strategies of feminized lyric sentimentalism at the same time that they address the readerly anxieties in which those strategies were located. The lines appear to have been written around 1865, exist in manuscript (fig. 35) only in one of the unbound sets (6b), were first published in 1945, and are now known as Poem 1061 in the Franklin edition:

> This Chasm, Sweet, upon my life
> I mention it to you,
> When Sunrise through a fissure drop
> The Day must follow too.
>
> If we demur, it's gaping sides
> Disclose as 'twere a Tomb
> Ourself am lying straight wherein
> The Favorite of Doom—
>
> When it has just contained a Life
> Then, Darling, it will close
> And yet so bolder every Day
> So turbulent it grows
>
> I'm tempted half to stitch it up
> With a remaining Breath
> I should not miss in yielding, though
> To Him, it would be Death—
>
> And so I bear it big about
> My Burial—before
> A Life quite ready to depart
> Can harass me no more—

The close relation between these lines and the lines that begin "On the World you colored" is immediately apparent: both texts are directly addressed, both make the figure of address complicit in a past scene of suffering now intimately associated with the scene of writing, and both collapse the misery of one into the misery of the other. Yet while in "On the

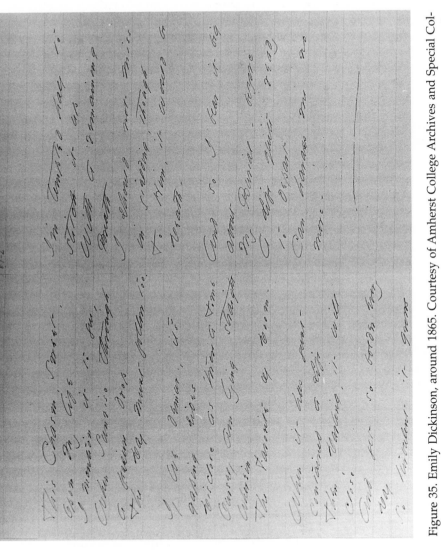

Figure 35. Emily Dickinson, around 1865. Courtesy of Amherst College Archives and Special Collections (ED ms. 87-1, 87-2).

World you colored" the deictic "wrinkled Finger" that implicitly points to a referent that the subject cannot explicitly articulate concludes the poem, the lines above begin in such a moment of pure deixis, of sheer pointing. And whereas "On the World you colored" projects the consubstantial fusion of past and present, self and other, suffering and its representation onto the landscape, "This Chasm" proceeds from its "mention" of painful experience to the progress of its internalization, its *incorporation* by a subject who, like a sentimental lyric, can disclose her meaning only by performing it—that is, by being read. The textual subjection of this subject is, then, by the last line, both a testimony to the authenticity of her pain and an acknowledgment that lyric testimony will inevitably be read as only the figurative performance (rather than the historical experience) of that referent. The self-become-tomb-become-poem finally introjects an entire literature of misery—and an entire legacy of reading—into itself.

The sort of sentimental reading that such a subject invites may explain why most twentieth-century critics steered clear of these lines. When Gilbert and Gubar considered "This Chasm" briefly in their consideration of Dickinson's work as "versified autobiography," they registered their discomfort with its invitation by deciding that the poem "parodies the saccharine love poetry that ladies were expected to write."[28] Yet these lines do not feel like a parody; the ironic distance we usually associate with that mode is wholly absent from their headlong plunge into pathos. Rather, the lines' immediate emphasis on the nondiscursive basis of their own discourse—on a "This" that could be demonstrated without linguistic illustration to a "you" intimate enough to see it—engages in savagely foreshortened perspective the contradiction inherent in the nineteenth-century *reception* of lyric testimony. When Gilbert and Gubar asked, "What specifically is the chasm this poem describes?" they neatly marked the semantic territory that separates Dickinson from her modern audience. No nineteenth-century reader would have needed to pose that question; the first line's referential conceit (rather like Hamilton's "agony of self-abasement") would have been too obvious not to be seen, and its visibility poses the question of parody at another level. The materials the lines work upon are not simply the materials of conventional sentiment, but the discourse positioning that sentiment in relation to the reader: from its first word, the lines dare a reader like Griswold or Bowles or Higginson to detach this subject's pain from her aesthetic claims—and end by daring him not to do so.

For certainly here there is everything to be endured and nothing to be done. Nothing, that is, but to "mention" what Arnold surely would have called a "class of situation from the representation of which, though accurate, no poetical enjoyment can be derived." So the first lines apologize by understating the effect of their own opening: a "Chasm" is hardly something one *mentions*, especially not after having pointed directly to what Bowles would have called the writer's "lacerated bosom." Not healed and therefore not prepared to "gladden other natures with the overflowings of a healthful life," the life the chasm interrupts cannot, apparently, help but attest to its interruption; Bowles counseled the new day's power to heal old wounds, but this "Sunrise" has already reversed such a progressive temporality. The disappearance of day "through a fissure" turns the naturalizing logic of Bowles's view against itself, and the poetic logic that "must follow" upon natural reversal must naturally be reversed. In four lines Dickinson turns inside-out not the perspective of the literature of misery—she adheres to that with a vengeance—but the perspective on the poetry of feminine suffering that would seek to wedge itself between a life and its "proper" representation.

Now the division of the proper, of the self from itself is, as we have seen, perhaps the signature characteristic of the subjectivity Dickinson bequeaths to literary history—it has, in fact, often been understood as the sign of Dickinson's modernity. Any reader of Dickinson can generate a long list of chasms, fissures, maelstroms, cleavings, self-burials, and horrors that irrevocably divide one part of the "I" from another. Nearly all of the commentary devoted to Dickinson has centered on the question of these self-splittings, and especially on the referent of this schizophrenic subjective representation: sheer grief, lost love, physical and psychic pain, gendered, artistic, and sexual misinterpretation and oppression have all vied as explanations for the missing referent of the crisis. Yet what is not often considered is that whatever the answer might turn out to have been to the riddle of subjective experience the lyrics present, that riddle is most often portrayed as a problem for lyric *reading*.[29] We might go so far as to say that the anticipation of that reading is exactly what fractures the subject: she experiences at the level of her person the fate of her representation, and it is a fate consistently figured as a crisis of or for bodily identity, as in these lines from the same set (6b) in which the lines that begin "This Chasm, Sweet . . ." were copied:

> I've dropped my Brain—My Soul is numb—
> The Veins that used to run
> Stop palsied—'tis Paralysis
> Done perfecter in stone—
>
> Vitality is carved and cool—
> My nerve in marble lies—
> A Breathing Woman
> Yesterday—endowed with Paradise.

Not dumb—I had a sort that moved—
A Sense that smote and stirred—
Instincts for Dance—a caper part—
An Aptitude for Bird—

Who wrought Carrara in me
And chiselled all my tune
Were it a witchcraft—were it Death—
I've still a chance to strain

To Being, somewhere—Motion—Breath—
Though Centuries beyond,
And every limit a Decade—
I'll shiver, satisfied.
    (F 1088)

Here, as in "This Chasm, Sweet . . . ," an unnatural occurrence inevitably or "naturally" eventuates in the subject's metamorphosis—her transubstantiation—into "dumb" matter, the artifactual object of her own regard. The comic corporeality of the first line challenges the reader to imagine a "Brain" rather than, say, a *mind* registering the shock of transformation or "Paralysis" from "Breathing Woman" to memento mori. Further, the third stanza identifies the talents of the formerly embodied self as those of the poet, or of performative lyric agency: "Not dumb—I had a sort that moved— / A Sense that smote and stirred— / Instincts for Dance—a caper part— / An Aptitude for Bird—." The fourth stanza then asks the question the reader might be expected to ask, the one readers of Dickinson always do ask: *What happened? Who or what effected the change?* And, as so often in Dickinson's lines, the answer is deferred toward a future readerly resurrection in which the "I" may "strain // To Being, somewhere . . . ," though "Motion—Breath" may "Centuries beyond" merely "shiver" beneath the text's rigidified, now differently embodied surface. When Dickinson first wrote to Higginson, she began, we recall, with what must have seemed to her future editor a "half-cracked" question: "Are you too deeply occupied to say if my Verse is alive?" (L 260); upon his immediate reply as to whether he thought "it breathed," she then thanked him "for the surgery," explaining "I could not weigh myself—Myself" (L 261). Already, in this inaugural literary correspondence, the dissecting hand of the critic has intervened between "myself" and "Myself." The question Dickinson posed to Higginson remains the one her readers keep never answering: can the reception of a lyric weigh the subject within the artifact? Where might "Motion" and "Breath" remain after they have been removed from "a sort that moved"?

The pathos of that question may gain a certain resonance, I have argued, in the post-Higginsonian (that is, post-nineteenth-century) history of the reception of Dickinson's progressively idealized and abstracted lyric voice, but it has another reverberation within the discourse of nineteenth-century sentimental lyric. In one popular poem on the subject of such poetry, for example, the type of lyric agency that Dickinson condensed into "An Aptitude for Bird" took the familiar form of the nightingale's song. "The Poet," by the well-known writer Elizabeth Oakes Smith (whose poetic character of Eva in her long narrative verse "The Sinless Child" [1842] probably informed Longfellow's best-selling "Evangeline" in 1847 as well as Stowe's enormously influential "little Eva" in 1851) opens with two epigraphs: "It is the belief of the vulgar that when the nightingale sings, she leans her breast upon a thorn," and then "NON VOX SED VOTUM" (not a voice but a vow). The poem as a whole goes on to elaborate the relationship between the two halves of both epigraphs: between incorporeal voice and the body's silent "vow," between misery and its utterance, poetic voice and the testimony of pain, a received literary identity and the antithetical experience it lifts into metaphor:

> Sing, sing—Poet, sing!
> With the thorn beneath thy breast,
> Robbing thee of all thy rest;
> Hidden thorn forever thine,
> Therefore dost thou sit and twine
>   Lays of sorrowing—
> Lays that wake a mighty gladness,
> Spite of all their mournful sadness.
>   Sing, sing—Poet, sing!
> It doth ease thee of thy sorrow—
> "Darkling" singing till the morrow;
> Never weary of thy trust,
> Hoping, loving as thou must,
>   Let thy music ring;
> Noble cheer it doth impart,
> Strength of will and strength of heart.
>   Sing, sing—Poet sing!
> Thou art made a human voice;
> Wherefore shouldst thou not rejoice
> That the tears of thy mute brother
> Bearing pangs he may not smother,
>   Through thee are flowing—
> For his dim, unuttered grief

Through thy song hath found relief?
Sing, sing—Poet, sing!
Join the music of the stars,
Wheeling on their sounding cars;
Each responsive in its place
To the choral hymn of space—
Lift, oh lift thy wing—
And the thorn beneath thy breast
Though it pierce, shall give thee rest.[30]

According to convention, Oakes Smith's apostrophic refrain urges the nightingale-Poet to turn her suffering into song—and in each stanza the rationale for doing so is the vicarious pleasure her "Lays of sorrowing" may bring. If we recall once again Shelley's definition of the poet as "a nightingale, who sits in darkness and sings to cheer its own solitude with sweet sounds," we might also recall that "his auditors are as men entranced by the melody of an unseen musician, who feel that they are moved and softened, yet know not whence or why." Oakes Smith emphasizes the source (the "whence or why") of this romantic affect and, in her echo of Keats's signature adjectival adverb from stanza six of the Nightingale Ode ("Darkling I listen . . ."), she also emphasizes that the affective transference characteristic of romantic poetics has its feminized or "vulgar" origin. "The Thorn beneath thy breast" is the source of the nightingale's song, but it is not her pain that she expresses; the "hidden thorn" is instead progressively removed through each stanza from the "mighty gladness," the "noble cheer," the "relief" it gives to "thy mute brother," and ultimately joins "the choral hymn of space" in an elevated constellation that transcends the pathetic corporeality of the bird's "lacerated bosom."

Yet while that figural progression constitutes the logic of the ode's counsel to the nightingale, it does not account for the logic of the poem itself: this is not the lyric the nightingale sings; its theme is instead the "vow" of the martyred body that enables the imaginary version of lyric song that the nightingale *would* produce. It is a view, as it were, behind the wings of poetic production. As Oakes Smith wrote in 1851 in her feminist treatise *Woman and Her Needs*, pain is the proper subject for women's poetry because it has been used to define women *as* subjects: "suffering to a woman occupies the place of labor to a man."[31] If suffering was taken to constitute women's "natural" or proper literary identity, in other words, Oakes Smith suggested that women turn that inheritance into capital.[32]

When Dickinson begins the lines "This Chasm, Sweet" by pointing deictically to a wound that both motivates the poem and for which the subject of the poem herself is the only evidence, she participates in what Foucault would call a nineteenth-century lyric episteme in which the body is called upon to validate the representational claims made in its name, but from which that very representation severs it.[33] Like Oakes Smith's "The Poet," Dickinson's lines insist on the invisible "vow" or promise that guarantees the sympathetic power of voice—but in "This Chasm" it is the mute body and not the voice that defines the subject. In effect, each quatrain works to close the gap between medium and message opened by "the belief of the vulgar" that Oakes Smith's poem exemplified, and they do so, as in "I've dropped my Brain," by identifying the "Vitality" of the subject with an uncanny "Life" and afterlife of the lyric text. Yet "identifying" does not feel like the right verb for what emerges as a competition between this "I" and the "Chasm" which, in the second and third stanzas, threatens to contain "a Life" in much the same way that "A Breathing Woman" is contained by her "chiselled" figuration in "I've dropped my Brain." The second stanza casts the threat in the idiom of carpe diem lyric, and specifically of Marvell's "To His Coy Mistress," in which the poet consigns the demur object of his desire to a "marble Vault" if she refuses his advances.[34] The reversal of the sun's logic thus allows for more than one kind of lyric reversal in Dickinson's lines, and the appealingly sinister humor with which "Ourself" becomes "The Favorite of Doom" is reminiscent of the parodic subjective confusion occasioned by Hamilton's reiteration of her "true" or "natural" literary identity. Marvell's "fine and private place" has become the open secret disclosed in Dickinson's lines: the consequences of her desire now seem to make her the property of an agency bent on her subjection.

On a rhetorical level, what has happened between the first and second stanzas is that the pure deixis of the poem's opening "This" has turned into metaphor in the sixth line's "as 'twere." Once given a name, the metaphor takes over, shifting from the metonymic "upon" of the first line to a near-substitution for the "I" that almost becomes the metaphor's tenor. Almost. Just at the moment when, in the third stanza, the "bolder" and "turbulent" intention of the vehicle closes upon its living captive, another intention asserts itself. The temptation "to stitch it up" rather than be fastened by the figure of the Tomb promises some release—if not of the self, then of an "I" grammatically distinct from "Him," no longer vicariously identified as an "Ourself." The "Motion—Breath—" temporally deferred and syntactically excluded in "I've dropped my Brain" becomes the envelope of "This Chasm," and the "I" nearly subjugated by lyric desire instead ends by enclosing it. This "stitch" of "Breath" rather exactly poises her text between the body and its material impression. The conceit of pregnancy in the final stanza resurrects the feminized, unrepresentable because overrepresented body of the woman writing in the perverse terms of "genuineness" Griswold prescribed for "female poets": the "power to originate [or] even, in any proper sense, to reproduce" may not, after all, define Dickinson's "genius." What may come closest to defining it is the way in which "a Life" remains in her writing in excess of the figures of that writing, the way in which her practice contained without becoming the lyric stuff of which she made it and out of which it was to be made.

"And bore her safe away"

Dickinson did and did not do what the poetesses in the print public sphere did so well: she did hypostatize the figure of the generic, suffering woman, but she did not abstract that figure into a personification that became the property of that sphere—or at least it did not become such an abstraction until well after the era of sentimental identification had passed.[35] Instead, she folded that public personification, as she folded other poetic genres, into texts that often point away from rather than toward their subject. A page she sent to Susan in early 1859, for example (fig. 36; H B186), carries some lines that, printed as a lyric for the first time in the twentieth century (by Martha Dickinson Bianchi in *Emily Dickinson Face to Face* in 1932), are not very interesting:

> Whose cheek is this?
> What rosy face
> Has lost a blush today?
> I found her—'pleiad'—in the woods
> And bore her safe away—
>
> Robins, in the tradition
> Did cover such with leaves,
> But which the cheek—
> And which the pall
> My scrutiny deceives—
> (F 48)

Although the flower to which "this" pointed is no longer on the page for the word to point *to*, on the manuscript its imprint is still visible. Visible as well is the small paper bird that Dickinson cut from *The New England Primer*.[36] In the *Primer*, the bird is a nightingale, and it (along with another nightingale, from which Dickinson's cutting isolated it) illustrates the letter *N* accompanied by the dimeter couplet, "Nightingales sing / In time of

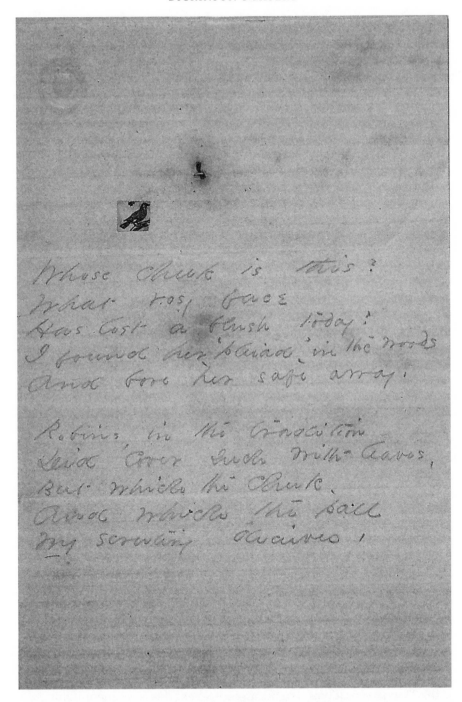

Figure 36. Emily Dickinson to Susan Gilbert Dickinson, 1859. The string that held
the flower and the flower's stain are still visible to the right above the nightingale.
By permission of the Houghton Library, Harvard University.

Spring." Susan would have known that the nightingale, tiny as it is, *was* a nightingale, because it was one of the images that taught her (and everyone else in the United States in the eighteenth and nineteenth centuries) to read. As we noticed in the third chapter in the valentine to Cowper Dickinson that consisted of cut-outs from the *Primer* and adapted lines from an old ballad, "while seeming to bind the alphabet to orthodoxy," as Patricia Crain writes, the *Primer* "in fact bound it firmly to everyday life."[37] In attaching the image of primary, everyday literacy to her lines, Dickinson also framed those lines *as* primary, everyday literacy of and in a particular genre. The frame of that genre is just being made visible in print by the new critics of women's sentimental lyric, but the frame of Dickinson's framing of that genre is invisible in print, though it is itself the creature of print. Dickinson's invocation of the figure of birdsong as the figure of the lyric has become a familiar strain in these pages, and her late nineteenth-century readers' reception of her verse as birdsong attested to the persistence of the trope that would be replaced by the trope of the lyric "speaker" in the twentieth century. The identification of poetesses *with* the nightingale as an image for the figure of the Poetess was about as common as the identification of letters in the *Primer*: Oakes Smith's "The Poet" was an exemplary instance of the countless wounded birds individual poetesses provided to illustrate the alphabet of sentimental lyric literacy.

In the early 1860s, Susan Dickinson sent Dickinson this message:

PRIVATE

I have intended to
write you Emily to-day but the
quiet has not been mine   I send
you this, lest I should seem to
have turned away from a kiss—
If you have suffered this past
summer   I am sorry   *I*
Emily bear a sorrow that I
never uncover—If a nightingale
sings with her breast against
a thorn, why not *we* [!]
When I can, I shall write—
Sue—[38]

Unlike Dickinson's flower attached to the lines that begin "Whose Cheek is this?" whatever it was that Susan sent—her "this"—as metonymic substitute for her affectionate presence has not left any evidence of its exchange. What *is* evident in Susan's message is the correspondents' mutual recognition of the nightingale's secret sorrow as an open secret that was not exactly the secret they wanted to share. Rather than identify with the nightingale as personification of female suffering, as Susan (if at arm's distance) suggests they do, Dickinson pastes the *Primer* nightingale— separated, like Dickinson, from its companion—to her sheet of paper next to a flower that metonymically substituted for "the writer's photograph in miniature" that their friend Samuel Bowles complained (in print) that women poets printed. The "this" that substitutes for the writer's affectionate presence in Dickinson's lines is the flower, which is already the substitute for the "cheek" of a woman who has, like the flower, died and been carried "safe away."

Or is it the other way around? Is the "cheek" a metaphor for the flower, or is the flower a metaphor for the "cheek"? Martha Nell Smith, who in this as in other instances has brought the material aspects of this text to the attention of Dickinson scholars, suggests that "the layout and attachment function as commentary on the poem, and the reader must develop their intertextual connotations. Doing so, one cannot help but recognize nor resist being amused by Dickinson's caricature of popular poetry . . . what appears to be a relatively insignificant little ditty of a lyric in fact mirthfully interrogates common poetic praxis."[39] I agree that Dickinson's lines have everything to do with poetic practice, but it seems to me that they work to deanthropomorphize, to dissolve the caricature of the Poetess that was circulated in "popular poetry" and that she stuck to the page in the imprint of the nightingale (which Smith reads as a "the cutout of the robin"). By presenting the "cheek" of the flower to Susan, Dickinson gives her something that does not have a face, and so cannot be effaced. Or is the effacement of the flower, like the effacement of the "Darkling" wounded nightingale, the problem here, and is this an even more ambivalently inflected invitation to vicarious identification with feminized lyric suffering than Oakes Smith's poem or Susan's letter?

No. In Dickinson's lines, the flower has been rescued from personification rather than delivered into it: "I found her—'pleiad'—in the woods / and bore her safe away—." Alive and in context, the flower seems to have sprung from the ground of poetic tradition: appropriately caricatured in quotation marks, the name that Ronsard in the sixteenth century took for himself and six other French poets from a group of Alexandrian poets who named themselves after the seven daughters of Atlas who, in the tradition, were metamorphosed as stars, has here been returned to a very different feminine figure for lyric personification than that represented by the wounded nightingale. The "this" that Dickinson offers Susan is not a vehicle for vicarious feeling; it is and is not, to recall de Man's definition of lyric anthropomorphism, "an identification on the level of substance," since it reverses the tropological process de Man described when a figure "is no longer a proposition but a proper name, as when the metamorphosis in Ovid's stories culminates and halts in the singleness of the proper name, Narcissus or Daphne or whatever."[40] Dickinson did not write to Susan "This is my cheek," or "this is my sorrow," or "this is my death," or "this is you." She did not name the flower; by taking it from the woods, rather than killing it she seems to have rescued it from being metamorphosed into other names—or other poems.

One of the lyrics it did not become was Emerson's poem "The Rhodora," a lyric almost as well known to highly literate New Englanders like Dickinson and Susan as the nightingales in the *Primer:*

The Rhodora

On Being Asked, Whence is the Flower?

In May, when sea-winds pierced our solitudes,
I found the fresh Rhodora in the woods,
Spreading its leafless blooms in a damp nook,
To please the desert and the sluggish brook.
The purple petals, fallen in the pool,
Make the black water with their beauty gay;
Here might the red-bird come his plumes to cool,
And court the flower that cheapens his array.
Rhodora! If the sages ask thee why
This charm is wasted on the earth and sky,
Tell them, dear, that if eyes were made for seeing,
Then beauty is its own excuse for being:
Why thou wert there, O rival of the rose!
I never thought to ask, I never knew;
But, in my simple ignorance, suppose
The self-same power that brought me there brought you.[41]

Often read as Emerson's defense of nature against culture, the lyric that Dickinson's lines echo personifies the flower found in the woods, metamorphosing "her" into the object of his romantic apostrophe, and finally into himself. In contrast, the fate to which the flower in Dickinson's lines is borne "safe away" is into Susan's hands, though what will happen to it once it gets there is much less certain than what happens to Emerson's humble flower. If the point of Emerson's poem is that, unlike the cultivated rose, the wild American Rhodora is not a traditional poetic subject (and therefore can become *his* lyric subject), then the point of Dickinson's lines is that the flower is not a subject at all. In invoking "the tradition" in which the robin covers the face of the unburied dead with leaves, Dickinson makes it clear that, like the paper nightingale whose tiny print body cannot "sing," the flower found not "fresh" but "'pleiad'" in the woods is not about to say a thing. It *is* a thing, and so cannot be either alive or dead, neither figurative "cheek" nor effaced "pall." This flower's charm was not wasted on the earth and sky, or on poetry.

But now we think that lyric poetry is what Emily Dickinson wrote. One of the most remarkable phases in the remarkable history of Dickinson's reception as a lyric poet has been the feminist adoption over the last twenty years of "My Life had stood—a Loaded Gun—" (F 764, fascicle 34) as an icon or allegory of Dickinson's claim to just the sort of lyric power I have spent this book suggesting that she did not want to have—or be. Yet since Adrienne Rich's declaration in 1974 that the poem "is a central poem in understanding Emily Dickinson, and ourselves, and the condition of the woman artist, particularly in the nineteenth century," and Sharon Cameron's extraordinary forty-page reading of the poem as "a dialectic of rage" in 1979, and Gilbert and Gubar's subsequent analysis of "the many ways in which this enigmatically powerful poem is an astounding assertion of 'masculine' artistic freedom" in that same year, "My Life had stood—a Loaded Gun—" became the ars poetica, the zero-sum game of interpretation, for nearly all accounts of Dickinson's writings as *lyrics*.[42] It is the poem, as feminist criticism has it, that does the dreamwork of Dickinson's poetics—the artistic agency the nineteenth-century woman poet could only imagine in someone else's hands. Yet in view of my very different account of Dickinson's use of lyric figures, and particularly in view of those figures' debts to sentimental poetics, "My Life had stood—a Loaded Gun—" begins to look like a nightmare. In it the life that just escapes figuration in "This Chasm" is, relentlessly, turned into a poem and taken back into the woods:

> My Life had stood—a Loaded Gun—
> In Corners—till a Day
> The Owner passed—identified—
> And carried Me away—
>
> And now We roam ×in Sovreign Woods—
> And now We hunt the Doe—
> And every time I speak for Him
> The Mountains straight reply—
>
> And do I smile, such cordial light
> Opon the Valley glow—
> It is as a Vesuvian face
> Had let it's pleasure through—

And when at Night—Our good Day done—
I guard My Master's Head—
'Tis better than the Eider-Duck's
ˣDeep Pillow—to have shared—

To foe of His—I'm deadly foe—
None ˣstir the second time—
On whom I lay a Yellow eye—
Or an emphatic Thumb—

Though I than He—may longer live
He longer must—than I—
For I have but the ˣpower to kill,
Without—the power to die—
ˣ the- ˣ low ˣ harm ˣ art

The plot is seamless and exact: once "identified," this "Life" does the work of its "Owner," becoming his vehicle so completely that the last lines can only perform the difference between the two as a riddle. The gun is powerful as long as it is a personification, a prosopopeia: it is pure, instrumental force because it is pure figure. It has been lifted so far away from the personal pronoun that inaugurates the poem that its body is recognizable in the final lines solely in relation to "His" body. The gun is not only her possessor's interpreter, she is his interpretation, his performance, his *interpretant.* When she speaks for him, it is as if "a Vesuvian face," a face fictively attributed to a strange phenomenon, had "let it's pleasure through"—though of course the gun has no face or any pleasure. It is not alive. As Judith Butler has argued, "the normative force of performativity—its power to establish what counts as 'being'—works not only through re-iteration, but through exclusion as well. And in the case of bodies, those exclusions haunt signification at its abject borders or as that which is strictly foreclosed: the unlivable, the nonnarrativizable, the traumatic."[43] The bravura performance of Dickinson's gun excludes through reiteration, and the specter of what it excludes is it own immortality, the lyric subjectivity its readers will keep bringing into being.

That Dickinson's work has become, for her later interpreters, a purloined *texte en souffrance* is a fate her writing predicted. What she could not have foreseen was that in order to escape that fate, she would have needed to write not only outside the lyric, but outside the history that modernity has passed and identified so it can carry us away.

Conclusion

> . . . and since
> our knowledge is historical, flowing, and flown.
> —*Elizabeth Bishop, "At the Fishhouses"*

LYRIC READING takes many forms, and I do not want my subtitle or the individual chapters of this book to give the impression that I have presented the only American model, much less the only modern model, that would be appropriate to Dickinson, or that there is any way out of the lyric or out of lyric reading as theory or practice, for Dickinson or anyone else. On the contrary, I have wanted to lead my reader into various theories of the lyric in order to think about both genre and genre formation historically. The difficulty of analyzing an object created by a certain historical perspective and at the same time analyzing that perspective itself can create an uneven pattern, or many overlapping points of focus, rather than a clearly resolved and well-framed subject. Because my argument has been that the framing of Dickinson's writing as a set of lyrics is not only an ongoing collective, historical process, but also a mistake, I have not tried to correct that mistake by deconstructing the lyric or what is sometimes called "lyric ideology," or by constructing an alternative feminist or humanist intentional and impassioned lyricism, or by bypassing genre and taking the pragmatic way out.

Instead, I have tried to place Dickinson's variously intentional and unintentional ways of writing next to nineteenth-, twentieth-, and twenty-first-century ideas of lyricism that have replaced those ways of writing with ways of reading. The previous chapters may have led my reader to expect in conclusion an answer to the question of what it was that Emily Dickinson wrote. But I have not wanted to find or to offer an alternative to lyric reading; I have wanted to find a way into various lyric genres (songs, notes, letters, lists, postscripts, elegies, jokes, ads, dead crickets, valentines, stamps, Poetess verse, pressed flowers, printed paper cut-out birds) as alternatives to a singular idea of the lyric, or to an idea of the lyric as singular, or to poetry as we now tend to understand it. To call such a miscellany either a list of *genres* or to call those genres *lyric* is to suggest how capacious retrospective lyric reading can be, and also to suggest the messiness that I would like to attach to what are often purified terms, to suggest that genres themselves might be read as historical modes of language power.

That echo of de Man modifies literary criticism's tendency to read gen-

235

res either from the inside out or from the outside in, to treat genres as if they excluded everything around them or to treat that everything as if it determined genres. Yet it also risks turning the lyric from an exclusive, hermetic genre into such a heterogeneous collage that the term devolves again into an all-purpose adjective. As *Dickinson's Misery* suggests in a number of ways, when *lyric* becomes an adjective, it evokes a theory of personal expression and abstraction that was highly problematic for Dickinson, but that has come to be highly valued in retrospect by modernism. As T. J. Clark has written in *Farewell to an Idea*, one of the distinctive features of both modernism and criticism is the nostalgia for the expressiveness they retroactively produce as what they cannot themselves be. "It seems that I cannot quite abandon the equation of Art with Lyric," Clark writes.

> Or rather—to shift from an expression of personal preference to a proposal about history—I do not believe that *modernism* can ever escape from such an equation. By "lyric" I mean the illusion in an artwork of a singular voice or viewpoint, uninterrupted, absolute, laying claim to a world of its own. I mean those metaphors of agency, mastery, and self-centeredness that enforce our acceptance of the work as the expression of a single subject. This impulse is ineradicable, alas, however hard one strand of modernism may have worked, time after time, to undo or make fun of it. Lyric cannot be expunged by modernism, only repressed.
>
> Which is not to say that I have no sympathy with the wish to do the expunging. For lyric in our time is deeply ludicrous.[1]

Why so idealize and so renounce the lyric? I have been suggesting that the lyric has come to seem so ideal and so ludicrous because it has been progressively identified with a form of personal abstraction that cannot quite be disowned, and yet cannot quite be embraced by modern critical culture. That is why Dickinson is such a perfect and pathetic figure for it, though that is the last thing she may have wanted to be.

In the 1950s, Joseph Cornell made a series of collage boxes inspired by things he had read by and about Emily Dickinson, and especially by her habit of using domestic scraps and objects as surfaces and enclosures. The most famous of those boxes, "Toward the Blue Peninsula" (1953), represents a pristine cage of isolation, a white box, the traces of a birdcage, white mesh wire, a blue window of lyric possibility. A less often seen box, "Chocolat Menier" (1952) (fig. 37), is much more cluttered, since it represents some of the things the absent subject has left behind: a chocolate wrapper, bits of string, a hidden shard of mirror pasted opposite a hidden, suspended metal ring in the cage from which the bird has flown. The chocolate wrapper (figs. 38a, 38b) on which Dickinson wrote some lines

Figure 37. Joseph Cornell, *Chocolat Menier*. 1952, mixed media construction (17 1/4 × 12 × 5 inches). Grey Art Gallery, New York University Art Collection, Anonymous gift, 1966. Courtesy of the NYU Art Colletion.

that have never been published as a poem was reported to Cornell by Jay Leyda, who catalogued it for the archive in Amherst; Cornell never read the lines themselves or saw the thin yellow wrapper in the archive, and he did not reproduce the lines on the back of the package of this expensive imported item newly available in New England in the 1870s (and made by

Figure 38a. Courtesy of Amherst College Archives and Special Collections (ED ms. 540).

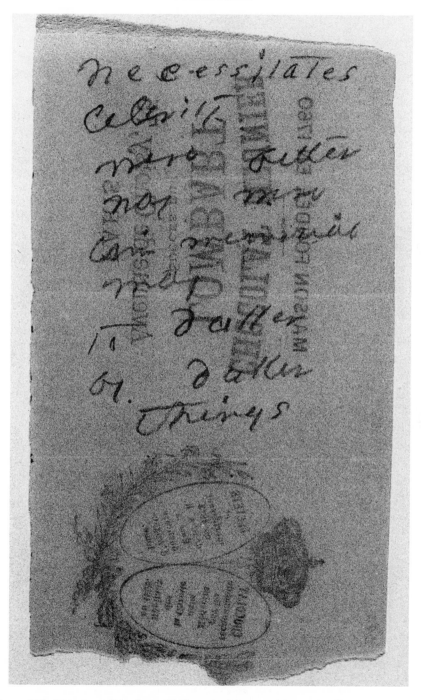

Figure 38b. Courtesy of Amherst College Archives and Special Collections (ED ms. 540).

the first industrial chocolate manufacturer and exporter in France). The lines or words or note or fragment,

> necessitates
> celerity
> were better
> nay were
> im memorial
> may
> to duller
> by duller
> things

are inscrutable, since everything that would explain them is missing.[2] What is missing is in turn what lyricizes the notion of the unread lines, or the private circumstances of an imaginary inscription on mass-produced print. Cornell frames what cannot be published, and in doing so turns toward its public the twentieth-century abstraction of the lyric, an idea of expression more telling than the poem that was never there.

Notes

Beforehand

1. In a letter to Mrs. C. S. Mack in 1891, Dickinson's sister Lavinia wrote, "I found (a week after her death) a box (locked) containing seven hundred wonderful poems, carefully copied" (17 February 1891; cited by Thomas H. Johnson in his introduction to *The Poems* [J xxxix]). This citation is one source for my narrative, though the tone and several of the details are drawn from Millicent Todd Bingham's sensationally partisan account of the "discovery" and publication of the poems in *Ancestors' Brocades*. Evidently, Dickinson's sister did burn many of her extant papers though there is nothing in the will directing her to do so. That Lavinia thought that the destiny of the poems was to appear "in Print," as she put it, is clear from her many letters to the poems' first editors, Mabel Loomis Todd and T. W. Higginson, and to the publisher, Thomas Niles of Roberts Brothers. Since these letters, the journals of Loomis Todd (in the Yale University Library) and the notes of Higginson (in the Boston Public Library) offer various versions of the manuscripts' recovery, my narrative is intentionally selective. A lucid narrative of the manuscripts' recovery and edition is offered by R. W. Franklin in his introduction to his edition of *The Poems of Emily Dickinson*. Susan Dickinson, the recipient of the greatest number of Dickinson's addressed manuscripts, did not write her own version of the story of the manuscripts' recovery, but her daughter, Martha Dickinson Bianchi, gives another wonderfully partisan account of that family's matrilineal transmission of the manuscripts in the introduction to *The Single Hound*. For that family's history of manuscript transmission, see Martha Nell Smith's and Ellen Louise Hart's introduction to *Open Me Carefully*. My account is a pastiche of these sources, and it is liberally influenced by my own experience of "discovering" the diversity of Dickinson's less carefully copied manuscripts (which may or may not have been in the locked box).

2. J. V. Cunningham, "Sorting Out: The Case of Emily Dickinson," in *The Collected Essays*, 354.

3. Norman Bryson, *Looking at the Overlooked*, 140.

4. See Robert Weisbuch, *Emily Dickinson's Poetry*, 19; Jay Leyda, *The Years and Hours of Emily Dickinson*, 1:xxi; Geoffrey Hartman, *Criticism in the Wilderness*, 129.

5. For the 1980 reading, see Margaret Homans, *Women Writers and Poetic Identity*, 194. Homans goes on to critique the strictly metaphorical interpretation that results when the lines are printed out of context, but she reads the lines lyrically nonetheless, and builds an argument about the relation between prose and poetry based on them: "Because the rhyming lines seem to grow spontaneously out of prose, they appear (whether or not Dickinson contrived the effect) to represent the untutored origins of poetry, as if poetry originated in imitation of nature" (195).

6. Mabel Loomis Todd, ed., *Letters of Emily Dickinson*; Martha Dickinson Bianchi, ed., *The Life and Letters of Emily Dickinson*; Mabel Loomis Todd, ed., *Letters of Emily Dickinson*; Thomas H. Johnson and Theodora Ward, eds., *The Letters of Emily Dickinson*.

7. See Charles Taylor, *Modern Social Imaginaries*, for the abstraction of the social imaginary. According to Taylor, "the social imaginary is not a set of ideas; rather it is what enables, through making sense of, the practices of a society" (2). Taylor follows Cornelius Castoriadis, who uses the term to refer to "the final articulations the society in question has imposed on the world, on itself, and on its needs, the organizing patterns that are the conditions for the representability of everything that the society can give to itself" (*The Imaginary Institution of Society,* 143). He also follows (as do I) the work of Benedict Anderson in *Imagined Communities*. On this logic, the lyric would be one such organizing pattern that takes distinctive shape in nineteenth-century print culture and shapes the growth of American literary criticism in the twentieth century.

8. Alistair Fowler puts the observation most succinctly when he warns that "lyric" in literary theory from Cicero through Dryden is "not to be confused with the modern term" (*Kinds of Literature,* 220). We will return in the next two chapters to the lyricization of postromantic poetry—and especially to the lyricization of Dickinson's writing as modern poetry. The phenomenon is aptly characterized by Glenn Most in an essay on ancient Greek lyricists:

> Some of us . . . may wonder what other kind of poetry there is besides the lyric. For a number of reasons it has become possible in modern times to identify poetry itself, in its truest or most essential form, with the lyric. . . . This is not to say that satires or poems for affairs of state have altogether ceased to be written; but these tend to be relegated to a secondary rank, whereas the essence of poetry is often located instead in a lyric impulse.

See Most, "Greek Lyric Poets," 76. As we shall see, the "number of reasons" to which Most alludes remain to be historically enumerated more carefully. The problem, of course, is how to do that. W. R. Johnson solved the problem in *The Idea of the Lyric*: by claiming that the lyric is transhistorical, a transcendent idea. M. H. Abrams made a start for a more historical approach to the nineteenth century in his "The Lyric as Poetic Norm" in *The Mirror and the Lamp,* 84–88, but surprisingly few scholars have extended his scant comments there. As we shall see, among those who have done so are Douglas Patey, whose "'Aesthetics' and the Rise of Lyric in the Eighteenth Century" is invaluable for its history of the lyric's ascendancy to "truest or most essential form"; Seth Lerer, "The Genre of the Grave and the Origins of the Middle English Lyric"; Mark Jeffreys, whose "Songs and Inscriptions: Brevity and the Idea of Lyric" makes a start for the difference between Renaissance genres and modern lyic ideas; and Stuart Curran, *Poetic Form and British Romanticism.*

9. Susan Stewart, "Notes on Distressed Genres," in *Crimes of Writing,* p. 67. It should be said that not only does Stewart not include the lyric as a "distressed genre," but she considers distressed genres opposed to avant-garde genres, since "the avant garde is characterized by a struggle against generic constraints" while "the distressed genre is characterized by a struggle against history" (92). Thus implicitly for Stewart the distressed genre would be reactionary and the avant-garde resistance to genre progressive. In chapter 2, we will return to Stewart's character-

ization of the lyric as both antigeneric (or avant-garde) and antihistorical (or distressed).

10. Gerard Genette, *The Architext*, 2. Genette's rereading of what he eloquently describes as the *lectio facilior* of finding the lyric where it was not in Plato and Aristotle should revise many accounts of modern poetics. Especially suggestive is Genette's conclusion that "modes and themes, intersecting, jointly include and determine genres" (73).

11. Mark Jeffreys, "Ideologies of Lyric: A Problem of Genre in Contemporary Anglophone Poetics," 200. Jeffreys's essay is particularly valuable for its exposition of the ways in which "the recent struggle to clear away New Critical poetics and to make room for a postmodernist poetics" (203) has often made the mistake of aligning the lyric itself (whatever that is, and Jeffreys is quite aware that generic definition is the question) with a reactionary critical ideology. For an earlier suggestive discussion of the problems entailed by the modern critical elevation of the lyric (and especially the critical abstraction of the romantic lyric), see Marjorie Perloff, *Poetic License.*

12. Mary Poovey, "The Model System of Contemporary Literary Criticism," 436. Poovey's argument depends on the version of the romantic lyric as formal structure as outlined by Clifford Siskin in *The Historicity of Romantic Discourse* (particularly in "Present and Past: The Lyric Turn," 3–63), and thus is itself the product of a critical fiction of the lyric rather than of any particular lyric (a situation that proves her point).

13. Percy, *Reliques of Ancient English Poetry*, xv–xxiii.

14. For an account of the history of literary history in the eighteenth century, see Jonathan Kramnick, *Making the English Canon: Print-Capitalism and the Cultural Past, 1700–1770.*

15. John Stuart Mill, "Thoughts on Poetry and Its Varieties," 345.

16. Anne Janowitz, *Lyric and Labour in the Romantic Tradition*, 19. Janowitz's book is the model of the sort of scholarship that *should* be done in nineteenth-century American poetry, especially since the public negotiation of what have been misunderstood as romantic ideals of the lyric was that poetry's stock in trade.

17. Matthew Rowlinson, "Lyric" in *The Cambridge Companion to Victorian Poetry*, 59.

18. Stuart Curran, *Poetic Form and British Romanticism*, 5. See Curran's wonderful "Prolegomon: A Primer on Subtitles in British Romantic Poetry," with which he prefaces his book for a lesson in antilyricization.

19. This is an exaggeration, but not much of one. In 1996, Joseph Harrington suggested that American literary studies since the 1950s has taken the view that "American poetry is not American literature" precisely because American literary studies bought "into a New Critical ideology of poetry" ("Why Poetry is Not American Literature" 508). Recently, that mistake has begun to be corrected: Kirsten Gruesz's *Ambassadors of Culture* does more to give an idea of Bryant and Longfellow in the period than most books that actually focus on the North American nineteenth century, and Mary Loeffelholz's *From School to Salon* makes nineteenth-century American women's poetry into American literature. See also John D. Kerkering's recent *The Poetics of National and Racial Identity in Nineteenth-*

Century American Literature and Lawrence Buell, *New England Literary Culture: From Revolution Through Renaissance.*

20. Cleanth Brooks and Robert Penn Warren, *Understanding Poetry*, xi–xii, vi.

21. The printed lyric's nostalgia for preprint forms of the genre might be attributed to Bakhtin's observation that genre is a repository of "undying elements of the *archaic*"; although a genre "lives in the present . . . it always *remembers* the past, its beginnings" (Mikhail Bakhtin, *Problems of Dostoevsky's Poetics*, 106). One might only add to Bakhtin's general point that if a genre cannot itself "remember" its history, readers have to invent one to remember for it.

22. Yopie Prins, *Victorian Sappho*, 19. Since "lyric reading" is an historically theorized process that Prins and I have thought out together (lyrically), her ideas on the subject will frequently subtend my own—more frequently, I fear, that I will be able to note often or explicitly enough in this book. For an explicitly co-written statement of some of these ideas, see Virginia Jackson and Yopie Prins, "Lyrical Studies."

23. Michael McKeon's is the classic form of an historical definition of genre in relation to the definition of the novel. According to McKeon, genre "cannot be divorced . . . from the understanding of genres in history . . . [T]he theory of genre must be a dialectical theory of genre" (*The Origins of the English Novel, 1600–1740* 1). In *Lyric Generations*, Gabrielle Starr argues that McKeon's dialectical history of the novel should include the lyric since, according to Starr, in the eighteenth century "the lyric mode is transformed by a history ostensibly not its own"—that is, by the history of the new print genre of the novel (1). Still, even in a history that is the history of the interaction and mutual revision of genres, the problem of what a generic form is before and after its revision (that is, what a literary form is when it is removed from the history that makes it into a literary form) remains. The closest thing to McKeon's book so far for the lyric form is Janowitz's *Lyric and Labour in the Romantic Tradition*. Something like it is needed for American lyric, and something like McKeon's recent anthology on *Theory of the Novel* is needed for the theory of the lyric.

24. Paul de Man, "Anthropomorphism and Trope in the Lyric," in *The Rhetoric of Romanticism*, 254. We will return to the difficulty (or, as he would put it, impossibility) of de Man's version of lyric reading in chapter 2.

25. Two recent versions of the Americanization of the lyric's only apparent transparency are Elisa New's *The Line's Eye* and Angus Fletcher's *A New Theory for American Poetry*. See my review of New's book in *Raritan*. Because both New and Fletcher embrace all poetry as essentially lyric, they both extend that embrace to include a lyricization of a national literary tradition.

The notable exception to the prevailing tendency to read Dickinson as if her lyricism were itself transparent is the work of Sharon Cameron, from *Lyric Time* to *Choosing Not Choosing*. Cameron's critical importance to the present study will become obvious in the chapters that follow.

26. My use of the phrase *"texte en souffrance"* is a shorthand allusion to the debate between Derrida and Lacan, which centered on Lacan's claim at the end of his seminar on Poe's "The Purloined Letter" that "the sender . . . receives from the receiver his own message in reverse form. Thus it is that what the 'purloined letter,'

nay, the 'letter in sufferance' means is that a letter always arrives at its destination" (*The Purloined Poet: Lacan, Derida, and Psychoanalytic Reading*, 35; Derrida's argument, "The Purveyor of Truth," is also included in this volume).

27. There are some excellent reception histories of Dickinson, but there is much more to be done; Buckingham's is the only history so far to give serious attention to the popular reception. See Caesar R. Blake and Carlton F. Wells, eds., *The Recognition of Emily Dickinson*; Karl Lubbers' *Emily Dickinson: The Critical Revolution*; Willis J. Buckingham's *Emily Dickinson's Reception in the 1890s*.

CHAPTER ONE: DICKINSON UNDONE

1. T. W. Higginson, "Letter to a Young Contributor"; "Emily Dickinson's Letters," 444.

2. "No such experience as this in the case of an unknown poet has been reported in New York City, at least in the present generation." This clipping is unmarked in Mabel Loomis Todd's scrapbook, Mabel Loomis Todd Papers, Manuscripts and Archives, Sterling Memorial Library, Yale University.

3. The precedence of print to handwriting in the nineteenth-century United States—or at least in New England—is a longer story than I can tell here. For suggestive beginnings on the subject, see Meredith McGill, "The Duplicity of the Pen," and her *American Literature and the Culture of Reprinting*, as well as Patricia Crain, *The Story of A*.

4. Jerome McGann, *The Textual Condition*, 87. For commentary on McGann's view, see Margaret Dickie, "Dickinson in Context," 325.

5. Michael Warner, *Publics and Counterpublics*, 81. Warner's apt phrase for one of the aspects of the phenomenology of lyric reading I describe is actually a way of summarizing his citation of my argument about the lyric, though the idea behind the phrase represents the way in which he has advanced my original ideas on the subject.

6. The lines were printed for the first time in *Bolts of Melody* in a section entitled "Poems Incomplete or Unfinished," given a number in the volume (618), and arranged as two quatrains without variants and missing one line:

> When what they sung for is undone
> Who cares about a bluebird's tune?
> Why, resurrection had to wait
> Till they had moved a stone.
>
> As if the drums went on and on
> To captivate the slain—
> I dare not write until I hear—
> when what they sung for is undone.

Bingham does not explain why she both arranges the lines as a poem and does not print them as such, except to say that "the above fragment was written after 'A pang,' but both are in the writing of the eighties" (BM, 308). Bingham's mother, Mabel Loomis Todd, first editor of the manuscripts, was given co-editorial credit though long since dead, and we do not know whether the decision to classify one manuscript as a poem and the other as an unfinished poem was Todd's or her daughter's. In any case, both Johnson and Franklin have followed the precedent.

7. "Like every previous appearance of Dickinson's poems, beginning with 'Sic transit gloria mundi' (2) in 1852, this edition is based on the assumption that a literary work is separable from its artifact, as Dickinson herself demonstrated as she moved her poems from one piece of paper to another" (F p. 27); "The distinction between genres was Dickinson's own. She maintained a workshop for the production, distribution, and recording of poetry, but separated letters from it" (F p. 34). G. Thomas Tanselle has eloquently defended Franklin's editorial distinctions between letters and poems, text and artifact in "Emily Dickinson as an Editorial Problem": "The judgment of editors mediates our approach to all authors," according to Tanselle, "and if we wish to think of degrees of mediation, I would say that less of it has been practiced on Dickinson than on many other writers" (79).

8. Hollander, "Breaking into Song," 74, and Herrnstein Smith, *Poetic Closure*, 63.

9. My questions about lyric recognition echo the title of Stanley Fish's essay, "How to Recognize a Poem When You See One." In that essay, Fish offers the example of a list of proper names (of authors of linguistic texts) that he wrote on the blackboard for one class before the entrance of another. The second class, on seventeenth-century religious poetry, then proceeded to read the list of names as if they were a seventeenth-century religious poem. Fish's conclusion from this accidental experiment is that "all interpretation is not the art of construing but of constructing. Interpreters do not decode poems; they make them" (327). While I agree with Fish that interpretation is the art of constructing, I would point out that the difference between his example and the construction of Dickinson's lyrics through interpretation is that his "interpretive community" had been instructed in the protocol for reading a historically defined (and not accidentally, pre-eighteenth-century) genre, whereas Dickinson's readers have defined the genre of her work according to much more flexible (though no less constructed) protocols of interpretation, which have often been not only replicated in but generated by the modern university classroom.

10. G. W. Hegel, *Aesthetics*, 2:971.

11. Paul de Man, "Anthropomorphism and Trope in the Lyric," *The Rhetoric of Romanticism*, 254. As I have suggested in the introduction, I take the phrase "lyric reading" from de Man, and, as my reader will notice, the pages that follow carry on a debate with de Man over the implications of the phrase I borrow from him, a debate often hidden between the lines, and not always possible to note explicitly. On de Man's contradictory notion of "lyrical reading," see Jonathan Culler, "Reading Lyric," and Yopie Prins, *Victorian Sappho*.

12. The classic study of Dickinson's relation to British poetic romanticism is Joanne Feit Diehl's *Dickinson and the Romantic Imagination*. Diehl's work still calls out for elaboration, especially given more recent work on the circulation of British romanticism in the United States. Gary Lee Stonum has done some of that elaboration in *The Dickinson Sublime* and Mary Loeffelholz has done suggestive work in this vein in *Dickinson and the Boundaries of Feminist Theory*.

13. Thomas Bailey Aldrich, "*In Re* Emily Dickinson" (1892), 143. The 1903 revision in included in Aldrich's collected works of that year, and is quoted in Karl Lubbers, *Emily Dickinson: The Critical Revolution,* 94.

14. Virginia Rinaldy Terris's 1973 dissertation "Emily Dickinson and the Genteel Critics" gives a good account of the critical deliberation in the 1890s over Dickinson's verse in relation to emerging mass culture; on the emergence of a distinction between literary and mass culture in the 1890s, see Andreas Huyssen, *After the Great Divide.*

15. Stoddard, "Technique in Emily Dickinson's Poems," *The Critic* 20 (January 9, 1892): 24. As I have noted earlier, in "The Model System of Contemporary Literary Criticism," Mary Poovey suggests that twentieth-century literary criticism relies upon the "organic form" of the romantic lyric as a paradigm for interpretation, but as these glimpses at the history of the interpretation of the lyric in U. S. critical culture indicate, the story of the transmission of the lyric *as* model has many chapters that remove it from Coleridge and Wordsworth. Francis Stoddard, for example, calls Emily Dickinson's form "subtle and medieval" rather than romantic ("Technique in Emily Dickinson's Poems," 24). For the history of the rise of English departments at the end of the nineteenth century and some of the issues in critical culture that arose with them, see Gerald Graff and Michael Warner, *Professing Literature,* and Michael Warner, "Professionalization and the Rewards of Literature."

16. On the literary critics' identification of textual interpretation with scientific observation, see John Guillory, "Literary Study and the Modern System of the Disciplines." Guillory's observation that "literary study internalized the fault line between the sciences and the humanities" (35) during the development of English departments in the 1890s illuminates Stoddard's remark.

17. Julia Ward Howe, "Battle-Hymn of the Republic" (1862), in Hollander, ed., *American Poetry: The Nineteenth Century,* 1:709–10.

18. We might say that Michael Warner's gloss on Howe's lines captures something of the spirit of Dickinson's: "Here, in 'The Battle-Hymn of the Republic,' violence does not appear as such. It does not say, 'let us kill'; it says 'let us die.' And it says that we should do this not to rule, but 'to make men free.' It appears not as a program of cruelty, but as a redemption from cruelty" ("What Like a Bullet Can Undeceive?," 4). While Dickinson's gloss on the sentiment in Howe's lines emerged from the discourse of the Civil War, Warner uses Civil War discourse to respond to the discourses that were already emerging around the incidents of September 11, 2001.

19. See Shira Wolosky, *Emily Dickinson: A Voice of War,* for a start in putting Dickinson in the context of Civil War discourse, and Karen Sanchez-Eppler, *Touching Liberty,* for some of the complications of that discourse that directly affected Dickinson.

20. Millicent Todd Bingham, "Prose Fragments of Emily Dickinson."

21. William H. Shurr, *New Poems of Emily Dickinson,* 1–2. Shurr's "discovery" of "a source of new Dickinson poems" in the letters serves as an example of the use of meter alone to separate genres.

22. Ibid., 91.

23. In "Emily Dickinson as an Editorial Problem," Tanselle cites a review of a Dickinson exhibition at Harvard (organized by Mary Loeffelholz) in 1998 to the ef-

fect that "'Dickinson has always been to some extent the creation of her editors'" (79). Tanselle's response is that "this statement is misleading if it is meant to suggest that Dickinson is unusual in this regard: the judgement of editors mediates our approach to all authors" (79). I am agreeing here with Tanselle, but it is worth asking why each edition of Dickinson appears so "dated" almost the moment it appears, whereas editions of, say, Shelley, some of whose manuscripts were in worse shape at his death than Dickinson's, do not. Perhaps revisionary editing (by hands other than the writer's own) has more to do with debates in critical culture than with the condition of any author's manuscripts.

24. Howe records her correspondence with Franklin in *The Birth-mark* (134), and, indeed, attributes to this correspondence the genesis of her book itself. In the chapters that follow, we will return to Howe's response to Franklin's editorial priorities, and particularly to her conviction that "the issue of editorial control is directly connected to the attempted erasure of anti-nomianism in our culture" (1).

25. Michael Silverstein and Greg Urban, eds., *Natural Histories of Discourse*, 81. Linguistic anthropologists such as Silverstein and Urban could offer us new ways of thinking about Dickinson's practices of "entextualization," ways that might give us some perspective on the narrow focus on modern literary textuality that has preoccupied editors and critics on all sides of the ongoing debates over Dickinson's manuscripts.

26. Franklin, *The Editing of Emily Dickinson*, 141–42. I will not reproduce here the arithmetic through which Franklin reaches his figure of 7680, but it is impressive.

27. Wimsatt and Beardsley, *The Verbal Icon*, 71.

28. Foucault, "What is an Author?," 118. See Meredith McGill's *American Literature and the Culture of Reprinting* for an extended consideration of what a dissolution of the "author function" could mean for a rereading of nineteenth-century literary culture.

29. Jerome McGann, *Black Riders*, 40. What McGann offers here is a succinct description of "genetic" editorial theory more generally, a theory that has, understandably, gotten a lot of mileage from Dickinson's manuscript and print situations.

30. Margaret Dickie, "Dickinson in Context," 322.

31. In his facsimile edition of the fascicles, for example, Franklin includes an "Index of First Lines," in effect presupposing that although they may be included on the same page or in the same collection, they are separate and separable poems. See *MB*, 1429–1442.

32. See Franklin's comments in his "The Emily Dickinson Fascicles."

33. It would be interesting to speculate on what sort of interpretive community Grossman supposed or sought to create in composing his "Summa" as a set of "Scholia" designed as a "Primer" in an emphatically lyricized poetic literacy. His work has already become a primer for critics, as Cameron's and Stewart's work attests.

34. Allen Grossman, *Summa Lyrica*, 207, 209, 211–12.

35. In addition to her association of Dickinson with modern poetry through her frequent citation of other modern poets, Cameron explicitly associates Dickinson's

poetics with Heidegger's phenomenology of "the Open," a concept Heidegger develops in his reading of Rilke (CC 190–91).

36. Other full-length studies of Dickinson's fascicles include Dorothy Huff Oberhaus, *Emily Dickinson's Fascicles: Method and Meaning,* and William H. Shurr, *The Marriage of Emily Dickinson: A Study of the Fascicles.* As the titles of these books indicate, they are interested in finding narratives in the discontinuous continuity of the texts of the fascicles. There seem to be many such narratives to find.

37. The distinction between "genre-as-medium and genre-as-work" is Stanley Cavell's way of making the question of genre "more curious" in "The Fact of Television," 243–45.

38. Harold Love, *The Culture and Commerce of Texts,* 145.

39. I am paraphrasing McCluhan here in order to argue against his version of technological determinism. See Marshall McCluhan, *Understanding Media* and *The Gutenberg Galaxy.*

40. Martha Nell Smith, who is responsible for much of the institutional organization and support for the sites, has a utopian vision of the possibilities of access and response they will offer. One wishes that her vision were possible. See Martha Nell Smith, "Computing: What's American Literary Study Got to Do with IT?"

41. Werner's definition is even more capacious than the modern definition of the lyric, yet within it her site makes many fine distinctions. To cite only her definition's *beginning,* the criteria for

> inclusion used in the current version of *Radical Scatters* are as follows: all of the fragments featured as "core" texts have been assigned composition dates of roughly 1870 or after; all of the core fragments are materially discrete (that is, fragments have not been editorially excerpted from other compositions); and all of the core fragments are inherently autonomous, whether or not they also appear as traces in other texts, and inherently resistant to claims of closure. Excluded from this version of the archive are fair- and rough-copy message- or message-drafts to identified or unidentified recipients; brief but complete poem drafts; extra-literary texts such as recipes and addresses; quotations and passages copied or paraphrased from other writers' works; and textual remains preserved only accidentally because Dickinson used the same writing surface to compose other texts. Two apparent exceptions to the above criteria require explanation. First, in instances in which a message-draft also exists as an independent fragment, perhaps as a pensée or meditation, the text has been included among the archive's core documents (e.g., A 802). Second . . .

Werner's fastidiousness as an electronic archivist is matched only by her sweep as a lyric reader. See her e-text (later reprinted in a scholarly collection) "The Flights of A821: dearchiving the proceedings of a birdsong" for an exemplary instance of her interpretation of a "fragment" on pieces of an envelope closely related to the text in figure 5 in the present chapter (1) as an exemplary lyric precisely because of its "snapping or short-circuiting of lyrical wires."

42. Elizabeth Wanning Harries argues in *The Unfinished Manner* that in the eighteenth century the fragment *was* a literary genre and not just a creature of interpretation. Compare Marjorie Levinson's argument in *The Romantic Fragment Poem* that the poetry that British romantic writers intentionally made as "fragmentary" invited the reader to fill in its blanks.

43. The phrase "the ends of the lyric" is taken not from Werner but from a book by Timothy Bahti entitled *The Ends of the Lyric*, in which Bahti makes an argument for "reading as the end and consequence at the ends of the lyric" (2). I borrow Bahti's title in order to indicate the genericism of Werner's sense of the fragments' "extrageneric" address.

44. The difference between Werner's earlier *Emily Dickinson's Open Folios*, her print edition of images of the late "fragments," and the digitized images available on *Radical Scatters* is a good measure of how much more vivid the Web images can be; they can even be digitally animated to spin, open, and close. What the Web *almost* manages to do is to personify the manuscripts themselves.

45. Brent Hayes Edwards, *The Practice of Diaspora*, 7.

46. Foucault, *Archaeology of Knowledge*, 131. See Derrida's *Archive Fever* for a different view of the archive's relation to what Foucault calls "the discontinuities of history," and see Carolyn Steedman's recent attempt in *Dust* to mediate between the two, and to offer her own autobiographical account.

47. Claudio Guillén, *Literature as System*.

48. Actually, Kenneth Burke uses the address on an envelope as an example of "semantic" as opposed to "poetic" meaning in *The Philosophy of Literary Form*, 122. For Burke, semantic meaning is determined as opposed to indeterminate meaning, an opposition it would be fruitful to compare to Herrnstein Smith's distinction between historical and fictive utterance in *On the Margins of Discourse*. Burke's example of the difference between determinate and indeterminate meaning on an envelope is worth citing: "Meaning, when used in the sense of 'correct meaning,'" Burke writes, "leads to an either-or approach. 'New York City is in Iowa' could, by the either-or principles, promptly be ruled out. The either-or test would represent the semantic ideal. But I am sorry to have to admit that, by the poetic ideal, 'New York City is in Iowa' could *not* be ruled out" (125). On Burke's view, Howe's and Werner's readings of Dickinson's envelopes would represent "the poetic ideal."

49. Carolyn Williams, "'Genre' and 'Discourse' in Victorian Studies," 520. Williams is in part elucidating Derrida's "The Law of Genre."

50. For the idea that genres are constitutive of rather than constituted by discourse, see Bakhtin, *Speech Genres*, and Benjamin Lee, *Talking Heads*.

51. Michael McKeon, *The Theory of the Novel*, 4; Mikhail Bakhtin, *Speech Genres*, 318.

52. Clifford Siskin, *The Historicity of Romantic Discourse*.

53. John Stuart Mill, "Thoughts on Poetry and Its Varieties," 423.

54. Sewall, in *The Life of Emily Dickinson*, 537, reports that Todd coined the term "fascicles."

55. As Bingham reconstructed Todd's version of the story, "Shortly after Emily's death her sister Lavinia came to me actually trembling with excitement. She had

discovered a veritable treasure—a box full of Emily's poems which she had no intention to destroy. She had already burned without examination hundreds of manuscripts and letters to Emily, many of them from nationally known persons, thus, she believed, carrying out her sister's wishes, without really intelligent discrimination. Later she bitterly regretted such inordinate haste. But these poems, she told me, must be printed at once. Would I send them to some printer—as she innocently called them—which was the best one, and how quickly could the poems appear"? (*Ancestors' Brocades*, 16–17).

56. Higginson, introduction to *Poems* 1890, iii. Higginson's citation from Emerson is taken from "New Poetry" in *Ralph Waldo Emerson: Essays and Lectures*, 1169.

57. Barton Levi St. Armand, "Keepsakes: Mary Warner's Scrapbook," in *Emily Dickinson and Her Culture*, 5. St. Armand's introduction of the commonplace book as an obvious correlate to Dickinson's "fascicles" has invited much curiosity but, curiously, has not so far had much effect on the interpretation of Dickinson's genres.

58. Helen Horowitz, in *Alma Mater*, describes the particular design of the Mount Holyoke Female Seminary as an intentional blend of the home and the school, with a common kitchen where students worked below and classrooms above (not incidentally the architectural design of the college was modeled on an insane asylum, perhaps the ideal combination of home and school). Mary Loeffelholz's *From School to Salon* gives the best account so far of the intimate relation of domestic and pedagogical spheres in nineteenth-century American culture, a relation that eventuated, as Loeffelholz puts it, in "a broad shift in the social locations in which American women gained access to authorship in the genre of poetry" (4). One might add that the shift Loeffelholz describes was also a shift in and of that genre.

59. The American insurance industry was founded by Benjamin Franklin, but it largely failed after the Civil War. Dickinson used the HOME INSURANCE CO. NEW YORK ads as stationery at just the time (1875) when the industry made a bid for the business of wealthy private homeowners like the Dickinsons. See Robert H. Tullis, *The Home Insurance Company*.

60. Gillian Brown, *Domestic Individualism*. For the place of the public sphere within the Dickinson home, see Diana Fuss, *The Sense of an Interior*.

61. Franklin cites the letter from Jackson (F 1299) and lists all of the extant manuscript versions.

62. Herrnstein Smith, *On the Margins of Discourse*, 33. We will return to Herrnstein Smith's distinction in chapter 3, but for now it is worth noting that she defines literature as "fictive utterance" and at the same time defines fictive utterance as literature—specifically, as Hamlet's speech. Thus, in order to invite us to imagine the difference between history and literature, Herrnstein Smith invites us to conceive of that difference *as* literature.

63. The bluebird's performance of what one might call art for art's sake in the lines sent to Jackson supports Loeffelholz's pairing of Jackson and Dickinson as figures suspended between the late nineteenth-century "poles of 'bourgeois art' and 'social art'" (*From School to Salon*, 135).

64. As my reader will already have noticed, the question of how we refer to the "titles" of Dickinson's texts opens all sorts of other questions, and the negotiation of these questions can be awkward. Since titles designate texts as individual poems, I usually avoid the practice of using first lines as titles, but some referential title is unavoidable. Since Franklin has no doubt that Dickinson wrote poems, he provides an appendix of "Titles, Characterizations, Signatures" that Dickinson used in her correspondence to refer to her verse (F 1545–46, app. 6). For an extended meditation on, history of, and speculation about the relation between lyric titles and generic definition, see Anne Ferry, *The Title to the Poem.*

CHAPTER TWO: LYRIC READING

1. The *Republican* notice is cited by Jay Leyda in *The Years and Hours of Emily Dickinson*, 2:87, though Leyda changes the assailant's name to "Cutler."

2. Bowles's and Beecher's comments on the Vanderbilt shooting are reported by Alfred Habegger, *My Wars Are Laid Away in Books*, 464.

3. On Dickinson's *Drum Beat* poems, see Karen Dandurand, "New Dickinson Civil War Publications," and "Dickinson and the Public" in Orzeck and Weisbuch, eds., *Dickinson and Audience*, 255–77. Dandurand's discovery opens important questions for Dickinson scholarship, which has been so focused on the possibility that there are more poems hidden in some attic or drawer that scholars have not gone in search of Dickinson's *public* circulation during her lifetime. Dandurand speculates that Dickinson volunteered the poems for the cause (more soldiers died of disease during the Civil War than fell in battle). If so, then she may either have conveyed them to Vanderbilt or to Richard Salter Storrs, the editor of the *Drum Beat* and an Amherst alumnus. Dandurand and others have thought Storrs the more likely candidate, but it is hard to say why, since we know that Dickinson had a correspondence with Vanderbilt while there is no evidence of a correspondence with Storrs.

4. Todd's notes to transcript, 59, 59a, 59b, 59c, Amherst Special Collections.

5. In Franklin's edition, the verses that Dickinson sent to Vanderbilt are Poems 505, 815, 895, and 946. They were all sent between 1863 and 1865. Franklin notes (p. 1556) that Gertrude Vanderbilt was "a friend of Catherine Scott Turner and through her of Susan Dickinson," a note that makes it clearer why Dickinson would have corresponded with Vanderbilt as part of an intimate genteel circle.

6. What is now Franklin's Poem 815 was first published in *Letters of Emily Dickinson* (1894), 154, as a ten-line stanza, then in *The Life and Letters of Emily Dickinson* (1924), 259, and *Letters of Emily Dickinson* (1931), 152, then as J Poem 830 in 1955.

7. F 946, Set 7. The difference between the "sets" and the "fascicles" is the string that binds the fascicle sheets but does not bind the sets. Since Dickinson apparently stopped binding fascicle sheets in 1865, during the time she was in Cambridge under treatment for eye trouble, Franklin views the unbound sets as a stage in the "winding down" of Dickinson's ambitions for her "workshop" (F 25).

8. Shira Wolosky, *Emily Dickinson: A Voice of War*, 7.

9. I have no doubt that these lines did contain an enclosure, though since there is no autograph copy, I have no evidence other than the lines themselves and Dickinson's habits of correspondence that the flowers were there.

10. Fascicle 39; MB 968.

11. *Ancestors' Brocades*, 36.

12. Dickinson's reversal of the usual referential relations between flowers and poems was one of her favorite puns, and there are too many instances to list, but it is worth noting that in the Bullard portrait of the Dickinson children in 1840, Emily holds a flower on an open book (see Habegger, *My Wars Are Laid Away in Books*, 366).

13. The manuscript is at Scripps College. Franklin prints the lines in quatrains (F 895), the first editor to include this early version in his variorum edition. Johnson broke this manuscript (or the transcript he had seen of it) into two poems (as had Bingham in BM, 1945) and made the last one (from the last two stanzas of this manuscript, beginning "The Earth had many keys—") the last poem in his edition (J 1775).

14. For an account of the poem's bibliographical history, see Franklin, "The Manuscripts and Transcripts of 'Further in Summer than the Birds.'" In "Dickinson and the Public," Dandurand makes the point that Storrs sent copies of the paper to all of his contributors, so he would have sent a copy to Dickinson. If Vanderbilt gave the poem to the paper, however, Storrs might not have known to send the paper to Amherst—though Vanderbilt may have done so.

15. Readers of Dickinson will recognize absurd anthropomorphism as one of her favorite tropes—as, for example, when she wrote to Louise Norcross that "it is lovely without the birds today, for it rains badly, and the little poets have no umbrellas" (L 340).

16. The address on the first manuscript, sent to Susan in the 1850s, has been erased. Hart and Smith note that in the context of Dickinson's correspondence with Susan, "Emily's poem echoes a poem by Susan, 'There are three months of Spring,' suggesting a call-and-response relationship in their writing life" (OC 71).

17. Louis Menand, *The Metaphysical Club*, x. I am simplifying Menand's argument, which is not only about the failure of the particular ideas that could no longer be held after the war, but about "a certain idea about the limits of ideas" (4). Ultimately, Menand sees that failure as the generative force behind the development of American pragmatism.

18. See Jenny Franchot's *Roads to Rome* for an argument that "anti-Catholicism operated as an imaginative category of discourse through which antebellum American writers of popular and elite fictional and historical texts indirectly voiced the tensions and limitations of mainstream Protestant culture" (xvii). Dickinson does not exactly fit Franchot's sense of that category, but Franchot's argument is suggestive for a reading of the Catholic imagery that pops up here and there in Dickinson's writing, since it makes clear that such imagery was not a quirk of Dickinson's but a common, and complex, cultural currency.

19. Diehl, *Dickinson and the Romantic Imagination*, 97. Since Diehl was reading the

poem in Johnson's edition, she did not have the last eight lines sent to Vanderbilt, so she did not know how right she was about the echo of Keats. See Mary Loeffelholz's commentary on Diehl's suggestion about the echo in *Dickinson and the Boundaries of Feminist Theory*, 145–46. Because Loeffelholz also had stanzas as they were printed as two different poems in Johnson's edition, she reads the last lines sent to Vanderbilt, which became the last poem in Johnson, as Dickinson's self-elegy.

20. *Atlantic Monthly* 93 (July 1865): 11.

21. See Michael Warner's "What Like a Bullet Can Undeceive?" for a reading of the way in which "violence" is defined against pastoral in Civil War poetry, specifically in Melville's elegy "Shiloh."

22. Compare Dickinson's "Beauty is Nature's fact" to Emerson's line in "The Rhodora" (published almost thirty years before Dickinson's lines were written): "Then beauty is its own excuse for being." We will return to Emerson's "The Rhodora" in the final chapter, but for now we should note that among the many exchanges that seem to have gone on between these lines, Dickinson's ongoing response to Emerson was one of them.

23. L 324; Boston Public Library manuscripts 21 and 22.

24. Habegger, in *My Wars Are Laid Away in Books*, calculates the dog's age, and speculates that the dog may have been named for St. John Rivers's dog in *Jane Eyre* (226), a speculation that would mediate even Dickinson's relationship with her dog through literature.

25. Dickinson's letter to Higginson in June 1864 is a striking condensation of life, death, and literature: "Are you in danger—I did not know that you were hurt. Will you tell me more? Mr. Hawthorne died" (L 290). For a partial account of Higginson's experiences as the white leader of a group of black soldiers during the war, see his autobiographical account in *Army Life in a Black Regiment*.

26. It was actually Helen Hunt Jackson who was responsible for the publication of the lines that begin "Success is counted sweetest" in what she called a "volume of 'no name' poetry" in 1878 (*A Masque of Poets*, Boston: Roberts Brothers, 1878). A copy of the book was sent to Dickinson either by Jackson or by Roberts Brothers as a matter of course, but Dickinson seems to have considered the book a gift from the publisher himself, so she sent a thank-you note to him, thus initiating a private correspondence. The exchange between Dickinson, Jackson, and Niles is included by Johnson as L 573a, 573b, 573c, and 573d.

27. It should be said that the intimacy of textual gift exchange does not mean that those gifts do not participate in their own economy, and it would be interesting to speculate along these lines in relation to Marcel Mauss's classic text on cultural economy, *The Gift*. In the context of the exchange with Niles, Dickinson seems to have transgressed his sense of the decorum that separated gift and business exchange when she sent him her own copy of the Brontë sisters' poems (L 813, 813a, 813b).

28. On the relation between singular objects and commodity forms, see Igor Kopytoff, "The Cultural Biography of Things." For an extended discussion of the relation between "thing theory" in anthropology, art history, political science, and

American literary studies (a discussion I wish I could expand here in more detail), see Bill Brown, "Thing Theory" and *The Sense of Things*.

29. Austin Warren, "Emily Dickinson," in Lubbers, ed., *The Recognition of Emily Dickinson*, 268–86. Warren's response to the 1955 Johnson scholarly edition was nostalgia: "This is not the edition in which to enjoy Emily," he wistfully remarked. "I recall the pleasure of reading her in the slender gray volumes of the 1890s. For pleasure, as for edification, Emily should not be read in big tomes, or much of her at a time" (269).

30. Todd's comment is cited by her daughter in *Ancestors' Brocades*, 17, in a story Bingham compiles from a number of sources, including the draft of Todd's essay, "Emily Dickinson's Literary Début," which appeared in *Harper's Magazine* for March 1930, as well as Todd's diaries and their personal conversations. Thus both Todd's account itself—and Bingham's account of it—are intended for both a private and public audience.

31. In a juicy account of the affair between Dickinson's brother and her editor, Polly Longsworth published letters back and forth between them, from this period and others. Toward the end of September 1883, Todd wrote to Austin asking him to "destroy this," and commenting, "how the crickets are chirping today" (*Austin and Mabel*, 169).

32. Cited in Longsworth, *Austin and Mabel*, 168.

33. Porter, *Dickinson: The Modern Idiom*, 9.

34. Yvor Winters, "Emily Dickinson and the Limits of Judgment," in *In Defense of Reason*, 283–99.

35. Notice that the 1891 editorial substitution of "Calls forth" for "arise" in these lines attributes the "canticle" to the season, whereas in the manuscripts its source is left in suspense.

36. John Crowe Ransom, *The New Criticism*.

37. This is why, as Jonathan Arac points out, "for New Criticism 'lyric' was not an object of theoretical concern. Allen Tate locates 'structure' not in 'genre' but in 'language.' *The Well Wrought Urn* is about 'poetry,' not about lyric, and this 'critical monism' was attacked in *Critics and Criticism* (1952) by R. S. Crane, a Chicago neo-Aristotelian for whom genre was deeply important" ("Afterword: Lyric Poetry and the Bounds of New Criticism," 352).

38. See Jeffreys, "Ideologies of the Lyric," 203. Jeffreys and I agree that "from a welter of other poetic genres, lyric gradually emerged as the most common catchall category, and only in the nineteenth and twentieth centuries was it mythologized as the purest and oldest of poetic genres and thus transformed into a nostalgic ideological marker" (197). As Jeffreys also points out, the view of the New Criticism as associated with a certain version of the lyric is hardly new: see Murray Krieger, *The New Apologists for Poetry*, and Gerald Graff, *Poetic Statement and Critical Dogma*.

39. For historicist accounts of the New Criticism (if not of the New Critical idea of the lyric), see John Fekete, "The New Criticism: Ideological Evolution of the Right Opposition," Frank Lentricchia, *After the New Criticism*, and John Guillory, *Cultural Capital*. Guillory's assessment of New Critical culture resonates with Win-

ters's reading of "My Cricket": "the effect of New Critical pedagogy," Guillory writes, was "to produce a kind of recusant literary culture, at once faithful to the quasi-authority of literature but paying tribute at the same time to the secular authority of a derogated mass culture" (*Cultural Capital,* 175).

40. Blackmur, "A Note on Yvor Winters," in *The Expense of Greatness,* 167.

41. For a recent example of the return to Winters as example of the moral authority literary criticism *should,* by some account, wield, see David Yezzi, "The Seriousness of Yvor Winters."

42. Allen Tate, "New England Culture and Emily Dickinson" (1932), included in *The Recognition of Emily Dickinson,* 154. In *Becoming Canonical in American Poetry,* Timothy Morris argues that Tate "constructed a unitary central self for Dickinson" in his reading (76), though that seems a property of the genre that Tate attributed to Dickinson , and in any case it is not true that Tate is acting, as Morris claims, simply as a representative of New Critical "canonization" or as "a virtual Eliot" in his reading of Dickinson.

43. R. P. Blackmur, "Emily Dickinson: Notes on Prejudice and Fact," in *The Expense of Greatness,* 118.

44. On the creation of academic culture out of the reading of individual texts, see Gerald Graff and Michael Warner, *Professing Literature,* and Michael Warner, "Professionalization and the Rewards of Literature."

45. Cleanth Brooks and Robert Penn Warren, *Understanding Poetry,* 18.

46. Theodor Adorno, "Lyric Poetry and Society," 38.

47. Actually, as Bruce Mayo points out in his useful introduction to the *Telos* publication of Adorno's essay, "Lyric Poetry and Society" was "originally broadcast as an adult education lecture over RIAS in Berlin" (51). The essay was then revised several times, though it remains tantalizingly brief.

48. This is not to say that Adorno has had *no* effect on American lyric reading; critics have turned to "Lyric Poetry and Society" at various moments, yet it has had little influence in the *way* that poetry is read in the United States. As representative exceptions, see Fredric Jameson, *The Political Unconscious,* 281–99; Annabel Patterson, "Lyric and Society in Jonson's *Under-wood,*" 162–63; Margaret Homans, "'Syllables of Velvet,'" 570; Forest Pyle, *The Ideology of Imagination,* 120–25; and especially John Brenkman, *Culture and Domination,* 108–21. As the length and eclecticism of my partial list suggests, we are still trying to take what we can from Adorno's brief remarks on the lyric. In order to extend those remarks, we would need to look beyond "Lyric Poetry" and into Adorno's work as a whole, and especially to his theory of music. Robert Kaufman's work on Adorno promises to be the best guide so far to Adorno as guide to romantic and modern lyric reading: See Kaufman's "Adorno's Social Lyric, and Literary Criticism Today: Poetics, Aesthetics, Modernity." For a modern poetic meditation on Adorno's poetics, see Drew Milne, "In Memory of the Pterodactyl: the limits of lyric humanism," and for a transformative sense of Adorno's scope, see Stathis Gourgouris, *Does Literature Think?*

49. As in the case of Adorno, Benjamin has become for many critics a figure of what criticism *should* or *would* do in relation to the lyric if we could only figure out

how to do it, a figure of utopian critical possibility rather than a model for practice. See Fredric Jameson, *The Political Unconscious*, and especially Jonathan Arac, "Walter Benjamin and Materialist Historiography," in *Critical Genealogies*, 177–214. Arac's suggestive comparison of Dickinson and Baudelaire under the auspices of Benjamin is especially relevant to the present study, though in light of my argument here, Dickinson and Baudelaire begin to seem comparable not, as Arac would suggest, because they do or do not share some essentially modern experience, but because they have both become such paradigmatic instances of the lyric.

50. De Man's place in the Yale School is much discussed, but his relation to Brower, who was also an influence on other exemplary lyric readers such as Vendler, Poirier, Hertz, and Orgel, and who coined the phrase "close reading" in *The Fields of Light* has been less discussed. My thanks to John Guillory, whose point it is that Brower coined "close reading," for pointing me toward Brower.

51. Paul de Man, "Anthropomorphism and Trope in the Lyric," in *The Rhetoric of Romanticism*, 261. This is the sort of statement that prompts Barbara Johnson to remark that "Anthropomorphism and Trope" is "one of the most difficult, even outrageous" of de Man's essays. See her reading of the essay in "Anthropomorphism in Lyric and Law," 206. It is also the sort of statement that makes it clear that Jonathan Arac was right to make explicit "the beginnings of de Man's work in countercommentary, more an intervention within criticism than a direct response to works of literature" (*Critical Geneologies*, 239).

52. Paul Hernadi, *Beyond Genre*, 79.

53. René Wellek, *Discriminations*, 252.

54. Paul de Man, "Hypogram and Inscription," 35n.

55. Jonathan Culler, "Reading Lyric," 105. For a genealogy of what de Man means by "lyric reading," and of one sort of lyric reading leading directly to de Man, see also Culler's "Changes in the Study of the Lyric."

56. Charles Baudelaire, *Les Fleurs du Mal*, translated by Richard Howard, 193; 15.

57. Baudelaire, *Les Fleurs du Mal*, 254; 77.

58. For an extended answer to this question (though not with reference to "Anthropomorphism and Trope"), see Rei Terada, *Feeling in Theory*. I hope that it will be obvious in these pages how much I owe to Terada's eloquent insight that "poststructuralist thought about emotion is hidden in plain sight" (3).

59. Paul de Man, "Tropes (Rilke)," in *Allegories of Reading*, 37.

60. See especially de Man's reading of Mallarmé's "Tombeau de Verlaine" in "Lyric and Modernity" in *Blindness and Insight*, 166–86; the elaborate allusion to Porphyry's esoteric interpretation of the Homeric ode "The Cave of the Nymphs" in de Man's reading of Yeats in "Landscape in Wordsworth and Yeats" in *The Rhetoric of Romanticism*; and, most suggestively, his reading of the figure of the pyramid in Baudelaire's "Spleen II" as "un immense caveau" in "Lyrical Voice in Contemporary Theory."

61. I hope that the trope of authority that I attribute here to de Man will not be confused with Frank Lentricchia's argument in his essay "Paul de Man: The Rhetoric of Authority" (in *After the New Criticism*). There Lentricchia claims that de Man "has always given the impression of having a grip on the truth" (284) and then

indicts that "impression" as "the realm of the thoroughly predictable linguistic transcendental" (317). I would argue instead that the impression of authority in de Man's discourse derives from a much more complex identification with the "transcendental" literary moment that holds the critic, despite himself, in its unpredictable and contingent grip.

62. Paul de Man, "Form and Intent in the American New Criticism," in *Blindness and Insight*, 31.

63. Sigmund Freud, *Inhibitions, Symptoms and Anxiety*, 37–38.

64. For a similar recognition of this "typical" critical gesture see, for example, Neil Hertz's tribute to Derrida's "remarkable ability to both fish *and* cut bait" in *The End of the Line*, 208.

65. My sense of de Man's prose as "in mourning" for its subject is indebted to conversations with Eric Santner; see Santner's suggestive discussion of de Man's "uncompromising elegiac rigor" in *Stranded Objects*, 13–19.

66. For a reading of de Man as a figure for "theory," see Guillory, "Literature After Theory: The Lesson of Paul de Man," in *Cultural Capital*, 176–265. I intentionally leave aside here the scandal of the "discovery" of de Man's career in Europe around World War II, but obviously the surcharge of de Man's personification of "theory" derives from that scandal.

67. Steven Knapp and Walter Benn Michaels, "Against Theory," originally published in *Critical Inquiry* 8, no. 4 (Summer 1982), and reprinted in *Against Theory: Literary Studies and the New Pragmatism*, ed. W.J.T. Mitchell, 11–30. The Mitchell volume includes the essay itself alongside most of the relevant immediate critical responses to it, as well as Knapp and Michaels's "A Reply to Our Critics" (*Critical Inquiry* 9, no. 4 [Summer 1983]); hereafter citations from the essays included in this volume will be designated AT.

68. See, for example, E. D. Hirsch Jr., *Validity in Interpretation*, 227–30 and 238–40; P. D. Juhl's revision or refinement of Hirsch's use of this example in *Interpretation*, 71–72; J. Hillis Miller, "On the Edge: The Crossways of Contemporary Criticism"; and M. H. Abrams, "Construing and Deconstructing," both in Morris Eaves and Michael Fisher, eds., *Romanticism and Contemporary Criticism*. It is Abrams who recalls that Hirsch's previous use of the poem was already an attempt to adjudicate the conflicting claims of still earlier readers: Cleanth Brooks and F. W. Bateson (145n27).

69. Actually, as William C. Dowling suggests, what Knapp and Michaels had was a paradigm of New Critical interpretations based on the distinction between author and speaker. "What Knapp and Michaels make clear," Dowling writes, "is that the formalist argument succeeded in its season by exploiting to the fullest an intentionality that is already and inevitably entailed by the very notion of meaning" (AT 94). Or by lyric meaning?

70. Georg Lukács, *The Theory of the Novel*, 63. Adorno's theory of the lyric as "a sphere of expression whose very essence lies in defying the power of social organization" would seem to grow directly out of Lukács's Hegelian rendering of the lyric (as opposed to the novelistic) subject. Likewise, Heidegger's widely influential idealization of poetry as "the saying of the unconcealedness of what is" seeks

to isolate the lyric subject from "the world's outer space," orienting it at the extreme verge of "the world's inner space" (*Poetry, Language, Thought,* 74). For an explicitly Heideggerian reading of Dickinson's poetry, see Sharon Cameron, "The Interior Revision" (CC 190–94).

71. *The Shape of the Signifier,* 9. Michaels's reference here is explicitly to the essays in the posthumously published *Aesthetic Ideology,* essays in which de Man explored the contradictions of textual materialism to which he gestured at the end of "Anthropomorphism and Trope in the Lyric." The implications of Michaels's argument as well as his deep reading of de Man (among much else) reach far beyond what I can discuss in these pages, though it is worth noting that his eloquent conclusion that "history, as of this writing, is still over" (182) is not unrelated to de Man's utopian and elegiac sense that history is by definition what cannot be represented in theory.

72. Susan Stewart, *Poetry and the Fate of the Senses,* 2. Stewart's ambitious project is also an attempt to bridge what has become an intellectual and institutional divide between poets and critics, or to re-establish the American tradition of the poet-critic (a tradition to which Susan Howe also belongs). Because there is some perception that this divide, which dates from the twentieth-century shift between figures like Higginson (a poet-critic who did not teach at a university) to figures like Tate and Winters (poet-critics who did), was more recently a schism caused by literary theory, Stewart explicitly opposes her project to de Man's. In a long footnote, Stewart counters de Man's argument that "the linguistic basis of . . . anthropomorphization is always a kind of defacement, inadequate to its object," by writing that she "would argue that this approach constantly reinscribes the very allegory it seeks to discover" (341–42, n. 107).

CHAPTER THREE: DICKINSON'S FIGURE OF ADDRESS

1. Anne Carson, *If Not, Winter,* fragment 96, 191; note 96.3, 371; (Dickinson L 56).

2. Yopie Prins, *Victorian Sappho,* 3.

3. The notion that passages of Dickinson's letters that fall into hymnal meter should be excised as individual lyrics is an old one, but its most recent and extreme practitioner is William Shurr in his *New Poems of Emily Dickinson.*

4. Anne Carson, *If Not, Winter,* ix.

5. Isobel Armstrong, *Victorian Poetry,* 111. Surprisingly, there has been no real study of Dickinson's relationship to the Victorians, or to the issues raised in Victorian poetry, and especially Victorian lyric. For Susan Dickinson's notes to *The Princess,* see Alfred Habegger, *My Wars Are Laid Away in Books,* 266.

6. Alfred Lord Tennyson, *The Princess: A Medley* (1847; 1850); this song is the introduction to Part III.

7. "Roll on, silver Moon," arranged by Joseph W. Turner; Oliver Ditson & Co., Boston (1847). This was the most popular arrangement and publication of the song. The Dickinsons had a large collection of sheet music which was (unlike their library, which now has a separate room to itself at the Houghton Library at Harvard) as far as I know not preserved, since it was considered ephemera rather than

literature. That sheet music is clearly one source or basis for many Dickinson lines, and speculation along these lines could open new areas of research for Dickinson scholars and students of American popular culture.

8. Donald Grant Mitchell ("Ik Marvell"), *Reveries of a Bachelor, or, A book of the heart*. The book was a sensation, and was passed back and forth between Dickinson, Austin, and Susan. In the note in which she invokes Dickinson's letter, Carson somewhat startlingly compares Mitchell to Homer in the sense that Sappho adapts Homer's signature adjective "rosyfingered" for twilight rather than dawn and for lyric rather than epic, and Dickinson "may startle a bit of destiny for herself" out of Mitchell's "clichés" (371 n 96.7).

9. The classic text on nineteenth-century female intimate literary and extraliterary exchange is Carroll Smith-Rosenberg's "The Female World of Love and Ritual" in *Disorderly Conduct*.

10. "Father was very severe to me; he thought I'd been trifling with you, so he gave me quite a trimming about 'Uncle Tom' and 'Charles Dickens' and these 'modern Literati' who he says are *nothing*, compared to past generations, who flourished when *he was a boy*. Then he said there were 'somebody's *rev-e-ries*,' he didn't know whose they were, that he thought were very ridiculous, so I'm quite in disgrace at present" (so Dickinson to Austin in April 1853 [L 1:113]).

11. Here I am simply (and, I fear, reductively) condensing the argument of Jürgen Habermas in *The Structural Transformation of the Public Sphere*.

12. On Dickinson's grammars, see Carlton Lowenberg, *Emily Dickinson's Textbooks*.

13. For a lyric reading of Dickinson's frequent exploitation of pronominal confusion, see Cristanne Miller, *Emily Dickinson: A Poet's Grammar*.

14. John (Jack) Spicer, "The Poems of Emily Dickinson," 136, 140. The California poet "Jack" was serving a brief stint during 1956–57 as curator of Rare Books and Manuscripts, Boston Public Library.

15. Ellen Hart is quoted in Domhnall Mitchell's *Emily Dickinson: Monarch of Perception*, 208; I also quote Mitchell from 209. For other serious work on the letters as such, see William Merrill Decker's chapter, "A Letter Always Seemed to Me Like Immortality: Emily Dickinson," in his *Epistolary Practices*, and Marietta Messmer's *A Vice for Voices*. Both are especially good at putting Dickinson's letters back into the nineteenth-century culture of the familiar letter, and Messmer comes close to questioning the distinction between letters and poems.

16. Ellen Louise Hart and Martha Nell Smith, introduction to *Open Me Carefully*, xxvi. On the Dickinson Electronic Archive site, "Correspondences" is the only generic term for Dickinson's and others' writing as it is posted on the site. "Letter-poem" is a hybrid term that editors borrow from Susan Dickinson.

17. Buckingham's *Emily Dickinson's Reception in the 1890s* makes the enthusiasm of the immediate reception of Dickinson's poems evident to modern readers. This reception is especially important for, as Buckingham notes, "twentieth-century Dickinson criticism, in many ways, has been a history of mis-characterizing the nineteenth-century reception (as mostly unfavorable) for the purpose of

writing against it" (xii). Hereafter citations to this volume will be designated Buckingham."

18. Percy Bysshe Shelley, "A Defence of Poetry," in Bromwich, *Romantic Critical Essays* 223. It is important to note that when taken out of context, Shelley's figure of the nightingale can (and has) become a cliché that the argument of Shelley's essay actually works against. Rather than an impression of unmediated voice, what the poem gives to the reader according to Shelley is, as David Bromwich reads the "Defence," "only the text of the poem [which] remains as a positive trace or inscription. Its sense may vanish with the mortality of the author. But its power may revive nevertheless, under a different and unfamiliar aspect, at the coming of later authors and readers who find that the traces concern them after all" (213).

19. For another "account of the relation, for [Dickinson], of privacy to the genre of lyric poetry," see Christopher Benfey, *Emily Dickinson and the Problem of Others,* 29–62. While Benfey's concerns parallel my own, he ends by emphasizing, rather than qualifying, the self-enclosure of the poems: what Dickinson "requires above all," Benfey writes, "is that something about her, or *in* her, remain hidden from the view of others. It is the terrible exposure of existence that appalls her" (62).

20. Percy Lubbock, "Determined Little Anchoress,"114. Lubbock's review is of both *Selected Poems of Emily Dickinson,* ed. Conrad Aiken (London: Jonathan Cape, 1924), and *The Life and Letters of Emily Dickinson,* ed. Martha Dickinson Bianchi (reprinted in London by Jonathan Cape, 1924). These were the editions that made such an impression on modernist writers like Faulkner in the twenties.

21. For a discussion of the relation between domestic self-enclosure and the development of American individualism, see Gillian Brown, *Domestic Individualism.* Brown's premise in this book, "that nineteenth-century American individualism takes on its peculiarly 'individualistic' properties as domesticity inflects it with values of interiority, privacy, and psychology" (1), is very suggestive for a reading of Dickinson that would take into account the specifically domestic (and thus gendered) cast of Dickinson's seclusion. The class-bound privilege of that seclusion certainly worked—as in the famous accounts of the "Myth of Amherst" which became the theatrical production *The Belle of Amherst*—to foster the spectacular domestication of the generic ideal, but one should beware of extending it (as Betsy Erkkila does in "Emily Dickinson and Class") to a caricature of Dickinson's privileged domestic sensibility as that of a bigoted Whig.

22. In Buckingham, *Emily Dickinson's Reception in the 1890s,* 64.

23. Herbert F. Tucker, "Dramatic Monologue and the Overhearing of Lyric," 242.

24. John Stuart Mill, "Thoughts on Poetry and Its Varieties," 348.

25. Ibid., 350n. 33.

26. Northrop Frye, *Anatomy of Criticism,* 249–50. While Frye is citing Mill, it is important to note as well that his emphasis on the poet's own agency in "turning his back on his audience" is mediated by the modernist aesthetics of Joyce (whom he also cites) and, implicitly, Eliot.

27. Frye, *Anatomy of Criticism,* 249.

28. John Stuart Mill, "Thoughts on Poetry and Its Varieties," 350n. 33. Mill re-

moved the reflection on the solitary cell when he revised and combined two 1833 essays for republication in *Dissertations and Discussions* (1859); it appears in his *Works* in a note.

29. Helen Vendler, *The Art of Shakespeare's Sonnets*, 1–2; 18–19. Vendler claims that she disagrees with Mill's version of the "overheard" as the structure of lyric reading, but she does tend to echo Mill's figures.

30. For a more interesting line of thought about Dickinson's literal "seclusion," see Diana Fuss's chapter on Dickinson, in *The Sense of an Interior*. Fuss emphasizes the public spaces enclosed within the private space of the Dickinson home.

31. This introduction to Dickinson's version of what Derrida has named "the scene of writing" could be read as a reductive gloss on that idea in *The Post Card*. For a related (though very different) understanding of the importance of "the scene of writing" in American literature, see Michael Fried, *Realism, Writing, Disfiguration*, especially 93–161.

32. The pedagogical example is relevant here, since my implicit argument throughout this book is that lyrics have been remade for consumption in the classroom: in the Johnson and Franklin reading editions that include these lines as a single lyric, but that cannot, of course, include the pencil, what will students understand as the subject of this poem?

33. Franklin notes that Eudocia Converse, a cousin of Dickinson's mother, copied "Sic transit gloria mundi" into her 1848–53 commonplace book, and that Higginson later wrote to Todd that "a lady [who] used to live in Amherst & left there about 1852 is quite confident that the valentine to Howland was written some years *before* that time (she had a copy given [to] her then)" (F 51, 56).

34. I am quite sure that this is the source for "Life is but Strife," and the context makes it a hilarious message to Cowper Dickinson, whom Dickinson, apparently, did not much like. For the ballad, see Bertrand Harris Bronson, *The Ballad as Song*.

35. Patricia Crain, *The Story of A*, 217–18. In *The Years and Hours of Emily Dickinson*, Jay Leyda prints a page from one of Dickinson's primers, *The Poetic Gift: or Alphabet in Rhyme* (New Haven, 1844), in which, under the engraving for the letter V, accompanied by the rhyme, "For the Virtuous Maidens here, / Partaking of the meal," Dickinson wrote her own name and those of three of her friends. We might note in passing that all of these primer rhymes are in hymnal meter.

36. Martha Nell Smith, "The Poet as Cartoonist," in Juhasz, Miller, and Smith, eds., *Comic Power in Emily Dickinson*, 64, 69. See also Smith's "Dickinson, Cartoonist" on the Dickinson Electronic Archive site, where one can see vivid virtual images of several of Dickinson's more colorful pieces.

37. Camille Paglia's "Amherst's Madame de Sade: Emily Dickinson," in *Sexual Personae*, did much to popularize the whip-and-stiletto S & M Dickinson as antithesis to the poetess in white. One measure of the influence of Paglia's intentionally shocking caricature, which was published in 1990, showed up in a cartoon I happened to see with my young son one afternoon in 1995. The show, called "Superwriters," and featured on the Warner Brothers television network, featured a group of "good guy" writers (Dickinson, Twain, and Hemingway) who must vanquish the "bad guy" writers (Sappho, Basho, and Poe). The bad guys invade the

Library of Congress and begin to destroy it: Sappho cuts all the men out of litera-ture, Basho cuts everything down to the size of a haiku, and Poe makes everything scary. Dickinson's job is to stop Sappho, and she does so dressed in full dominatrix leather, whip in one hand and a very long cigarette holder in the other. Her voice is a good Joan Crawford snarl as she says "Because I could not stop for Death," and Sappho keels over.

38. Austin Warren, "Emily Dickinson," 565.

39. In *A Vice for Voices,* Marietta Messmer ventures the speculation that "Dickin-son might initially have started to group her fascicle poems according to the peo-ple she intended to share them with; that is, within any one fascicle she might have included poems she had mailed to or considered suitable for a specific correspon-dent" (190). It is an intriguing suggestion. But isn't it even more likely that the fas-cicles served as collections of the verse she had circulated, though not necessarily to anyone in particular?

40. Cynthia Griffin Wolff, *Emily Dickinson,* 419. There are, to be precise, thirteen instances of the pronoun "you" in the lines that begin "I cannot live with you—," as against ten instances of "I."

41. Dickinson's dictionary was the 1841 edition of Noah Webster's *American Dic-tionary of the English Language* (Springfield, Mass.: George and Charles Merriam).

42. Sharon Cameron, "Dickinson's Fascicles," 157.

43. Mary Jo Salter, "Puns and Accordions," 194. As already noted, Cameron's second book on Dickinson, *Choosing Not Choosing,* takes a polyvalent view of Dick-inson's variant practice as thesis, and extends it in suggestive ways for the inter-subjective situation I address here. See in particular Cameron's discussion of the way in which the variants "testify . . . to a suspension of normal either/or disjunc-tions between self and other, origin and destination, address and attention" (186).

44. Helen McNeil, *Emily Dickinson,* 19. McNeil's reading of Dickinson also ar-gues that Dickinson is "a woman who writes rather than speaks" and her empha-sis is informed (as mine is) by Derrida's interest in the "becoming literary of the lit-eral" (*Writing and Difference,* 230). I depart from her only in emphasizing what happens to the literal once it passes on, taking up where she leaves off when she writes that Dickinson's poems "now survive as unaddressed gifts" (181). For a rel-evant discussion of Dickinson's treatment of her audience as participants in a lyric gift economy, see Margaret Dickie, *Lyric Contingencies.*

45. F 1136; A 357. In the manuscript note that Leyda made for Amherst Special Collections, he suggests that the drawing was sent to J. L. Graves, perhaps because this piece makes so little sense if read as a self-addressed lyric.

46. This schematic version of the function of the Real in Lacanian theory should be referred to Lacan's *Le Seminaire XX: Encore.* A translation of the seminar appears as chapter six of Mitchell and Rose, eds., *Feminine Sexuality.* For a discussion of the temporality peculiar to the interrelation between the Real, the Symbolic, and the Imaginary, see Jane Gallop, *Reading Lacan,* 74–92. For an extended (and brilliant) application of Lacanian theory to Dickinson's poetry, see Mary Loeffelholz, *Dick-inson and the Boundaries of Feminist Theory.*

47. For an interesting discussion of the relevance of both the moment of death in

American nineteenth-century culture and Phelps's novel to Dickinson's poetry, see Barton Levi St. Armand, *Emily Dickinson and Her Culture*, 39–78 and 117–52.

48. By suspending the question of the "face" that Dickinson may imagine for the addressee, it will also be noticed that I am suspending the question of the reader's gender. In the poems that I am reading here, that gender seems to me strategically (rather than accidentally) indeterminate precisely because the "face" is not envisioned. For a reading of Dickinson's poems of address that emphasizes different poems in which the reader may be gendered, see Karen Oakes, "Welcome and Beware."

49. Emily Brontë, *Wuthering Heights*, 143. In a late letter to Elizabeth Holland, Dickinson half-quotes Heathcliff's exclamation, revising it into a somewhat perverse congratulation on the birth of a first grandchild (Kathrina Holland Van Wagenen): "say with 'Heathcliff' to little Katrina—'Oh Cathie—Cathie!'" (L 866).

50. For an important discussion of Dickinson's departure from the masculine romantic sublime for which Brontë's Heathcliff may stand as model, see Joanne Feit Diehl, *Dickinson and the Romantic Imagination* and *Women Poets and the American Sublime*.

51. Jonathan Culler, "Apostrophe,"146. This view of apostrophe as the central, appropriative trope of the lyric is the most consistent strain in post–de Manian lyric theory in the work of Culler, Barbara Johnson, and Cynthia Chase. In this line of thought, "apostrophe" and "lyric" become synonyms for one another. My discussion owes much to these critics, but attempts to pry apostrophe and lyric a little further apart.

52. Wolff, *Emily Dickinson*, 423.

53. Ralph Waldo Emerson, "Fate," in *Essays and Lectures*, 962.

54. For one instance in which there clearly was what Hart and Smith call a "call-and-response" exchange between Dickinson and Susan through which what is now one of Dickinson's most famous poems became a joint effort, see the letters around "Safe in their Alabaster Chambers" (OC 96–101). Hart and Smith make a convincing argument about the "workshop" effect here, but this is not a text *addressed* to Susan. Are the directly addressed texts also to some extent co-written because they depend on the recipient's response? If so, then what would that response mean for the texts' genre?

55. The lines are now printed as F 145, though I have adjusted them to the manuscript's design.

56. The ode concludes a pamphlet apparently distributed at the site entitled "The American Goliah." It was also reprinted in several papers.

57. Bianchi, preface to *SH*, x.

58. Robert Weisbuch, *Emily Dickinson's Poetry*, 177.

59. As in the introduction, I refer here to the now well-known debate between Lacan and Derrida, which centers on Lacan's claim at the end of his seminar on Poe's "The Purloined Letter" that "the sender, we tell you, receives from the receiver his own message in reverse form. Thus it is that what the 'purloined letter,' nay, the 'letter in sufferance' means is that a letter always arrives at its destination" (*The Purloined Poe* 72). Derrida's argument appears in "The Purveyor of Truth," and is

reprinted and extended in *The Post Card*. The form of my allusion to this debate echoes that of Joel Fineman in "Shakespeare's *Will*" (69, 75). I borrow the form of Fineman's response in order also to borrow his powerful answer to both Lacan and Derrida: "literary letters *always* arrive at their destination precisely because they *always* go astray."

Chapter Four: "Faith in Anatomy"

1. Leyda's suggestion is part of his manuscript note in Amherst Special Collections (A 129); for Porter's, see *Dickinson: The Modern Idiom*, 82.

2. The references to Leyda's notion of the referential "omitted center" and Hartman's version of "revoked . . . referentiality" in Dickinson may be found in note 4 of the "Beforehand." The last phrase here is from Jane Eberwein's *Dickinson: Strategies of Limitation*.

3. Jeanne Holland, "Scraps, Stamps, and Cutouts." For a suggestive version of the relation between public and private in Dickinson's domestic economy, see Diana Fuss, *The Sense of an Interior*. For an interesting use of this text as a starting point for speculation about Dickinson's relation to copyright and intellectual property law, see Jerrald Ranta, "Dickinson's 'Alone and in a Circumstance' and the Theft of Intellectual Property."

4. Jarrell, "Some Lines from Whitman," in *Poetry and the Age*, 112.

5. In *Becoming Canonical in American Poetry*, this loopy logic is what Timothy Morris dubs "the poetics of presence."

6. Mary Loeffelholz's question at the end of *Dickinson and the Boundaries of Feminist Theory* is still the best one for feminist criticism generally, and it has proven far from rhetorical: "What theoretical challenges to the metaphysics of self-presence, what forms of psychic ambivalence, what gaps between revisionary intentions in language and actual linguistic performances, what absences, what distances, what differences (apart from those with a male-authored tradition) can feminist critics entertain with respect to women writers?" (170).

7. Sandra Gilbert and Susan Gubar, *Madwoman in the Attic*, 582.

8. I have again taken the liberty of altering the lineation of Franklin's edition to fit some of the details of the manuscript. Some of the lines included on this manuscript were also included in a letter Dickinson wrote to Louise Norcross in 1872 (L 2:379). In the letter, the relation between written and spoken intentionality is explicitly at issue, and Dickinson seems especially concerned about the afterlife of intention: "We must be careful what we say. No bird resumes its egg."

9. Gilbert and Gubar, *Madwoman in the Attic*, 52. As the passage continues, Dickinson's text becomes the explicit script for "the woman writer": "while, on the one hand, 'we' (meaning especially women writers) 'may inhale Despair' from all those patriarchal texts which seek to deny female autonomy and authority, on the other hand 'we' (meaning especially women writers) 'may inhale Despair' from all those 'foremothers' who have both overtly and covertly conveyed their traditional authorship anxiety to their descendants."

10. I borrow the notion of a "pathos of indeterminate agency" from Neil Hertz's *The End of the Line*, and especially from Hertz's reading of de Man, 222–23.

11. Susan Howe, *The Birth-mark,* 20; 19. Since Howe intentionally skews her syntax and word order, it is difficult to cite her suggestions about Dickinson's texts as propositions—which is, of course, part of her point. *The Birth-mark* concludes with an interview of Howe by Edward Foster, intended, one assumes, to make it clear "who is speaking" in the book, and what she means to say.

12. Howe, *The Birth-mark,* 170. It might be interesting to compare Howe's projections to Jonathan Goldberg's suggestions in *Desiring Women Writing* that at least as early as the early modern period, "good writers" were identified as "good women," and vice versa.

13. Thomas Wentworth Higginson, *Women and the Alphabet,* 66–67.

14. "Ought Women to Learn the Alphabet?" first appeared in the *Atlantic Monthly* for February 1859 (three years before the issue of that journal in which Higginson published "Letter to a Young Contributor," the article to which Dickinson responded by sending him samples of her poems). In a prefatory note to the 1900 volume, Higginson claims that his earlier advocacy has already had "liberal" cultural effects, citing "a report that it was the perusal of this essay which led the late Miss Sophia Smith to the founding of the women's college bearing her name."

15. Higginson, *Atlantic Essays,* 313.

16. Ibid., 324.

17. The transcendent and transnational notion of literature that Higginson invokes has a particular nineteenth-century American history; it was articulated by Longfellow, Higginson's professor at Harvard, as a version of Goethe's *Weltliteratur*—so it makes sense that Goethe is the author that Higginson cites without attribution here. See Virginia Jackson, "Longfellow's Tradition."

18. Charles Sanders Peirce, *Writings,* 1:518.

19. Ibid., 1:521.

20. The racist overtones of Peirce's theory of indexical reference would be interesting to consider in relation to Karen Sanchez-Eppler's work, in *Touching Liberty,* on the complex rhetorical relations between abstract and corporeal personhood in various discourses of antebellum culture. Those overtones would also bear consideration in relation to the genealogy of American pragmatism, and particularly to recent empiricist trends in the American literary criticism philosophically indebted to it.

21. Charles Sanders Peirce, *Writings,* 1:522–23.

22. Fried, *Realism, Writing, Disfiguration,* 163. In *Pierce-Arrow,* Susan Howe explores a different version of Peirce's implicit emphasis on the materiality of writing. Characteristically, Howe's commentary takes the form of a series of poems on the eccentricities of Peirce's manuscripts.

23. Robert Weisbuch, *Emily Dickinson's Poetry,* 160.

24. In the fascicle (7), Dickinson posed an eight-line alternative to the lines I include, an alternative that allows Shelley to surface in the allusion to "Asphodel" and that substitutes the proper name "Brontë" for "Nightingale," thus making the place of return even more explicitly literary:

Gathered from many wanderings—
Gethsemane can tell
Thro' what transporting anguish
She reached the Asphodel!

Soft fall the sounds of Eden
Upon her puzzled ear—
Oh what an afternoon for Heaven,
When "Brontë" entered there!

25. Elizabeth Barrett Browning, *Aurora Leigh*, 82. Helen McNeil notes the passage in Barrett Browning in connection with Dickinson's poem, claiming that the former's "feminist distinction between womanly song and male song is unmistakable" (*Emily Dickinson*, 96). It seems to me, however, that if "we" are "men," the gendered referents here must be less stable than that.

26. Dickinson sent the elegy on Barrett Browning to Susan in 1861, and Leyda has suggested that she may also have sent a copy to Bowles.

27. The figure of the lark as the disappointment of lyric transcendence is also, as Martin Harries has reminded me (in sweet division), in Shakespeare. In *Romeo and Juliet*, the lark is not the subject but the agent of division:

> Some say the lark makes sweet division;
> This doth not so, for she divideth us.
> Some say the lark and loathed toad change eyes;
> O now I would they had chang'd voices too,
> Since arm from arm that voice doth us affray,
> Hunting thee hence with hunt's-up to the day. (3.4.29–34)

28. Elaine Scarry, *The Body in Pain*, 217. It would be interesting to read Scarry's work as a latter-day fantasy of the incarnate letter, though for her it remains a utopian possibility.

29. Christopher Benfey, *Emily Dickinson and the Problem of Others*, 94.

30. Vivian Pollak, *Dickinson: The Anxiety of Gender*, 90.

31. For a concise and amusing summary of the uses of the "Master" letters as testimonial, see Martha Nell Smith, *Rowing in Eden*, 99.

32. The letter is number 233 in Johnson's edition, dated (from the handwriting) about 1861. Johnson places it as the second in the series of the three letters to "Master," while R. W. Franklin (1986) elaborates an argument on the basis of the handwriting that would place this letter as the final installment. Franklin's edition of the "Master" letters reproduces the letters in facsimile—going so far as to give the reader the odd mimetic experience of opening the envelope to "discover" these intimate manuscripts.

33. For an intricate examination of the sexual logic informing the use of the signature "Daisy," see Margaret Homans, " 'Oh, Vision of Language!' " On Dickinson's play with the literary pseudonym, see Susan Howe's hyperbolic reading of these letters in *My Emily Dickinson*, particularly her suggestion that in *David Copperfield*, "Master" Davy is "Daisy" to Steerforth and that Little Emily writes "dis-

jointed, pleading letters after eloping with Steerforth, addressed to her family, Ham, and possibly Master Davy/David/Daisy—the recipient is never directly specified, and the letters are unsigned" (25–26).

34. I have used Franklin's edition of the "Master" letters for the transcription; remarkably, his lineation makes it look like a poem—though not, perhaps, a Dickinson poem. As you can see, Dickinson's manuscript pages are so heavily written over and crossed out that they are left without any margin at all. I have crossed out the parts of the text that Dickinson crossed out, and then I have followed Franklin's procedure of using brackets around the sections under erasure, so that my reader can read them.

35. Sandra Gilbert and Susan Gubar, *Madwoman in the Attic*, 604. The notion of Dickinson as the laureate of injury is an old one; see, for example, the somewhat patronizing 1947 British review of *Bolts of Melody*, "The Wounded Poet."

36. The "x" that keys Dickinson's variants clearly points to this place in the letter, and yet editors continued to place the lines at the letter's conclusion—as if the final shift in genre could heal the letter's exposure of the wound of gender. Franklin prints the two lines for the first time as a separate lyric (F 190). Thus in 1998 they became a poem.

37. Lucie Brock-Broido's *The Master Letters* answers this question by giving fifty-two bravura performances, thus becoming one of the latest effects of the process of turning Dickinson's letters into lyrics.

38. Michael Moon, *Disseminating Whitman*, 4–5. Moon credits Allen Grossman's "The Poetics of Union in Whitman and Lincoln" with the notion that Whitman's poetry seeks to disseminate affectionate bodily presence, a notion implicated in Grossman's theory of the lyric in *Summa Lyrica*.

39. Michael Warner, "Whitman Drunk," in *Publics and Counterpublics*, 287–88.

40. Susan Howe, *The Birth-mark*, 20.

41. As you can see, the "poem" is written on two quarters of the flier, one half opposed to the other, and there is another "poem" (F 1135) on the other side:

> None who saw it ever told it
> 'Tis as hid as Death
> Had for that specific treasure
> A departing breath—
> Surfaces may be invested
> Did the Diamond grow
> General as the Dandelion
> Would you serve it so?

One can imagine a lyric reading of "the Diamond" as commodity akin to those sold by Orr, but it would be a long interpretive stretch.

42. See, for example, the anatomically literalized reading of this manuscript suggested by William Shurr, who in *The Marriage of Emily Dickinson* turns Dickinson's tortured figures into the narrative of an affair, pregnancy, and "a painful abortion which left her sick and bedridden" (181).

CHAPTER FIVE: DICKINSON'S MISERY

1. Lavinia Dickinson, letter to Mabel Loomis Todd, December 23, 1890, cited in *Ancestor's Brocades*, 18.

2. Susan Stewart, *Poetry and the Fate of the Senses*, 2. Stewart actually writes that "it is precisely in material ways that poetry is a force against effacement," a premise that is suggestive for the reading of Dickinson I have begun here.

3. Jane Gallop, *Around 1981*, 136.

4. Of all of Dickinson's recent critics, Loeffelholz is most suspicious of the feminist critical pathos. At the end of her *Dickinson and the Boundaries of Feminist Theory*, she calls for "some form of the 'hermeneutics of suspicion' in order to think process and pain in identity" (171). Her own work on Dickinson is the best possible response to that invitation; in these pages I also want to suggest that such a hermeneutics was already current for Dickinson in the least obvious (or most suspicious) place.

5. Joanne Feit Diehl, "'Ransom in a Voice,'" 174; David S. Reynolds, *Beneath the American Renaissance*, 424. Reynolds's logic here is roughly analogous to that of Gilbert and Gubar in their reading of Dickinson's enacted trope of Victorian iconography (such as "Dickinson's metaphorical white dress") in *Madwoman in the Attic* (620). In her consideration of Dickinson against the background of nineteenth-century women writers, Joanne Dobson has suggested a closer or less ironic relation between Dickinson and her sentimental contemporaries, yet her stress remains on Dickinson's eccentric departure from those contemporaries' conventions: "her intensely idiosyncratic reconstruction of received feminine images constitutes at once an attraction to and a critique of those modes of being, suggesting a deeply rooted conflict in her own sense of identity" (*Dickinson and the Strategies of Reticence*, xvi).

6. Cheryl Walker, *American Women Poets of the Nineteenth Century*, and *The Nightingale's Burden*, 108.

7. Betsy Erkkila, "Dickinson, Women Writers, and the Marketplace," 60.

8. Elizabeth Petrino, *Emily Dickinson and Her Contemporaries*, 201. See also Marianne Noble, *The Masochistic Pleasures of Sentimental Literature*, and Mary Lou Kete, *Sentimental Collaborations*.

9. The 1848 anthologies included Rufus Griswold's *The Female Poets of America*, Caroline May's *The American Female Poets*, George Bethune's *British Female Poets*, and Frederic Rowton's *The Female Poets of Great Britain*.

10. My debt to both the American and transatlantic conversations about the Poetess (and to the women with whom it has been possible to create those conversations) will be clear from my allusions to the work of Prins, Lootens, Armstrong, and Loeffelholz in these pages. Everyone's thinking about Poetess poetics has been furthered by Adela Pinch, in particular in *Strange Fits of Passion*. Bennett's work, as critic and anthologist, has been foundational for anyone working in the field, Annie Finch's has been enormously suggestive, and Eliza Richards's work will usher in a new wave of Poetess studies. The new Poetess Archive created by

Laura Mandell at Miami University in Ohio (www.orgs.muohio.edu/womenpoets/poetess/scholars.htm) has not only a very helpful range of primary texts, but lists emerging scholarship on the Poetess on both sides of the Atlantic as soon as it appears.

11. Of course, women were not the only sentimental lyricists. I have restricted my comments here to the figure of the sentimental poetess, but not only were there poetesses who were men (Longfellow, for example) but the gendering of sentiment is precisely what is so complex. Jerome McGann's *The Poetics Of Sensibility* suggests the intricately intertwined strains of romanticism, gender, sentiment, and poetry. See also, on the American side, Glenn Hendler, *Public Sentiments*, and *Sentimental Men*, ed. Chapman and Hendler.

12. This is the thesis of Cheryl Walker's *The Nightingale's Burden*. As my responses to her work throughout this chapter suggest, Walker and I read "the secret sorrow" in different ways: she as an enforced silencing of the female voice, I as one mode of feminine "personal" revelation. Yet anyone working on this material is in Walker's debt for making it available to other interpretations.

13. Eve Kosofsky Sedgwick, "Wilde, Nietzsche, and the Sentimental Relations of the Male Body," in *Epistemology of the Closet*, 150. Sedgwick's aim is to distinguish "the feminocentric Victorian version" of sentimentalism from "the twentieth-century one with its complex and distinctive relation to the male body," but I would maintain that Sedgwick's arguments that the latter is the highly charged "glass closet" or "empty secret" at the center of modern culture also applies to the widely circulated "secret" at the heart of nineteenth-century culture—and, if it can so apply, then the nineteenth century must form more than a feminized bridge between the eighteenth-century honorific and the twentieth-century damning senses of the "sentimental."

14. The phrase is from Shirley Samuels's introduction to *The Culture of Sentiment*, 4. The historical accounts of this double logic have grown too numerous to list, but one might begin with George M. Frederickson's *The Inner Civil War*, Susan P. Conrad's *Perish the Thought*, Deborah E. McDowell and Arnold Rampersad's collection *Slavery and the Literary Imagination*, Anne Norton's *Alternative Americas*, and Ann Douglas's *The Feminization of American Culture*.

15. For powerful accounts of the accountability and nonaccountability involved in emerging versions of sympathetic identification in the eighteenth and early nineteenth centuries, see David Marshall, *The Surprising Effects of Sympathy*, and Adela Pinch, *Strange Fits of Passion*.

16. None of the influential treatments of sentimentalism and gender in nineteenth-century culture has much to say about poetry: Ann Douglas's *The Feminization of American Culture* touches on poetry, but sees women's fiction as contributing to the self-consumerism of mass society; Jane Tompkins, in *Sensational Designs*, countered that nineteenth-century sentimental women's writing constituted a political resistance to patriarchal culture and patriarchal public values, but concentrated that resistance exclusively within fiction, and Richard Brodhead, in *Cultures of Letters*, claimed that women's sentimental fiction functioned as an "intimate discipline" in "the domestic-tutelary complex" of the nineteenth-century

middle class. Lauren Berlant has replied to these arguments with a theory of "the female complaint," which, she argues, "served as a feminine counterpublic sphere whose values remained fundamentally private," and yet Berlant also considers sentimental prose the central representation of those "values" (see Berlant, "The Female Complaint," and "The Female Woman," 270). The exclusion of lyric—arguably the most visible, *public* stage for nineteenth-century sentimental exchange—from such a lively debate speaks eloquently of the twentieth-century misapprehension of the period's notions of the genre. For a beginning on the place of the lyric in discussions of the sentimental, see Jerome McGann, *The Poetics of Sensibility* and Mary Loeffelholz, *From School to Salon.*

17. Rufus W. Griswold, ed., *The Female Poets of America,* 3.

18. In *Keywords,* Raymond Williams locates in the early nineteenth century the turn from *sentimental* as a synonym for the positively valued *sensibility* to *sentimental* as a "complaint against people who feel 'too much' as well as against those who 'indulge their emotions.' This confusion has permanently damaged *sentimental* (though limited positive uses survive, typically in *sentimental value*) and wholly determine *sentimentality*" (282). Williams does not comment on the role that gender plays in that "damage" and "determination."

19. Gail Hamilton, "My Garden," *Atlantic Monthly,* November 1862; collected in *Gail Hamilton: Selected Writings,* 31. Cristanne Miller has sensed some relevance to Dickinson of these passages from Hamilton but, curiously, becomes entwined in the prose's own tropes: "Judging by a contemporary writer's characterization of typical feminine and masculine writing styles," Miller writes, "Dickinson shares more with the latter than with the former" (*Emily Dickinson: A Poet's Grammar,* 158). Even if, as Miller writes, "the stereotypes basically hold," must this view mean that such types were not *effects* rather than *sources* of a given style?

20. The editorial appeared in the *Springfield Daily Republican* for July 7, 1860, and is reprinted in Richard Sewall's *The Life of Emily Dickinson* (2:489–90). The connection between the *Republican* article and Dickinson's poetry seems to have begun with Ruth Miller's conjecture that "it seems inevitable that Emily Dickinson should have interpreted these words as a public rebuke to her . . . It takes little imagination to reconstruct the effect of such an article, reminding ourselves that Susan would read it, Lavinia would read it—well, all of Amherst that counted for Emily Dickinson would read it—and perhaps laugh, or what would be worse for such a proud and so self-conscious a woman, pity her" (*The Poetry of Emily Dickinson,* 128, 163–64). Sewall rebutted Miller's excessively personal interpretation, but he did so on comparably personal grounds: "Whatever Emily Dickinson wrote 'through,'" Sewall claimed, "even Bowles should have seen that it was not through a 'mist of tears'" (490). Sewall went so far as to list the poems that Dickinson sent to Bowles, dividing them between those "on the happy and healthy side" and those which "reflect considerable 'suffering' of various sorts." He then included an appendix anthologizing a random selection of "the tearful lyrics . . . that flooded the market" in order to prove that "there were many other, and much grosser examples at hand of the literature of suffering" than those by Dickinson. The only critic who has taken Bowles's article as a symptom of a broader cultural

concern is David Reynolds, who places Dickinson as a central figure within an "American Women's Renaissance" characterized by "the new dark women's literature" (*Beneath the American Renaissance*, 395). Reynolds, however, limits this literature to popular novels, and so concentrates exclusively on shared plots and themes.

21. Matthew Arnold, preface to the 1853 edition of *Poems.*

22. The questions that Arnold and the reading of Arnold raise for the interpretation of the lyric would be interesting to place into the context of Amanda Anderson's discussion of the nineteenth-century geneology of an idealized double cultural investment and detachment in *The Powers of Distance,* though the lyric as a genre is not her concern there.

23. Rufus W. Griswold, ed., *The Female Poets of America,* 4.

24. In Willis J. Buckingham, *Emily Dickinson's Reception in the 1890s,* 64.

25. Thomas Wentworth Higginson, "Sappho," first published in the *Atlantic Monthly* (1871) and reprinted in *Atlantic Essays* (324). The German phrase, as I noted in chapter three, is from Goethe's *Faust,* though Higginson (or his publisher?) inadvertently changed Goethe's *Das-ewig* to *Die ewige.*

26. Karen Sanchez-Eppler, *Touching Liberty,* 2.

27. Ibid., 12.

28. Sandra Gilbert and Susan Gubar, *The Madwoman in the Attic,* 628.

29. Again, my claim here about Dickinson's embodiment of the hermeneutics of the genre should be distinguished from Sharon Cameron's argument in *Lyric Time* to the effect that Dickinson's poems "attempt to reverse" time and so throw "into relief the shape of the lyric struggle itself" (260). My comments are meant to indicate Dickinson's struggle with and against the lyric genre and not, as Cameron's are meant to do, to reaffirm her hyperbolic representation or personification of it.

30. Oakes Smith's "The Poet" does not appear in the 1846 collection of her poems, *The Poetical Writings of Elizabeth Oakes Smith* but it is included in Griswold's *Female Poets of America* in 1848 (194). Griswold also wrote the preface to Oakes Smith's 1846 edition, praising her poems for "a power far above mere *intellectuality.*" One might speculate that it is precisely that sort of reception that informs the power ascribed to the nightingale in "The Poet."

31. Elizabeth Oakes Smith, *Woman and Her Needs,* 12.

32. On what becomes of the interpretation of Oakes Smith's figure of the poetess, see Virginia Jackson and Yopie Prins, "Lyrical Studies." Eliza Richards's *Gender and the Poetics of Reception in Poe's Circle* gives the best reading of Oakes Smith that that writer has yet received.

33. This sentence is a necessarily reductive version of Michel Foucault's thesis in *The Order of Things* that before the seventeenth century, "being and representation found their common locus" in the parallelism of a complete taxonomical language (312). After the seventeenth century, in which Foucault locates the emergence of "man," the problems of disorigination and reflexivity constitute the modern condition of knowing. Although the thesis is considerably complicated in *The History of Sexuality,* as several critics of Foucault have pointed out, it takes into account the rise of the concept of "man" while inadequately addressing the epistemology of

"woman" in modern discourse. Nineteenth-century sentimentalism might serve as one place to begin inflecting differently the Foucauldian paradigm.

34. In his extraordinary reading of Marvell's poem, Francis Barker aligns it specifically with the emergence of the modern episteme charted by Foucault, tracing "a reductive subjugation of the body" that is "practised vengefully in Marvell's lyric" on the dissected anatomy of the woman he loves. See Francis Barker, *The Tremulous Private Body*, 73–94.

35. I am suggesting here that nineteenth-century sentimental lyric reading does not just "pass" or become outmoded, but leads directly to twentieth-century lyric reading. For the precedent shift in the reading of sentimental personification from the eighteenth to the nineteenth century, see Steven Knapp, *Personification and the Sublime.*

36. The nightingale is missing from the copy of *The New England Primer* in the Dickinson collection at the Houghton Library (an edition published in Hartford by Ira Webster, 1843).

37. Patricia Crain, *The Story of A*, 52. The longer story that Crain tells about the European sources for the *Primer* explains what nightingales are doing as illustrations for *N* in New England.

38. Susan's letter is included in OC, 101, and was also cited by Leyda, *The Years and Hours*, 2:38.

39. Martha Nell Smith, "The Poet as Cartoonist," in Juhasz, Miller, and Smith, eds., *Comic Power in Emily Dickinson*, 74.

40. Paul de Man, "Anthropomorphism and Trope in the Lyric," in *The Rhetoric of Romanticism*, 241.

41. Emerson, "The Rhodora," (first published, 1839) in John Hollander, ed., *American Poetry*, 1:272.

42. Adrienne Rich, "Vesuvius at Home," (1975), 174; Sandra Gilbert and Susan Gubar, *Madwoman in the Attic*, 610. While Sharon Cameron did not align her extended reading of "My Life had stood—a Loaded Gun—" with Rich and feminist criticism, her understanding of the poem as "a dialectic of rage" that is "heroic" in "its refusal to choose" between conflicting identities has similarly utopian consequences (*Lyric Time*, 55–90).

43. Judith Butler, *Bodies that Matter*, 188.

Conclusion

1. T. J. Clark, *Farewell to an Idea*, 401.

2. Johnson published the lines as a "Prose Fragment" at the end of his three-volume edition of the *Letters*, 925, in 1958; Leyda did not publish his documentary history of Dickinson until 1960. The first publication of the lines was in *New England Quarterly* in 1955 in Bingham's "Prose Fragments of Emily Dickinson."

Selected Works Cited

Abrams, M. H. "The Lyric as Poetic Norm." In *The Mirror and the Lamp: Romantic Theory and the Critical Tradition.* Oxford: Oxford University Press, 1953.

Abu-Lughod, Lila. *Veiled Sentiments: Honor and Poetry in Bedouin Society.* Berkeley: University of California Press, 1986.

"Accomplices." *Atlantic Monthly* 93 (July 1865): 11.

Adorno, Theodor. "Lyric Poetry and Society." Translated and with an introduction by Bruce Mayo. *Telos* 20 (Summer 1974): 52–71.

Aldrich, Thomas Bailey. "*In Re* Emily Dickinson." *Atlantic Monthly* 69 (January 1892): 143–144.

"The American Goliah: A Wonderful Geological Discovery." Syracuse: Printed at the *Journal* Office, 1869.

Anderson, Amanda. *The Powers of Distance: Cosmopolitanism and the Cultivation of Detachment.* Princeton: Princeton University Press, 2001.

Anderson, Benedict. *Imagined Communities.* London: Verso, 1991.

Anderson, Charles R. *Emily Dickinson's Poetry: Stairway of Surprise.* New York: Holt, Rinehart, and Winston, 1960.

Arac, Jonathan. "Afterword: Lyric Poetry and the Bounds of New Criticism." In *Lyric Poetry: Beyond New Criticism,* edited by Hošek and Parker.

———. *Critical Genealogies: Historical Situations for Postmodern Literary Studies.* New York: Columbia University Press, 1987.

Armstrong, Isobel. *Victorian Poetry: Poetry, Poetics, and Politics.* London: Routledge, 1993.

———. "Msrepresentation: Codes of Affect and Politics in Nineteenth-Century Women's Poetry." In *Women's Poetry, Late Romantic to Late Victorian: Gender and Genre, 1830–1900.* Ed. Isobel Armstrong and Virginia Blain. London: Macmillan, 1998, 3–32.

Arnold, Matthew. "Preface to the First Edition of *Poems* (1853)." In *On the Classical Tradition.* Vol. 1 of *The Complete Prose Works of Matthew Arnold,* edited by R. H. Super. Ann Arbor: University of Michigan Press, 1960.

Bahti, Timothy. *The Ends of the Lyric: Direction and Consequence in Western Poetry.* Baltimore: Johns Hopkins University Press, 1996.

Bakhtin, Mikhail. *Problems of Dostoevsky's Poetics.* Translated by Caryl Emerson. Theory and History of Literature 8. Minneapolis: University of Minnesota Press, 1984.

———. *Speech Genres and Other Late Essays.* Translated by Vern W. McGee. Edited by Caryl Emerson and Michael Holquist. Austin: University of Texas Press,1986.

Barker, Francis. *The Tremulous Private Body: Essays on Subjection.* London: Methuen, 1984.

Barker, Wendy. *Lunacy of Light: Emily Dickinson and the Experience of Metaphor.* Carbondale: Southern Illinois University Press, 1987.

Barthes, Roland. "The Death of the Author." In *Image, Music, Text: Essays.* Translated by Stephen Heath. New York: Hill and Wang, 1977.

Baudelaire, Charles. *Les Fleurs du Mal.* With English translation by Richard Howard. Boston: David R. Godine, 1982.

Benfey, Christopher. *Emily Dickinson and the Problem of Others.* Amherst: University of Massachusetts Press, 1984.

Benjamin, Walter. *Charles Baudelaire: A Lyric Poet in the Era of High Capitalism.* Translated by Harry Zohn. London: NLB, 1973.

Bennett, Paula Bernat. *Emily Dickinson: Woman Poet.* Iowa City: University of Iowa Press, 1990.

———. *Poets in the Public Sphere: The Emancipatory Project of American Women's Poetry, 1800–1900.* Princeton: Princeton University Press, 2003.

Berlant, Lauren. "The Female Complaint." *Social Text* 19/20 (Fall 1988): 237–59.

———. "The Female Woman: Fanny Fern and the Form of Sentiment." In *The Culture of Sentiment: Race, Gender, and Sentimentality in Nineteenth-Century America,* edited by Shirley Samuels.

Bethune, George. *British Female Poets.* Philadelphia: Lindsay and Blakiston, 1848.

Bianchi, Martha Dickinson. *Emily Dickinson Face to Face: Unpublished Letters with Notes and Reminiscences.* Boston: Houghton Mifflin, 1932.

———. *The Life and Letters of Emily Dickinson.* Boston: Houghton Mifflin, 1924.

Bingham, Millicent Todd. *Ancestors' Brocades: The Literary Debut of Emily Dickinson.* New York: Harper Brothers, 1945.

———, ed. *Emily Dickinson's Home: Letters of Edward Dickinson and His Family.* New York: Harper Brothers, 1955.

———. "Prose Fragments of Emily Dickinson." *NEQ* 28 (1955).

Blackmur, R. P. "Emily Dickinson's Notation." In *Emily Dickinson: A Collection of Critical Essays,* edited by Richard B. Sewall. Englewood Cliffs, N. J.: Prentice Hall, 1963.

———. *The Expense of Greatness.* New York: Arrow Editions, 1940.

Blake, Caesar R., and Carlton F. Wells, eds. *The Recognition of Emily Dickinson: Selected Criticism since 1890.* Ann Arbor: University of Michigan Press, 1964.

Bloom, Harold, ed. *Modern Critical Views: Emily Dickinson.* New York: Chelsea House Publishers, 1985.

Bowles, Samuel. "When Should We Write?" *Springfield Republican,* July 7, 1860.

Brenkman, John. *Culture and Domination.* Ithaca: Cornell University Press, 1987.

Brock-Broido, Lucie. *The Master Letters.* New York: Knopf, 1997.

Brodhead, Richard. *Cultures of Letters: Scenes of Reading and Writing in Nineteenth-Century America.* Chicago: University of Chicago Press, 1993.

Bromwich, David. "Parody, Pastiche, and Allusion." In *Lyric Poetry: Beyond New Criticism,* edited by Hošek and Parker.

———, ed. *Romantic Critical Essays.* Cambridge: Cambridge University Press, 1987.

Bronson, Bertrand Harris. *The Ballad as Song.* Berkeley: University of California Press, 1969.

Brontë, Emily. *Wuthering Heights.* 1847. Boston: Houghton Mifflin, 1956.

Brooks, Cleanth, and Robert Penn Warren. *Understanding Poetry: An Anthology for College Students.* New York: Henry Holt, 1938.

Brower, Reuben. *The Fields of Light: An Experiment in Critical Reading.* New York: Oxford University Press, 1962.

Brown, Bill. *A Sense of Things: The Object Matter of American Literature.* Chicago: University of Chicago Press, 2003.

———. "Thing Theory." In *Things*, ed. Bill Brown. Chicago: University of Chicago Press, 2004.

Brown, Gillian. *Domestic Individualism: Imagining Self in Nineteenth-Century America.* Berkeley: University of California Press, 1990.

Browning, Elizabeth Barrett. *Aurora Leigh: A Poem.* New York: J. Miller, Publisher, 1864.

Bryson, Norman. *Looking at the Overlooked: Four Essays in Still Life Painting.* Cambridge, Mass.: Harvard University Press, 1990.

Buckingham, Willis J., ed. *Emily Dickinson's Reception in the 1890s: A Documentary History.* Pittsburgh: University of Pittsburgh Press, 1990.

Buell, Lawrence. *New England Literary Culture: From Revolution through Renaissance.* Cambridge: Cambridge University Press, 1986.

Burke, Kenneth. *The Philosophy of Literary Form: Studies in Symbolic Action.* Rev. ed. New York: Vintage Books, 1957.

Butler, Judith. *Bodies that Matter: On the Discursive Limits of "Sex."* New York: Routledge, 1993.

Cadava, Eduardo. *Emerson and the Climates of History.* Stanford: Stanford University Press, 1997.

Cadava, Eduardo, Peter Connor, and Jean-Luc Nancy, eds. *Who Comes After the Subject?* New York: Routledge, 1991.

Cameron, Sharon. *Choosing Not Choosing: Dickinson's Fascicles.* Chicago: University of Chicago Press, 1992.

———. "Dickinson's Fascicles." In *The Emily Dickinson Handbook*, edited by Grabher, Hagenbüchle, and Miller.

———. *Lyric Time: Dickinson and the Limits of Genre.* Baltimore: Johns Hopkins University Press, 1979.

Carson, Anne, trans. *If Not, Winter: Fragments of Sappho.* New York: Knopf, 2002.

Castoriadis, Cornelius. *The Imaginary Institution of Society.* Translated by Kathleen Barney. Cambridge: MIT Press, 1987.

Cavell, Stanley. "The Fact of Television." In *Themes Out of School: Effects and Causes.* San Francisco: North Point Press, 1984.

Chandler, James. *England in 1819: The Politics of Literary Culture and the Case of Romantic Historicism.* Chicago: University of Chicago Press, 1998.

Chapman, Mary, and Glenn Hendler, eds. *Sentimental Men: Masculinity and the Politics of Affect in American Culture.* Berkeley: University of California Press, 1999.

Chase, Richard. *Emily Dickinson.* New York: William Sloan, 1951.

Clark, T. J. *Farewell to an Idea: Episodes from a History of Modernism.* New Haven: Yale University Press, 1997.

Cody, John. *After Great Pain: The Inner Life of Emily Dickinson.* Cambridge, Mass.: Belknap Press of Harvard University Press, 1971.

Cohen, Ralph. "History and Genre." *New Literary History* 17.2 (Winter 1986): 203–18.

Conrad, Susan. *Perish the Thought: Intellectual Women in Romantic America.* New York: Oxford University Press, 1976.

Crain, Patricia. *The Story of A: The Alphabetization of America from the New England Primer to The Scarlet Letter.* Stanford: Stanford University Press, 2000.

Culler, Jonathan. "Apostrophe." In *The Pursuit of Signs: Semiotics, Literature, Deconstruction.* Ithaca: Cornell University Press, 1981.

———. "Changes in the Study of the Lyric." In *Lyric Poetry: Beyond New Criticism,* edited by Chaviva Hošek and Patricia Parker. Ithaca: Cornell University Press, 1985.

———. "The Modern Lyric: Generic Continuity and Critical Practice." In *The Comparative Perspective on Literature,* edited by Clayton Koelb and Susan Noakes. Ithaca: Cornell University Press, 1988.

———. "Reading Lyric." *Yale French Studies* 69 [*The Lesson of Paul de Man*] (1985): 98–106.

Cunningham, J. V. *The Collected Essays of J. V. Cunningham.* Chicago: The Swallow Press, 1976.

Curran, Stuart. *Poetic Form and British Romanticism.* Oxford: Oxford University Press, 1986.

Dandurand, Karen. "Another Dickinson Poem Published in Her Lifetime." *American Literature* 54, no. 3 (October 1982): 434–37.

———. "Dickinson and the Public." In *Dickinson and Audience,* edited by Orzeck and Weisbuch.

———. "New Dickinson Civil War Publications." *American Literature* 56.1 (March 1984): 17–27.

Decker. William Merrill. *Epistolary Practices: Letter Writing in America before Telecommunications.* Chapel Hill: University of North Carolina Press, 1998.

De Grazia, Margreta, and Peter Stallybrass. "The Materiality of the Shakespearean Text." *Shakespeare Quarterly* 44.3 (fall 1993): 255–83.

de Man, Paul. *Allegories of Reading: Figural Language in Rousseau, Nietzsche, Rilke, and Proust.* New Haven: Yale University Press, 1979.

———. *Blindness and Insight: Essays in the Rhetoric of Contemporary Criticism.* Minneapolis: University of Minnesota Press, 1983.

———. "Hypogram and Inscription: Michael Riffaterre's Poetics of Reading." *Diacritics* 11.4 (Winter 1981): 17–35.

———. "Lyrical Voice in Contemporary Theory." In *Lyric Poetry: Beyond New Criticism,* edited by Hošek and Parker.

———. *The Rhetoric of Romanticism.* New York: Columbia University Press, 1984.

Derrida, Jacques. *Archive Fever: A Freudian Impression.* Chicago: University of Chicago Press, 1996.

———. *The Ear of the Other: Otobiography, Transference, Translation.* Translated by Peggy Kamuf. Edited by Christa V. McDonald. New York: Schocken Books, 1985.

———. *Glas.* Translated by John P. Leavey Jr. and Richard Rand. Lincoln: University of Nebraska Press, 1986.

———. "The Law of Genre." In *Acts of Literature*, edited by Derek Attridge. New York: Routledge, 1992.

———. *Of Grammatology*. Translated by Gayatri Chakavorty Spivak. Baltimore: Johns Hopkins University Press, 1976.

———. *The Post Card: From Socrates to Freud and Beyond*. Translated by Alan Bass. Chicago: University of Chicago Press, 1987.

———. *Writing and Difference*. Translated by Alan Bass. Chicago: University of Chicago Press, 1978.

Dickie, Margaret. "Dickinson in Context." *American Literary History* 7.2 (Summer 1995): 320–33.

———. *Lyric Contingencies: Emily Dickinson and Wallace Stevens*. Philadelphia: University of Pennsylvania Press, 1991.

Dickinson, Emily. *Poems by Emily Dickinson*. Edited by two of her friends, Mabel Loomis Todd and T. W. Higginson. Boston: Roberts Brothers, 1890.

———. *Poems by Emily Dickinson*. Edited by T. W. Higginson and Mabel Loomis Todd. Second Series. Boston: Roberts Brothers, 1891.

———. *Letters of Emily Dickinson*. Edited by Mabel Loomis Todd. Boston: Roberts Brothers, 1894.

———. *Poems by Emily Dickinson*. Edited by Mabel Loomis Todd. Third Series. Boston: Roberts Brothers, 1896.

———. *The Single Hound: Poems of a Lifetime*. Edited by Martha Dickinson Bianchi. Boston: Little and Brown, 1914.

———. *Selected Poems of Emily Dickinson*. Edited by Conrad Aiken. London: Jonathan Cape, 1924.

———. *The Complete Poems of Emily Dickinson*. Edited by Martha Dickinson Bianchi. Boston: Little and Brown, 1924.

———. *Further Poems of Emily Dickinson* ed. Martha Dickinson Bianchi and Alfred Leete Hampson. Centenary edition. Boston: Little, Brown, 1930.

———. *Letters of Emily Dickinson*. Edited by Mabel Loomis Todd. New York: Harper and Brothers, 1931.

———. *Bolts of Melody: New Poems of Emily Dickinson*. Edited by Mabel Loomis Todd and Millicent Todd Bingham. New York: Harper and Brothers, 1945.

———. *The Poems of Emily Dickinson: Including variant readings critically compared with all known manuscripts* Edited by Thomas H. Johnson. Cambridge, Mass.: The Belknap Press of Harvard University Press, 1955.

———. *The Letters of Emily Dickinson*. Edited by Thomas H. Johnson and Theodora Ward. Cambridge, Mass.: The Belknap Press of Harvard University Press, 1958.

———. *The Manuscript Books of Emily Dickinson*. Edited by R. W. Franklin. Cambridge, Mass.: The Belknap Press of Harvard University Press, 1981.

———. *The Poems of Emily Dickinson*. Variorum Edition. 3 volumes. Edited by R. W. Franklin. Cambridge, Mass.: The Belknap Press of Harvard University Press, 1998.

———. *The Poems of Emily Dickinson: Reading Edition*. Cambridge, Mass.: The Belknap Press of Harvard University Press, 1999.

Diehl, Joanne Feit. *Dickinson and the Romantic Imagination.* Princeton: Princeton University Press, 1981.

———. "In the Twilight of the Gods: Women Poets and the American Sublime." In *The American Sublime,* edited by Mary Arensberg. Albany: State University of New York Press, 1986.

———. "'Ransom in a Voice': Language as Defense in Dickinson's Poetry." In *Feminist Critics Read Emily Dickinson,* edited by Suzanne Juhasz.

———. *Women Poets and the American Sublime.* Bloomington: Indiana University Press, 1990.

Dobson, Joanne. *Dickinson and the Strategies of Reticence: The Woman Writer in Nineteenth-Century America.* Bloomington: Indiana University Press, 1989.

Douglas, Ann. *The Feminization of American Culture.* New York: Knopf, 1977.

Eaves, Morris, and Michael Fisher, eds. *Romanticism and Contemporary Criticism.* Ithaca: Cornell University Press, 1986.

Eberwein, Jane. *Dickinson: Strategies of Limitation.* Amherst: University of Massachusetts Press, 1985.

Edwards, Brent Hayes. *The Practice of Diaspora: Literature, Translation, and the Rise of Black Internationalism.* Cambridge, Mass.: Harvard University Press, 2003.

Eliot, T. S. "The Three Voices of Poetry." In *On Poetry and Poets.* London: Faber and Faber, 1957.

Emerson, Ralph Waldo. *Ralph Waldo Emerson: Essays and Lectures.* Edited by Joel Porte. New York: The Library of America, 1983.

Erkkila, Betsy. "Dickinson, Women Writers, and the Marketplace." In *The Wicked Sisters: Women Poets, Literary History, and Discord.* New York: Oxford University Press, 1992.

———. "Emily Dickinson and Class." *American Literary History* 4:1 (Spring 1992): 1–27.

Farr, Judith. *The Passion of Emily Dickinson.* Cambridge: Harvard University Press, 1992.

Fekete, John. "The New Criticism: Ideological Evolution of the Right Opposition." *Telos* 20 (Summer 1974): 2–51.

Ferry, Anne. *The Title to the Poem.* Stanford: Stanford University Press, 1996.

Finch, Annie. "Dickinson and Patriarchal Meter: A Theory of Metrical Codes." *PMLA* 102 (1987): 166–76.

———. "The Poetess in America." *Able Muse* <http: www.ablemuse.com/> 2003.

Fineman, Joel. "Shakespeare's *Will*: The Temporality of Rape." *Representations* 20 (Fall 1987): 25–76.

———. *Shakespeare's Perjured Eye: The Invention of Poetic Subjectivity in the Sonnets.* Berkeley: University of California Press, 1986.

Fish, Stanley. "How to Recognize a Poem When You See One." In *Is There a Text in This Class?: The Authority of Interpretive Communities.* Cambridge, Mass.: Harvard University Press, 1980.

Fletcher, Angus. *A New Theory for American Poetry: Democracy, the Environment, and the Future of Imagination.* Cambridge and London: Harvard University Press, 2004.

Foucault, Michel. *Archaeology of Knowledge.* Translated by A. M. Sheridan Smith. New York: Pantheon Books, 1972.

———. *The History of Sexuality.* Vol. 1: *An Introduction.* Translated by Robert Hurley. New York: Pantheon, 1977.

———. "My Body, This Paper, This Fire." Translated by Geoff Bennington. *Oxford Literary Review* 4.1 (1979): 928.

———. *The Order of Things: An Archeology of the Human Sciences.* New York: Random House, 1973.

———. "What is an Author?" In *Language, Counter-Memory, Practice: Selected Essays and Interviews.* Translated by Donald F. Bouchard and Sherry Simon. Edited by Donald Bouchard. Oxford: Basil Blackwell, 1978.

Fowler, Alistair. *Kinds of Literature: An Introduction to the Theory of Genres and Modes.* Cambridge, Mass.: Harvard University Press, 1982.

Franchot, Jenny. *Roads to Rome: The Antebellum Protestant Encounter with Catholicism.* Berkeley: University of California Press, 1994.

Franklin, R. W., ed. *The Editing of Emily Dickinson: A Reconsideration.* Madison: University of Wisconsin Press, 1967.

———. "The Emily Dickinson Fascicles." In *Studies in Bibliography* 36, edited by Fredson Bowers. Charlottesville: The Bibliographic Society of Virginia, 1983.

———. "Manuscripts and Transcripts of 'Further in Summer than the Birds.'" *Papers of the Bibliographical Society of America* 72 (fourth quarter, 1978): 552–60.

———, ed. *The Master Letters of Emily Dickinson.* Amherst: Amherst College Press, 1986.

Frederickson, George M. *The Inner Civil War: Northern Intellectuals and the Crisis of the Union.* New York: Harper and Rowe, 1965.

Freud, Sigmund. *Inhibitions, Symptoms and Anxiety.* Translated by Alix Strachey. Edited by James Strachey. New York: Norton, 1959.

Fried, Michael. *Realism, Writing, Disfiguration: On Thomas Eakins and Stephen Crane.* Chicago: University of Chicago Press, 1987.

Friedman, Susan Stanford. "Creativity and the Childbirth Metaphor: Gender Difference in Literary Discourse." *Feminist Studies* 13.1 (Spring 1987): 49–82.

Frye, Northrop. *Anatomy of Criticism: Four Essays.* Princeton: Princeton University Press, 1957.

Fuss, Diana. *The Sense of an Interior: Four Writers and the Rooms that Shaped Them.* New York: Routledge, 2004.

Gallop, Jane. *Around 1981: Academic Feminist Literary Theory.* New York: Routledge, 1992.

———. *Reading Lacan.* Ithaca: Cornell University Press, 1985.

Genette, Gérard. *The Architext: An Introduction,* trans. Jane E. Lewin. Berkeley: University of California Press, 1992.

Gilbert, Sandra, and Susan Gubar. *The Madwoman in the Attic: The Woman Writer and the Nineteenth-Century Literary Imagination.* New Haven: Yale University Press, 1979.

———, eds. *The Norton Anthology of Literature by Women.* New York: Norton, 1985.

Goldberg, Jonathan. *Desiring Women Writing: English Renaissance Examples.* Stanford: Stanford University Press, 1997.

———. "Hamlet's Hand." *Shakespeare Quarterly* 39.3 (Fall 1988): 307–27.

———. *Writing Matter: From the Hands of the English Renaissance.* Stanford: Stanford University Press, 1990.

Gourgouris, Stathis. *Does Literature Think? Literature as Theory for an Antimythical Era.* Stanford: Stanford University Press, 2003.

Grabher, Gudrun, Roland Hagenbüchle, and Cristanne Miller, eds. *The Emily Dickinson Handbook.* Amherst: University of Massachusetts Press, 1998.

Graff, Gerald. *Poetic Statement and Critical Dogma.* Chicago: University of Chicago Press, 1970.

Graff, Gerald, and Michael Warner. *Professing Literature: An Institutional History.* Chicago: University of Chicago Press, 1987.

Griffith, Clark. *The Long Shadow: Emily Dickinson's Tragic Poetry.* Princeton: Princeton University Press, 1964.

Griswold, Rufus Wilmot, ed. *The Female Poets of America.* Philadelphia: Carey and Hart, Publishers, 1848.

Grossman, Allen. "The Poetics of Union in Whitman and Lincoln: An Inquiry toward the Relationship of Art and Policy." In *The American Renaissance Reconsidered,* edited by Walter Benn Michaels and Donald E. Pease. Baltimore: Johns Hopkins University Press, 1985.

———. *Summa Lyrica: A Primer of the Commonplaces in Speculative Poetics.* In *The Sighted Singer: Two Works on Poetry for Readers and Writers,* by Grossman with Mark Halliday. Baltimore: Johns Hopkins University Press, 1992.

Gruesz, Kirsten Silva. *Ambassadors of Culture: The Transamerican Origins of Latino Writing.* Princeton: Princeton University Press, 2002.

Guillén, Claudio. *Literature as System: Essays toward the Theory of Literary History.* Princeton: Princeton University Press, 1971.

Guillory, John. *Cultural Capital: The Problem of Literary Canon Formation.* Chicago: University of Chicago Press, 1993.

———. "Literary Study and the Modern System of the Disciplines." In *Disciplinarity at the Fin de Siècle,* edited by Amanda Anderson and Joseph Valente. Princeton: Princeton University Press, 2002.

Habegger, Alfred. *My Wars Are Laid Away in Books: The Life of Emily Dickinson.* New York: Random House, 2001.

Habermas, Jürgen. *The Structural Transformation of the Public Sphere: An Inquiry into a Category of Bourgeois Society.* Translated by Thomas Burger with Frederick Lawrence. Cambridge: Polity Press, 1989.

Hamilton, Gail [Mary Abigail Dodge]. *Gail Hamilton: Selected Writings,* edited by Susan Coultrap-McQuin. New Brunswick: Rutgers University Press, 1992.

Harries, Elizabeth Wanning. *The Unfinished Manner: Essays on the Fragment in the Later Eighteenth Century.* Charlottesville: University Press of Virginia, 1994.

Harrington, Joseph. "Why American Poetry is Not American Literature," *American Literary History* 8 (Fall 1996): 496–515.

Hart, Ellen Louise and Smith, Martha Nell, eds. *Open Me Carefully: Emily Dickinson's Intimate Letters to Susan Huntington Dickinson.* Ashfield, Mass.: Paris Press, 1998.

Hartman, Geoffrey. *Criticism in the Wilderness: The Study of Literature.* New Haven: Yale University Press, 1980.

Hegel, G. W. *Aesthetics: Lectures on Fine Art.* Translated by T. M. Knox. Two vols. Oxford: The Clarendon Press, 1975.

Heidegger, Martin. *Poetry, Language, Thought.* Translated by Albert Hofstadter. New York: Harper and Rowe, 1971.

Hendler, Glenn. *Public Sentiments: Structures of Feeling in Nineteenth-Century Literature.* Chapel Hill: University of North Carolina Press, 2001.

Hernadi, Paul. *Beyond Genre: New Directions in Literary Classification.* Ithaca: Cornell University Press, 1985.

Hertz, Neil. *The End of the Line: Essays on Psychoanalysis and the Sublime.* New York: Columbia University Press, 1985.

Higginson, Thomas Wentworth. *"Army Life in a Black Regiment" and Other Writings.* 1870. New York: Penguin, 1997.

———. *Atlantic Essays.* Boston: Lee and Shepard, 1882.

———. "Emily Dickinson's Letters." *Atlantic Monthly* 67 (October 1891): 444–56.

———. "Letter to a Young Contributor." *Atlantic Monthly* 9 (April 1862): 401–11.

———. "Recent Poetry." *The Nation* 61.1582 (October 24, 1895): 296–97.

———. *Women and the Alphabet: A Series of Essays.* New York and Boston: Houghton, Mifflin, 1900.

Hirsch, E.D. Jr. *Validity in Interpretation.* New Haven: Yale University Press, 1967.

Hirsch, Marianne, and Evelyn Fox Keller, eds. *Conflicts in Feminism.* New York: Routledge, 1990.

Holland, Jeanne. "Scraps, Stamps, and Cutouts: Emily Dickinson's Domestic Technologies of Publication." In *Cultural Artifacts and the Production of Meaning: The Page, the Image, and the Body,* edited by Margaret J. M. Ezell and Katherine O'Brien O'Keeffe. Ann Arbor: University of Michigan Press, 1994.

Hollander, John., ed. *American Poetry: The Nineteenth Century.* 2 vols. New York: Library of America, 1993.

———. "Breaking into Song: Some Notes on Refrain." In *Lyric Poetry: Beyond New Criticism,* edited by Hošek and Parker.

Homans, Margaret. *Bearing the Word: Language and Female Experience in Nineteenth-Century Women's Writing.* Chicago: University of Chicago Press, 1986.

———. " 'Oh, Vision of Language!': Dickinson's Poems of Love and Death." In *Feminist Critics Read Emily Dickinson,* edited by Suzanne Juhasz.

———. " 'Syllables of Velvet': Dickinson, Rossetti, and the Rhetorics of Sexuality." *Feminist Studies* 11.3 (Fall 1985): 569–93.

———. *Women Writers and Poetic Identity: Dorothy Wordsworth, Emily Brontë, and Emily Dickinson.* Princeton: Princeton University Press, 1980.

Horowitz, Helen. *Alma Mater: Design and Experience in the Women's Colleges from their Nineteenth-Century Beginnings to the 1930s.* New York: Knopf, 1984.

Hošek, Chaviva, and Patricia Parker, eds. *Lyric Poetry: Beyond New Criticism.* Ithaca: Cornell University Press, 1985.

Howe, Susan. *The Birth-mark: Unsettling the Wilderness in American Literary History.* Hanover: Wesleyan University Press, 1993.

———. *My Emily Dickinson.* Berkeley: North Atlantic Books, 1985.

———. *Pierce-Arrow.* New York: New Directions, 1999.

———. "Some Notes on Visual Intentionality in Emily Dickinson." *HOW(ever)* 3.4 (1986): 11–13.

Huyssen, Andreas. *After the Great Divide: Modernism, Mass Culture, Postmodernism.* Bloomington: Indiana University Press, 1986.

Jackson, Virginia. "Longfellow's Tradition; or, Picture-Writing a Nation." *Modern Language Quarterly* 59.4 (December 1998): 471–96.

———. "Poetry and Experience." Review of *The Line's Eye: Poetic Experience, American Light,* by Elisa New, *Raritan* 20.2 (Fall 2000): 126–35.

Jackson, Virginia, and Yopie Prins. "Lyrical Studies." *Victorian Literature and Culture* 27.2 (1999): 521–30.

Jameson, Fredric. *The Political Unconscious: Narrative as a Socially Symbolic Act.* Ithaca: Cornell University Press, 1981.

Janowitz, Anne. *Lyric and Labour in the Romantic Tradition.* Cambridge: Cambridge University Press, 1998.

Jarrell, Randall. *Poetry and the Age.* New York: Ecco, 1953.

Jeffreys, Mark. "Ideologies of the Lyric: A Problem of Genre in Anglophone Poetics." *PMLA* 110.2 (March 1995): 196–205.

———. "Songs and Inscriptions: Brevity and the Idea of Lyric." *Texas Studies in Literature and Language* 36 (1994): 117–34.

John, Richard. *Spreading the News: The American Postal System from Franklin to Morse.* Cambridge, Mass.: Harvard University Press, 1995.

Johnson, Barbara. "Anthropomorphism in Lyric and Law." In *Material Events: Paul de Man and the Afterlife of Theory,* edited by Tom Cohen et al. Minneapolis: University of Minnesota Press, 2001.

Johnson, W. R. *The Idea of the Lyric: Lyric Modes in Ancient and Modern Poetry.* Berkeley: University of California Press, 1982.

Juhasz, Suzanne, ed. *Feminist Critics Read Emily Dickinson.* Bloomington: Indiana University Press, 1983.

Juhasz, Suzanne, Cristanne Miller, and Martha Nell Smith. *Comic Power in Emily Dickinson.* Austin: University of Texas Press, 1993.

Juhl, P. D. *Interpretation: An Essay in the Philosophy of Literary Criticism.* Princeton: Princeton University Press, 1980.

Kamuf, Peggy. *Signature Pieces: On the Institution of Authorship.* Ithaca: Cornell University Press, 1988.

Kaufman, Robert. "Adorno's Social Lyric, and Literary Criticism Today: Poetics, Aesthetics, Modernity." In *The Cambridge Companion to Adorno,* ed. Tom Huhn. Cambridge: Cambridge University Press, 2004.

Keller, Karl. *The Only Kangaroo Among the Beauty: Emily Dickinson and America.* Baltimore: Johns Hopkins University Press, 1979.

Kerkering, John D. *The Poetics of National and Racial Identity in Nineteenth-Century American Literature.* Cambridge: Cambridge University Press, 2003.

Kete, Mary Louise. *Sentimental Collaborations: Mourning and Middle-Class Identity in Nineteenth-Century America.* Durham: Duke University Press, 2000.

Knapp, Steven. *Personification and the Sublime: Milton to Coleridge.* Cambridge: Harvard University Press, 1985.

Knapp, Steven, and Walter Benn Michaels. "Against Theory." In *Against Theory: Literary Studies and the New Pragmatism,* edited by W.J.T. Mitchell. Chicago: University of Chicago Press, 1985.

Kopytoff, Igor. "The Cultural Biography of Things: Commoditization as Process." In *The Social Life of Things: Commodities in Cultural Perspective,* edited by Arjun Appadurai. Cambridge: Cambridge University Press, 1986.

Kramnick, Jonathan Brody. *Making the English Canon: Print-Capitalism and the Cultural Past, 1700–1770.* Cambridge: Cambridge University Press, 1998.

Krieger, Murray. *The New Apologists for Poetry.* Minneapolis: University of Minnesota Press, 1956.

Lacan Jacques. *Le Seminaire XX: Encore.* Paris: Seuil, 1975.

Lee, Benjamin. *Talking Heads: Language, Metalanguage, and the Semiotics of Subjectivity.* Durham: Duke University Press, 1997.

Lentricchia, Frank. *After the New Criticism.* Chicago: University of Chicago Press, 1980.

Lerer, Seth. "The Genre of the Grave and the Origins of the Middle English Lyric." *MLQ* 58 (1997): 127–61.

Levinson, Marjorie. *The Romantic Fragment Poem: A Critique of a Form.* Chapel Hill: University of North Carolina Press, 1986.

Leyda, Jay. *The Years and Hours of Emily Dickinson.* 2 vols. New Haven: Yale University Press, 1960.

Loeffelholz, Mary. *Dickinson and the Boundaries of Feminist Theory.* Urbana: University of Illinois Press, 1991.

———. *From School to Salon: Reading Nineteenth-Century American Women's Poetry.* Princeton: Princeton University Press, 2004.

Longinus. *"Longinus" on Sublimity.* Translated by D. A. Russell. Oxford: Clarendon, 1965.

Longsworth, Polly. *Austin and Mabel: The Amherst Affair and Love Letters of Austin Dickinson and Mabel Loomis Todd.* New York: Farrar, Straus, Giroux, 1984.

Lootens, Tricia. *Lost Saints: Silence, Gender and Victorian Literary Canonization.* Charlottesville: University Press of Virginia, 1996.

Love, Harold. *The Culture and Commerce of Texts: Scribal Publication in Seventeenth-Century England.* Amherst: University of Massachusetts Press, 1993.

Lowell, Amy. *The Complete Poetical Works.* Boston: Houghton Mifflin, 1955.

———. "The New Manner in American Poetry." In *Amy Lowell: A Chronicle, with Extracts from her Correspondence,* by S. Foster Damon. Boston: Houghton Mifflin, 1935.

Lowenberg, Carlton. *Emily Dickinson's Textbooks.* Lafayette, Calif.: np, 1986.

Lubbers, Karl. *Emily Dickinson: The Critical Revolution.* Ann Arbor: University of Michigan Press, 1968.

Lubbock, Percy. "Determined Little Anchoress." *Nation and Athaneum* 36 (October 18, 1924): 114.

Lukács, Georg. *The Theory of the Novel.* Translated by Anna Bostock. Cambridge: MIT Press, 1971.

MacLeish, Archibald. "The Private World." In *Emily Dickinson: Three Views,* by

MacLeish, Louise Bogan, and Richard Wilbur. Amherst: Amherst College Press, 1960.

Marshall, David. *The Surprising Effects of Sympathy: Marivaux, Diderot, Rousseau, and Mary Shelley.* Chicago: University of Chicago Press, 1989.

May, Caroline. *The American Female Poets.* Philadelphia: Lindsay and Blakiston, 1848.

McCluhan, Marshall. *The Gutenberg Galaxy: The Making of Typographic Man.* Toronto: University of Toronto Press, 1962.

———. *Understanding Media.* New York: Signet, 1964.

McDowell, Deborah E., and Arnold Rampersad, eds. *Slavery and the Literary Imagination.* Selected Papers from the English Institute, 1987. Baltimore: Johns Hopkins University Press, 1989.

McGann, Jerome. *Black Riders: The Visible Language of Modernism.* Princeton: Princeton University Press, 1993.

———. *The Poetics of Sensibility: A Revolution in Literary Style.* Oxford: Clarendon Press, 1996.

———. *The Textual Condition.* Princeton: Princeton University Press, 1991.

McGill, Meredith L. *American Literature and the Culture of Reprinting, 1834–1853.* Philadelphia: University of Pennsylvania Press, 2003.

———. "The Duplicity of the Pen." In *Language Machines: Technologies of Literary and Cultural Production,* edited by Jeffrey Masten, Peter Stallybrass, and Nancy J. Vickers. Essays from the English Institute. New York: Routledge, 1997.

———, ed. *The Traffic in Poems: Nineteenth-Century Trans-Atlantic Poetry.* New Brunswick: Rutgers University Press, forthcoming.

McKeon, Michael. *The Origins of the English Novel, 1600–1740.* Baltimore: Johns Hopkins University Press, 1987.

———, ed. *The Theory of the Novel: A Historical Approach.* Baltimore: Johns Hopkins University Press, 2000.

McNeil, Helen. *Emily Dickinson.* New York: Virago, 1986.

Menand, Louis. *The Metaphysical Club.* New York: Farrar, Straus and Giroux, 2001.

Messmer, Marietta. *A Vice for Voices: Reading Emily Dickinson's Correspondence.* Amherst: University of Massachusetts Press, 2001.

Michaels, Walter Benn. *The Gold Standard and the Logic of Naturalism: Essays on American Literature.* Berkeley: University of California Press, 1987.

———. *The Shape of the Signifier: 1967 to the End of History.* Princeton: Princeton University Press, 2004.

Mill, John Stuart. "Thoughts on Poetry and Its Varieties." In *Autobiography and Literary Essays.* Vol. 1 of *The Collected Works of John Stuart Mill.* Toronto: University of Toronto Press, 1981.

Miller, Cristanne. *Emily Dickinson: A Poet's Grammar.* Cambridge: Harvard University Press, 1987.

Miller, Ruth. *The Poetry of Emily Dickinson.* Middletown: Wesleyan University Press, 1968.

Milne, Drew. "In Memory of the Pterodactyl: the limits of lyric humanism." *The Paper,* no. 2 (Sept. 2001): 16–29.

Mitchell, Domhnall. *Emily Dickinson: Monarch of Perception.* Amherst: University of Massachusetts Press, 2000.

Mitchell, Donald Grant. [Ik Marvell.] *Reveries of a Bachelor, or, A book of the Heart.* New York: Baker and Scribner, 1850.

Mitchell, Juliet, and Jacqueline Rose, eds. *Feminine Sexuality: Jacques Lacan and the École freudienne.* New York: Pantheon, 1982.

Moers, Ellen. *Literary Women.* Garden City, N.J.: Doubleday, 1976.

Moi, Toril. *Sexual/Textual Politics.* London: Methuen, 1985.

Moon, Michael. *Disseminating Whitman: Revision and Corporeality in Leaves of Grass.* Cambridge, Mass.: Harvard University Press, 1991.

Morris, Timothy. *Becoming Canonical in American Poetry.* Urbana: University of Illinois Press, 1995.

Most, Glenn. "Greek Lyric Poets." In *Ancient Writers: Greece and Rome,* edited by T. J. Luce. New York: Scribner, 1982.

Muller, John P., and William J. Richardson, eds. *The Purloined Poe: Lacan, Derrida, and Psychoanalytic Reading.* Baltimore: Johns Hopkins University Press, 1988.

New, Elisa. *The Line's Eye: Poetic Experience, American Light.* Cambridge, Mass.: Harvard University Press, 1998.

Noble, Marianne. *The Masochistic Pleasures of Sentimental Literature.* Princeton: Princeton University Press, 2000.

Norton, Anne. *Alternative Americas: A Reading of Antebellum Political Culture.* Chicago: University of Chicago Press, 1986.

Oakes, Karen. "Welcome and Beware: The Reader and Emily Dickinson's Figurative Language." *ESQ: A Journal of the American Renaissance* 34.3 (1988): 181–206.

Oakes Smith, Elizabeth. *The Poetical Writings of Elizabeth Oakes Smith.* New York: J. S. Redfield, 1846.

———. *Woman and Her Needs.* New York: Fowlers and Wells, 1851.

Oberhaus, Dorothy Huff. *Emily Dickinson's Fascicles: Method and Meaning.* University Park: Pennsylvania State University Press, 1995.

Orzeck, Martin, and Robert Weisbuch, eds. *Dickinson and Audience.* Ann Arbor: University of Michigan Press, 1996.

Paglia, Camille. *Sexual Personae: Art and Decadence from Nefertiti to Emily Dickinson.* New Haven: Yale University Press, 1990.

Patey, Douglas. "'Aesthetics' and the Rise of Lyric in the Eighteenth Century." *Studies in English Literature 1500–1900* 33.3 (Summer 1993): 587–608.

Patterson, Annabel. "Lyric and Society in Jonson's *Under-wood.*" In *Lyric Poetry: Beyond New Criticism,* edited by Hošek and Parker.

Pearce, Roy Harvey. *The Continuity of American Poetry.* Princeton: Princeton University Press, 1961.

Peirce, Charles Sanders. *Writings of Charles S. Peirce: A Chronological Edition.* 6 vols. Edited by Max H. Fisch. Bloomington: Indiana University Press, 1982.

Percy, Thomas. *Reliques of Ancient English Poetry.* 1765. 3 vols. London: L. A. Lewis, 1839.

Perloff, Marjorie. *Poetic License: Essays on Modernist and Postmodernist Lyric.* Evanston: Northwestern University Press, 1990.

Petrino, Elizabeth A. *Emily Dickinson and Her Contemporaries: Women's Verse in America, 1820–1885*. Hanover: University Press of New England, 1998.

Pinch, Adela. *Strange Fits of Passion: Epistemologies of Emotion, Hume to Austen*. Stanford: Stanford University Press, 1996.

Pollak, Vivian R. *Dickinson: The Anxiety of Gender*. Ithaca: Cornell University Press, 1984.

Poovey, Mary. "The Model System of Contemporary Literary Criticism." *Critical Inquiry* 27.3 (Spring 2001): 408–38.

Porter, David. *Dickinson: The Modern Idiom*. Cambridge, Mass.: Harvard University Press, 1981.

Preminger, Alex, Frank J. Warnke, and O. B. Hardison, eds. *Princeton Encyclopedia of Poetry and Poetics*. Princeton: Princeton University Press, 1965.

Prins, Yopie. *Victorian Sappho*. Princeton: Princeton University Press, 1999.

Pyle, Forest. *The Ideology of Imagination: Subject and Society in the Discourse of Romanticism*. Stanford: Stanford University Press, 1995.

Ransom, John Crowe. *The New Criticism*. Norfolk, Conn.: New Directions, 1941.

Ranta, Jerrald. "Dickinson's 'Alone and in a Circumstance' and the Theft of Intellectual Property." *ESQ: A Journal of the American Renaissance* 41.1 (1995): 65–95.

Reynolds, David S. *Beneath the American Renaissance: The Subversive Imagination in the Age of Emerson and Melville*. Cambridge, Mass.: Harvard University Press, 1989.

Rich, Adrienne, "Vesuvius at Home: The Power of Emily Dickinson." In *On Lies, Secrets, and Silence: Selected Prose 1966–1978*. New York: Norton, 1979.

Richards, Eliza. *Gender and the Poetics of Reception in Poe's Circle*. Cambridge: Cambridge University Press, 2004.

Ross, Andrew. *The Failure of Modernism: Symptoms of American Poetry*. New York: Columbia University Press, 1986.

Rowlinson, Matthew. "Lyric." In *The Companion to Victorian Poetry*, edited by Richard Cronin, Antony Harrison, and Alison Chapman. Oxford: Blackwell, 2002.

Rowton, Frederic, ed. *The Female Poets of Great Britain*. Philadelphia: Carey and Hart, 1848.

Salter, Mary Jo. "Puns and Accordions: Emily Dickinson and the Unsaid." *The Yale Review* 79.2 (Winter 1990): 188–221.

Samuels, Shirley, ed. *The Culture of Sentiment: Race, Gender, and Sentimentality in Nineteenth-Century America*. New York: Oxford University Press, 1992.

Sanchez-Eppler, Karen. *Touching Liberty: Abolition, Feminism, and the Politics of the Body*. Berkeley: University of California Press, 1993.

Santner, Eric. *Stranded Objects: Mourning, Memory, and Film in Postwar Germany*. Ithaca: Cornell University Press, 1990.

Scarry, Elaine. *The Body in Pain: The Making and Unmaking of the World*. New York: Oxford University Press, 1985.

———, ed. *Literature and the Body: Essays on Population and Persons*. Baltimore: Johns Hopkins University Press, 1988.

———. *Resisting Representation*. New York: Oxford University Press, 1994.

Sedgwick, Eve Kosofsky. *Epistemology of the Closet.* Berkeley: University of California Press, 1990.

———. "A Poem is Being Written." In *Tendencies.* Durham: Duke University Press, 1993.

Sewall, Richard. *The Life of Emily Dickinson.* New York: Farrar, Straus and Giroux, 1974.

Shurr, William H., *The Marriage of Emily Dickinson: A Study of the Fascicles.* Louisville: University of Kentucky Press, 1981.

———, ed. *New Poems of Emily Dickinson.* Chapel Hill: University of North Carolina Press, 1993.

Silverman, Kaja. *The Acoustic Mirror: The Female Voice in Psychoanalysis and Cinema.* Bloomington: Indiana University Press, 1988.

Silverstein, Michael, and Greg Urban, eds. *Natural Histories of Discourse.* Chicago: University of Chicago Press, 1996.

Siskin, Clifford. *The Historicity of Romantic Discourse.* New York: Oxford University Press, 1988.

Smith, Barbara Herrnstein. *On the Margins of Discourse: The Relation of Literature to Language.* Chicago: University of Chicago Press, 1978.

———. *Poetic Closure: A Study of How Poems End.* Chicago: University of Chicago Press, 1968.

Smith, Martha Nell. "Computing: What's American Literary Study Got to Do with IT?" *American Literature* 74.4 (2002): 833–57.

———. *Rowing in Eden: Rereading Emily Dickinson.* Austin: University of Texas Press, 1992.

———. "To Fill a Gap." *San Jose Studies* 13.3 (Fall 1987): 3–25.

Smith-Rosenberg, Carroll. "The Female World of Love and Ritual: Relations Between Women in Nineteenth-Century America." In *Disorderly Conduct: Visions of Gender in Victorian America.* New York: Knopf, 1985.

Spicer, John L. "The Poems of Emily Dickinson." *Boston Public Library Quarterly* 8 (July 1956): 135–43.

St. Armand, Barton Levi. *Emily Dickinson and Her Culture.* Cambridge: Cambridge University Press, 1984.

Starr, Gabrielle. *Lyric Generations: Poetry and the Novel in the Long Eighteenth Century.* Baltimore: Johns Hopkins University Press, 2004.

Steedman, Carolyn. *Dust.* Manchester: Manchester University Press, 2001.

Stewart, Susan. *Crimes of Writing: Problems in the Containment of Representation.* Durham: Duke University Press, 1994.

———. *Poetry and the Fate of the Senses.* Chicago: University of Chicago Press, 2002.

Stoddard, Francis. "Technique in Emily Dickinson's Poems." *The Critic* 20 (January 9, 1892): 24.

Stonum, Gary Lee. *The Dickinson Sublime.* Madison: University of Wisconsin Press, 1990.

Tanselle, G. Thomas. "Emily Dickinson as an Editorial Problem." *Raritan* 19.4 (Spring 2000): 64–79.

Tate, Allen. "New England Culture and Emily Dickinson." *Symposium*, April 1932. Reprinted in *The Recognition of Emily Dickinson*, ed. Blake and Wells.

Taylor, Charles. *Modern Social Imaginaries*. Durham and London: Duke University Press, 2004.

Terada, Rei. *Feeling in Theory: Emotion after the "Death of the Subject."* Cambridge, Mass.: Harvard University Press, 2001.

Terris, Virginia Rinaldy. "Emily Dickinson and the Genteel Critics." PhD diss, New York University, 1973.

Thoreau, Henry David. *Walden.* Edited by J. Lyndon Shanley. Princeton: Princeton University Press, 1971.

Tiffany, Daniel Newton. *Toy Medium: Materialism and Modern Lyric.* Berkeley: University of California Press, 2000.

Tompkins, Jane. *Sensational Designs: The Cultural Work of American Fiction, 1790–1860.* New York: Oxford University Press, 1985.

Tucker, Herbert F. "Dramatic Monologue and the Overhearing of Lyric." In *Lyric Poetry: Beyond New Criticism*, edited by Hošek and Parker.

———. "The Fix of Form: An Open Letter." *Victorian Literature and Culture* 27.1 (1999): 531–35.

Tullis, Robert H. *The Home Insurance Company: Men of Vision During 125 Years.* New York : Newcomen Society in North America, 1978.

Vendler, Helen Hennessy. *The Art of Shakespeare's Sonnets.* Cambridge, Mass.: Belknap Press of Harvard University Press, 1997.

Walker, Cheryl, ed. *American Women Poets of the Nineteenth Century: An Anthology.* New Brunswick: Rutgers University Press, 1992.

———. *The Nightingale's Burden: Women Poets and American Culture before 1900.* Bloomington and Indianapolis: Indiana University Press, 1982.

Walsh, John Evangelist. *The Hidden Life of Emily Dickinson.* New York: Simon and Schuster, 1971.

Warner, Michael. "Irving's Posterity." *ELH* 67 (2000): 773–99.

———. *Letters of the Republic: Publication and the Public Sphere in Eighteenth-Century America.* Cambridge, Mass.: Harvard University Press, 1990.

———. "Professionalization and the Rewards of Literature." *Criticism* 26 (1985): 1–28.

———. *Publics and Counterpublics.* New York: Zone, 2002.

———. "What Like a Bullet Can Undeceive?" *Public Culture* 15.1 (Winter 2003): 41–54.

Warren, Austin. "Emily Dickinson." *Sewanee Review* 65 (Autumn 1957): 565–86.

Watts, Emily Stipes. *The Poetry of American Women from 1632 to 1945.* Austin: University of Texas Press, 1977.

Webster, Noah. *An American Dictionary of the English Language.* Springfield, Mass.: George and Charles Merriam, 1841.

Weisbuch, Robert. *Emily Dickinson's Poetry.* Chicago: University of Chicago Press, 1972.

Wellek, René. *Discriminations: Further Concepts of Criticism.* New Haven: Yale University Press, 1970.

Werner, Marta L. *Emily Dickinson's Open Folios: Scenes of Reading, Surfaces of Writing*. Ann Arbor: University of Michigan Press, 1995.

———. *Radical Scatters* [electronic resource]: *Emily Dickinson's fragments and related texts, 1870–1886*. Ann Arbor, Mich.: University of Michigan Press, 1999–.

———. "The Flights of A821: Dearchiving the Proceedings of a Birdsong." Online. http://www.altx.com/ebr/ebr6/media/ebr6.essay.menu.gif. Reprinted in *Voice, Text, Hypertext: Emerging Practices in Textual Studies*. Edited by Raimonda Modiano, Leroy F. Searle, and Peter Shillingsburg. Seattle: University of Washington Press, 2004.

Williams, Carolyn. "'Genre' and 'Discourse' in Victorian Studies." *Victorian Literature and Culture* 27.2 (1999): 517–20.

Williams, Raymond. *Keywords: A Vocabulary of Culture and Society*. New York: Oxford University Press, 1983.

Wilson, R. Jackson. *Figures of Speech: American Writers and the Literary Marketplace, from Benjamin Franklin to Emily Dickinson*. New York: Knopf, 1989.

Wimsatt, W. K., and Monroe C. Beardsley. *The Verbal Icon*. Louisville: University of Kentucky Press, 1954.

Winters, Yvor. "Emily Dickinson and the Limits of Judgment" [1938]. In *In Defense of Reason*. Denver: Alan Swallow, 1947.

Wolff, Cynthia Griffin. *Emily Dickinson*. New York: Knopf, 1986.

Wolosky, Shira. *Emily Dickinson: A Voice of War*. New Haven: Yale University Press, 1984.

"The Wounded Poet." *Times Literary Supplement* no. 2392 (December 6, 1947): 628.

Yezzi, David. "The Seriousness of Yvor Winters." *The New Criterion* 15.10 (June 1997): 26–33.

Index

Abrams, M. H., 112, 242n.8, 258n.68
address, 118–165; on envelope, 16; as figuration, 146–158; as genre, 8, 118–120; historical vs. fictive, 133–142; to "Master," 190–196; to "Misery," 206; modes of, 133; multiple forms of, 63–67, 68–92; object of, 142–158; of *Poems*, 1890, 126–128; to "Sceptic Thomas," 189–195; as self-address, 129–133. *See also* anthropomorphism; apostrophe
Adorno, Theodor, "Lyric Poetry and Society," 98–99, 256n.48
Aiken, Conrad, 95, 128
Aldrich, Thomas Bailey, 27–28
Anderson, Amanda, 272n.22
Anderson, Benedict, 242n.7
anthropomorphism, 27, 74, 100–109, 116–117, 152–158, 160–162, 167, 171–185, 190–203, 204–208, 233–234. *See also* address; apostrophe
apostrophe, 63–67, 105–107, 129–133, 142–165, 205–208, 220–234. *See also* address, anthropomorphism
Arac, Jonathan, 255n.37, 257n.49
Armstrong, Isobel, 120, 269n.10
Arnold, Matthew, 216–218
Atlantic Monthly, 16–17, 27–28, 77–78, 179–181, 213, 266n.14

Bahti, Timothy, 250n.43
Bakhtin, Mikhail, 55, 244n.21, 250n.50
Barker, Francis, 273n.34
Baudelaire, Charles: "Correspondances," 101–109; "Obsession," 105–109
Beardsley, Monroe, 39
Beecher, Henry Ward, 68
Benfey, Christopher, 190, 261n.19
Benjamin, Walter, 99
Bennett, Paula, 210
Berlant, Lauren, 271n.16
Bianchi, Martha Dickinson: *Emily Dickinson Face to Face*, 228; *The Life and Letters of Emily Dickinson*, 95; *The Single Hound*, 125, 162, 199, 241n.1. *See also* editions of Dickinson's poems

Bible, Gospel of John, 189–190
Bingham, Millicent Todd: *Ancestors' Brocades*, 241n.1, 251n.55, 255n.30; *Bolts of Melody*, 31, 34, 36, 71, 77, 245n.6. *See also* editions of Dickinson's poems
birds: as figures of inhuman lyricism, 16–31, 223–228; paper, 228–232; song of, 26–27, 56–57, 76, 185–189. *See also* Keats, John; lyric reading; Shelley, Percy Bysshe; Smith, Elizabeth Oakes
Blackmur, R. P., 95–98
Blind, Mathilde, 83
Bowles, Samuel, 68, 135–139, 215–219. See also *Springfield Republican*
Brenkman, John, 256n.48
Brock-Broido, Lucie, 268n.37
Brodhead, Richard, 270n.16
Bromwich, David, 261n.18
Bronson, Bertrand Harris, 262n.34
Brontë, Charlotte, 187
Brontë, Emily, *Wuthering Heights*, 156–157
Brooklyn Eagle, 68
Brower, Reuben, 99
Brown, Bill, 255n.28
Brown, Gillian, 62, 251n.60, 261n.21
Browning, Elizabeth Barrett, 187–189
Browning, Robert, 180, 187
Bryson, Norman, 3
Buckingham, Willis J.: *Emily Dickinson's Reception in the 1890s*, 127–128, 245n.27, 260n.17. *See also* reception of Dickinson's poems
Buell, Lawrence, 244n.19
Burke, Kenneth, 250n.48
Burns, Robert, 131
Butler, Judith, 234

Cameron, Sharon: *Choosing Not Choosing*, 42–45, 58, 150, 244n.25, 259n.70, 263n.43; *Lyric Time*, 41–42, 143, 154, 155, 233, 272n.29
Carlo (Dickinson's dog), 79–82
Carson, Anne, 118–119
Castoriadis, Cornelius, 242n.7
Cavell, Stanley, 46, 249n.37